Of The M...

W9-CDP-448

JAN 0 8 2003

944.08
In9   D04708

In search of France   8.95

Date		Due	

**MID-CONTINENT PUBLIC
LIBRARY SERVICE**

**Antioch Branch
5217 Antioch Road
Kansas City, Mo.**   **AN**

Books circulate for four weeks (28 days)
unless stamped otherwise.

No renewals are allowed.

Books will be issued only on presentation of
library card.

A fine will be charged for each overdue book.

In Search of France

CENTER FOR INTERNATIONAL AFFAIRS

HARVARD UNIVERSITY

STANLEY HOFFMANN

CHARLES P. KINDLEBERGER

LAURENCE WYLIE

JESSE R. PITTS

JEAN-BAPTISTE DUROSELLE

FRANÇOIS GOGUEL

In Search of France

HARVARD UNIVERSITY PRESS

Cambridge · Massachusetts · 1963

AN

D04708

944.08 IN9   AD
IN SEARCH OF FRANCE
1963   AN MCPL

3 0000 00087378 0 ..

© COPYRIGHT 1963 BY THE PRESIDENT AND FELLOWS OF HARVARD COLLEGE
ALL RIGHTS RESERVED

DISTRIBUTED IN GREAT BRITAIN BY OXFORD UNIVERSITY PRESS · LONDON

LIBRARY OF CONGRESS CATALOG CARD NUMBER: 63-9549

PRINTED IN THE UNITED STATES OF AMERICA

THIS BOOK HAS BEEN PREPARED UNDER THE AUSPICES OF THE
CENTER FOR INTERNATIONAL AFFAIRS, HARVARD UNIVERSITY

Created in 1958, the Center fosters advanced study of basic world problems by scholars from various disciplines and senior officers from many countries. The research at the Center, focusing on the processes of change, includes studies of military-political issues, the modernizing processes in developing countries, and the evolving position of Europe. The research programs are supervised by Professors Robert R. Bowie (Director of the Center), Alex Inkeles, Henry A. Kissinger, Edward S. Mason, and Thomas C. Schelling.

Book-length studies prepared thus far under the Center's auspices include:

The Soviet Bloc, by Zbigniew K. Brzezinski, 1960 (jointly with Russian Research Center). Harvard University Press.

The Necessity for Choice, by Henry A. Kissinger, 1961. Harper & Brothers.

Strategy and Arms Control, by Thomas C. Schelling and Morton H. Halperin, 1961. Twentieth Century Fund.

Rift and Revolt in Hungary, by Ferenc A. Váli, 1961. Harvard University Press.

United States Manufacturing Investment in Brazil, by Lincoln Gordon and Engelbert L. Grommers, 1962. Harvard Business School.

The Economy of Cyprus, by A. J. Meyer, with Simos Vassiliou, 1962 (jointly with Center for Middle Eastern Studies). Harvard University Press.

Entrepreneurs of Lebanon, by Yusif A. Sayigh, 1962 (jointly with Center for Middle Eastern Studies). Harvard University Press.

Communist China 1955-1959, with a foreword by Robert R. Bowie and John K. Fairbank, 1962 (jointly with East Asian Research Center). Harvard University Press.

In Search of France, by Stanley Hoffmann, Charles P. Kindleberger, Laurence Wylie, Jesse R. Pitts, Jean-Baptiste Duroselle, and François Goguel, 1963. Harvard University Press.

Contents

vii

Contents

FOREWORD

THE hallmark of the period since World War II has been drastic change in the domestic order and international position of countries all over the world. In the vast regions of Asia, Africa, and Latin America this period has seen the birth of some fifty new nations and the beginning of an epic drive to modernize traditional societies. But the mature societies of Western Europe, long at the hub of international affairs, have also felt the impact of radical change. In less than two decades Europe has gone through a cycle from the postwar stagnation to the current dynamism. Diverse pressures have been reshaping societies, economies, and external relations. The nations of Western Europe have rapidly adapted to the conditions of the postwar world and are on the road to the creation of a European Community. These domestic and external changes are as sweeping as anything happening in the emerging continents of Asia and Africa.

The study of change in Western Europe, as in the developing countries, has been a part of the research program of the Harvard Center for International Affairs since its inception. It was early realized that a penetrating analysis of the interacting changes affecting Europe would require the pooling of the knowledge and insights of experts in domestic politics and foreign relations, economists, social historians, and sociologists. It was also felt that one fruitful approach, though not the only one, would be to analyze the experience of individual countries. The choice of France for the first such study was prompted by the presence in the Cambridge area of a number of well qualified specialists from different disciplines who were eager to undertake it together. Each, in the course of his own work, had come to feel the need for a reappraisal of the changing French situation. All recognized that "shocks" from outside France—the war, the defeat of 1940, the occupation and liberation—had shaken the foundations of pre-1939 France and had released forces pent-up for some years. But many questions re-

ix

mained. Each specialist was anxious to discover the thinking of fellow students of France in other fields.

The present book is the tangible result of this joint interest. The group wanted to go well beyond the usual symposium of separate essays. From the outset its aim was to combine individual analysis and interpretation with the benefits of joint criticism. In pursuit of this purpose the group worked together continually for more than two years, developing their thinking by mutual "challenge and response."

The laboratory for this group experiment was a Seminar on France, which was held at the Center during the academic years 1959–60 and 1960–61. About half the seminar meetings were devoted to discussing papers written especially for the seminar by members of the group and distributed in advance. The other meetings were held with outside specialists, usually academic or diplomatic; about half of these submitted papers on aspects of contemporary France,* and all offered themselves as targets for questions from the regular members. These meetings were also attended by Fellows of the Center (career officials) and a small number of invited guests whose fields were germane to the project. During the second year, the group also held a number of closed meetings to allow the members to examine where they stood on the basic problems and to discuss organization of the material for the book.

The culmination of the Seminar was a three-day colloquium held at the Fondation Nationale des Sciences Politiques in Paris in July 1961, when earlier versions of the present chapters were discussed by the authors with a group of French specialists on contemporary France, who were invited to criticize and offer suggestions.

By training and background the authors are well equipped for sympathetic but critical analysis of their subject. Stanley Hoffmann was educated in France and has taught both at the Institut de Hautes Etudes Internationales in Geneva and at the Institut des Sciences Politiques in Paris. He has also written for a variety of

* Two of these papers deserve special mention because the authors have drawn on them in writing the book: "The Structure of French Business," by Maurice A. Adelman, Professor of Economics, Massachusetts Institute of Technology; and "Recent Trends in French Education," by William Johnston.

periodicals in Europe and in the United States. Charles P. Kindleberger has done extensive research in Europe and is currently working on a comparative study of the British and French economies since 1850. For Laurence Wylie, interest in French society traces back to work at the Institut des Sciences Politiques under André Siegfried, and was carried on in studying the French mind through the national literature. His *Village in the Vaucluse* resulted from a year's sojourn with his family in a village in southeastern France; and he is now at work on a book based on a similar stay in a village in western France. Jesse R. Pitts, with one parent French, was educated partly in France and has written extensively on French social structure, especially on the bourgeoisie. Jean-Baptiste Duroselle, an authority on international relations in the twentieth century, directs the Centre d'Etudes Internationales at the Fondation Nationale des Sciences Politiques. He has taught at Harvard, Brandeis, and Notre Dame Universities. François Goguel, currently Secretary-General of the French Senate, is a leading French political scientist.

Several people, who do not appear as authors, have contributed to the study in major ways. Most important is our debt to Jo W. Saxe, formerly Research Associate at the Center, who first organized the seminar and presided over its meetings until he left to join the staff of the Organization for Economic Cooperation and Development in November 1961. Nancy L. Roelker, Instructor in Modern European History, specializing in French History, at the Winsor School in Boston, has served as Secretary of the Seminar. She has been tireless and invaluable in maintaining the momentum of the project and in coping with many of its practical problems. In addition, she translated the chapters by Jean-Baptiste Duroselle and François Goguel. (In the other chapters translations from French sources are the responsibility of the authors.) Three others who participated in the Seminars for extended periods had an important influence on the development and content of the essays: Raymond Aron, Professor at the Sorbonne and distinguished French political analyst; Michel Crozier of the Centre National de la Recherche Scientifique whose work on the French concept of authority greatly influenced the authors; and Nicholas Wahl of the

Harvard Department of Government. Max Hall, Editor of Publications at the Center and Social Science Editor of the Harvard University Press, has materially improved the clarity and style of the book by his meticulous and skillful editing. Stephen Graubard, of the Harvard Department of History and Editor of *Daedalus*, offered criticism and editorial advice which was helpful in shaping the volume.

Finally, the Center and the authors are deeply grateful to the many specialists, both here and in France, who criticized the papers, asked provocative questions and shared their knowledge and experience. These included members of the United States Departments of State and Defense, French and other European diplomats and scholars, Fellows of the Center, and faculty members from various departments and graduate schools of Harvard and other American universities. Especially helpful were the participants in the colloquium in Paris: Michel Crozier, whose contribution to the Seminar has already been noted; Alfred Grosser and Georges Lavau, who share in the Direction d'Etudes at the Fondation Nationale des Sciences Politiques; Marcel Maget, Conservateur des Musées Nationaux; Jean Mayer, Inspecteur des Finances; Jean Stoetzel, Director of the Institut Français d'Opinion Publique and Professor of Sociology at the Sorbonne; Jean Touchard, Secretary-General of the Fondation Nationale des Sciences Politiques; and Philip M. Williams, Nuffield College, Oxford University. Among the benefits of the colloquium, besides a renewed stimulus, were answers to certain questions, the sharpening of many issues, some changes of opinion, and help in revision of the chapters.

In their search to understand the emerging France, the authors are unanimous in believing that their thinking has greatly benefited from the give and take with one another and with the many others who have cooperated so generously both at the Center and in France. But, in the final analysis, each author has been responsible for his own essay—for its content, its appraisals, and its judgments.

As the title suggests, any analysis of a rapidly changing, complex society is a continuing quest. No study can ever be definitive. These essays do not pretend to be so: they are an attempt to assess some significant strands of the change in France between the 1930's and the 1960's. Nor are they an exhaustive study. Some important aspects of the French scene receive only incidental treatment; another group of observers would doubtless emphasize other factors and interpret differently those presented here. The aspects discussed reflect the competence and judgment of these authors, who continue "in search of France."

Robert R. Bowie, *Director*
Center for International Affairs

November 1, 1962

PARADOXES OF THE FRENCH POLITICAL COMMUNITY

Stanley Hoffmann

In the three decades of French history from the early 1930's to the early 1960's, a combination of deliberate policies and external shocks produced almost revolutionary changes in France's society and in France's role in the world. Those changes, stormy and massive, kept France's political system out of joint with the times. The political system, to be sure, has not been totally unreformed and unadapted (for if this had been the case the impact of economic and international blows would have been almost uniformly disastrous) but it shows, so to speak, a new scar for every new sign of strength, a new wound for every convalescence. During this period the nation, faced with a challenge to its very survival, responded far more impressively than many of its critics would have predicted, but time and again had to sacrifice its rudder to the storms it was weathering. If the observer looks at French society and French external policy, he may well exclaim that miracles happen; if he looks at France's political system he will be tempted to fall back on *plus ça change, plus c'est la même chose*. He may be right both times, and my objective is to say why.

This essay is about the transformation of France as a political community. I use the word "community" in its purely formal meaning of a group of people living together, whose relations with one another are intense, and who have developed common habits and rules—rather than in its substantive meaning of a group sharing the same values, attitudes, and objectives. Indeed, the fundamental question I must try to answer is whether France *is* a political community in the substantive sense. But in either case, formal or substantive, the study of a political community implies more than an analysis of what is usually called the political *system:* the pattern of power, interests, and policies, the activities of institutions, parties, pressure groups, and bureaucracy. It requires a look at the nation as a whole. The role which the political system plays is to a large extent determined by the economic and social structure of the nation and by the values of the main social groups. Inversely, society is molded by political decisions and processes. Both society and the political system, in turn, are affected by international events. Therefore the three spheres—society, political system, foreign policy—must be examined over and over as the story proceeds. I assume them to be relatively autonomous, but heavily influencing one another in ways that must be pointed out.

The examination will be carried out in three parts. In the first, I will try to describe briefly the main characteristics of the French political community under the Third Republic. I submit that there existed a "Republican synthesis" which gradually emerged in the century after the French Revolution and flourished in the period 1878–1934. I call it a synthesis because of the way in which the main features of society, the political system, and the French vision of the outside world fitted together.

In the second part, I will examine the impact of the war years on this synthesis. The harmony which was the Third Republic was destroyed by a number of shocks of which World War Two was the culmination. The war itself brought to a climax a number of trends, some of which were quite ancient; but it is in the period 1934–1940 that they began to become dangerous; the hard knocks suffered by the French political community in those years became the death-blows of the Republican synthesis in 1940–1945. Many of the political, economic, and social forces which have carried postwar France increasingly further from the prewar pattern have their origin in the war years.*

---

* Parts I and II are a revised and much expanded version of my article, "The Effects of World War II on French Society and Politics," *French Historical Studies,* Spring 1961, pp. 28–63.

In the third part, I will discuss the stage reached by the French political community at the present time. The very forces unleashed during the war, while they have destroyed the old harmony, have also prevented, so far, the appearance of a new synthesis. Although it is easy to see what France's new economic and social pattern will be, and it is already possible to guess what its new place in the world may be, the road which has been traveled has been so painful that the political system has not adjusted to those changes. In the long run, barring serious new external shocks, they may of course affect and heal the political system's diseases; but in the short run they rather complicate the cure.

I

THE REPUBLICAN SYNTHESIS

◇◇

SOCIETY

The basis of the Republican synthesis was a peculiarly complex society, which may best be called the stalemate society, and which had three essential features. In the first place, the stalemate society was a unique mixture of socio-economic systems. Second, it was characterized by a peculiarly French style of authority. Third, its associational life was poor; the actors were mainly individuals rather than organizations.

Socio-economic system

Two models developed by sociologists may be useful here. One is the model of the feudal-agrarian society. It is marked by a small degree of division of labor. There is little specialization of roles, and society is likely to be fragmented into segments; the basic groups—family or corporations—embrace most of the individual's life; the social hierarchy is based on status, deference, tradition; such a society is both hierarchical and static. The other model is the model of industrial society, where division of labor is extensive, roles are specialized, and communications hasten the unification of

3

the market and the process of social mobilization. Groups too are more specialized; the social hierarchy is functional, access to the top being the result of competence rather than kinship; such a society is marked by social mobility and economic dynamism.

French society was a surprising mixture of the two models. It could be called neither dynamic nor static. It was not dynamic; for the French bourgeoisie, in its very struggle for emancipation from the feudal order of the old regime, had adopted many features of that order and therefore showed little enthusiasm for the logic of economic rationality. There was a tradition of entrepreneurs whom one might call Schumpeterian if Saint-Simon had not been their original prophet, but it was not the dominant tradition. The basic motivation of business was social rather than economic: to insure the continuity of the family and its social predominance rather than to produce the greatest amount of goods. Consequently social mobility was not considered to be necessarily beneficial. It was not a static society either, however, for it accepted social mobility within limits which will be indicated below, and it did not resist deliberately the introduction of new techniques of production. France did become an important industrial country.

The explanation of the blend can be found in the existence of a very broad consensus on a form of "equilibrium" which accepted social mobility and evolution toward a more industrialized order, but only within sharp limits and along well-defined channels. Economic change was welcome only if new factors (such as techniques) were fitted into pre-existing frameworks, so that the traditional way of life would be affected very slowly. As John Clapham has put it, there was industrialization without an industrial revolution. Social mobility presented some very special features. In Edmond Goblot's words, class barriers could be crossed but not destroyed.[1] When one jumped over such a barrier one had to leave one's previous way of thinking and living, and accept for oneself and for one's family the values and attitudes found on the other side of the fence. Thus a certain equilibrium among agriculture, services, and industry was maintained by thwarting or diluting industrial expansion. Industry could coexist with an agrarian economy, whose links with the national market were tenuous, and the industrial sector itself was shot through with nonindustrial features. In particular, the social hierarchy remained more traditional than functional, and the family kept its pervasive importance at every level of the hierarchy.

The groups which participated in this consensus were the peasantry and middle classes composed largely of "independents" (non–wage earners). The very size of the peasantry and middle classes before the age of industry, and the fact that France's population growth slowed down earlier than in other European countries, favored the establishment and preservation of such a consensus.

The key to the system was the French bourgeoisie. It was the product of three influences. The first was its peasant background, which had determined the nature and role of the family, the bourgeois conception of work and thrift, and the bourgeois sense of the limits of work. The second influence was the prerevolutionary bourgeois tradition which had promoted the progress of the bourgeoisie along two lines: the conquest of wealth—business careers—and the conquest of prestige—intellectual ones requiring a gift for orderly abstract reasoning. A final influence was the feudal hangover, already mentioned; it meant that traditional Catholic doctrines (notably concerning the evils of capitalist accumulation) left their mark even before much of the bourgeoisie, in the nineteenth century, staged a return to Catholicism; it also meant that the bourgeoisie in many ways imitated the aristocracy, and that the practices of mercantilism persisted. All of these influences contradicted or at least diluted the values of capitalism. The stalemate society was the perfect expression of this delicate balance of forces.

The bourgeoisie controlled almost all the ruling groups, spiritual and temporal, economic and political. In order to preserve its supremacy it used two bulwarks.

One was the over-all structure of society itself, in which passageways for entrance into the bourgeoisie were left open. As before, they were the line of wealth, passing through the petite-bourgeoisie of artisans and shopkeepers, and the line of prestige, which passed through the professions and the civil service.[2] These *antichambres* were protected by state policy. So was the peasant reservoir, which was kept large so as to provide a regular supply of future bourgeois.

A second bulwark was to be found in the values of society as shaped by the bourgeoisie. The bourgeoisie identified itself with French society as a whole: it was the model and the matrix for the rest of society.[3] Thus it emphasized values generally acceptable to most groups in France, stability, harmony, permanence—rather than competition, which means both mobility and elimination. It stressed values and attitudes which were dissolvers of class solidarities so that society would appear to be a collection of individuals psychologically alike, of whom the bourgeois would seem the perfect average. Among the values, the most significant were resistance to the machine age and emphasis on moderation and equilibrium. France was thus presented and seen as a spiritual as well as a physical hexagon. The school system, with its sharp distinction between the equalitarian primary *écoles publiques obligatoires et gratuites* and the bourgeois quasi-monopoly of the secondary schools (*lycées*), was the best example of the structures of individual ascent and of the values of the stalemate society.

It is easy to understand how such structures and such values would slow down economic transformation. France's "economic retardation" was certainly not caused by lack of capital: on the whole, supply exceeded demand. It may have been aggravated but was not created by a lack of sufficient coal and by the location of industry. Ultimately what was responsible was the nature of the French bourgeoisie—its beliefs, its attitudes, its way of life—and this nature was reflected not only in the family firm but in many other firms as well.[4] This celebrated "freezing of the capitalist spirit," which may have kept France behind in the world race, had at least domestic advantages from the viewpoint of the all-important equilibrium. The consensus of the bourgeoisie, its two preserves and its reserves, was perpetuated through a tight and somewhat cramped solidarity of all its members. In business, social considerations prevailed over economic ones, so that small firms were protected against cut-throat competition. In the relations between the business world and the landed notables, the two groups indulged in joint investments in land—or in protectionism—a solidarity which distinguished France from England. In the relations between business and civil servants, there developed practices of intermarriage, social mixing, and the passage of state officials into more lucrative private enterprises (*pantouflage*). The timidity of entrepreneurial drives was a prerequisite for the conciliation of the interests of the groups included in the consensus.

This agreement left out, indeed it pushed out, the industrial proletariat, relegated to a social ghetto. The French working class was in a most unhappy position; there was a much-celebrated community of values between peasants and bourgeois, but all that the bourgeois offered the workers was the prospect of individual ascent through hard work and thrift. That was the method of ascent which the peasants had used, but it seemed to the workers a betrayal of the solidarity of industrial labor. Living in a society which praised the peasant's work—individual, free, "in the perspective of time"—the industrial worker could not but strongly resent the nature of his own labor, which was exactly the reverse. Furthermore, as Georges Sorel had seen, the very slowness of economic progress and the mediocrity of many of the firms could not fail to exacerbate the opposition of the proletariat to a capitalism which was not even productive. If the peasantry was the reservoir of French society, the working class was its swamp. As a result severe tensions poisoned the relations between the workers and the consensus groups, and in accordance with Proudhon's final advice a tradition of noncooperation developed among the labor unions.

The explanation of the peculiar balance of French society—the halfway house between the old rural society and industrialization—could be sought in that matrix of modern France, the Revolution. If it is true that European nations have been shaped by the character of the relations between the aristocracy and the bourgeoisie, then the French blend can be seen as the product of the defeat-and-resistance of the aristocracy. The bourgeoisie triumphed through a battle, and the battle explains both the continuation of industrial development as an element of bourgeois drive and the energy with which the bourgeoisie defended itself against any push from the new lower class, the proletariat. The aristocracy had

7

offered a long and heated resistance: hence both the bitter equalitarian suspiciousness which pervaded French society and the deep impact which aristocratic values nevertheless made on bourgeois and even on workers' attitudes. Neither social reaction nor social revolution became the imperative that shaped French society.

The style of authority

A second essential characteristic of the stalemate society could also be defined in terms of "neither-nor." This is the style of authority in the relations not only between people in groups but also between groups, and, consequently, the style in which conflicts were solved in society. It has been admirably analyzed by Michel Crozier and, with reference to its matrix, the school, by Laurence Wylie.[5]

Once again let us start with contrasting models. The first would be the model of democratic authority, which emphasizes initiative, cooperation, open discussions, and compromise, and which, at the national level, would be the mark of what Louis Hartz calls a liberal society, i.e., one that is informed by egalitarian values, disdainful of ranks and castes, intellectually homogeneous and pragmatic. At the other extreme we would find an authoritarian society, in which conflicts are settled by fiat, and which is quite likely to be seething with repressed tensions.

Again, neither of our two models applies to the French style of authority. It comes closer to a third model: the "noninterventionist" style of authority, that is, not so much the blend as the coexistence of *limited* authoritarianism and *potential* insurrection against authority.[6] What is most striking is the dislike of face-to-face discussions leading to compromises through participation of all parties involved in a problem. As in the authoritarian model, conflicts are referred to a higher central authority instead. However, the other essential aspect of this style is the sharp set of limits imposed on such authority: power is delegated to it so that the drama of face-to-face personal relations can be avoided but only in order that, and as long as, the exercise of power from above remains impersonal and curtailed both in scope (subject-matter) and in intensity (means of action) by general rules, precedents, and inhibitions. Without such exercise of authority from above, the group or the society could hardly function—as in the authoritarian model —but the group does not display at all the solidarity found in that model, solidarity achieved through either common efforts to carry out the leader's orders or joint resistance to his commands. Since the only legitimate sources are the superior ones, but since the role of the leaders is also strictly limited, all associations below have an air of illegitimacy or conspiracy: this applies to peer groups in high school as well as to business associations or political parties.

Thus, such a system preserves the independence of each member, since it protects him from that responsibility for the outcome which democratic authority relations entail, and it safeguards his right to protest more effectively than in the case of authoritarian relations, which place fewer restraints on the leaders. The often noted tendency of the French to dissociate the "real," inner, private life from the façade of official life is a by-product of such a style. Such a tendency is far more difficult to perceive either in democratic or in authoritarian patterns: there it is the inner life which takes on the suspicious shade of clandestinity, and which flourishes only if self-restraint is exercised by the group in one case, the elite in the other. Here, restraint is built-in: hence the perpetuation of French "individualism" and what Jesse Pitts calls the cult of prowess, for in a system in which ends are determined higher up, men tend to put their energy and care into the means. Another famous aspect of French life which such a style fosters is centralization.

There is a close connection between the pattern of authority relations and the mixture of socio-economic systems in French society. The higher authorities in that pattern are very often traditional notables who owe their position to "social" power—family, money, land; and the distrust which meets them below reflects the egalitarian feelings mentioned above. Thus the style of authority embodies both the hierarchical and the "revolutionary" features of French society.

The explanation of the persistence of this style is, therefore, to be found in a historical experience which developed both the need for and the fear of authority. The need for authority had been inculcated by the Old Regime, whose patient destruction of autonomous sources of power had tended to make all groups dependent on the state, as Tocqueville has shown. Subsequently, the tensions between the consensus groups and the workers, the tensions produced among the consensus groups themselves by the slow rate of economic growth and by the coexistence of opposite socio-economic systems, the bourgeoisie's attempt to stabilize society by favoring individualism and fragmentation—all these factors made it impossible for society to solve its countless conflicts by methods of "face-to-face" compromises. But this society had emerged from a revolt against the bonds of personal dependence left behind by feudalism, and against the Old Regime. The revolt had been staged just at the time when the old bonds had lost any justification, and when the monarchy, precisely because of its own blend of authoritarian and "noninterventionist" features, had managed to lose touch with a changing society, thus forfeiting its usefulness as a common frame of reference and appearing increasingly arbitrary. Furthermore, any new swing toward authoritarianism could not but revive fears of social change, either in the direction of reaction or in that of industrialization. The danger of aristocratic revenge or proletarian revolution nourished a fear of the very authority which the need to prevent both disasters made necessary. The complex hierarchical character of French society kept groups at every level looking above for authority, and suspicious of the authority that came from above. Postrevolutionary France was an attempt to replace the straitjacket of the Old Regime with a society whose structure and values would make it possible to dispense with an authoritarian state, but postrevolutionary France was also a construction so delicate that the pattern of centralized authority had to be preserved both in society and in the state.

When the tasks a group has to perform exceed its capacities or when the group is too deeply divided, democratic relations of authority are almost useless. When, however, the group is at least capable of a negative consensus against authoritarianism, the "noninterventionist" style becomes the least disadvantageous. Its main drawback is that it entails delays; also, precisely because it does not try to overcome the fundamental divisions in the group or between the groups, it is essentially conservative. But those flaws happened to be quite consonant with the desires of the bulk of society.

Associations

The last major characteristic of the stalemate society is its peculiar associational life. "Individualism" reigned here too—and it meant that interests were barely organized. This was another large difference between France and the other main Western nations. It can be traced back to the two factors previously discussed.

Thus, this "atomism" of French society can be explained by the slowness of industrialization and the isolation of agriculture. The defense of the various interests in the consensus could be undertaken through more traditional structures and "notables." To crystallize such interests in well-organized groups could easily have heightened tensions within the stalemate society. As a result, pressure groups were more effective on a local than on a national or regional scale. Neither business nor other middle-class nor peasant organizations had large memberships or solid structures. The only exceptions were the labor unions, but even they did not speak for the bulk of France's workers. This individualism was the corollary of the fragmentation of French society, which the diversity of French landscapes and the Paris-centered nature of the communications network have encouraged. Rather than a national market there was a conglomeration of small ones; industry was dispersed among countless small and medium-sized enterprises. The French school of electoral sociology, which is actually a school of electoral *geography*, reflects and illuminates such fragmentation. Moreover, the style of authority, which stressed the function of resistance rather than common positive tasks, was also responsible for the traditional brittleness of French organizations.

The weakness of those "intermediate bodies" in turn contributed to the peculiar balance of socio-economic systems and to the resilience of the style of authority. It slowed down industrialization and consolidated a social hierarchy capped by traditional notables or "new notables" who made it to the top through education, competitive examinations and individual prowess, rather than "organization men" distinguished by their service to the group. Social mobility was also slowed down by the lack of transmission belts. Moreover the weakness of intermediate bodies prevented France's style of authority from becoming fully democratic, for a liberal society requires vigorous associations in which many citizens join for positive purposes. But the fragmentation of society also prevented the French style from becoming too authoritarian, for the power of the central decision-makers was never spread over too broad a range of issues or too large a section of the population, and checks could therefore be enforced despite the absence of organized associations.

POLITICAL SYSTEM

For more than a century the political problem of France was to devise a political system adapted to the stalemate society.

The problem

There were two constants in the various political systems that followed the Revolution: centralization and the limitation of the state's role. Centralization was the foundation stone of all political edifices. The French bureaucracy shaped the style of authority described earlier; the lasting importance of the civil service in turn reflects and perpetuates this style on the political plane. With only temporary exceptions, however, the scope of bureaucratic action has been limited, for, as we have seen, the stalemate society wanted to preserve its hard-won emancipation from the Old Regime, and not be encased in a straitjacket again. Hence the role of the state has been a narrow one, meeting the individual's desire not to become a mere instrument of the state, especially in economic affairs, and the desire of the consensus groups for a sharp separation between state and society. Indeed, as exemplified by French administrative law, the justification for the privileges granted to the state rests upon the extent to which the state's functions are different from those of individuals. Administrative law is concerned both with stating the prerogatives of the state and with defining the limits on arbitrary action by the state.

In a way, then, the centralized but limited state was a faithful translation of two of the key features of the stalemate society. But establishing a political system remained a very complicated task; for, between a society and a political system, there is a crucial problem of transmission belts and institutional arrangements.

It is true that there are authority patterns in all groups, from the family to the state. But, precisely because the state is the "group of groups," the way in which authority relations prevalent in society will or will not operate in the political system depends to a large extent on what may be called the political formula, or political legitimacy: the way in which political leaders are selected and power distributed among them. There will usually be strong connections, of course, between the style of authority and the political formula; however, a given style of authority in society is compatible with a variety of political formulas.

It is also true that in studying the question of political legitimacy one must take into account the presence or absence of a social consensus. But its mere existence is not a guarantee of political stability, because a consensus on the nature of society does not determine the regime which will be based on it. Thus, in France, the previously described *social* consensus was not enough—a political consensus was missing; there was no agreement either on the objectives for which political power is to be used, or on the procedures through which disputes over such objectives can be resolved. Whoever undertakes to arrange the political institutions and the transmission belts to society ought to consider not only the main features of society but also the main political opinions—and to remember that his work is at the mercy of the most unmanageable of all variables: events.

France, ever since the Revolution, had been split into rival schools of thought, differing not only in their judgment of the merits of the stalemate society but also in their views about how society should be governed. It is a Marxist and pseudo-Marxist fallacy to believe that a class or social group must have a single conception about how its interests will best be protected, i.e., about the political system. This is false for two reasons: there can be sharp splits within the same group on such an issue, and furthermore political opinions are concerned not only with the defense of social interests but also with purely ideological questions, irreducible to "class." France is the best example. Its political history is largely the history of the political divisions of the bourgeoisie—an over-all division between the counterrevolutionaries who refused to accept government by consent and those persons who wanted it, and a further division among the latter, split into conservatives afraid of too much democracy, democrats closer to Rousseau than to Locke, and socialists dissatisfied with the stalemate society.

Between the Revolution and the establishment of the Third Republic in 1875, all kinds of political systems were tried. On the whole these were congruent with the authority patterns existing in society, but they gave a variety of answers to the question of political legitimacy: they differed as to the mode of selection of leaders, and appealed to different schools of thought. There were, so to speak, two opposite poles: the regimes that stressed primarily the need for authority and the liberal regimes that reflected the fear of authority. The first type was characterized by a mixture of authoritarian and "noninterventionist" traits—authoritarian in the personal character of the leader, who derived his power from heredity or plebiscites, and in infringements of the rule of law, noninterventionist in the attempt to rule above and despite political and social divisions, rather than trying to eliminate them, and to operate within the framework of the limited state. Such regimes could be thought of as nothing but the civil service capped by a powerful leader. At the other pole, the liberal regimes were characterized by a blend of noninterventionist and "democratic" features—democratic in the limited sense of putting power into the hands of elected representatives, and allowing a free interplay of political forces. But the experience with the two types was not satisfactory. Regimes of the first type lapsed into arbitrariness and carried much too far the downgrading of representation; regimes of the second type were plagued in the earlier times by the narrowness of their electoral basis and harmed at all times by the divisions in French political thought.

The solution

The genius of the Third Republic was the devising of an institutional set-up more effectively adapted to French society.

First of all the role of the state was kept strictly limited, in accordance with the requirements of the style of authority, the desires of the "consensus groups," and the wishes of most schools of French political thought. What the stalemate society needed was state protection, not domination; it wanted an instrument, not a master. Economic intervention was justified only when it operated to preserve the economic equilibrium, either through legislation (especially on tariffs and taxes) or through piecemeal administrative intervention.[7] Otherwise the state's function was an ideological one. It was a state wedded to the social *status quo;* it was neither industrial (à la Saint-Simon) nor reformist nor laisser-faire, but politically doctrinaire and economically beleaguered.

The organization of this state was such that an effective executive, clear-cut economic or social alternatives, and a strong party system could not emerge. Parliament was supreme but immobile; its supremacy, well reflected in the French doctrine of delegated national sovereignty, freed it from any mass pressures from below. Its role was deliberative rather than representative; law was the product of a compromise between opinions rather than the result of a weighing of forces.[8] In such a way, the risks for the social and political stability of France which many had seen in universal suffrage and in the representation of all opinions were minimized, since the scope of what Parliament could do was restricted, and the sharp edges of political opinions could be worn out in the *"camaraderie"* of Parliamentarism. The decision of Léon Gambetta and his friends to woo the peasants rather than the urban workers was of decisive importance in dissociating the Republic from "disorder." The political notables of the Third Republic represented quite faithfully the core of the stalemate society, i.e., the bourgeoisie (with a significant underrepresentation of business) and its two preserves, i.e., Gambetta's *"nouvelles couches."*

Parties, thanks largely to the electoral system, were primarily parliamentary collections of "fief-holders"; their function was to occupy power rather than to govern. The characteristic weakness of French associations was thus reflected here too—except on the extreme left, whose parties addressed themselves largely to those groups which were outside the social consensus and which had a much greater interest in a reformist state. Political life came close to the model of a pure game of parliamentary politics—the government of the nation by a Parliament which put the life of cabinets constantly at stake, dictated policy-making, and knew no effective institutional restraints on its powers. But this game, played in isolation from the nation-at-large by a self-perpetuating political class, saw to it that the fundamental equilibrium of society would not be changed by the state.

The limits of stability

A recent theory of stable democracy suggests that for a political regime to be stable, there must be "congruence" between authority relations in the government and authority relations in society.[9] Such congruence existed in France. The style of political life under the Third Republic corresponded admirably to the style of authority of French society. Participation of the electorate was strictly limited to election day: the referendum was banned from the constitution, dissolution never used after 1877. Decisions were left to the civil service on the one hand, to the parliamentarians on the other. The task of the parliamentarians was to supervise the civil service, and thereby to protect the citizens from arbitrariness. In the beginning the system worked well; the first generation of republican leaders, behaving as Burkean representatives, were men of stature and faith. After an era of scandals had destroyed the façade of purity and brought back cynicism, a new link was introduced: the Radical *"comités."* In the post-Dreyfus phase of the regime, these acted as intermediaries between the electorate and the parliamentarians, but they tended not so much to increase popular participation as to supervise the parliamentarians in turn. Alain's "Radical doctrine" of obedience without love and distrust without revolt bears a strong resemblance to the style of authority analyzed by Crozier and to the school system described by Wylie. The Third Republic was indeed, as Thiers said, the regime which divided the French least.

However, under the criteria set up by the "congruence" theory of stable democracy, the Third Republic—France's most stable regime—fared badly. The votes of the electorate did not decide the outcome of the competition for power among the parliamentarians; decisions were not democratically made; and the regime, so long on words, was short on actions. All those flaws were real enough, but were not due to a lack of "congruence."

First, it is true that the elections resulted regularly in a rule of the Center rather than a genuine and creative alternation of Left and Right. This excessive stability can be traced, curiously enough, to a germ of instability. The ideological formula of the regime included the Extreme Left but kept out the counterrevolutionary Extreme Right, whereas the social formula—the preservation of the stalemate society—entailed the opposite. This is what condemned the regime to the rule of the Center from the beginning. The real danger in such a pattern was that it would be jeopardized the day the Center stopped being strong and numerous.

Secondly, it is true that to a large extent the Republic was a façade behind which the bureaucracy made decisions. This I have already traced to the nature of the social consensus, to the style of authority, and to the weaknesses of French associational life. The danger here was in the remoteness of the political system from the "real country." Inevitably, the citizens of a regime which so faithfully applied the "noninterventionist" pattern of authority on the level of the political community as a whole were bound to fall into cynicism and to slip from obedience without love to contempt. For they had little participation in local government, their parliamentary representatives were playing a rather byzantine game of pure politics in the house without windows, and there was no strong executive to serve as a focus of attention and as a rallying point for action.

Thirdly, it is true that the regime had plenty of brakes and not much of a motor. Democratic mixed government, which requires that the executive be both reasonably strong and the expression of the popular will, did not emerge. Representative government was never reconciled with effective executive leadership.[10] "Game" politics meant the triumph of representation over leadership. Here again the explanation can be found in the political divisions of Parliament and of the country, in the nature of the social consensus, in the style of authority whose more negative side, the fear of authority, was so much more sharply reflected in the regime than the craving for it. The Republic was well designed to *resist* —for instance, to overcome the onslaught of the Right at the time of the Dreyfus case, or to break the "revolutionary" actions of the workers in the first decade of the century. The social and the political consensus made such feats quite possible. But how would the regime handle emergencies? World War One performed the miracle of suspending, rather than aggravating all divisions. However, even before the great challenge of the thirties, there were quite a few alarms. The parliamentary game with its endless debates, its painful compromises, its loose parties and heterogeneous party system, its frequent cabinet crises, was bound to antagonize people who celebrated the values of activism and violence and who resented an atmosphere of verbalism and stagnation—intellectuals, workers, and even many members of the urban lower middle class. Hence the development of antiparliamentarianism among syndicalists, nationalists, and numerous writers. Throughout French political history, in addition to the schools of thought I have mentioned and to shifting, countless parties or movements, born as much out of circumstances as of ideologies, there have been two "tempers" which may be called Jacobin and Girondin: both can be found at the same time or in rapid succession in every sector of French opinion. It was the Jacobin temper which the parliamentary game left out, and which, at each crisis, the regime found in the opposition.

FRANCE AND THE WORLD

The social and political system rested also on a certain *vision of the outside world.*

A consensus: universality, rank, and power

Despite the defeat of 1871, the French generally felt that the outside world was distant enough to allow them to care primarily about their own affairs. The defeat itself had insured that there would be no great dissent from hostility-to-Germany as the categorical imperative of French foreign policy; and this is why World War One did not become the occasion of a split in French opinion. Victory plus new alliances served to plaster over the cracks opened by the shock of invasion. Thus, in the Third Republic, the outside world was neither feared as a major threat nor taken as an invitation to hegemony; and foreign policy was not an important subject of contention among domestic factions. And what made this possible was a large consensus on the role of France in the world—a role which would not be so demanding that domestic tranquility (or perhaps domestic turmoil) would have to be sacrificed to its exigencies, but which would nevertheless keep France in the very forefront of nations. The French, no different from many other well-established nations, like *une grandeur sans histoires;* but *la Grandeur dans l'Histoire,* they quite definitely liked.

All French *"familles d'esprit"* displayed considerable pride in the universality of French values. Here, Michelet, Jaurès, Maurras were not too far apart. The emphasis may have been different: Maurras stressed the example given by France as the oldest national state; Jaurès and others preferred to identify France with civilization. But it was always the same underlying belief—that France was a pace-setter for the rest of the world.

A crucial preoccupation, especially after 1871, was the concern for rank: France had to remain a major power. The Republic achieved some of its greatest triumphs in this respect, since it maintained France in the race for colonial conquest as well as in European alliances. Since there could be no enjoyment of rank without security, those alliances were of particular importance.

The statesmen of the Republic, like their predecessors, never doubted that power was the currency which would allow France to buy rank and prestige. Their conception of power reflected the values of the stalemate society. From the Old Regime, the leaders of France had inherited the concern for military might and an essentially Roman notion of greatness—assessed in terms of territory occupied. No economic drive explains the spread of French colonization. France exported little capital to her colonies and was not much concerned with their economic development. France's colonization was triple: military, peasant, and administrative. The French civil servant rather than the merchant became the symbol of French rule. Obviously, France would not easily disengage from an empire acquired as a means toward rank and as a way of spreading France's universal values, rather than as a source of wealth; an empire subjected to the French instinct of centralization, applied to areas where central authority found or brooked no limits to its commands.

Signs of trouble

Despite such national harmony, some of the sharpest storm signals of the Third Republic originated in the field of foreign policy.

A first crisis developed in the decade before World War One. French nationalists became obsessed with France's relative decline (and especially with her demographic stagnation). They blamed the regime, in accordance with one of the most fundamental political reflexes of citizens of a nation which has known many regimes, none of them strong enough to have its legitimacy totally divorced from its efficiency. At the same time, one of the regime's leaders, Caillaux, began to wonder whether France's world ambitions did not exceed her resources. Both warnings were drowned out, however. Caillaux at first had almost no followers, and the nationalist campaign was undercut by the very revival of nationalism among the Republicans.[11]

After World War One the weakness of France's position came from the fact that all her aspirations had been fulfilled just as all her resources had been taxed to the limit—she could go only one way: down. Sharp tactical divisions appeared almost at once between those who wanted to preserve France's rank and security by nationalist policies (including a kind of permanent distrust of Germany) and those who put more faith in international cooperation. The breach was not yet irreparable, since many of the heralds of the League of Nations were trying hard to turn the League into an instrument of, and a supplement to, French power and a means toward security, but it was an indication of a switch to a defensive state of mind.

THE PARADOX OF IMMOBILITY

Such was the Republican synthesis. The system made it possible for the Left and the Right to fight pitched ideological battles such as the Dreyfus case without endangering the social balance. But the paradox of this synthesis was that its survival depended upon the absence of drastic change in France's economic and international positions. France's invocation to the *status quo* might have been expressed in Faust's words, *"Verweile doch! Du bist so schön."* For it was obvious that if the stalemate society were to be severely affected by economic depression or by inflation, tension would mount among all groups (and of course between the consensus groups and the workers) because of the competition for a share in the national income or against shouldering the financial burden. The political system was not strong enough to deal with these issues. French parties were neither equipped to cope adequately with them nor capable of reacting coherently to a deterioration of France's international status. This first became apparent in the twenties when Poincaré had to step in and save the parliamentary system from impotence.

The only world for which French politics was made was the golden age of the Third Republic. The other side of this paradox was, of course, that only an external shock could provoke a radical change in France's social and political system

II

THE DESTRUCTION OF THE
REPUBLICAN SYNTHESIS

◇◇

THE SHOCKS OF THE THIRTIES

The challenge of the thirties did what previous crises such as *boulangisme*, the Dreyfus case, or the financial troubles of the mid-twenties had been unable to do. It undermined all the foundations of the Republican synthesis.

Society in crisis

The depression, an event "imported" from the outside world, came to France late, but hit hard. Characteristically, the reaction of most political groups was to cut public expenditures and to decree a thorough deflation, instead of devaluating the franc. The policy of balanced budgets and cuts in wages and salaries was an attempt at preserving the stalemate society, which, one feared, would be upset both by monetary manipulations and by an extension of the role of the state in economic affairs. The beliefs that inspired the Republican synthesis expressed themselves in various ways. The sanctity of contracts became a "mystique." The outside world was said to be out of joint, so that naturally France could not be expected to devaluate in order to fall into line. Freezing the stalemate society at a low level of economic activity was thought preferable to experimentation which might upset both the social hierarchy and the well-established relation of society to the state.

The consequence, however, was the worsening of all the latent tensions of the stalemate society, and finally the shattering of its equilibrium. The loss of purchasing power and the fear of unemployment pushed the issue of social reform and the workers' grievances to the highest danger level since 1848. But now, the workers also found allies among the "consensus groups," which joined in a mass protest against what their respective situations had become during the depression. Peasants, civil servants, small businessmen, and shopkeepers thus supported the Popular Front for a while. The fact that the workers' allies wanted a return to the *status quo ante* rather than a jump to the *"Grand Soir"* of workers' dreams meant, however, that tensions between the consensus groups and the workers would soon reappear in acute form. Indeed they did, shortly after the Popular Front's financial and economic policies became an obvious fiasco.

The outside world intrudes

As in other countries earlier, the citizens finally crawled out of the depression largely by grasping the rope of rearmament. But the tragic irony of the French case was that the measures which helped France overcome the effects of the first shock were prompted by a second one, ultimately far more devastating. For the outside world intruded not only to disturb the delicate balance of French society but to ruin the consensus on France's international role.

During the thirties the stream of history seemed to be leaving France behind, and even to condemn the values and the procedures of the French political system. The world had become a world of motion, indeed revolution. Stalin, Mussolini, Hitler, Scandinavian experiments in socialism, Roosevelt's experiment in muscular liberalism stood in glaring contrast to France's immobility. Even to the most musty readers of the *Revue des deux mondes*, France and England began to appear like dead wood. Moreover, the regimes which repudiated the principles of constitutional democracy were the ones that seemed to be the wave of the future. Finally, France, with its stagnant population, was hopelessly overcommitted. Once Germany went on the move again, France's victory of 1918 appeared not only hollow but treacherous; for it had condemned France to equally disastrous choices.

Almost inevitably, the collapse of the order of Versailles had a divisive impact within France. It would have been painful even if the domestic situation had been more harmonious, but the political and social tensions of the thirties further distorted people's reactions to international events. On the left, pacifism was the refuge of some who made the reform of the stalemate society and its limp political system their first imperative, and the cause of many who made anti-Communism their overriding concern. On the right, although many continued to believe that France's rank and civilization must be defended against the new threat from Germany, others felt that a war would only either destroy a nation which had already fallen behind and whose population had not recovered from its World War One losses, or else prolong for a while a regime which was seen as a major cause of decline. Consequently they thought the best France could do to hold her own was to dig in behind her fortified wall—and give herself institutions more attuned to the new world around her. Thus, arguments which the Extreme Right had made for a long time became much more popular at last—but in a period and situation in which their effect, by another tragic irony, was to discourage France from defending her position in Europe, instead of goading her to fight. The fear of permanent decline led to the advocacy of present with-drawal, with the hope of future *redressement*. Now that the na-tionalists were turning to various branches of pacifism instead of jingoism, their appeal could no more be undercut by a "nationalist revival" among Republican leaders: on the contrary. Whatever the specific arguments used by the various types of appeasers, and to whatever degree they were moved by domestic considerations, one fact remains: never before had so many Frenchmen doubted about all the aspects of France's past vision of the world, and ques-tioned so sharply her power, her claim to a high rank, and the relevance of her values.

The political system in confusion

The institutions proved too weak to weather such a storm. The prerequisites for that peaceful coexistence of all French political tendencies which was the Third Republic had disappeared. The future of the stalemate society had been put at stake—obliquely, through financial policies, directly, through Popular Front ideology. And now the role of France in the world had become a political issue. The result was the worst possible combination of explosive-ness and paralysis.

Throughout French history, the conservatives had tended to take refuge in the antiparliamentary shelter of the Extreme Right whenever the balance of society appeared to be threatened. There had again been strong symptoms of such a switch in the twenties. It was not the first time that the Radicals had governed with So-cialist support, but there were good reasons why the reaction of the Right, around 1924, was so much more vigorous than before. This time the government had to deal with a financial crisis, and there was a major difference between a left-wing majority concerned only with ideology (as around 1900) but not with the order of society, and one which had to tinker with this order. The Right objected to the Left's philosophical doctrines, but left-wing eco-nomic and social ideas the Right would not tolerate at all, for it feared that in this somber area the Radicals would be the dupes of the more sophisticated Socialists. Furthermore, there now were

Communists at the left of the Socialists, so that any move in the direction of what the Socialists advocated for the French economy seemed but a prelude to total subversion. Finally, fascism had already appeared as the model of what resistance to such disorder can achieve. Consequently, the first "Leagues" since the turn of the century sprang up around 1924 at the time of the *Cartel des gauches,* and the campaign of the Right soon led to the break-up of the Cartel. The same phenomenon occurred again in 1934 and in 1938—but each time at a higher pitch of violence. In 1936–37 the French political "community" looked rather like two armed camps preparing for a fight.

On the other hand, most French parties had not been created around the issue of economic and social balance or around foreign affairs, since these had been the pillars of French consensus. Consequently, when these became the major *political* issues, the parties proved both incapable of agreeing on coherent measures and unable to get their own members to agree. Precisely because France had a multiparty system, she became the victim of a remarkable paradox: her parties were ideological but at the same time resembled pressure groups in the sense that each one represented only a small section of the population and was tempted to behave as a spokesman for the interests of that small section. This did not make either for easy compromise or for intelligent policies. The Socialist Party, which was not wedded to the social *status quo* originally, had, however, been pushed in that direction by two developments. First, as a minority party operating in the stalemate society, it had become permeated by the atmosphere of caution, immobility, and "equilibrium" which characterized this society; it put infinitely more emphasis on changes in the distribution of the national income than on the need to create a spirit of enterprise so as to increase the total product.[12] Secondly, especially after it had been shoved further to the right by the Communists, many of its voters were not at all interested in overhauling the stalemate society and voted for the Socialists for general ideological reasons rather than out of economic or social discontent. All the parties were inept in economic and financial affairs, and, this being so, they naturally turned to the experts, whose advice throughout the period was consistently wrong; the same experts often served Laval and Blum.

Consequently, the French political system tried to handle the depression through a succession of faulty policies, marked by party bickerings, internal contradictions (deflation without devaluation, wage increases with a sharp cut in the length of industrial work), and final failure. The foreign issue cut across all parties, producing a strange alliance of "appeasers" versus "warmongers" irrespective of party label. This led first to Munich, then to a war whose preparation had been disastrously hampered by such splits and doubts, and by the prolonged depression. At a time when executive action was needed, the deep divisions within Parliament condemned cabinets to shorter lives than ever before, and to immobility or incoherence during their brief existence. The impotence of Parliament itself was underlined by the abdication of legislative power through decree-laws.

THE PROCESS OF DESTRUCTION

Let us examine now the process of destruction in the period 1934–1940. The shocks I have mentioned encouraged centrifugal forces in every respect. Until then, the Republic had functioned neatly enough, because most of France's political and social forces had accepted both the regime and the society which it expressed. The rest, i.e., the Extreme Left, representative of the proletarian swamp, and the Extreme Right had been kept in their ghettos. Suddenly, confusion and flux replaced the tidy, if cramped, order of Alain's *République Radicale*. All the types of attack which had been launched *seriatim* in the past against the regime, at the time of Boulanger, Panama, Dreyfus, or the Cartel, reemerged, converged, and expanded.

The assailants

In a period of major trouble the citizens, and especially those who feel the pinch of a depression, rediscover the function and importance of politics. Robert de Jouvenel's famous sentence (politics in France was a luxury, not the condition of men's lives) was true only as long as the bases of the system were not threatened. The return to politics of previously indifferent groups can have more than one meaning. It can mean that the existing political system will be reactivated because the malcontents have found easy access to power through the political parties and pressure groups available. But when those parties do not fulfill their task and when the pressure groups are able only to increase the weaknesses of the state by milking it at the expense of the common good, the existing political system will be in danger of collapse.

The latter situation is the one which obtained in France. Existing political parties simply did not adjust to the new issues: they locked themselves in the traditional Republican fortress, instead of rebuilding it. A look at the program of the parties in 1936 shows the extent of sclerosis on both sides of the political fence. The Left, in 1934, had prevented constitutional reform, a prerequisite of political reconstruction, and, instead of building a positive alliance for the solution of the new problems enumerated above, it threw together a negative one against the forces which attacked the regime for its incapacity to solve those problems. Anti-League feelings were merely put in the place of former anticlericalism: 1935 was 1899 revisited. The economic program of the Popular Front christened with the new slogan of "purchasing power theory" the old practice of promising benefits to a huge quantity of groups.

The consequent movement of dissent from, or revolt against, the Republic included a large segment of the already politically active forces of France. They were a highly heterogeneous crew. For example, people, groups, and reviews, originally identified with the Republican parties, became restless and found that they could not get their views across within those parties; so they dissented and started to float away. Many of them swam vigorously as far as they could from the Communists, whose sudden reformism, recent nationalism, and subtle infiltrations they distrusted. In the middle of the ocean, they found all those men of the Right—the conservatives—who had made it clear that their support of the Republic was conditional upon the preservation of the kind of society the regime now seemed unable to save. They also found those men, movements, and journals of the Extreme Right, who had never had any faith in the Republic anyhow and had attacked it all along from their age-old ghetto. All these people became, on the whole, outspoken enemies of the regime. Thus the regular institutions became more and more a façade; the real life—suddenly most turbulent—seemed somewhere else.

Among the dissidents from Republican political parties, the most notorious were the three men, who, ironically enough, had been the first to speak of a Popular Front, only to be kept away or to turn away from it later: Jacques Doriot (ex-Communist), Marcel Déat (neo-Socialist) and Gaston Bergery (ex-Radical). At their right, André Tardieu switched also from being one of the chief statesmen of the regime to being one of the main publicists against it.

The conservatives among the assailants were a highly interesting mass of people. They felt almost permanently deprived of majority support in the electorate; to many of the voters *la République* ever since its beginning had been identified with the Left. In the government, the best the conservatives could usually hope for was to share control with the Radicals. As long as political power did not matter because the dominance of the middle classes in society was secure, this insufficient control was not a major nuisance; as long as the conservatives' Bastilles in society (civil service, industry and banks, the professions, the salons) still stood, it was not very important that left-wing parties were better organized than rightist parliamentary clans, and that labor unions were more real than business or peasant groups. But when the traditional positions were threatened by economic chaos and the political "disorder" of the Popular Front, access to power had to be reopened. Moreover, such access was to be sought in anti-Republican ways rather than through the organization of new, but Republican, parties and pressure groups, for a variety of reasons of which the most important was that such an effort would have gone against the grain. It presupposed a total change of heart among people who had supported (or tolerated) the Republic only because the regime required no big organizational work or apparatus from notables who wanted to dominate society as elites, not as political parties or as special interests.[13] Antiparliamentarism came infinitely more naturally—as had been shown by so many historical precedents.

It was not too difficult for those men to rub elbows with various political figures who had turned antiparliamentary before or around February 1934; the Maurrassiens, the Jeunesses Patriotes of Pierre Taittinger, men like Philippe Henriot, Xavier Vallat, Georges Scapini. One can put into the same category, or into a neighboring one, the newspapers which came more and more to support the themes of anti-Republicanism and played such a crucial role in bringing to France the climate of Vichy before Vichy.[14]

In addition to all these forces that had a prior history of political activity, the assailants included many new faces. The 1930's were marked by the "politization" of various groups of men who, in happier days, would not have dreamed of singing the *"garstig Lied"* of politics. Intellectuals, ending a period in which they had been singularly nonpolitical, poured into the arena—hence the mushrooming of new reviews and sects with grandiloquent programs and spiritual verbiage. There were equally surprising numbers of engineers, especially from the Ecole Polytechnique, where the old Saint-Simonian tradition of illuminism-cum-technology flourished again.[15] There were students, who built up impressive-sounding but short-lived youth movements (at a time when the parties also reactivated or created youth sections); veterans' associations, who substituted the jargon of national overhaul for the vocabulary of special financial complaints (the *Croix de Feu* are of course the biggest example); union leaders and businessmen who turned from their previous attitudes of nonparticipation in, or no-comment on, politics, to studies of general reform and examples from other countries.[16]

The assailant groups, coming from so many different milieux and counting so many people whose sudden discovery of public affairs had gone to their heads like extra-fine champagne, were more confused than coherent in their attack on the Republican synthesis. Indeed, if there is one characteristic of these movements in the period under consideration, it is the bitterness of their own divisions. For a few months in 1934–35 all these people fraternized in astonishment at their common feelings and slogans. At first, their quarrels were not more than yelps of dissent among dissenters (although, of course, French yelps can be a mighty strain on any ear). Soon they began to excommunicate one another and to raise nuances to the dignity of abysses once again. Later, once the Republic fell into the trap the Germans, plus Laval, had opened, the disputes among the former critics of the regime led to a quasi-civil war between Vichy and the Resistance, both being composed essentially of the malcontents of the 1930's.

The themes

Nevertheless in the thirties they had common grievances against the Republican synthesis, and since these themes announce the changes of postwar France, it is important to list them.[17] They all express a revolt against the kind of society and state which had been entrenched for decades. To a striking degree, the ideologies of both Vichy and Resistance would repeat those themes. They broke the mold of traditional French political thought; of the four main "spiritual families" of the bourgeoisie, only the counterrevolutionaries were represented here *en masse*—often by young disciples whose respect for Maurras' orthodoxy was far from complete. The members of the other three schools of thought, that is, the conservatives, democrats, and socialists, were not at home in the company I have described. Two new clans, however, made an impressive appearance on the stage. One was the Christian Democrats, whose voice had long been little more than a whisper. The other was the fascists, sons of the nationalists of the previous generation, but sons both prodigal and degenerate, who had turned their fathers' dream of renovation into a nightmare of hatred and destruction, and whose despair of France and admiration for foreign examples led them straight into nihilism.

The first common theme was a critique of French parliamentarism. The most interesting example is probably Tardieu's set of volumes composed between 1934 and 1936. Tardieu's remark that if one wants to be heard by the country it is best not to be a parliamentarian is significant enough. Practically all the dissenters from the Republic argued in favor of a stronger state, one less dependent on the whims of the representatives and less submissive to the pressures of the voters on the parliamentarians. This was a turn toward the more authoritarian version of France's political system, advocated either because of a felt need for action or because of a fear of "subversion"—i.e., a felt need for *reaction*. The advocates of action were concerned with closing the gap between the nation and the political system; the advocates of reaction wanted to increase the distance.

A deeper theme was an attack on the "individualism" of the stalemate society. This meant two things.

It meant in the first place an attack on the neglect of groups in French "official" thought and public law. The various aspects of this revival of group thinking were: the proliferation of youth movements, the concern for new formulas of organization and representation of interests, and the rediscovery in contemporary "public philosophy" of man-as-a-social-being under the loftily vague name of *Personnalisme*, championed by two new periodicals, *Esprit* and *l'Ordre nouveau*. The revival was led by men opposed to the doctrine of Alain or of the "Jacobin" state, but they in turn were split between advocates of democratic organizations and doctrinaires for elitist, authoritarian groups.

The attack on individualism meant in the second place an attack on French capitalism. Here of course ambiguity was supreme, and misunderstandings were most juicy, for some of those attackers wanted (at least they thought so) to overthrow the private-enterprise economy, whereas others criticized French capitalism only because it had not succeeded in freezing the stalemate society once and for all. Thus one wing argued for greater socialization of the economy, for more state intervention and planning, i.e., an extension of the scope of state authority. But the other wing still feared state dabbling more than anything except Communism (although that was about the same in their eyes); therefore they merely wanted France's consensus groups to organize solidly at last, and to coordinate their policies among themselves, in order precisely to prevent the state from using the present lack of organization as a pretext for "*étatisme*." They favored an increase in the *intensity* of state authority, i.e., the above-mentioned switch toward authoritarianism, but a restriction of its *scope*. What all nevertheless agreed upon, was that present disorganized capitalism (neither state-regulated nor officially self-regulated) was rotten. It wasted national resources through the excesses of competition; it demoralized the nation through its materialism; it encouraged uprooted adventurers and nomadic speculators; [18] it crushed "*les petits*" and benefited only "*les gros*"; it built new "feudal orders" in France. There is a marvelous irony in the spectacle of so many people denouncing the fiasco of French 1934–35 capitalism as the discomfiture of "*l'économie libérale*," if one remembers how little free competition and indeed how much self-regulation there was in this most restrictive economy. But it was well-concealed self-regulation, and what the partisans of "organized professions" (such as Claude-Joseph Gignoux, the new head of the Business Confederation) wanted was officially proclaimed and sanctioned self-regulation, giving to business groups powers snatched away from the state or from unions.[19]

In both these attacks on individualism, all the groups involved addressed themselves primarily to the French lower middle classes and to the peasants: this was as true of Colonel de La Rocque or Doriot as it was of men like Déat, Bergery, or the labor leader René Belin.

Another theme, which went perhaps even deeper, was a universal lament about the moral climate of France. This was the generation of *péguysme*—the worship of poor Péguy, on whom Emmanuel Mounier, the founder of *Esprit*, had just written a book. Péguy's search for a *mystique* away from the *politique* of the regime, his disillusionment with the Republic, his mixture of "social" inspiration and nationalism, his quest for innocence and communion, had made him the inevitable, if involuntary, hero of all the *déclassés* of politics. It was also the epoch of activism: Sorel and Proudhon were the patron saints of many of the new reviews. André Malraux was of course a shining hero-witness of the revolt against the climate of mediocrity and immobility. The examples afforded by other countries were continually displayed, discussed, and sometimes even studied.

The battle

The ways in which the attackers of the Republican synthesis pushed France out of the drydock in which she had been waiting for permanently postponed repairs are far too complicated to be described in detail, but certain points are of major interest.

Two blocs. The confusing mass of dissenters ultimately split into two blocs (heterogeneous ones, to be sure). On the one hand there were all the people who ended on the side of Vichy, or rather those whom de Gaulle calls "les amants inconsolables de la défaite et de la collaboration." These included: most of the *Maurrassiens*, those hermetically sealed counterrevolutionaries; the fascists of occupied Paris (literary types, like Drieu la Rochelle, or gangsters, like Doriot's pals); the fascists of Vichy France (muddleheaded activists like Joseph Darnand or schemers like Jacques Benoist-Méchin); the much bigger group of disgruntled conservatives, trembling sheep with wolves' voices, like La Rocque, Pétain's Legion of Veterans, and so many of his civil servants, business or peasant leaders; and those pacifists (like Belin and many of Déat's friends) whose left-wing origins had been erased by their prolonged fight against Communism and for appeasement. On the other hand, we find all those dissenters from the Third Republic who nevertheless hated defeat and Nazism more than a French form of democracy and who became the political leaven in the Resistance organizations, where they met thousands of intellectuals, students, journalists, doctors, lawyers, military men, and others who had had no political activity before 1940. Those *Résistants* belonged largely to two groups: (1) a relatively tight one, the Christian Democrats, whose *Personnalisme* was politically liberal, not authoritarian, and whose pluralism was democratic, not elitist; and (2) a much more loose group, the former *planistes* from business or from the unions.[20] It was only later in the Resistance that many but of course not all members of the parties of the Third Republic joined those former dissenters (who were most inhospitable to their belated companions), gradually submerged them, and turned the Resistance into a second version of the Popular Front.

Two phases. If one looks at the direction taken by France after 1940, one can distinguish, with some exaggeration, two phases. First there was, under Vichy, a movement of contraction. This brief triumph of a reactionary's delirium broke with the "individualistic" society of the Third Republic in order to establish a *"société communautaire,"* whose organized and self-regulating groups were even more restrictive in economic practice, and more dominated by the anti-industrial, anti-urban ideal, than the Republic had ever been. Then, after 1944, the pendulum rushed in the opposite direction toward economic expansion, a loosening up of society instead of the tight and petrified moral order of Vichy.

TWO REVOLUTIONS: VICHY AND THE RESISTANCE

We now have to establish a balance sheet of the effects which the process we have just sketchily described produced during World War Two. The central fact is that the two movements—contraction and renovation—converged on a number of very important points. This strange dialectic can be explained without any recourse to the invisible hand of history. The participants in the two revolutions of Vichy and the Resistance had some common (if often negative) ideas, and since many of Vichy's dreams were beyond realization—"ce qui est exagéré ne compte pas"—many of Vichy's reforms inevitably turned into directions Vichy neither expected nor desired, or even produced effects contrary to those which the authors of these reforms had hoped to obtain.

Toward a new society

If we look at developments in society at the end of the war, we see that the groundwork of postwar change was laid during the war years.

The phenomenon which was perhaps of greatest importance was a kind of rediscovery of France and of the French by the French, because of the defeat and later in reaction against Vichy. An essentially psychological change, it was the necessary condition of the more tangible transformations of the major features of the stalemate society. Common sufferings did a great deal to bridge over, if not to close, some of the fissures which the social fabric of France had suffered before the war. This rediscovery took many forms, some of which had been anticipated in the thirties—either in the literature of the dissidents I have mentioned or even in the initiatives of the Popular Front and of Edouard Daladier; but at that time political divisions had not allowed such efforts to go very far. One of the most ironical symbols of the new mood was the celebration of Péguy by Vichy as well as by the Resistance; but wasn't Péguy a symbol of love for *"la France charnelle"* apart from political ideologies or philosophical abstractions? It is important to remember that after the orgy of self-lacerations and doubts which had marked the 1930's, both the Resistance forces and the non-fascist elements of Vichy fostered a nationalist revival. The kind of civic education that Vichy's youth camps and youth movements offered to their members, the *veillées* at which Barrès or Péguy were read, the cult of Joan of Arc, the intense, generous, and somewhat confused social nationalism of the *Ecole des Cadres* at Uriage,[21] pointed in the same direction as the nationalism of much of the Resistance which tried to reconcile "Jacobinism" with chivalry, the revolutionary heritage with the themes of the thirties, planning with decentralization, the call to arms against the hated invader with the need for solidarity among nations.

When Vichy finally became a shrunken, isolated, and fascist-dominated little clique, common opposition to the German occupants and the collaborators brought together people and groups that had remained separated both in prewar France and in the period of Vichy which preceded Laval's return to power. The collaborators played in 1944–45 the sad but useful role of scapegoats, and the shrillest of their enemies were often men who had first put their faith in Pétain and shared in Vichy's integral nationalism of 1940–41. The myth which the Resistance men gladly endorsed—that almost all of France was *résistante* in 1944—contributed to healing some of the wounds which the clash between Vichy's forces and the Resistance had opened. If Vichy was a localized cancer, and the rest of the body of France was healthy, then a reunion in nationalism was possible for all except the black sheep. The extraordinary nationalist fervor of the Communists in the Resistance and Liberation days [22] was far more than a tactical shift: it constituted in many cases a genuine emotional wave of relief after (or should I say expiation for) the somber period 1939–1941, when Communist opposition to the war had pushed the Party's members and sympathizers outside of the national community—or out of the Party. The executions of collaborators in the summer and fall of the Liberation were examples of ritual murders far more than evidence of civil war.

The emphasis so heavily put on youth and on the family by Vichy was intended to contribute to the rebirth of a sense of community. The Resistance did nothing to reverse the movement. Were not its organizations dominated by young men who acceded to responsibilities which French youth had been deprived of since the days of the Revolution? As for the stress on family life, the Christian Democrats saw to it that it would not disappear with the Vichy regime.

It is obvious that the revival of community was far from complete or final, and it is impossible to measure the degree of community in a nation. But I would maintain that it has been higher after 1944 than in the 1930's, despite the return of the Communists into their ghetto and despite such phenomena as poujadism or the *putschs* and bombs of 1960–1962. The tone of public arguments has been milder; the hysteria so characteristic of debates in the 1930's has been limited to lunatic fringes. France as a *political* community may have been almost as pathetic after 1946 as before 1939. But there are other levels or forms of community as well, and those, which had been badly damaged in the 1930's, were in much better shape after the Liberation.

A second major change affected an area whose poverty in prewar France had been so striking: "intermediate" bodies. Two forces contributed to the change. From below, there was a spectacular growth of Catholic influence—both a cause and an effect of the rediscovery of France as a community. From above, there were measures taken by the Vichy regime and later preserved by the Liberation government.

As for the spread of Catholic influence, the groundwork had been prepared long before 1940. The separation of Church and

State, by divorcing Catholicism from political battles, had made it easier for the Church to put more attention on action in society. To the consolidation of such a trend, both Vichy and the Resistance did indeed contribute. Catholic action groups and Catholic youth movements benefited greatly from the encouragements received from Vichy during the war years. Vichy-created youth movements, in search of *cadres*, turned to men obligingly placed at their disposal by Catholic movements. Consequently, although most of the youth organizations created by Vichy were fiascos almost from the start (in the sense that they never succeeded either in attracting the bulk of the nation's youth, or in bringing their members to endorse Vichy's brand of ideology),[23] the Catholic Association of French Youth did become a link between the movements operating in France during the Vichy period, and postwar French youth associations.[24] The role of Catholics in the Resistance needs hardly to be stressed. Whereas the Catholic element in the making of France had been more and more minimized by official political leaders and by textbook writers and Sorbonne representatives of the prewar Republic, the Resistance movements reversed the trend. "Celui qui croyait au ciel, celui qui n'y croyait pas"— Aragon's famous poem testifies to the reconciliation which had taken place thanks to Christian Democracy. This rehabilitation of Catholicism has been of tremendous and lasting importance. It has contributed to the break-up of the traditional pattern of French thought by dissociating Catholicism from the right. Furthermore it has accelerated the replacement of the old individualistic society with an "organized" one, particularly among peasants; for those parts of France where the Catholic Agricultural Youth Movement has been most active have been the ones where the scope and solidity of social organization have been most impressive.

Under Vichy, various other associations were launched in order to bring the French closer together. For one thing, roving companies of young comedians and groups of young music lovers were supposed to bring art back to non-Parisians and to shake the French out of their individualism.[25] But the main innovations largely due to Vichy's impact were elsewhere: a number of interests in society emerged from prewar chaos or confusion with the kind of organization which made them possible levers for economic and social change. Alain's individualistic society has indeed been left behind.

Vichy's motives in setting up these bodies were mixed. One of the drives was corporatist ideology—the "restitution" to organized groups in society of powers which the Republican state had supposedly usurped. But there was also the need to set up bodies which could administer the restrictions forced upon the French economy by defeat and occupation. Furthermore, some of Vichy's authorities wanted to prevent the Germans from controlling the French economy, as the Germans could otherwise have done either by benefiting from its lack of organization or by setting up German-directed organizations.[26] The result was, in business, the creation of "Organization Committees" which became the mold of the postwar Conseil National du Patronat Français.[27] Among peasants, Vichy set up the Corporation Paysanne, whose impact has been considerable, though complicated. The Confédération Générale Agricole (CGA), instituted at the Liberation in reaction against the Corporation's ideology and leaders, nevertheless kept the Corporation's structure. The leaders whom the Resistance teams put in charge of the CGA were gradually ousted as the peasants moved politically back toward the right and as the Fédération Nationale des Syndicats d'Exploitants Agricoles grew out of the ill-starred CGA. Many of the Corporation's former key men now became the leading lights of this new organization; thus the "men of Vichy" were sent back to the jobs from which M. Tanguy-Prigent, the Socialist Minister of Agriculture of 1945, had expelled them.[28] Embryonic organizations of *cadres* created within the Labor Charter of Vichy have flourished since. The professional orders (lawyers, doctors, etc.) established between 1940 and 1944 have been preserved and consolidated.

Continuity here has been most striking. The Resistance movements, in spite of their revulsion against Vichy corporatism, did not propose a return to prewar "individualism." The economic shortages of the Liberation made a continuation of the Vichy-created organizations (under different names) inevitable anyhow. But, more significantly, the programs of the main Resistance move-

ments and parties contained, in addition to ritual attacks on
"*féodalités économiques*" and "corporative dictatorship," a plea
for a new economic system in which the economy would be directed by the state after consultation with the representatives of
economic interests.[29] The Resistance also wanted representatives of
the professionals to play a part in the management of the free
sector of the economy. The pluralism advocated by the new Christian Democratic party, the Mouvement Républicain Populaire
(MRP), in particular contributed to remove any tinge of illegitimacy from the organized groups which had survived the
Vichy period. Vichy certainly did not create these bodies for
purposes of industrialization, economic modernization, or education toward a less fragmented society. But such institutions, after
having served as transmission belts for Vichy's philistine propaganda or for the German war machine, could do the same for the
Monnet plan.[30]

Besides the rediscovery of France and the creation of intermediate bodies, Vichy initiated a third major social development;
this one affected the mixture of socio-economic systems which was
at the core of the stalemate society. The business and peasant organizations set up in these years were put under the direction of
men far less reluctant to break away from protection and restriction than the spokesmen for "organized" business and farmers before the war—the Claude-Joseph Gignoux of the Confédération
Générale de la Production Française or the Joseph de Pesquidoux
of the Société des Agriculteurs.

In the Organization Committees, delegates of big business,
not of small enterprises, were put in charge; furthermore, these
men were managers rather than owners. The age-old solidarity
between small and large businesses—the large protecting the small,
the small accepting in return the leadership of the large in trade
associations—was severely tried by the circumstances of 1940–
1944. Spokesmen for small business and representatives of certain
traditional, patrimonial family enterprises expressed considerable
hostility toward the Committees.[31] They realized that in these
bodies men with bolder ideas, who were far from scared by the
thought of planning and of economic cooperation with the gov-

ernment, were entrusted with more means of action than the leading businessmen had ever had in France's predominantly nonorganized economy before the war. Under German pressure, but with less resistance from some of the Committees' leaders than from some of Vichy's officials, measures of concentration of enterprises were put into effect.[32] After the Liberation, the sense of shame or embarrassment which many of the leaders of business felt, at a time when the business community was widely accused of having collaborated wholesale with the Germans, probably contributed to making these men almost eager to prove their patriotism by cooperating with the new regime for economic reconstruction and expansion.

In Vichy's Peasant Corporation, the men in control were neither small peasants representing the more backward areas of rural France, nor big old-fashioned landowners—members of the aristocracy whose farms were really in the hands of tenants. Instead, they were commercially-minded men more concerned with markets and remuneration than with status. Or rather, they were aware of the fact that the traditional *économie familiale* of French peasants could be preserved best through technical improvements, professional education, the regrouping of excessively divided lands, extended credit facilities, a better organization of markets, and (inevitably) price supports.[33] Those men were in control of the French peasants' movements throughout the 1950's, but are now being challenged by younger leaders.

Thus the more dynamic elements of the economy were given effective positions, instead of remaining dispersed or submerged. The ideas of groups such as the Jeunes Patrons or the prewar Nouveaux Cahiers received in these institutions a kind of official blessing they had never had before. The Saint-Simonian tradition was no longer underground. Of course these men were still primarily interested in obtaining advantages for their respective constituencies. As shown by the postwar record of continued milking of the state by pressure groups, an old history of state intervention designed to give privileges to all had not ended by 1945.[34] In particular, the peasants' representatives have continued to demand price supports, state subsidies, and protection against outside competition. Nevertheless, one major change of outlook had taken place: the "new men" of business and agriculture had a less parochial and less compartmentalized view of the economic problems of their professions and of the nation than their predecessors. One of the parodoxical results of a period which saw wartime France divided into more administrative zones and separate realms than at any time since the Revolution—in part because of the restrictions on (and later the breakdown of) communications—was to inject a greater awareness of the nationwide scope of economic problems. Consequently, the need for attacking these problems at least from within the framework of a whole profession, rather than through reliance on individual and local pressures, also became understood. The physical fragmentation of 1940–1944 dealt a heavy blow to the economic and social fragmentation of prewar France.

However, the Achilles heel of the stalemate society was not cured, despite a flood of pronouncements about the need for a cure. Relations between workers and other social groups were not improved. Indeed, they did not improve at all under Vichy, where the policy practiced both by the state and by business organizations was one of reaction and repression. The legislation which the Popular Front had adopted in order to bring classes closer together had failed almost completely.[35] The bitterness with which Resistance platforms denounced business attitudes toward labor indicated how deep this fissure had become. The bad memories left, on the workers' side, by the Labor Charter and the rump unions sponsored by Vichy or by Paris collaborators, and, on the management side, by the reforms of the Liberation, doomed legislative attempts such as the *comités d'entreprises* (needless to say, Communist domination of the labor movement contributed to the failure). Not even the postwar nationalization of industries has noticeably contributed to the "reintegration of the proletariat into the nation" which the Resistance wanted to achieve and which socialists saw as one of the main advantages of public ownership. What Crozier calls "*l'horreur du face à face*" has remained a basic obstacle.

Politics in flux

Developments on the political front have been much more contradictory than those in society.

A major change, consonant with the transformation of the balanced French society, was the acceptance of an interventionist state—at last. Vichy's philosophy was, to start with, diametrically opposed to it. Vichy's dream was the "absolute but limited" state, so dear to counterrevolutionaries ever since Bonald—absolute enough in its means of action to crush any attempts at subverting the stalemate society, but limited in the scope of its activity to the protection and perpetuation of the stalemate society. But Pétain's regime, despite its theory of decentralization aimed at reducing the scope of state intervention, and despite its dream of corporations running the economy under a distant and discreet check from the state, was unable to practice what it preached. In the business organizations that Vichy set up, civil servants and managers learned to run the show together. Here the influence of Jean Bichelonne, Vichy's Minister of Industrial Production, was considerable. One of his associates calls him the father of professional statistics in France.[36] His all-encompassing activity marked a break with the past tradition of a civil service whose interventions in economic affairs were largely limited to measures protecting vested interests, defending them against competition but never challenging their privately decided policies. Bichelonne's selection of the bosses of the Organization Committees contributed mightily to the replacement of businessmen for whom the state could only be either an enemy or a servant with managers for whom the state could be a guide. Thus Bichelonne's administration initiated practices of cooperation which the Monnet plan later institutionalized.

Indeed, on the other side of the political fence, the need for a more active state had become one of the main planks of Resistance platforms. The platforms called for planning by the state, nationalization, big public investments, "economic and social democracy," and state control over cartels, prices, or capital movements; all those proposals showed that the revulsion against the lopsided "economic liberalism" of prewar times had become irresistible. The measures taken in 1944–1946 in order to put them into effect are well known. It is worth noting that none of the "conquests of the Liberation" has been seriously threatened since. The attacks against *"dirigisme"* by Radicals and conservatives were successful only when they were directed against price controls and at those measures of intervention into the affairs of rural France which the peasant organizations themselves had not requested.

A drastic shift in public issues resulted—from the old ideological issues to economic and social ones. It had been foreshadowed even before 1939. The key ideological issue of the Third Republic had begun to fade away; even the Popular Front showed no official hostility to the Church.[37] As a recent report stresses, the rapprochement between Catholics and *laïcs* under the Resistance led to various attempts to eliminate permanently the stumbling block of *laïcité*.[38] Although they failed, it is worth remembering that the projects which were discussed in 1943–44–45 shied away from the old *laïc* objective of a pure and simple elimination of private schools; a blunt *monopole* was rejected, and some kind of pluralism advocated. Except for the years 1945–1951, private schools have received help from the state since 1941.

On the other hand, since the late 1930's the state has promoted measures of income redistribution which went far beyond what the theory of the stalemate society allowed. It showed concern for social welfare on a scale unknown before; the *"politique de la famille"* has been followed by every regime since Daladier's decrees of July 1939. Vichy gave tremendous publicity to its main contribution to social insurance: the old-age pensions for retired workers. Resistance platforms emphasized the need for extending protection against social risks, and the social security system of the Liberation was built by a man who had been one of the main drafters of the law of August 1940 setting up Vichy's Organization Committees.[39] The participation of workers' delegates in at least some of the activities of the firm became the subject of various laws, from the Popular Front's shop stewards to Vichy's *comités sociaux* and the Liberation's *comités d'entreprises*.

Thus, the shift in issues contributed to the "nationalization" of opinion and issues which proportional representation accelerated.

The fragmentation of the political scene into "fiefs" and local issues began to fade just as economic fragmentation did. Society and the state began moving simultaneously, and in the same direction.

A second series of changes affected France's traditional schools of political thought. The origins of these changes can be found both in the social transformations already mentioned and in the realm of political events. Again, the main influences were, on the one hand, the fiasco of Vichy, and on the other, the fact that the Resistance was dominated by dissidents from the regular old "spiritual families" and by Christian Democrats, whose ideas influenced those men in the Resistance who had never been politically active before. Thus, Christian Democracy became one of the main postwar forces, owing its importance less to the coherence or precision of its doctrine than to its concern for the problems raised by the new direction of French society—rather than by the standard issues of the stalemate society—and to its penetration in various milieux such as youth, peasants, and workers.

One of the unexpected results of the Vichy *Götterdämmerung* has been the almost complete elimination of the Maurras counterrevolutionaries as a political force, and the weakening or transformation of those social groups which had been sympathetic to the shrill shrieks of hate that came from the deaf old man. The army, the navy, the fashionable salons, the provincial academies, old family doctors, and *notaires*—all have been affected by purges, inflation, or simply the heavy toll of natural deaths. There is little left of *Maurrassisme* in metropolitan France; traces are still visible in Algeria and in certain circles of "integral Catholicism," but they are quaint relics rather than politically significant phenomena.

Another of the prewar groups, the cautious conservatives (in other words the bulk of the conservatives who had followed La Rocque, had read more and more the anti-Republican press of the 1930's, and had joined Pétain's Legion), discovered in the last, tragic months of Vichy that Thiers had been right after all: it is still the Republic that best protects them against disorder. That is, in a country where the majority is composed of members of the middle classes or of peasants who have no interest in social subversion, it is majority rule that has the best chance of defending the *status quo* against the revolutionaries of the far left and the nihilists of the far right. These conservatives came to realize that they were far closer to the political system of prewar France than to the totalitarian delirium of the Laval-Darnand period. After all, not only the conservatives who had deserted *"la vieille maison"* but also the Radical and the Socialist politicians believed that politics meant primarily legislation, and that authority meant education rather than police. Hence a new *Ralliement* to the Republic in 1944; it was from those conservative groups that the MRP received much of its unexpected support in 1945–46. Ever since, conservatives, having understood the lesson of 1934–1944, have concentrated on organizing their parties and pressure groups more effectively than before the war, so as to gain better access to power. When the challenge of Communism seemed too strong for the Fourth Republic around 1947–48 only some of those elements deserted to de Gaulle's Rassemblement du Peuple Français (RPF), and many of these men either deserted the RPF in turn when the danger seemed over, or simply used the RPF as an elevator which would carry them back up to the level of power from which they had been pushed down by the politicians of Communist-Socialist-MRP *tripartisme*. Indeed, antiparliamentary movements since 1944 have found more recruits among the groups which had provided the social basis of the "Republicans" of the Third Republic (peasants and shopkeepers), or among the new middle classes of engineers, modern businessmen and white-collar workers, than among the former *pétainistes*.[40]

This phenomenon points to a final aspect of the change in France's political ideologies. The democrats of the Radical tradition have lost much of their influence, in part because their own role in the Resistance was limited, in part because both their ideas and their social basis were too closely tied to that society of anti-clerical, socially satisfied, and ideologically "advanced" notables to which the war has delivered fatal blows.

It is when we turn to the crucial problem of the organization of the state that we find the most baffling story of failure—baffling because a series of events corresponding to almost overwhelming, if contradictory, desires for a change led to a new political system so disturbingly close to the Third Republic.

The story starts with a turnover in political personnel. In 1940, power fell into the hands of the previous "minorities"—those groups of men who, for one reason or another, did not belong to, or had become separated from, *"la République des Camarades";* the fall of France was the "divine surprise" of many of the dissenters or enemies whom we have mentioned before. Metropolitan France became the battlefield between the factions into which those groups split: corporatists against *"belinistes,"* pro-Pétain Christian Democrats against *Maurrassiens,* and of course fascists against conservatives or technocrats or other fascists. Those dissenters who either refused to support Vichy or abandoned Vichy after a few months of hesitation (as did many Catholics, who were first taken in by institutions such as the Uriage school or youth camps) [41] became the backbone of the early Resistance. One of the paradoxes of the restoration of 1945–46 is that although it brought back many of the parties discredited in 1940, the political personnel of the Third Republic never succeeded in coming back *in toto.* Of course there were Henri Queuille and Robert Schuman; but Schuman had hardly been a star before the war: he had belonged to a party which never fit the system of the Third Republic. Neither of these two men, nor Herriot—more a monument now than a leader—gave the Fourth Republic its tone. In the old parties which reemerged, purges eliminated many of the prewar leaders; thus in the Socialist Party men like Guy Mollet, Daniel Mayer and the syndicalists (Robert Lacoste, Christian Pineau) took over from the generation of Blum and Paul Faure. The MRP was dominated by "men of the Resistance" rather than by the leaders of the tiny prewar Christian Democratic parties.

Nevertheless, no new political equilibrium has been found. Practically the same institutions that had proved fatal to the lethargic Third Republic were seen again in the far more active state of the Liberation. The connection between the functions of government and its internal organization, between the scope and the intensity of public authority was overlooked by the assemblies which drafted the constitution of the Fourth Republic. One might have hoped that a transformation in the social and economic conditions of French life, fostered by and in turn acting upon the institutions of the state, would result in a corresponding "modernization" of political conditions; [42] but it has not. At the root of the failure, we find an incapacity to take advantage of the change of political personnel, issues, and doctrines in such a way as to change French parties as well. If there was one theme which Vichyites and Resistance men pursued more shrilly than any other, it was the need for a "renewal of elites," but neither Vichy nor the Resistance could bring this about. Vichy usually meant thereby a depolitization of France, and the assigning of state powers to business representatives, peasant leaders, civil servants, and local notables—a redistribution, hardly a renewal. At the end, the reformers or dissenters of the 1930's who had sailed on the Vichy liner and did not jump off in time were drowned when their ship sank.

As for those in the Resistance who asked for new and more democratic political elites recruited from all classes of society, they never thought through the problem of how to produce them. The problem got lost in the chaos of Resistance thinking about postwar political movements—a chaos which resulted from a number of factors: one was the moralism of Resistance thinking, produced by newcomers to political reflection and dissenters from prewar politics; another was the almost messianic hopes which were indispensable for the morale of men who risked their lives under incredible circumstances; and still another was the ideological heterogeneity within each movement, for each owed its existence not to a community of ideas but to the vagaries of geography or friendships and to a common but negative desire to liberate the country. As is well known, there were those who hoped that a big Resistance movement would supersede prewar parties, and that the Resistance would thus provide the new political personnel—but how such a movement would evolve and provide for its own renewal was left unclear.[43] There were also those who worked toward the reemergence of a party system: the Communists, who saw in the idea of a Resistance bloc a major threat; the Socialists, whom the Communists urged only too successfully to preserve their party identity;

the Christian Democrats, as soon as they saw that the two "Marxist" parties would continue as in the past; and—paradoxically enough —de Gaulle himself, for reasons of foreign policy and because at the time his authority was accepted more easily by the parties, which needed him, than by the movements, which did not owe their existence to him and tended to resent his heavy hand.[44] The tendency toward reemergence of parties won, and the problem of insuring a continuous supply of political elites became a mere corollary of the problem of preserving the vitality of the party system.

The very widespread hope of preserving it through a modern sort of contract theory, i.e., through agreements between strong parties on a program which would become the charter for the executive, was to be frustrated soon enough, when it appeared that the parties were anything but strong. The tragedy of Resistance thinking on making parties strong was that it had remained terribly superficial. Regeneration-through-suffering simply was not enough. Blum repeatedly stressed that his party needed a change in structure, but not in doctrine; hence it did not open its gates to men who were more interested in broad *travaillisme* than in socialism.[45] The new men whom the Resistance had attracted to politics redistributed themselves among multiple chapels often more concerned with doctrinal purity than with efficiency in action. Therefore, the chances of this new generation of leaders to provide better political leadership than before the war and to keep their parties dynamic and appealing enough to recruit younger members in the future, depended entirely upon a second set of factors: not the party system itself, but the constitutional order.

The tragedy, here, was the return to unreformed parliamentarism. For it insured that the reformers in the Resistance would be gradually brought back to orthodox parliamentary behavior by "*le système.*" The comeback of what I have called the pure "game model" of politics inevitably led to public disenchantment, to the withering of parties, and finally to massive indifference or distaste for politics.

In this area, the solidarity of Vichy and the Resistance was of a rather devilish nature. After the fall of France, dissatisfaction with parliamentarism had become general; Blum's soul-searching book *For All Mankind* proves this far more conclusively than the various statements of contrition issued by men like Herriot just after the shock of defeat. The first pronouncements of Resistance movements about postwar politics were just as harsh on the late Republic. But gradually all the alternatives to parliamentarism—drastic ones like the presidential system and milder ones like Michel Debré's scheme—were discarded.[46] Two factors were crucial here: first, the tactics of the Communists, who skillfully appealed to the Republican tradition and subtly exploited Resistance fears about de Gaulle; secondly, Vichy's rabid antiparliamentarism, which, after Blum's defense of the Third Republic at the 1942 Riom trial, gradually made France's former brand of parliamentarism look good by contrast. Indeed, responsibility for pushing the Resistance away from its own initial ideas must rest largely on the failure of the Vichy regime to establish either the "strong but limited state" of original Vichy orthodoxy or the presidential system which Pétain ultimately endorsed on paper (and which was less democratic than, but not fundamentally different in its institutions from, various Resistance schemes). Instead it turned into a masterpiece of arbitrary, incoherent, and repressive dictatorship.

Of course, the drive to "reform" the prewar system did not disappear, but instead of going in the direction of drastic *institutional* change designed to make the state more capable of surviving the divisions of the representatives, it tried on the contrary to make the system even more representative; it took refuge in the effort against restoring a new Senate, and in the unfounded hope of a "better" (i.e., stronger) party system. The degree to which a party system depends on the organization of power was minimized or overlooked. The combination of a parliamentary regime so closely patterned after that of the Third Republic and of proportional representation was about as regressive as one could have invented. Those of the "new men" of the Resistance who saw in this pseudo-reform a mistake, and in the restoration of parliamentarism a recipe for certain failure, became de Gaulle's postwar supporters—and thus remained in the unhappy position of dissenters.

Consequently, the stability of French democracy was made more elusive than ever. During the Third Republic, when a major crisis arose, the parliamentary game had to be suspended, and power had to be entrusted temporarily to a savior: Clemenceau, Poincaré, Doumergue. Until 1940 the oscillations between game and saviors had been moderate; the interruptions of the game never amounted to a collapse of the regime. Before 1934 the Republic had been able to provide a sufficient amount of executive leadership—either because weak executives sufficed as long as the sky was blue, or through temporarily strong and stable cabinets during the crisis years of the Dreyfus case, or through a brief suspension of the rules in favor of a savior. Thus the permanent opposition between two conceptions of politics—politics as a rally around one man, and politics as free splintering—had been relatively subdued.

Since 1940, however, the oscillations have become more ample and more violent. Twice, in 1940 and in 1958, the appeal to a savior has entailed the demise of the previous constitutional order. Also, whereas in the past both the more authoritarian and the more liberal types of political leadership operated within the narrow context of the limited state, ever since 1940 France's political regimes, as we have seen, have intervened in society not merely to protect it but to transform it. The collapse of 1940 ushered in a period, lasting to this day, in which compromise between the two types of politics seems impossible but more necessary than ever. Vichy, trying ruthlessly to eliminate all vestiges of representative government, gave enormous powers to the executive. The hope of achieving a better balance between executive action and representative government collapsed when, after Jean Moulin's death in 1943, de Gaulle's concept of *l'Etat* and the Resistance emphasis on *politics* proved to be irreconcilable.[47] The Resistance, reacting against both Vichy and de Gaulle, pushed the triumph of representative government to the utmost degree of executive impotence, at a time when the revolution in the scope of the state's functions made this a particularly serious mistake.

Paradoxically, each extreme has doomed its own principle by pushing it so far. The main flaws of the Third Republic were not only preserved, but aggravated. First, both Vichy and the Fourth Republic, when faced with emergencies, proved once again more capable with words than with acts. Vichy's executive was powerful in theory, but by 1943 it was a paper tiger. Secondly, the distance between the electorate and the political system kept growing. Both Vichy and the Fourth Republic helped to alienate the people from politics; if there was any continuity, it was in keeping "*le peuple absent*," as Maurice Duverger has written.[48] The post-Resistance parties thus ended by compromising their representative character, as demonstrated both by the lack of public support and by the increase in the size of an unstable floating vote. One reason why the electorate has stayed remote from the political system has been the resilience of centralization; for another irony of our period lies in the parallelism between Vichy and the Resistance in their originally proclaimed intentions to decentralize and their subsequent moves in the opposite direction. With Vichy the move was from "provinces" to *préfets regionaux* and the centralization of the police, with the Resistance from the promise of self-government for local units to "*superpréfets*."

Thirdly, once the people in 1945 recovered the right to vote, the old problem of the "efficiency" of elections reemerged. After 1947, the permanent rule of the Center became once again a basic precept of the game, contributing both to the sterility of the parties and to the alienation of the electorate, which was more convinced than ever that its votes did not affect the competition for power. At this point, there was no longer a danger that the Center would become too narrow, because, though the Extreme Left was large indeed, the Extreme Right had shrunk. The trouble with the "Third Force" governments was the multiple splits that paralyzed them on every important issue.

Another crucial deficiency resulted from the war years, and created an entirely new threat to the stability of the political system. One group has emerged from World War Two both split and largely alienated from the rest of the national community: the army. The breach between army elements which remained faithful to Pétain and those which followed de Gaulle was never completely repaired. Under Vichy the armed forces found themselves increasingly unpopular in a country which was put under quasi-military control by a defeated army and navy. At the same time the Gaullist military leaders who fought outside France (and often against other Frenchmen) found it difficult to adjust to the political and moral climate of France after the war ended. Their dream of a France *"pure et dure"* was cruelly shattered, and the famous clash of December 1945 between the Constituent Assembly and General de Gaulle indicated that in the new regime, once de Gaulle was eliminated, the army would not have a major role. In a way, both Vichy's misuse of its armed forces and the Resistance's predominantly civilian character contributed to discredit the army, despite de Gaulle's attempts at an *amalgame* between Resistance, Free French, and formerly Vichyite forces.[49]

Furthermore, the relation of the army to politics has inevitably been transformed. After all, Vichy was largely a military regime whose officers were at first given a taste of power and later severely punished for having sworn an oath of loyalty to Pétain, and the military elements of the Resistance were composed of men who had disobeyed in order to follow their idea of France's honor. Thus the kind of unconditional loyalty to the state which even politically hostile leaders like Lyautey had observed toward France's regime was shattered. De Gaulle's grandiose gesture of defiance and Vichy's resort to the broken sword unleashed forces which are far from tamed today.

It is not the smallest irony of our story that the new army which emerged from the trials of the war years, and whose loyalty has been so fragile, is an army whose officers have been more representative of France's social structure than the largely aristocratic or upper bourgeois officer corps of the past. The more "feudal" army of the Third Republic had remained loyal to the very unfeudal political system. A much more democratic army was going to challenge France's new democracy.

France and a world in motion

The war years also resulted in drastic new changes in the French image of France in the world. This is a subject which is very difficult to treat, for there is little evidence to back one's statements; it deserves much further study. At the start, we find another strange convergence between Vichy and the Resistance—again an involuntary one, to be sure, since the battle between those two groups of forces was fought largely because of their different views of the world and of France's role. Many of the original supporters of Vichy were nationalists, determined to restore France's pride and to protect what was left of French power; and their impact was far from nil. Later, the abject submissiveness of Vichy cured many Frenchmen of those prewar doubts which had so devastated French morale. And the Resistance, of course, was a nationalist revival. The rediscovery of community that I have mentioned was to a vast extent a quest for power, rank, and prestige. Thus no contrast was sharper than that between the sinister mood of the thirties and the vigor of France's postwar attitude toward the world. But the troublesome question was: what could power, rank, and prestige mean in the new world after 1940? Granted that the temptation of *repli, abandon,* folding up and shrinking had been overcome, what adjustments would have to be made to insure that France could play her role with maximum effectiveness?

Adjustments. In two important areas of national life, the need for such adjustments was clearly being felt by many, both in Vichy and in the Resistance. These were again points on which their antagonism was far from complete.

The first area was the national economy. Even before 1940 the need to put an end to the alarming economic retardation of France in order to restore or preserve France's position in the world had been understood by a large number of the dissenters from the Third Republic. Now, many of the civil servants who joined in Resistance movements, or served in the Vichy regime to its end, were in close touch with the formidable German war economy and came to realize how strong was the link between industrial organization and political power.[50] Many of the business leaders and engineers of Vichy and Paris were also thrown into contact—often collaboration—with Germany's extraordinary dynamism; they negotiated with German business leaders and officials, and many of them visited German plants and business offices. As a consequence, these men became far more aware of the need for organization, concentration, higher productivity, improved statistical equipment, better industrial relations, and more cooperation between the business community and the state. In the last period of the war and in the months which followed its end, the contact with America's war machine, industrial economy, and bureaucratic efficiency provided the same groups of Frenchmen with another compelling display of the prerequisites of influence in the modern world. Thus, there came to be an understanding of a new component of power.

Secondly, civil servants and businessmen during the occupation had also realized—often under duress—the amount of interdependence of Western European economies and the possibilities of cooperation across borders. This point, like the preceding one, had been made by some dissenters before the war: the businessmen and engineers of the Nouveaux Cahiers or X-Crise, Déat and his *"planistes."* Now interdependence became a matter of daily life. Moreover, within a different context, postwar European unity became a theme of many Resistance movements which were either looking forward to a European holy alliance of the peoples against trusts and munition-makers or dreaming of a powerful Europe playing once again a major role in world affairs. Despite this more ideological or political approach, the "European" feelings of the Resistance buttressed the practical concern of the more technocratic Vichyites; indeed it is thanks to such Resistance dreams that the idea of European unity survived its exploitation by Nazi propaganda.[51] Finally, General de Gaulle also looked forward to a European political force that would play its own part in world affairs.[52] Of course, the officials and businessmen of Vichy thought primarily in terms of Franco-German cooperation, whereas the Resistance thought about the links forged among the victims of Germany by Nazi domination, and General de Gaulle thought about the avenues which Europe could open to French leadership and shut to German *revanche*. But these conceptions were not mutually exclusive.

With the demise of Vichy, the quest for rank became a vital imperative again, but the nationalism of the Resistance and of General de Gaulle was modified by their understanding of the impossibility for France to recapture "grandeur" outside a context of European solidarity, in an age dominated by extra-European giants. Thus the technocratic "realism" of the Vichy period, purged of its defeatist connotations, could survive the collapse of Vichy.

After the war the Fourth Republic decided to scrap its policy of revenge and to replace it with a Franco-German partnership; and although the new approach met with numerous protectionist objections from French businessmen, there was not much opposition (outside the Communist Party) to the basic idea of the need for reconciliation and cooperation between the two former enemies. Many Resistance platforms and de Gaulle himself had mentioned the need for cooperation after the war and denazification. In a way, Laval's statement that, whatever the result of the war, France and Germany would remain neighbors and would therefore have to find a *modus vivendi* was more widely understood than one realized at first. The contacts which had been established during the occupation period between elites of the two countries, especially in the business world, were probably far from wasted. Within the *Festung Europa* which waited for its liberation from the outside, occupied peoples and temporary masters discovered that they had a lot in common which distinguished them from outsiders.

Maladjustments. The separation between Nazi-dominated Europe and the outside world, however, had some far less constructive effects, which were probably more important, at least in the immediate postwar period.

The main factor here could be described as follows. At the very time when many Frenchmen came to understand that a deep economic transformation was needed in order to preserve France's importance in the world, the trauma of the war years blinded them to changes which made France's restoration to the status of a world power highly problematic, even in case of domestic overhaul. They overlooked forces which were making a delusion out of the old French image of a world responsive to the universality of French values, and out of the vision of a map in which French colors would occupy almost as much place as England's. Thus there was insufficient awareness, not just of the weakening of French power (for it is a perfectly legitimate goal to try to regain power), but of the need for a more drastic revision of past French concepts of power than the new emphasis on industrialization. And there was insufficient awareness of the fact that rank could not be won without adjustments more extensive than the emphasis on Europe. Here again, many elements contributed to the blindness: Vichy's fantasy of neutral France mediating in the war;[53] the Resistance's lack of concern for foreign affairs; the inevitable reaction of desperate pride which the humiliation of submission to the occupant was bound to provoke; the tremendous effort by de Gaulle in 1944–45 to restore French self-respect by emphasizing France's contribution to the allied victory; the huge numbers of war prisoners herded into German camps. Alfred Grosser has remarked, quite rightly, that even though de Gaulle's dogma of priority to foreign affairs disappeared with him when he resigned in 1946, his conception of foreign affairs and of France's role was inherited uncritically by his successors.[54] On colonial affairs in particular, the curtain which separated France from the world outside Europe prevented both the Vichy elites and the future leaders of the Fourth Republic who were in the metropolitan Resistance from realizing the depth of the revolt in the empire against a simple restoration of prewar colonial rule, or even against half-hearted liberal measures. As for the Free French, they needed the base provided by the empire too desperately to envisage "self-government," as their Brazzaville statement of 1944 made clear.

Consequently a deep psychological abyss opened between France and the rest of the world. France was eager to regain her rank, and to do so through economic efforts and European cooperation. However, two obstacles were going to make the task almost impossible.

On the one hand, many of France's postwar leaders had deep inferiority feelings—a sense of failure and shame for the defeat of 1940 and the behavior of Vichy, a passionate desire to erase those memories by political and psychological means. They tried to increase France's role in the last months of the war and in the peacemaking process. And they tried to reestablish the control of France over her empire; in this effort the leaders of the MRP played a major role just after the war. Certainly, the behavior of many of France's postwar politicians, such as Bidault or Debré—and even more of top army leaders from de Lattre to Navarre and Challe—indicates how widespread the inferiority feelings were.

On the other hand, many of the Resistance leaders who fought in France never even got an inferiority complex. They were simply ignorant of the outside world; they were primarily interested in domestic issues. When they took over, they found themselves in many ways even less prepared to face the postwar world than the men who, shamed by what had happened, wanted to restore France's greatness. The behavior of leaders like Mollet, Lacoste, and Maurice Bourgès-Maunoury reveals depths of innocence and layers of good conscience untainted by anything like a sense of guilt or an understanding of the world at large. They found themselves in a world they neither made nor really watched making. Instinctively they operated on the old assumptions about France-in-the-world.

It is probably not an accident that the men who found it least difficult to adapt to the postwar world were Pierre Mendès-France, whose very pragmatism and essentially economic approach to politics turned him into a mixture of Cassandra and hermit in French affairs; Jean Monnet, whose outlook was not very different, whose knowledge of the world was deep, and who had the good sense to remain at the back of the stage; and men like Robert Schuman and Antoine Pinay, who had not been either deeply involved in the bitter battle for status fought by Free France in London and Algiers or engulfed in the passionate and soul-filling struggles of the Resistance against Reaction, Fascism, and Hitler.

The force which was least likely to adjust to the change in the international position of France was of course the army. Its very humiliations, its internal splits, and its traditions made it incapable of doing so. Those elements that remained on the side of Vichy were both subjected to, and willing partners in, continual xenophobic propaganda; those elements that joined de Gaulle or re-entered the war after the Giraud detour wanted more than anything else to erase the memory of the defeat of 1940 and to restore France to an uncontested position of eminence. Many of the most dangerous recent aspects of *le Malaise de l'Armée* had their roots in World War Two. Those aspects—the tendency to see a plot against France behind every incident, the readiness to see defeatism in every concession—have never been brought out more sharply than in the trials which followed the abortive *putsch* of April 1961 and which struck at a number of officers who had distinguished themselves on de Gaulle's side during the war.

PARADOXES OF THE WAR EXPERIENCE

This part of my study can be summarized by offering a few paradoxes for our meditation.

First, Vichy and the Resistance, which fought each other so bloodily, cooperated in many ways without wanting or knowing it, and thus carried the nation to the threshold of a new social order. It can be said that the two groups that gained most from the war years were business and the Catholic Church—a far cry from the France of 1936. Vichy brought into existence social institutions which could become the channels for state action, and it thereby gave a considerable boost to the latter-day Saint-Simoniens, men who were willing to serve as agents of the Count's old dream of organization, production, industrialism. The Resistance brought to power teams of engineers, civil servants, and politicians determined to use those agents and those channels for economic and consequently for social change. Had these new teams not arrived, it is quite possible that the social institutions erected by Vichy would have withered away just as the consortiums of World War One had vanished after 1919. Without readily available transmission belts and without the shock of discovery produced on French economic elites by sudden and brutal contact with foreign economies, postwar planning might have failed. The transformation of the French economy and society since 1952 is due to the combination of the wills of a statist, de Gaulle, and a Saint-Simonien, Monnet; they used instruments prepared by Vichy and strengthened them by adding quite a few of their own, such as nationalizations, the Planning Commission, and a reform of the civil service. The meekness of business, which was unwilling to oppose the government of the Liberation, and the big production drive of the Communists in 1944–1947, which contrasted with labor's prewar attitude, both contributed to the initial success of the movement. The process is far from completed, and no transformation of French political life has resulted from it so far. But World War Two had on French society effects opposite from those of World War One.

Secondly, both Vichy and the Resistance provide us with choice examples of serendipity. Vichy, which wanted to coax the French back to the land and back to rule by traditional notables, consolidated instead the business community and demonstrated conclusively that the elites of "static" France could not provide leadership any more. Vichy also wanted to restore old provincial customs and dialects and peculiarities—instead of which it put into motion powerful forces of further economic and social unification. The Resistance, which wanted to purify French political life and was prone to proclaim the death of the bourgeoisie, ended as a political fiasco but was the lever of an economic modernization which has certainly not meant the demise of the bourgeoisie. Indeed, those of the dissenters from the Third Republic who turned against it because they wanted to save the stalemate society which the Republic seemed unable to defend—an order based on the preponderance of the middle classes—could remark today that French society is still dominated by those classes. The proportion of industrial workers has barely increased. It is the composition of the middle classes which has changed.

Thirdly, the continuity between Vichy and the Resistance—a continuity which manifested itself in economic alterations, family protection, the "rediscovery" of youth, and the revival of Catholicism—appears also, in more ironic fashion, in a number of failures. The hope of reconciling the workers and the employers has not been fulfilled; neither the paternalistic solutions of the Vichy Labor Charter nor the social measures of the Liberation have succeeded in overcoming a long tradition of mutual suspicion, although it is possible that the old antagonisms will be gradually overcome by new attitudes among businessmen concerned with "human relations" and by the increasing hierarchy and specialization within the working class—all resulting from economic change. In agriculture, both Vichy and the Resistance movements emphasized the need to preserve the traditional family units, but their postwar decline has been spectacular and no amount of protection from the state has been able to suspend it; indeed, mechanization of the farms has often contributed to the decline by increasing the financial difficulties of farmers whose products sell at prices which remain at a lower level than the cost of the machines, and by worsening the plight of peasants whose land is too small for efficient production. As for the army, both regimes have failed to preserve its morale, its unity, and its strength. Finally, both have failed to stabilize the French political system, for the new society of France still awaits a political synthesis comparable to the early Third Republic; it has enjoyed only a respite. In Robert de Jouvenel's days, politics was the hobby of Frenchmen, but not the condition of their lives. Today, unfortunately, it has become the condition of their lives, but also the object of their dislike. I suggest that the effects of World War Two have something to do with this reversal. Whether these effects came through serendipity, through some Hegelian dialectic in action, or through some invention of my own is something I shall not decide.

III

FRANCE IN 1962:
JUDGMENT SUSPENDED

◇◇

The cramped old equilibrium is gone, but the new dynamic France, growing in population again, is marked by contradictions which explain why so many different judgments can be made in good faith about her. Rarely has Marianne so strongly resembled Janus.*

SOCIETY TODAY

France's society in the early 1960's is a mixture of the old and the new. The changes which are taking place are the most far-reaching since the French Revolution; the stalemate society is dead. But these changes are too recent to have destroyed completely the old pattern and too sweeping to take place without tensions. They

* In this final part of the essay I have incorporated many points made during our Paris meeting of July 1961 by my colleagues and by the discussants, especially Messrs. Crozier, Grosser, and Georges Lavau. I have also taken into account subsequent comments by Professors Henry Ehrmann, Gavin Langmuir, and Stephen Graubard.

are being studied in greater detail elsewhere in this volume; what I want to emphasize here are those aspects and effects which concern the French political community.

Changes in the socio-economic system

The transformation of the old balance of French society, begun in the war years, has been drastic.

Innovations. If we take an over-all look we find that the combination of "new men and new attitudes" inherited from the war period has made French society much less different from the societies of other industrial nations. Insofar as the stalemate society still had the marks of France's old feudal order, one may say that the final elimination of feudalism is in progress. Let us not decide at this point whether the old values have been eliminated with it; what we can observe is a thoroughly new set of attitudes, which may correspond either to new values or to the need to adjust to a new situation created from the outside even though the old values themselves have not disappeared. It is certain that should such attitudes persist, the new behavior will ultimately affect the values as well. But we are dealing here with a "revolution" which is both recent and incomplete, and values can be assessed only over a much longer time.

What has happened in France has been happening almost all over Western Europe, particularly in Northern Italy and in West Germany. Everywhere, as in France, the percentage of the population employed in agriculture goes down and the percentage of managers, executives, and employees goes up. In the civil service, in business, in professional organizations, even in the military forces, new groups of "technocrats" appear—men who specialize in the management of a highly industrialized and bureaucratic society, men who earn high incomes without necessarily owning much capital.

A hierarchy based on skills and performance is beginning to emerge in France. Expansion has at last attracted public attention to economic matters. Within the business world, a kind of managerial revolution has led to a new conception of profits, in which management and ownership are less tightly fused and in which the firm's power counts more than the owner's fortune. Increasing concern for forecasting has led to internal reorganization of management. The productivity of labor has increased by around five percent a year since the war.[55] Outside business, a revolution in the way of life has begun. An increasing proportion of the Frenchman's income goes for health, housing, and transportation; a decreasing one is lavished on food. The village is less important as an economic unit. The family is less tightly closed: there is growing cooperation between families in order to share the comforts and gadgets of industrial society, and the spectacular "car rush," which has given to France the highest ratio of cars per population in Western Europe, has increased the circle of acquaintances of family members far beyond the village or small town. The spread of television has lifted their horizons. The attitudes toward credit and savings have been reversed. There is less distance than before between ranks and statuses, although there may be even more distance between incomes. More students choose scientific or technical courses instead of the traditional liberal education. The transition which is being crossed here is the transition from *la France bourgeoise* to *la France des classes moyennes,* from the *Revue des deux mondes* to *Réalités.*

Although these developments are not characteristic of France alone, the way in which they have taken place in France is unique and fascinating. Given the classical style of authority and France's resulting centralization, the change could occur only if the initiative came from the top. The state took over the direction of the economy in 1944–1946 and thus gave the decisive impulse—a major revolution indeed by comparison with the Third Republic's limited state, whose interventions were merely those of a watchdog of the stalemate society. The role of the state has been double.

On the one hand, it has taken direct responsibility for an important public sector, modernizing it and increasing its production; also the rate of public investments and expenditures for family allowances, housing, professional training, school construction, and other "economic and social action" has been kept high enough to encourage and speed up France's economic conversion (the provisions of the Fourth Economic Plan and the budget for 1962 are particularly impressive in this respect).

On the other hand, the state has put pressure on the private sector of the economy to force that sector out of past habits. Here, the Planning Commission has been of special importance, since its role consists of connecting the state with the leaders of French business, and thus transmitting the state's impulse. The state has promoted change by exploiting that very craving for security which had previously slowed down change. That is, the state has done its best to lower the risks of change. Having to deal with notoriously reluctant swimmers, it has warmed the water so that the swimmers would not be afraid to catch cold, and it has multiplied the incentives to convince them that swimming would not only be harmless but profitable. Thus, the old practices of state aid continued—but such aid was now serving as a crutch instead of a wheelchair. The incentives include depreciation allowances which encourage businessmen to increase their investments; other tax measures which favor industrial mergers; financial aid to incite businessmen to move out of Paris; priority access to credit; subsidies for research projects; special agreements to facilitate the start of new manufactures; and equipment subsidies in depressed areas.[56] Also, the state has put its own statistical and forecasting services at the disposal of businessmen. Many of the decisions on agriculture published in 1961 were designed to orient the farmers toward production for which demand is likely to increase (such as meat, milk, fruits, and vegetables) and help them to organize a better distribution of their products.

The leaders of French business (and, to a much lesser extent, those of French agriculture) have in turn transmitted this impulse downward. What has convinced them of the need for expansion was, first, the fact that in 1945 the choice was no longer between the risks of expansion and the comforts of stability, but between modernization and extinction; secondly, the push and the incentives from the state's credit and investment policies; and thirdly, the compelling momentum of the state's decision to create a common Western European market. In this last area French business did not give in without a battle; the opposition of the steel industry to the Schuman plan for a coal and steel community was quite spectacular. But the failure of this opposition helped convince the leaders of French business that adaptation was the best part of wisdom. Here again, the way in which the European Communities have gently reduced risks for the swimmers has complemented the lessons of the failure to prevent the birth of those Communities; for the European "technocrats" have been extremely lenient toward cartel agreements, at least in the decisive first years of the Communities' existence. As a result, the old "static equilibrium" has been replaced with a forward-rolling "bicycle equilibrium," as someone has called it. Planning and forecasting had to be adopted both by the state and by business. In a nation with a rising population and with a growing desire to improve its way of life after many years of stagnation and deprivation and with new outlets opening in Europe, it was no longer possible either to treat demand as static or to consider only the local or regional market. Businessmen have kept the rate of investment high, and a number of industries have pushed their exports considerably. The compelling logic of economic rationality began to win out, not because of myriads of individual decisions of independent entrepreneurs, but because of the machinery set up from above. The impulse was transmitted downward (especially in the steel and electronics industries) by the large firms, on which the state relied; the movement has led in turn to further concentration, in industry and now also in commerce. It has also led to a further weakening of the prewar solidarity between big and small business, for in most industries (with the significant exception of textiles) the bigger firms have been the most productive and the most eager to get out of past routines. Thus, even determined or nostalgic defenders of the old restrictive order have had to give in or give way. Businessmen, shopkeepers, and peasants alike are more dependent now on the national economy than on a mere segment of it; it is striking to hear the peasants' organizations today demand what amounts to long-term national planning of agricultural production, even at the expense of private property.

Another important aspect of the change can be seen in the industrial workers—both their way of life and their conduct. Their way of life has moved noticeably toward that of the bourgeois, thanks to the rise in the standard of living, to gradual improvements in housing, to paid holidays and household appliances, and to the ownership of cars in which to escape from the suburbs on weekends and to experience the "glorious uncertainty" and equality of this national sport, driving. The increasing specialization of industrial tasks fragments the workers as a class and diversifies their reactions to other groups or to the state. The proportion of factory workers among wage-earners is going down. The nature of much industrial labor today integrates the worker's life into the plant; his wages depend on the prosperity of the business much more than on his own individual efficiency; his job security has become a matter of joint interest for management and labor.[57] Willingness to buy on the installment plan integrates many workers into the rest of society. As a consequence, their enthusiasm for strikes and their militancy in unions or parties have considerably decreased; the unions have compromised with employers in numerous collective agreements, including the famous "Renault contract." The social activities of the *comités d'entreprises* have been impressive.[58] There is also evidence of an increasing willingness to change jobs or residence, at least among workers who are relatively well off and who want to preserve or improve their standard of living.[59] Between bourgeois and workers there seems to be even a partial rapprochement in values—the bourgeois having left behind the ideal of thrift and the fear of industrialization or proletarianization, the workers having on the whole given up the apocalyptic dream of collective ascent out of the proletarian ghetto.

Tensions of growth. The changes so far in the old economic and social system have not been easy. Some of the difficulties stem from the very process of economic growth. Three kinds of problems have arisen in that connection.

First, the process has inevitably created tensions between "ascending" and "descending" groups. The descenders include inefficient producers of industry, agriculture, and commerce who feel that they are losing the protection of the old society and of its state, and who are obliged to give up what they are doing; this may well mean becoming someone else's employee—a genuine "fall" within the value system of the old society to which they have remained faithful. The "new spirit" in the organizations which represent France's various economic activities has impelled the major ones sooner or later, with varying degrees of enthusiasm, to plead with their members against fruitless resistance to adaptation. Partly as a consequence, dissident associations or movements of protest have appeared—the poujadists, for example, among the shopkeepers and artisans (and among the peasants of various areas), and other groups among the underprivileged farmers of central France and Brittany. There was also the spectacular resistance of Decazeville's miners to any reconversion which would not preserve the special rights they owed to being miners. The policy of regional development (*aménagement du territoire*) has so far been a failure; west of a line drawn from Marseille to Le Havre, the average income is smaller by half than the income east of that line where eighty percent of France's industrial activities are concentrated (hence the vigor of Brittany's charge of neglect). It is ironical that the maldistribution of growth has brought signs of a new fragmentation based on geographical unevenness, in place of the fading fragmentation of the stalemate society.

Secondly, even among the ascending groups, tensions appear because of the differing rates of growth among the various prosperous sectors and regions. Thus, in addition to those peasants whose farms are too poor or too small to keep above subsistence level, many peasants are deep in debt because they bought tractors and chemical fertilizers, or switched production in order to improve both their output and their income. These too have found good reasons to rebel. They observe that the result of their efforts is an overproduction which brings prices down. They note that their products are less protected than others (such as wheat and beets) which constitute a far smaller share of total agricultural income but which are sponsored by wealthy representatives of big-farm areas. They find that the antiquated system of distribution penalizes producers and consumers alike for the benefit of a whole series of intermediaries. They realize that the increase of the peasant's income in the past twenty years has remained much below that of the rest of France—largely because this is the area in which state protection has remained far too long of the wheelchair variety. Similarly the employees of nationalized enterprises protest when they notice that wages go up faster in the private sector. Since the state has to watch constantly the danger of inflation, there has inevitably been unevenness between sectors, which has led to recurrent troubles.

Finally, there have been traces of a kind of contest between the young and the old, or rather signs of a push of the suddenly much increased population under thirty or thirty-five years old against a society ill-prepared for them. In the civil service, in politics, and at the head of the main private collective organizations, far younger men than before the war are in control, and this circumstance encourages such a push, rather than making the young men more patient. Thus, there is a movement of young peasants who advocate a scheme for the retirement of peasants over sixty-five and for a drastic regrouping of small farms. Students and professors have vociferously called for a much higher educational budget, for crash plans of school construction, and for state allowances to students at the university level.

Such tensions are not exceptional by themselves: any industrial society which is not ruled by a totalitarian regime is marked, as Raymond Aron puts it, by "querulous satisfaction." [60] However, there are many reasons why in France the margin between satisfaction and general protest is so slim. Without even mentioning now the flaws of the political system which contribute to reducing the margin, one must note that France experiences at the same time the quarrels of an industrial society and those of industrialization.

Residues of the past. In addition to these difficulties growing out of the process of growth, France is bothered by traditional forces and attitudes which are the residue of the old stalemate society. This is a second vast category of difficulties. Here again, several kinds of problems can be distinguished.

First, there are all the groups which resist change by exploiting privileges of old standing, which the state has been unwilling or unable to dismantle—usually for political reasons. For instance, France's fiscal legislation is remarkable not so much for the huge proportion of indirect to direct taxes (it has been argued that

France's indirect taxes are far less regressive than other indirect tax systems) but for the way in which the income tax is levied on small businessmen, on farmers, on shopkeepers and artisans. The *forfait* method—the basing of taxes not on actual net income but on estimated net income, in an amount determined by agreement between the taxpayer and tax authorities—results in a considerable undervaluation of income. Designed to avoid "fiscal inquisition," it saves such taxpayers from the need to keep complicated accounts, but it also saves them from any fiscal pressure to modernize; justified by the underdevelopment of those sectors, it perpetuates their underdevelopment and thus preserves a surplus of inefficient enterprises.[61] Similarly, a celebrated report [62] has recently denounced the obstacles to expansion represented by "closed" professions (pharmacists, *notaires*, millers) or by past laws which give inexpugnable property or tenure rights to owners of commercial enterprises, to owners of real estate, or to farmers, and thus slow down mobility and modernization. Here again, no reform has taken place. As a result, what an official publication politely calls the "spontaneous protectionism" of France's domestic commerce has been kept intact.

Secondly, another residue of the past has been a persistence of social fragmentation. Thus, France's social security consists of a maze of special systems which try to adapt to the peculiar needs of various elements of the population, but also tend to preserve traditional distinctions of questionable usefulness, and increase the profits of intermediaries.[63] The school system suffers heavily from being fragmented into too many compartments; despite recent reforms, the barrier between primary and secondary education has not been removed. Another example is the sharp distinction between various categories of housing—between high-rent modern apartments and low-rent housing, and, within the low-rent category, between postwar housing projects and old houses still benefiting from interwar rent-control measures.

The examples of the school and housing systems point to a third residue: factors which slow down social mobility and perpetuate a social hierarchy definitely not based on technical skills alone. The range of social inequality remains excessively high. Studies of expenditures for health and holidays are revealing. The austerity measures decided upon by the government in December 1958 have hit the workers (especially those with large families and those working in the public sector) and the small civil servants more than most other groups. The social security program has not been used as an instrument of income redistribution, both because of the fragmentation I have mentioned and because of the fact that the contributions to the program are not proportional to income. Even housing projects created in order to help the poorer citizens have often been "diverted" toward the middle classes. The most effective and resilient barrage on the road toward greater mobility and equality remains the school system: the percentage of sons of workers and farmers gets smaller and smaller as one looks successively at the higher grades in secondary schools and at the university. This discrepancy is due not merely to inequality in income and the insufficiency of the state's scholarship program, but also to structural obstacles (such as too scanty transportation of school children to secondary schools in rural areas) and to traditional attitudes. The son of a small white-collar employee is more likely to get to secondary school than the son of a worker with the same income, because of the past ideology, among the "consensus groups," of individual social ascent through education. As a result, even though the effects of change are beginning to be felt—the social origins of the new technical executives are far from limited to the middle classes—an industrial worker's son has only one chance out of five of becoming anything but a wage-earner, and two chances out of five of being anything but an industrial worker.[64]

A final residue, resulting in large part from such persistent inequality, is the disaffection and distrust which the industrial workers continue to feel, and with which they keep talking about the rest of society. Though their behavior expresses far less opposition than before, surveys, interviews, and more importantly, votes in political and union elections [65] show that the old resentments are not dead. Grudging resignation and a willingness to accept individual escape into middle-class status may have replaced the former impulse toward "collective organized resistance," [66] but far from erasing a sense of frustration, they are the contemporary expressions of such a feeling. To realize that no regime will ever abolish hierarchical work and consequently to want to escape from it by one's own means is very different from accepting one's present status as a fair one and endorsing a society whose system of education does not appear to create real equality of opportunity. The failure of the *comités d'entreprises* in their economic tasks has kept alive the unions' dream of "management supervision" by the workers but has also shown its infeasibility at present. The fiasco of Gaullist-sponsored schemes of "labor-capital association" also points to continuing refusal on the workers' part to accept the legitimacy of capitalist enterprise—at least on the local level.

The growing importance of associations

Along with the socio-economic system, the associational life of the stalemate society has been transformed, also under the momentum of the war years and as a consequence of France's demographic and economic changes. The influx of young men and women into higher education has strengthened the French Students Union (UNEF), whose role has been impressive, though controversial. In the new economy, the importance of organized interests has risen continually, especially in agriculture as a consequence of modernization and in industry as an effect of the Common Market—indeed has risen so much that a recent writer has compared present-day France with Tocqueville's America.[67] The impressive increase in textile production and exports has largely resulted from the systematic effort of the producers' organizations. France's planning procedure, which brings business representatives into close association with the state, has generally contributed to the tightening of business organization. The measures of 1961 concerning agriculture are explicitly designed to put pressure on the farmers to work together in order to find outlets for their products. Both in business and in agriculture, the role of Catholic leaders has continued to be crucial. Private *sociétés mutualistes*, challenged by the development of public social security programs, have expanded to twelve million members. As a result of all these changes, the family, though strengthened as a biological unit by the state's policy of allowances, has lost some of its dominant importance as a social cell.

There remain many sectors in which associations are flimsy, or in which a wealth of *groupements* conceals a scarcity of active members: for instance, in commerce and among consumers. The labor unions continue to suffer from widespread disaffection, which reflects both their political divisions and their failure to adjust to the new society. Also, the development of new, well-organized interests has meant the proliferation of big and powerful pressure groups, frowned upon by many political scientists. But in order to assess the role of those groups, we have to turn to the third main feature of French society.

The style of authority challenged

The traditional style of authority has recently—and almost for the first time since Tocqueville—come under scrutiny and attack. This is an indication both of change and of continuity.

There is no question that the familiar pattern is beginning to show signs of wear and tear. The authority of the parents in the family is weaker, and the other members become more self-reliant. Centralization, though not reversed, has been affected by the creation of regional expansion committees, by the state-supported policy of industrial decentralization, by the procedures of consultation and cooperation which the Planning Commission follows, and by the revival of some provincial universities. As a result of such developments, and also of the economic changes and the growth of the new associations, the role of groups in French society has tended to be less negative and defensive; a switch from mere protectionism to adaptation, from mere resistance to cooperation with public authorities, has been noticeable. The decline of fragmentation has corresponded to the rise of an *économie concertée* which simply does not allow for the kind of semiclandestine independence and separatism that groups enjoyed before. The principal associations realize that their special interests cannot be isolated from those of the other groups. Even among agricultural associations the change could be detected during the confusing months of peasant agitation in 1961. As for leaders, including civil servants in the plan-

7 1

ning committees and heads of the various economic associations, their role has far exceeded the previous limits of "noninterventionist" authority, but it has not been purely and simply authoritarian either, for they have sought the cooperation of their associates and subordinates.

The system of education, which was so decisive in shaping the traditional style, is being less reformed than submerged by the tremendous increase in enrollment in secondary education, so that several new curricula are now surrounding the old system of essentially nontechnical and bourgeois *lycée* education. In those new programs, there is less emphasis on abstract principles, competition, and individualism, more on sports, teamwork, and "concrete methods." The secondary school teacher is less frequently an *agrégé*, member of the intellectual elite. A similar development is taking place in university education, especially in the sciences, through piecemeal measures such as the new *doctorats de recherche*.[68]

On the other hand, the traditional style of authority has proved to be singularly resilient. Although the role of the state has changed from "noninterventionist" to "active leadership," this change has come about in the time-honored way—from the top—and not in response to initiatives from below. Such initiatives have been uneven; they have come mainly in economic affairs, where the pressure from the top was strongest, and have been rarest in social affairs, where the state left little room for them. Survival of the traditional style in society is illustrated by the continued "apoplexy at the center," that is, the apparently irreversible and alarming growth of the Paris area.[69] The old pattern of authority is apparent even in the new planning machinery, since the directives are drafted by a relatively small number of men, composed primarily of representatives of the top civil service and of the business associations; the final say remains with the civil servants, and the participation of labor delegates is often minimal or nominal. France's traditional style is not one which makes cooperation between "leaders" and "public" easy; observers have noted that the associating of family organizations to social security programs has, so to speak, sterilized their representative function. The unions are reluctant to switch from grievances to cooperation. Even in business, the conspiratorial air of French associations has not vanished entirely; businessmen, when making agreements, continue to prefer secrecy to candor. Thus there is a lag of social behavior behind economic structures. Precisely because the traditional style was the product of a social hierarchy inherited from the feudal order, the fact that this hierarchy has not yet entirely disappeared delays the change in authority relations.

But it is in the system of education, despite the changes I have mentioned, that the old style can still be found to reign supreme. Here is the root of the lag. There is still too much emphasis on individual perfection rather than on the common good, too much competition and too little teamwork, too much *culture de la différence* and not enough study of the world around the individual. The traditional secondary education, that of the *lycées*, may be submerged but it is not defeated. It remains privileged as long as the *baccalauréat* is not abolished; and the *baccalauréat* is still the prerequisite to university education and thus to the top functions of society. Therefore this system continues to recruit France's future leaders from a rather narrow section of the population, just as it did under the stalemate society which, however, needed smaller elites than the industrial society of today with its extensive division of labor.[70] Characteristically, it is the fear of arbitrary decisions by the students' own school teachers which contributes to preserve the *baccalauréat* examinations, where cramming is "redeemed" by the fact that examining board and candidate are anonymous and unknown to each other. In higher education, the *agrégation*, necessary for obtaining the top teaching jobs, recruits fewer and fewer people precisely because the boards refuse to lower their standards; consequently, more and more teachers are not *agrégés*—a sign of change—but the *agrégation* remains the most coveted goal and the old hierarchy is jealousy preserved, even at the cost of increasing irrelevance. Only a drastic reform of secondary and higher education will be able to affect decisively, though gradually, France's traditional style of authority.

Thus, all the residues and tensions of the new French society point in the same direction: the need for state measures to break resistance and to preserve the momentum of change. Hence the importance of the political system.

ADJUSTMENT TO THE POSTWAR WORLD

The same conclusion can be drawn from the story of France's relation to the postwar world. This has been the central problem of postwar politics. As the old domestic ideological issues declined, the major crises were produced by the impact of external developments on the French. Charles Morazé and Alfred Grosser have pointed out with a characteristic mixture of sorrow and pride that France was the only nation in which the great international problems of the period—the cold war, decolonization—became the dominant domestic issues, the main sources of party conflicts and divisions.[71] The causes of purely domestic crises are difficult to remember, but nobody has forgotten the battles over the European Defense Community, Indochina, Morocco, and of course Algeria.

The drama of French external policy can be termed a crisis of adjustment. But this is a highly ambiguous expression. The mood of adjustment can be defensive—*repli*—or it can be dynamic and aggressive. Both moods existed here. What has marked the French crisis has been the clash between the vigorous and very widespread determination to recapture power, rank, and prestige, and the fact that in a crucial area of world affairs an irresistible tide has forced the French to fight a defensive battle just as they were overcoming their prewar doubts and moving with considerable success in other respects. Besides, it is important to realize that there is nothing mechanical about the process of adjustment. It implies far more than submission to irrefutable facts. The very task of statesmanship consists of selecting the most favorable interpretation of the facts, whenever the lessons they carry are ambiguous; of choosing the most subtle and dignified form of submission, when the lesson is beyond debate; and most importantly, of trying to change the facts whenever they are intolerable but it is in the nation's power to transform them. The tragedy here has been that in the colonial area the best that statesmanship could have done was to bring about as painlessly as possible precisely the kind of submission which the nation did not want.

The commentators who have derided France's quest for new forms of grandeur, who have pointed at its high cost and at its fragility, and who have stressed that the money could be better used to accelerate economic progress at home, have both made a point and missed a point. Their valid point is that even though decolonization ought ideally to have been handled in such a way that many advantages could be salvaged from the shipwreck of empire, yet no force could have prevented the shipwreck, or made the change from domination to influence something else than a decline in power and rank. The crucial truth that such writers have forgotten is this: for many Frenchmen, the basic reason for liquidating the stalemate society was not that a higher standard of living could be attained thereby, but that only through economic and social change could France hope to rescue some of her international prestige and power from the previous shipwreck of 1940. It would not be wrong to describe French policy in the last two decades as a battle against humiliation. At no point until now have the advocates of "little France" won their argument. Although some of the "Europeans" have presented European integration in such a light,[72] this was not the line followed by them in Parliament. Mendès-France has sometimes sounded like a "little Frenchman" since he has been out of office, but in 1954 "Mendèsisme" was a modern form of nationalism calling upon the nation to adapt its economic and colonial bases of power to the new conditions of history so as to play a more effective role in the world.[73] On the whole, the French have not seemed determined to jump suddenly from great-power status to minor-power resignation, from the world scene to the hermitage. It is not surprising that a Swiss like Herbert Luethy should look with a mixture of anger, amusement, and amazement at a nation which obstinately refuses to behave like Switzerland and which sees in the Swiss form of happiness a solitary confinement rather than a solitary delight. This is why France's behavior and stature in the world have been the decisive domestic issues.

Stanley Hoffmann

Successes of adjustment: power, rank, universality

Let us start with those areas in which adjustment has been most successful. They are those in which France could choose a course that was neither resignation to mediocrity nor nostalgic pretensions of anachronistic grandeur. Even here the road has been difficult. The substitution of new concepts for the traditional means and goals of French foreign policy has been groping and far from deliberate. The decision to become a member of the Atlantic coalition was met with opposition both from nationalists and neutralists —nationalists who feared that France's role would be that of a satellite to a power whose wisdom and leadership ability they questioned, and neutralists who feared that the alliance would divert France from accomplishing the social revolution which required an alliance with the Communist Party. Nor was the problem of Germany initially seen in Paris as it was seen in Washington or even in London; indeed, the first temptation was that of a return to the policy of the twenties—a temptation which marked both the cabinets of General de Gaulle in 1944–1946 and those of his successors. Even after the French government had switched from a policy of repression, dismemberment, and reparations to a policy of European unity, diffidence remained the key-word. The strength of anti-German feelings in the French Parliament was such that even the "good Europeans" had to stress the negative side of their program by showing that the main virtue of European integration was that it would "never leave Germany to herself." However, much has been accomplished in the way of adjustment.

The revision of France's conception of power has continued. Here the change which resulted from the war years has been of crucial importance. Industrialization has succeeded in making the French feel that their rate of progress and their technical achievements have put them back among the mightier nations of the world. To this extent the sense of failure bred by the shocks of the thirties, by the occupation, and by the postwar financial disorders has been eliminated. One remembers the feeling of discouragement which determined business opposition to the Coal and Steel Community and to the European Defense Community at a time when

76

Germany seemed so much more dynamic than France. It is striking to compare that feeling with the tone of confidence after 1955 which underlies business acceptance of the Common Market, and which I have tried to explain earlier by looking at the techniques used by the state and the European Communities. Thanks to such techniques, the Europe of the Six has been accepted as preferable either to the old protectionist French outlook or to ruthless, un-limited competition. The peasants, whose resentment against the Common Market ("dupes' market") had been greatest, were brought in line with business by the spectacular bargain negotiated among the Six in December 1961 and January 1962.

Nobody has insisted more than General de Gaulle on the need for France to be "a great industrial power" so as to be *"une grande puissance tout court."* His repeated allusions to industrialization as the new common undertaking are not at all a switch from his previous conviction that only by giving priority to foreign affairs could the French escape domestic bickering. On the contrary they are a reassertion of his belief that only through economic strength can France pretend to a *"grande réussite"* (a great success) and avoid *"un abaissement sans recours"* (a decline without appeal).

Along with industrialization, France's traditional faith in mili-tary power has reemerged—in part because industrial and mili-tary strength are so strongly connected. The reemergence has been exemplified by de Gaulle's multiple objections to military integra-tion with other countries and by the decision of French govern-ments even before de Gaulle to build an independent nuclear de-terrent—whose industrial by-products have been stressed even by French critics of the deterrent. This move is to a large extent a reflection of France's new sense of vitality. Just as the doctrine of *offensive à outrance* expressed, in 1914, the dynamism of the pros-perous and nationalist country of Poincaré and Péguy, just as the Maginot defensive dogma translated the defeatism of a stagnant and divided society, the request for atomic power reflects the be-lief that as an economically much stronger nation, France ought to have her hand on the sword as well as a better role behind the shield. Moreover, these claims are by themselves a form of recon-version to a role in international affairs which is far from mediocre;

they are an attempt to analyze the new conditions of political power in the atomic age, and to make France meet those conditions. Americans may regret France's decision because of the peril of nuclear diffusion; but if they point at the waste of money involved, the French can easily answer by putting the blame on the American atomic legislation which denies to allies secrets already known to the enemies, and by stressing that the power relationships within NATO, between the United States and England, or France, or Germany, are no longer what they were in 1949. France's atomic policy is not an anachronism, but the kind of adjustment that entails an effort at changing unpleasant but not irresistible facts.[74]

Power, as in the past, is seen as an elevator, which should lift France toward the heights of "rank." "Rank" depends today not entirely on armies or on the control of territory but also on the possession of what remains the *ultima ratio* in international affairs, that is, nuclear weapons. But the quest for rank has entailed other policies far more popular in the United States (although not at all less controversial in France). The outbreak of the cold war has convinced French cabinets, backed by the bulk of the nation, that French security would best be preserved by the Atlantic alliance rather than by a neutralist policy, and that only by being a member of the alliance could France pretend to "rank." Europe being the hottest stake in the cold war, a neutral European power in an age of giants could hardly play any other role than that of a pawn. The strength of authentic neutralism has decreased because many of its previous adepts have come to recognize the seriousness of the Soviet threat and the primacy of foreign affairs. The evolution of *Le Monde* and *Esprit* since 1950–51 is most interesting in this connection. Nationalism has gradually turned from bitter nostalgia to a quest for prestige, from straight opposition to efforts at improving France's status within the Atlantic alliance.

Besides, the French have gradually come to recognize what had started to appeal to many during the war, that "rank," so hard to recapture for a nation of France's size, could nevertheless be claimed by a new Western European Community. And the fiasco of the regressive policy toward Germany convinced many that the security from Germany which this policy had failed to obtain could best be sought by tying Germany to Western Europe. At present, France has definitely accepted her commitment to a European community.

There remain divergences among Frenchmen on all three aspects of the making of Europe: purposes, functions, institutions. Should the new Europe try to be an independent force in world affairs, or should it remain at all times America's faithful partner? Should it strive to define common foreign and military policies, or should its functions be economic, social, financial, and cultural only? Should its policy-making organs be essentially intergovernmental or should supranational institutions become the norm? Such disagreements are not insignificant, but they must be kept in perspective. The peculiar style of French political argument makes them appear far worse than they are. As to the purposes, no one really wants to break away from the Atlantic alliance, but the desire to redeem the "political collapse of Europe" and to make the Atlantic partnership less uneven has been alien to nobody. As to functions, the scope of the commitment among the Six has never ceased to grow—before as well as after de Gaulle's return to power —and the line between purely "internal" European policies and a European "external" policy is rather thin. As for the institutions, the practical difference between supranational and intergovernmental ones has become gradually smaller. Two facts are clear: first, governmental agreements must be prepared by the careful work of the supranational commissions; second, even those commissions require government support to forge ahead. The more ambitious the purposes are, and the more vital the functions of the European enterprise, the less the national governments will actually be ready to leave the last word to "technocratic" authorities —even if the last word which those governments insist on keeping is really just an assent to such authorities' suggestions. The billows of smoke produced by the debates between the supporters of a supranational Europe and those of *"l'Europe des patries"* should not make one forget that de Gaulle's insistence on clear-cut and precise intergovernmental agreements have led to an impressive result in the most difficult area of agriculture; that de Gaulle has

79

taken initiatives for closer political cooperation; and that the main opposition has come from Holland and Belgium, which fear a Franco-German predominance and the exclusion of England.

Moreover, disagreements among the French have continually been narrower than divergences between France and Britain. At first the issue between the two countries was supranationality. Later, as the importance of supranational institutions among the Six decreased, the issue between the Six and England became a functional one. In the days of the Free Trade Area the British did not accept as broad a scope of commitment to cooperation as the Six had consented to. When the same reasoning which had led France eleven years earlier on the way to integration finally determined England to accept the broader commitment and to apply to all the European communities, the Franco-British rift centered on the purposes of the European entity. For the British do not want to give up either their ties with the Commonwealth or their position as America's privileged ally, whereas de Gaulle looks forward to a highly self-conscious Europe in which no member would be America's Trojan horse. There is some truth in the charge that de Gaulle's Europe would be a "French" Europe, but in this respect de Gaulle differs from other French leaders in his style more than in his ambition. France's European policy has served since 1950 both to hasten France's economic rejuvenation and to reconvert France for "*grandeur*" in a partial way; for Europe was the most logical and almost the only available avenue of leadership.

The old concern for the universality of French values has also been "redirected" after the shock of World War Two. France could not affect decisively the relations between East and West and had to be satisfied with a secondary role in the cold war, but previous French pride in the universality of France could be diverted toward, and grafted on, the making of Europe.

The reconversion of France's empire in Black Africa, through Defferre's *loi-cadre* of 1956 and de Gaulle's wise decisions of 1958–1961, has been in part an attempt at preserving the image of France as an emancipator, and de Gaulle's frequent emphasis on the duty to aid underdeveloped countries has had the same purpose. But here we come to a much more somber side of the picture.

The traumas of decolonization

To many Frenchmen adaptation was suspiciously close to resignation and therefore they criticized every step on the road to European integration and to decolonization in Black Africa. But the deepest tragedy lay elsewhere.

In Indochina and North Africa, adaptation seemed hardly possible without the very humiliation which Frenchmen were trying to exorcise. When it came to the dispute between East and West, or to the policy in Europe, France seemed to have almost no liberty of choice; the means may be and still are open to debate, but the direction was written on the wall and it was easy to show that a nationalism which refused to adapt was bound to lead to isolation and further humiliation. On the contrary, in the colonies, largely because of the effects of the war, France acted as if the choice were still open. She was forced into the tragic error of trying to hang on in order to offset the inevitable losses she had suffered elsewhere. Adaptation was equated with humiliation in the minds of millions of Frenchmen and, consequently, in the facts.

The nationalist revolt in the colonies deeply affected the French because it seemed to challenge the very core of French values. It denied to French ideals and practices the universality of which the French were so sure, and it threatened to reduce France's power and rank in the world even more than the cold war; for the limits imposed by coalition diplomacy might be temporary, but the shrinking of France on the map would be beyond denial and repair. The traditional conception of France's role in the world— pride in the civilizing mission, concern for the possession of land, a Roman conception of greatness—seems to have taken refuge in this remaining area of France's past power and resisted the more desperately for having had to give way in so many other respects. As in society, but with far worse effects, the residue of old beliefs and attitudes has come to plague the process of change.

It is fascinating to compare France and England in their attitudes toward Europe and decolonization. England, having escaped occupation and ended the war as a major power, did not realize until very recently that the sense of independence she had toward Europe—the belief that she was free not to join so as to preserve her liberty of action in the world—was largely illusory. France, occupied, weakened, and reduced to a very minor role in the allies' counsels of 1945–1947, recognized necessity and did the best she could with it.[75] But in colonial matters England identified the "winds of change" and bowed to necessity while it was still an opportunity and not yet a disaster; the Indian crisis of 1942 played a role comparable to the collapse of France's position in Europe. In the affairs of empire the French were the ones who nursed illusions. It took Dien Bien Phu to jolt them, and even then many Frenchmen became simply more determined to hold on to the rest of the empire by forcibly preventing any such new debacles. There are two decisive explanations of the difference between France's decolonization and England's. First, in wartime the French were humiliated whereas the English were not. Second, before the war the two countries' conceptions of power had stood in vivid contrast—the Roman version versus the more commercial tradition of indirect rule, which, paradoxically enough, not only made withdrawal easier but was also accompanied by much greater attention to overseas affairs.

The residue of the French imperial past not only has slowed decolonization but also has threatened to undo much of what has been done in other areas of international and French affairs. In this respect, the Algerian War, both by its length and because it has involved Frenchmen far more than the war in Indochina ever did, dealt three heavy blows to the process of France's adaptation to the postwar period.

The first blow has been inflicted upon France's relations with other countries—with her former colonies or protectorates, with her allies, and with the uncommitted nations. Humiliation could be overcome only if the resentments and suspicions which colonialism had left behind in the new states and in many of the NATO powers were to vanish fast. The Algerian War, however, put France in a vise. For a long time the Algerian nationalists (FLN) stuck to the most extreme *politique du pire*, seeming to prefer chaos and a clean break with France to the concessions with which an orderly transition would have to be bought. Because of their prolonged intransigence, France was unable to reach the kind of negotiated solution which would not have left among the French and especially in the French army any bitter taste of shame. De Gaulle's policy consisted of trying to cover retreats through unilateral concessions in order to save face and to add to those concessions a mixture of threats (for instance, of partition) and blandishments (economic aid), with the hope that ultimately the FLN, having obtained most of what it wanted, would make in turn some concessions to French pride. This policy consumed enormous amounts of time. Meanwhile the strains on the new ties with the independent French-speaking states of Africa became increasingly heavy. For example, relations with Morocco and Tunisia deteriorated. France became the ritual target at meetings of the non-aligned states. The Bizerte affair of 1961 was a tragic but logical by-product; giving in to Bourguiba's demand would have meant one more humiliation, but firing back resulted in a weakening of France's position in Africa. As long as the Algerian War lasted, so did the danger of a French nationalism of resentment and frustration aimed at the United States because of America's obvious impatience with and dislike of the war. It was François Mitterrand, a generally liberal minister of the Fourth Republic, who lamented in 1957 that France's allies had not sufficiently understood that now it was the Mediterranean and not the Rhine which was the axis of French foreign policy.[76]

The second blow dealt by the Algerian War has severely damaged France's relations with her own professional army. Its officers—particularly the colonels, majors, and captains—have been carrying the humiliating burden of France's defeats since 1940. What they wanted was a victory, and what made them fluctuate from strained discipline to actual revolt was the feeling that the politicians and indeed the people in metropolitan France were throwing away the military successes achieved by the army in Algeria. However, one may well ask whether the very nature of the Algerian problem would not have driven any army to despair, whatever the regime; for the army was asked to do something which had no precedents anywhere (certainly not in Indochina, where defeat both aggravated and simplified matters, or in Malaya) —i.e., to achieve as much of a military victory as any *guerre révolutionnaire* against nationalist rebels allows, and then to let the country thus "pacified" be turned over to the enemy. Many of France's officers—entrusted, especially by Mollet, with a task which was not only military, but political, economic, social, and administrative—tended to build up the romantic dream of a radically transformed Algeria, in which vaguely thought-out land reform, extensive relocation of the population, and the continued presence of the army would altogether improve the Moslems' lot and political status, starve off the FLN, and maintain France's control. This dream resulted in cutting off the regular army from practically all the civilians. It divorced the army from the government, whose policy of self-determination was a stinging repudiation of any Algerian integration into France; from the nation, which tended to look forward to accommodation with the FLN, whereas many officers saw in such talks the very touchstone of "betrayal" and "abandon"; from the conscripts, whose attitude in April 1961 sealed the fate of Challe's and Salan's adventure; from the settlers, who were not concerned with agrarian reform and Moslem "promotion"; and even from right-wing politicians, treated by the plotting officers with some distrust and contempt after the repeated failures of the right in France and the fiasco of January 1960 in Algiers.

More and more, the career officers are recruited among sons of officers; the army is becoming an alien body in France's midst. Some writers have equated the officers' "internal emigration" with a military form of poujadism—the reaction of men who know that the evolution of military technology is going to eliminate them and replace them with technicians of nuclear war. This explanation strikes me as much too simple. One finds rebellious army officers coming from practically every service, age group, and shade of political opinion; moreover, many of them believe that the war of the future is more likely to be a "revolutionary war" against subversion than a thermonuclear one. However, de Gaulle's determination to build a new atomic army has ambiguous results: it attempts to divert the French army from its Algerian hypnosis, so as to restore a more proper perspective; but at the same time it underlines and worsens the plight of those officers whose whole careers have been spent on guerrilla warfare and what de Gaulle has contemptuously termed boy-scout activities. Their personal reconversion to modern techniques of war is highly unlikely. France thus faces a new problem of embittered *demi-solde*, often full of rancor against a nation which they describe as soft and corrupt,[77] and a new problem of subversive and rebellious soldiers, who have proved only too ready to use terror and force on a massive scale to impose their view of the world.

The third blow has interfered with the adjustment of the Frenchmen's image of their role in the world to the realities of the postwar scene. Nationalism of resentment has grown out of the Algerian War in two opposite forms. Their effect is tragic not only because each one is an obstacle to satisfactory adjustment but also because the two forms, by being antithetic, have aggravated France's predicament. In one form of nationalism France appears as a frustrated crusader, in the other an embittered recluse.

On the one hand, the Algerian War has continually fed the tortured fantasies of those who thought that France's role in the world could remain what it had always been. The behavior of so many elements of the army in recent years shows that the half-baked doctrine of "psychological warfare" has gained hold precisely because of its thesis that France is the one nation crusading for the defense of Western values against the barbarians from the East. This is France in her traditional posture, although on a bigger scale than ever, and more crucified than ever. The decline of France's position was thus made synonymous with the decline of Christian civilization; once more France's cause was that of honor, justice, and freedom. The army was not alone in rationalizing its sentiments this way. Among members or sympathizers of the terrorist Secret Army there are—significantly enough—former poujadist shopkeepers for whom the death of France's former grandeur and the extinction of their former way of life are somehow connected—a link which reminds one of Nazism. Even outside the lunatic fringe, Socialist leaders from 1956 to 1958 often painted the bleakest picture of "racist nationalisms" and denounced the meaninglessness of self-determination before the individual native has become—through education and welfare—the Kantian master of his soul; they defined France's mission as the one that should promote such liberation, including liberation from nationalist obscurantism. How widespread the nostalgia for this hallowed tradition has been, was shown by the popular support Mollet got at the time of Suez.[78] Extreme pretensions breed inevitable rebuffs. Accumulated frustrations foster the search for domestic and foreign scapegoats. The wounds of humiliation remain open.

On the other hand, the very cost and the very vanity of such attempts tend to produce reactions that go too far in the opposite direction. Readaptation in order to play an effective role in the world could be jeopardized also if a mood of isolationism should develop, that is, if all sense of mission or external ambition should be discarded along with colonization, and if hostility toward an ungrateful world should bring a return to the defensive and a switch to a "little France" policy. French funds then would be withdrawn from such attempts to meet present-day conditions as aid to underdeveloped countries and nuclear capacity, and would be applied to domestic tasks such as aid to the underdeveloped parts of France, the building of more houses, schools, and hospitals. This mood has been growing; peasants and parliamentarians have complained about the contrast between the Constantine plan for Algeria and the absence of any plan for Brittany. France may well ultimately come to such a policy, if the evolution of Africa brings about a more complete divorce between the new states and their former masters, and if atomic strength proves unattainable. Indeed, one could argue that the deliberate selection of a "little France" policy by a united country determined to give up once and for all the quest for rank and the temptation of world influence (except through cultural or commercial channels) could be a sound formula for national happiness. But to be forced into such a corner by a succession of disasters, and amidst clashes among advocates of the old grandeur, proponents of a new grandeur, and supporters of a *repli* would be quite a different thing, and hardly a prelude to harmony.

Critics of de Gaulle's concern for grandeur have often pointed at the public's apparent indifference. But what is far more significant is the fact that every new humiliation, real or imaginary, has brought about reactions of frustration and indignation of one kind or another. De Gaulle's concern was entirely justified—but not even he could succeed in "disengaging" France from the Algerian War without sounding at times either like a die-hard nationalist (for instance in his comments on the United Nations) or like an advocate of withdrawal from "ungrateful" or uncooperative areas.

Uncertainties of adjustment

The battle of adaptation obviously is not concluded. In the early 1960's a number of important uncertainties remain. De Gaulle's foreign policy has consisted of trying to find a mean between anachronism and *repli*. He has also tried to act in such a way that his successor—whoever he is, and barring a violent coup—would find France irreversibly committed to the road selected by de Gaulle. It cannot be said at this stage that he has entirely succeeded.

I do not mean to say that either of the two extremes is likely to be followed. In Gaullist language, neither the "mediocrities" who want "things to be the way they desire, and the opposite of what they are," nor the "sirens of decadence" are probably going to prevail. But there is more than one "middle of the road." Although de Gaulle and most of the politicians who led the Fourth Republic share the ambition to restore France's grandeur, there are significant areas of contention.

In the first place, the objectives are not quite the same. De Gaulle considers that power and rank must entail the maximum amount of autonomy for the nation; should Europe and the Atlantic community limit such autonomy by removing vital decisions from the French government, they would become harmful; similarly, military independence is pursued as a goal. Hence the General's obstinate hostility to military and political integration, which he equates with national decadence—*"effacement"*—even though he accepts extensive commitments as long as they are enforced through traditional intergovernmental negotiations. Most of France's political leaders disagree; they are quite willing

87

to provide France with nuclear weapons, but largely in the hope of prodding France's major allies into some scheme of nuclear sharing. To many of those leaders, European integration and Atlantic unity are goals valuable for themselves, whereas autonomy seems to them beyond reach, and they have nothing but sympathy for supranational institutions, so long as France is not discriminated against. De Gaulle tends to dismiss their views as a brand of abdication; they tend to describe his policies as a form of anachronism. Each side exaggerates the position of the other, but it is true that each of these two "middles" of the road bears some resemblance to one of the two extremes. De Gaulle points out that his predecessors were willing to accept for France, in Europe and NATO, a back-seat position which Great Britain would not have taken. But they remark that even measures acceptable to Britain (the double control of nuclear warheads, for instance) are not accepted by him. Neither with respect to European integration nor with respect to the atomic striking force are Gaullist policies safe from some revision.

In addition to the clash of objectives, there is the matter of money. The very costs of grandeur may lead to a reappraisal. The ambitious role which most French political figures have tried to define since the war is an expensive one. The costs of atomic development are well known. So are those of France's rejuvenated policy with respect to her former colonies, in particular Algeria under the Evian agreements of March 1962. This policy preserves for the time being France's privileged position in large parts of her former empire; there are treaties which safeguard her interests in defense, economics, and education, and the civil service of the new nations continues to depend heavily upon French advice and participation. But the price France has to pay is heavy, in terms of financial and technical assistance; only at such cost can bygone power be transformed into continuous influence. Whether de Gaulle's successors will always be willing and able to pay such a price is far from clear.

As already suggested, it may well be that the evolution of international affairs will force France to accept a much more limited role in world politics. France's resources, whatever the regime, will not be unlimited and furthermore, as one of the Western powers, she shares the fate of all the others. But why should her allies summon her to resign herself to such a shrinkage in advance of necessity—a trend which until now has been bitterly resisted and whose French advocates have been motivated by a most unhealthy feeling of pent-up frustration and rage against the outside world? In particular, why summon France to give up worldwide claims for a more limited European role? If they are genuine interests, she should keep them. If they are mere pretenses, they will evaporate in due course. No state which was once of the first order likes to limit its efforts all at once to a narrow area only. France's problem in this respect is not different from England's. France's care for her "north-south" axis across the Mediterranean is comparable to Britain's preoccupation for the Commonwealth: the concrete significance of such associations may be hard to define but there is a role for intangibles as well as for hard cash in world affairs. The task of diplomacy is to keep the various zones of national concern in harmony, to smooth transitions, to keep the nation's visiting card at places where it once had its feet on the table, and to avoid all those clear-cut choices and sacrifices which are not absolutely indispensable. Precisely because the process of adaptation has been a cruel one, the wounds will heal most effectively if France is able to cling to all available symbols or shreds of worldwide interest even if, as seems likely, Western Europe becomes the main focus of her concerns. The less she feels imprisoned in the Western European community, the more likely she will be to contribute to integration. It will do no good to push her into it, for she does not want a cage but a home—and a home is, by definition, a place one can leave in order to go to one's offices.

THE POLITICAL SYSTEM TODAY

The outcome of the search for grandeur is likely to be affected not only by external events but also by domestic developments in France's political system. And France's political system continues to be a graveyard of hopes, a denial of cherished theories, a puzzle to the most expert analysts.

Hopes have at times been high because of three historic developments which were discussed earlier and which have continued in recent years: the revolution in France's economy and society, the general acceptance of a sweeping extension of the scope of state authority, and the decay of the old ideological issues and consequently of traditional distinctions in French political thought. The range of fundamental disagreements has indeed been narrowed. The old debates lost most of their relevance when the stalemate society that was their frame of reference was overhauled —debates between champions of the individual and socialists; between both, as supporters of *le peuple*, and defenders of the old elites; between clericals and anticlericals. France's right-wing *Indépendants* can hardly challenge the growth of industry any more. The Socialist Party has long ago abandoned the idea that nationalization was a panacea. Nobody really thinks of a public monopoly of education.

However, various theories [79] which have flourished in the early 1960's, and which have in common the belief that the age of political peace and quiet could easily be reached because of those developments, are wide of the mark. Nothing remains further from the truth than the notion that economic modernization produces political rationalization and that it would be easy to devise stable institutions adapted to the new society. The story of recent years in France shows just the opposite.

The fate of the political institutions

The story could be called: The Death of French Political Institutions, Killed by the Very Issues with Which Those Institutions Have Had to Deal. It was pretty obvious that the nature of the problem faced by France required strong and stable political institutions—an increase in the *intensity* of state authority to match the extension of its scope and the size of the challenge. The nation's leaders needed the capacity to take the necessary measures and to enforce them despite all obstacles. They needed procedures for the settlement of conflicts between the groups engaged in the process of development—an arbitral function without which a nation becomes a jungle of competing interests. They should have had the means to deal with the balance-of-payments problem, with inflation, with the difficulties resulting from the resistance of marginal producers. Only a strong and efficient state had any chance of wresting votes from the Communist Party. In external affairs, it was obvious that only institutions capable of giving stability and coherence to the executive had any chance of keeping the accidents of decolonization from becoming national traumas. But the lesson of the postwar period is that the reactions of the French to the problems they faced have prevented a strong and stable state from emerging.

The Fourth Republic started with a major handicap. A multiparty system preserved by proportional representation had no chance of developing stable and coherent governments if the problems to be dealt with prevented the formation of lasting majorities. This was soon demonstrated. But the story of the Fourth Republic goes further: it shows that the regime established in 1946 itself, weak as it was, was gradually destroyed by its incapacity for dealing with the issues. The problems of economic and social change were handled by the bureaucracy rather than by Parliament; what came before the nation's representatives were the incidents and crises in the process—budgetary or taxation difficulties, claims by special interests. In those cases, French parties, as in the thirties, tended to behave more like pressure groups and to defend the interests of their principal voters. Their incapacity for defining coherent policy resulted in multiple cabinet crises and undermined the parliamentary system once again.

But it was, of course, the fiasco of decolonization which ultimately destroyed the regime. In economic affairs, parliamentary incompetence or confusion could detract from, but not destroy, what a dynamic bureaucracy was setting in motion in the way I have mentioned. On the contrary, in colonial affairs the natural tendency of the civil servants was to go on administering as before; and here the bureaucratic routine added its dead weight to that of parliamentary paralysis. In economic affairs the civil service had been put on its new course by the political decisions of 1944–1946. In colonial affairs the bureaucracy received no such new impulse, and therefore perpetuated an obsolete tradition of direct and centralized rule.[80] Thus, it was the political failure that proved to be decisive. Decolonization has been so painful not only because of the parliamentary arithmetic—the opposition of a large Communist group and of a sizable number of irreconcilable die-hards —but also because the center parties themselves, ever since the early debates in the Constituent Assemblies of 1946, were deeply divided over this issue. It took either a disaster such as Dien Bien Phu, or a temporary breakthrough such as Mendès-France's (which followed Dien Bien Phu), or tortuous maneuvers such as Edgar Faure's in 1955, to push the political machine out of the ditch. The issue of Indochina was met by *immobilisme* until the Assembly had no choice but to turn, temporarily, to a strong leader and let him settle the inglorious end of a long and hopeless adventure. The issue of Algeria put an end to any pretense of internal unity in most parties, and in May 1958 led to the coup of Algerian *activistes*, army leaders, and Gaullist advocates of a strong state.

In the cases of both Indochina and Algeria the regime had been embarrassed by the presence in the permanent opposition of a huge Communist group whose behavior reflected the fact that the workers remained politically irreconcilable despite the transformation of society. It is not by accident that Poujade embraced all the themes of chauvinistic and imperialistic nationalism, mixing up the plight of the shopkeepers with the humiliation of France; for those were the two issues which *"le Système"* had been unable to resolve. The political class of the Fourth Republic—not fundamentally different from the notables of the Third—had become doubly irrelevant. It was no longer sufficiently representative of the new French society, and it had been shown incapable of solving the main problems of that society. On the whole, over modernization the regime was left *hors-circuit*, whereas over decolonization it produced nothing but *courts-circuits*.

The story of the Fourth Republic had been forecast, precisely because the parallel with the thirties was obvious. But the story of the Fifth Republic has been a surprise. I certainly do not want to deny or belittle its impressive achievements. The financial measures of December 1958 averted a major disaster for France's balance of payments and consequently for France's domestic and international economic position. De Gaulle's systematic pedagogy has stressed the imperative of economic progress and of *"épouser le siècle"* far more consistently than the premiers of the Fourth Republic. The patient inching toward an honorable Algerian settlement has been finally, though grimly, rewarded. Above all, de Gaulle has been the shield of the nation against those extremist politicians, military men, and terrorists who might otherwise have seized power and ruined all the work done since 1944. But the founders of the Fifth Republic had far bigger ambitions, and it is in this light that the balance sheet is depressing.

Here was a regime carefully designed by its constitution to be capable of governing despite the divisions of the nation and the representatives. Here was an executive endowed with all the requirements of stability and efficiency. At the same time here was an attempt at genuine mixed government, since the executive derived its powers from the nation's representatives and since Parliament was formally left with considerable legislative and political powers. The whole enterprise was based on the hope that the benefits of strong executive action would speed the transformation of French political attitudes and alignments more surely than economic and social changes could do it by themselves, and more safely than such a risky surgical operation as a genuine presidential system could do. Consequently, one hoped, the new regime might even become the beginning at last of the synthesis of France's opposed political traditions.

The leaders discovered, however, that France contained not one but two layers of paralysis. The parliamentary one had been discarded, but the deeper causes were in the country itself, that is, in the reactions of the various groups when hit by the processes of modernization, and above all, in the divisions of the French over Algeria. The difficulties of economic change and the tragedy of decolonization have proved too strong not only for the parliamentary procedure of settling disputes through discussion and delay, but also for the Gaullist procedure based on authority, especially the authority of the bureaucracy. The parliamentary procedure operated as an echo-chamber for all of the various complaints. The Gaullist procedure is plagued by a triple illness. First, authority is often unable to follow its brave words with decisive moves because it is too affected by national uncertainties and divisions as reflected within the ranks of the decision-makers, and too anxious to avoid adding to France's divisions by siding openly with any one faction against another. Second, authority is often too high to deal with the disputes before they are at the crisis stage. And third, authority is too personal to grow roots, without which no sap will rise in the French political plant which became desiccated under the Fourth Republic.

The first illness—the limits on decisive action—lingers because the executive has wanted to remain a democratic one. De Gaulle wants to rule by consent rather than by coercion, and has therefore often relied on cunning rather than on clear-cut commands. The new constitutional setup assures permanence, but cannot guarantee efficiency; here, as in the United Nations, legal power can at times coexist with political impotence. Of course, executive stability is in many ways a blessing (especially from the viewpoint of prestige abroad) but it has not been enough to bring back to the government all that sense of duration, that broad perspective of time for its operations and calculations, which so many critics of the Fourth Republic had looked forward to. One obstacle is that de Gaulle's quest for unanimity has entailed frequent changes of direction, depending on the shifting winds of domestic opinion and foreign pressures. Moreover, the dizzying turnover of individual ministers, partly a consequence of those changes of direction, partly a characteristic of many French regimes of "saviors," is about as great as it was during the cabinet crises of the Fourth Republic.

As for the second illness—inability to see disputes before they are inflamed—what military theorists call "escalation" has taken place: never before has resort to violence been so widespread and treated so casually. The ungodly spectacle of party squabbles and cabinet crises had been eliminated, only to be replaced by an even ungodlier one. If the institutions of yesterday were too close to a shaky ground, those of today are too far removed, and dissent tends to express itself through direct action—strikes, plots, bombs, and coups. Other channels are lacking. It is fascinating to see that the tactics used by the young peasants in their strikes have been influenced by their experiences in the Algerian guerrilla war during their military service. It is startling to see with what indulgence French juries and judges have treated acts of violence committed for political reasons by Frenchmen against other Frenchmen or against North Africans. Of the prewar schools of thought, the most durable is the most volatile; it is the one I would call fascist— a nationalism which is informed not by the counterrevolutionary dogmas of Maurras but by the rage of humiliation, marked by the call for direct and violent action, expressed in plots against the false elites, and obsessed by decadence. The groups which have been particularly susceptible to its appeal are the familiar clientele of the Leagues: students, shopkeepers, veterans, and soldiers.[81] When postwar veterans' movements have been tempted by political intervention, they have leaned more toward this extreme than toward the conservatism which often came close to the line of *l'Action française* between the wars. Nor are the activists of the Secret Army any longer disciples of Maurras: they behave like heirs of Baltic or Silesian *"Freie Korps"* desperados, and some of them (or their friends) lean toward a kind of National Socialism full of anticapitalist slogans. This tendency can be explained in part by the accumulation of political disappointments in the last thirty years and the seriousness of the issues. But whereas in the past it was the impotence of the state that excited such people's fury, now it is the haughty and imperial way in which France's leader defines her policy. Ironically enough, some of the die-hards accuse him of dictatorship.

The third and by far the most disturbing illness is General de Gaulle's inimitably personal way of exercising power and of demanding loyalty to himself. This has sealed once more the fate of mixed government and affected all of France's political institutions. Theoretically, the very flexible constitution of the Fifth Republic could evolve in one of three ways: a return to traditional French parliamentarism, a cabinet system with a strong and stable premier, a genuine presidential system.[82] Under General de Gaulle, the road has been a fourth one: the predominance of the President at the expense of every other institution. The Fifth Republic seems to have systematically thrown away its chances of putting an end to the swing of the pendulum from the extreme of a savior outside party politics to the extreme of representative politics almost without a government. Because Parliament is often more concerned with local and special interests than with the issues of "national ambition," its role has been diminished until it is no longer even able to play the useful role of safety valve and watchdog of bureaucracy.[83] The regime has used every means, from the refusal to summon special sessions to the manipulation of the agenda, to keep Parliament down.[84] Even the procedure for revising the constitution now has been twisted for that purpose.

France is in a unique situation among Western democracies. Traditional channels of political expression, the networks of representatives extending from municipal councils to Parliament, are dried up. As usual this discredit is being rationalized by some. A modern society, so goes the story, needs no "intermediaries." They may have been useful when communications were slow and poor, when access to central power could be obtained only through such notables and when the state was to be a "nomocracy"; but now that the state's function is "teleocratic," now that the citizen has a television or radio which keeps him informed of what goes on in Paris, now that the old ideological debates are over, all that the citizens need is a popular leader and an efficient bureaucracy.[85] The trouble with such optimism is that it is of the Pangloss variety. French "intermediaries" have lost their role not because there is no role for them any more, but because they proved unable to settle the problems of France in the Fourth Republic and have been stripped of any importance in the Fifth. However justified the repudiation of the old system may be, the absence of intermediaries assures neither that the leader (so far above) will be strong, nor that the bureaucracy (left to itself) will be efficient. Indeed, the sabotage of executive policies which French parties and parliaments used to undertake has at times become the property of new kinds of "intermediaries," hidden in the civil service or even in the staffs of cabinet members.

For it is not only the representatives who have been weakened. Many other heads and hands have been unsteadied by the feeling that the regime suspended to the life of an aging leader, is just a parenthesis in French history. The mushrooming of *lois d'exception*, of special tribunals and of special police powers, both before and after the use of the emergency provisions of Article Sixteen of the present constitution, has done much to detract from the serenity of the civil service. The prolonged resort to the powers of Article Sixteen by the president has been paradoxical, for the measures taken did not amount to a drastic reform of the regime or even to a thorough shake-up of the civil service despite the alarming discoveries of April 1961, and yet the long duration of "emergency legality" has been enough to create a climate of arbitrariness. Such traditional state institutions as the judiciary, the Council of State, and the prefects, having suffered thirty years of political shocks, tend to serve all regimes with the same lukewarmth. Thus, the only political channel remaining is the plebiscitary one—which depends on one man alone.

The crumbling of France's postwar political institutions has had damaging effects on the nation. It has meant, for one thing, that the political system has often stood in the way of social change and adaptation to the world. I have indicated previously that the protection of questionable economic activities has persisted, especially under the Fourth Republic. Encouragement to such products as wine, beets, and wheat, despite the danger of overproduction, and the failure of multiple attempts at fighting the *"bouilleurs de cru"* (small distillers of wine) are well known. The tendency of the Fourth Republic to let *faits accomplis* settle France's colonial problems deprived France of the benefits that an earlier settlement might have entailed. Ever since the war, those political leaders who were aware of the imperative necessity of decolonization found themselves in a cruel dilemma: open concessions to overseas nationalists stiffened the resistance of many Frenchmen to any further move, and oblique maneuvers convinced the French of the dishonesty of the leaders in power—not of the wisdom of the policy's goal. Paradoxically, General de Gaulle's peculiar insistence on preserving the style of grandeur in less than glorious circumstances has sometimes resulted in making matters worse by provoking—as in Bizerte, or in relations between France and the U.N.—the very loss of prestige which he was trying to prevent. Nothing has made adaptation to the world more difficult than the attitude of the two regimes toward the army. Under the Fourth Republic, "the government failed abysmally to give the Army direction; the Army gradually assumed, and then was tempted to usurp, prerogatives of the government." [86] Under the Fifth Republic, the government chose a direction, but did not care enough, or early enough, to make this direction clear to the army, whose grip on Algerian affairs was at first even strengthened in a war which could not but encourage delusions and prepare revulsion.

The most crucial effect of France's political weaknesses, however, has been to turn the ideal of a stable and democratic political system into a mirage.

The mirage of political stability

Even if the optimists are right when they say that economic and social progress must ultimately be reflected in the establishment of such a political system, the obstacles are formidable. The present autonomy of the political system rests on a triple foundation.

The first factor consists of residues of France's past political life. One of the most troublesome is the army which fought in Algeria, and whose reconversion is so highly problematic. Another is the style of political behavior, which reflects and perpetuates the traditional but now changing style of authority in society. The old doctrines may be dead, but new issues are treated in the old style. The end of ideology does not mean the end of ideological attitudes; it may merely mean the replacement of the old coherent and stable positions in conflict by utterly erratic and nonetheless explosive ones. Certainly issues such as the European Defense Community and especially Algeria, were tackled with the same resort to mythology, obstinacy, disregard for facts, and contempt for concessions as the old battles of the Third Republic. After all, politics is not made only of deep and "structural" conflicts; there are many incidental or accidental issues, and the drama of France's politics is that the attitudes which have grown out of the old fundamental issues get grafted, so to speak, on the new occasional ones, and put gangrene into mere scratches. Consequently, the growing consensus on, or indifference to, the old substantive issues of French politics is not enough to assure political stability.

Neither of the postwar regimes has fostered participation; instead the Fourth Republic reverted to the tradition of parliamentary occupation of power and the Fifth Republic reduces participation to popular approval of the leader's words. Their failure on this score has helped to preserve the style of authority of traditional French society and has strengthened the citizens' ancient tendency to behave as angry subjects. The state remains the enemy—the expression of what Laurence Wylie has called "*les ils*" [87]—even though it still is the natural distributor of benefits to whom one turns at the slightest trouble and whose help is expected as a right. This mixture of diffidence and dependence, resulting from the state's emphasis on its own mixture of importance and distance, has rarely been more manifest. Groups hit by the incidents of modernization react by asking for state protection, and by threatening the state with their fists, tractors, or strikes. Even when their purpose is not to resist change, but to demand a greater share in economic progress, their grievances are presented not as requests for participation but as a bitter outsider's protests.

Thus, even though the new generation of peasant leaders, largely Christian Democrats, is more concerned with the expansion and organization of the nationwide market than with price supports and immediate relief, nevertheless in their choice of methods they behave exactly as if they were disciples of the extreme right-wing prewar agitator, Henri Dorgères—only more efficiently. In the case of the workers, even though their methods are less radical than in the past, their over-all attitude toward the state has not changed; too often reduced to a very minor position in national or local planning boards, they too often in turn continue to interpret efforts to integrate them or their unions into state bodies—bureaucratic or parliamentary—as a threat to their independence and an insinuating attack against their tradition of protest.[88] The intellectuals of the two extremes and the little parties of the left persist in refusing even to consider the point of view of those who have to govern, and thus turn irresponsibility into a dogma. They have advocated either a holy Western crusade to keep Algeria French or an all-out cooperation with the FLN as the only force capable of saving France from fascism! The National Union of Students sided with the FLN in the middle of the negotiations at Evian. Parliament itself, with its wings clipped and its nails cut off, has tended to behave at times as a large protest group, reacting to executive leadership in a way quite typical of the traditional model of French authority relations. After the *putsch* of April 1961, the more the executive refused to recognize that it owed any debt to anyone but itself, the more bills were presented to it by parties, movements, and individuals eager to cash in. The bloody incidents of December 1961 and February 1962, which followed government attempts to ban public demonstrations against the Secret Army, have shown the same vicious circle of official demands that the "passengers stay at their place" and the passengers' itch to rock the boat so as to impress the captain.

Moreover, as indicated above, the difficulties of decolonization have engendered among many Frenchmen not only the certainty that they have been betrayed by allies or politicians, but also contempt for the state. De Gaulle's caution in handling the Algerian issue has not contributed to keeping untarnished the vision of a strong state. His attempts at appeasing those who he knew would resist his policy and at cajoling his enemies in order to disarm their hostility without provoking new crises, his policy of making gradual and unilateral concessions in order to preserve as much as possible France's self-respect and the impression that she was freely setting the pace—none of this has given the citizens any greater sense of responsibility for public affairs.

One could argue that what has kept the style of French politics so alarmingly traditional is precisely the isolation and the personal character of France's present leadership. However, there is another residue we must take into account: France's parties. Although the death of the old ideologies around which they were built and the devastating impact of postwar issues have left the parties in a state of chaos and coma, they are still alive. They have been pushed aside—first by events, then by a man too great for them—but they are watching in the wings. They have had no incentive to reform, being sandwiched between the haughty contempt of a regime which distrusts them on principle and the sarcastic contempt of a public which remembers their antics and observes their present disgrace. The appearance of new parties has only added new sources of confusion and entailed neither a burial nor a *regroupement* of the old ones. The legislative elections of 1958 and subsequent by-elections have shown that the electorate preferred those candidates who stood for de Gaulle's policies. But the downgrading of Parliament has caused the parties to treat the regime as an interlude which requires them to have staying power but not to make any effort at reform. As a result there has been no consolidation, at the level of France's representatives, of a consensus matching the one whose existence in the electorate had been shown by the people's votes. Consequently the duality of a merely latent "general will" among the people and of a fragmented will among the people's representatives has survived. Whatever the well-known faults of France's parties, it is hard to imagine a stable and democratic political system which could dispense with them. Their weaknesses brought their disgrace. Their elimination brought no solution. A system which would try to perpetuate their present "internal exile" would erect them into permanent instruments of irresponsible discontent, and provoke at some stage a "return of the parties" comparable in its effects to the Visit of Dürrenmatt's Old Lady and to their own previous return of 1945–46. Indeed, such effects may well be felt again as soon as the Guide who chooses to lean only on the general will and to discard the divided will is removed—unless the parties are reformed in the meantime.

But we find here the second obstacle to reform: the present vacuum. Political life under de Gaulle has been a kind of limbo. De Gaulle either keeps the public at arm's length or seeks it out *en masse* for presidential tours and for plebiscitary referendums in which the substance of the measures proposed disappears under the personal appeal for confidence. Angry citizens express themselves against the state in one of the striking ways that I mentioned. Prosperous citizens prefer the joys of home to the excitement of rallies, and become the spectators of their collective fate. The complacency of a prosperous electorate, the temptation of vio-

lence and nihilism among the fanatics, milder forms of irresponsibility and frustration on the left, students divided between those
groups but not attracted to parties and party reform—this is what
can be observed at the grass roots. Many people have remarked that
the new generation of Frenchmen is quite indifferent to its elders'
battles—Algeria included—and looks at politics with a healthy
mixture of pragmatism and coolness, as one area of problems to be
solved, among others, not as a field for clashing conceptions of
le sacré. But the effect of such an attitude is to divert young men
from the political system, since there are no ready-made channels
and transmission belts.

As for the "new notables," leaders of the big private interest
groups, of civil servants' unions, youth movements, civic associations, it is they who more and more play the role of intermediaries,
but they do so from outside the political system, and very often
with the peculiarly ferocious brand of irresponsibility that such a
situation traditionally breeds in France. They no longer address
themselves to the old political intermediaries, since such a detour
would be a waste of time. Thus the silencing of the old political
class has led to the appearance of new political voices, but since
they are voices without political experience or *encadrement* their
intrusion has resulted mainly in cacophony. Higher up, one constitutional provision which might have been used to fill the vacuum
has been a failure—the provision according to which cabinet
ministers must resign their seats in Parliament. This measure might
have preserved cabinet stability without eliminating parliamentarians from the government, or it might have encouraged a resort
to men coming from all sorts of milieux and thus prepared the
entry of the "new notables" into the political system. Instead, the
result has been the gradual extinction of parliamentarians and their
replacement with civil servants.

The worst aspect of the present vacuum is that France is left
without any legitimate (i.e., generally accepted) set of institutions.
De Gaulle's cavalier violation of his own constitution in both of the
referendums he called in 1962 has made this startlingly obvious.
Consequently, more than ever the nature of the political system is
one of the major stakes in political contests. France remains a bizarre
patient whose stomach is too weak to digest political crises, but

who throws out his stomach each time he throws up. Nothing has pointed up this gap of legitimacy more dramatically than the army *putsch* of April 1961 and the trials that followed—not least that of Raoul Salan—for they revealed how much the army's allegiance had been divorced from the state. The leaders of the rising—either seasoned officers who had fought on de Gaulle's side during World War Two or young men whose first experience of battle had been in Indochina—claimed that they had sworn an oath of fidelity to the population of Algeria or to the dead comrades of Indochina and Algeria, or followed their sense of national interest and honor. They seemed to have forgotten completely about the regime and about the endorsement it had received from the nation in the referendums. It cannot be said that their military judges have always repudiated them.

Even if the present vacuum could somehow be filled, there would remain a third obstacle to the establishment of a stable political system—the weight of the problems with which it will have to deal. True, one can argue that the worst is over, that the long and tragic thirty-year tunnel is behind France, that with the end of the Algerian War the ordeal of decolonization is overcome, and that on the economic and social front few issues seem capable of testing to the limit the strength of the French state. However, notes of caution must be made. Politics is events, the world of the twentieth century is notoriously tough, and we should not forget that it was primarily the impact of the outside world that upset one French regime after another in the last twenty years. Furthermore, nothing guarantees that even a problem of minor intrinsic significance will not be inflated beyond recognition. The way in which a nation reacts to an issue depends on its political habits and institutions; England and France would perceive and handle quite differently the same kind of problem. What has made French issues so explosive has been the amplification of their impact through domestic dissension.

Such are the obstacles to the creation of a stable political system. They are huge enough to make one understand why changes in society and in France's role in the world are not enough to provoke a corresponding reform in politics. The residues of yesterday and the vacuum of today help one realize (with little pleasure) that the present alternatives are the familiar extremes of the pendulum.

At one extreme there is General de Gaulle's change in the mode of election of the President of the Republic, so that he will be chosen by universal suffrage. This development only confirms the *reductio ad absurdum* of Parliament, and it implies that a strong state is possible only if the executive is given an overwhelming preponderance and kept high above the representative factions. Such an imbalance being unacceptable to the parties, the presidential reform is not likely to reach its goals—to increase direct popular participation, to shock the parties out of their rut, or to make government possible without them. It is not likely to prove definitive.

Precisely because the political pendulum has swung so far already and the "new notables" are still outside the door, the risk is great that parties and parliamentarians, now lying low and unreconstructed, will try to get their revenge by carrying matters back to the other extreme. They may challenge General de Gaulle as in 1945—smoke him out, so to speak, by denying him a majority in Parliament. Or they may wait until after his disappearance and then build a regime which may be to the Fourth Republic what the Fourth was to the Third, that is, a new parliamentary game with a few provisions for executive strength, provisions no more likely to be effective than were those of the constitution of 1946. De Gaulle may not be wrong in fearing that after he has gone France may be the victim not of a vacuum but of an overflow. Once again, French politicians, especially on the left, having noticed that constitutional reforms are not the complete answer, may fall back on the equally old illusion that the only thing needed to make the political system work is a "contract," an alliance between the major parties on a program of action, as in 1936, and in 1946 . . .

Let us then go back to Harry Eckstein's conditions of democratic stability: *primo*, a government capable of action; *secundo*, decisions made by the representatives of the people, not by other forces; *tertio*, an electorate provided with genuine alternatives. Whether those conditions can be met depends on the problems, the institutions, the parties, and the electorate. We have seen that the problems may not cooperate. France's institutions will be ultimately shaped by her parties; but the only political forces to which the French electorate will be able to turn after de Gaulle are France's unreformed parties, and they are not likely to tolerate institutions capable of reforming the parties.

The lesson is only too clear. In a nation with no tradition of political consensus and legitimacy, "spontaneous democracy" leads to the peculiar kind of politics which consists of the parliamentarians' confiscation of power for themselves, and "corrected democracy" leads to confiscation by the correcting Guide.[89] As we saw earlier, both types of political systems, resting on the same Procrustean bed of bureaucratic centralization,[90] are in accordance with the national style of authority. Both maintain the traditional distance between the leader and the led which protects them all from "*l'horreur du face à face.*" Both excuse the leaders from having to mobilize the led for action and preserve the happy irresponsibility of the led. Both avoid the blend of leadership and participation which mixed government aims at. But both types would have to operate in the context of a new economy which fosters participation, and of a state whose scope has considerably increased. Modern France has become a society in which the problems to be dealt with by the state embrace such a wide range of social activities—and in which the number and scale of social organizations whose functions affect the public welfare have increased so much —that the very simple patterns of plebiscitary or parliamentary rule no longer suffice. Inevitably, those patterns result in arbitrariness, and then provoke protest and revolt. Complaints about "*le peuple absent*" in French political life did not begin until the thirties; the theme was used then by Tardieu, today by Duverger and René Capitant. The people were just as "absent" before, but in those days the range of public affairs was much narrower. It is therefore not surprising that recent discussions center on the question: how can the nation be reintegrated into its political system?

PARADOXES OF THE PRESENT

Having examined today's society, external relations, and political system, I must trace the present condition of the French political community.

Stanley Hoffmann

The paradox of political lag

The most obvious paradox is the political lag. Social change remains behind economic change; political change is even further behind. Social and international changes affect but slowly the political system, and seem indeed more affected by *it*. Observers who have noticed the solidarity of French regimes in such misdemeanors as centralization, keeping the public out, and treating the voters like children, want to *"donner la parole au peuple"* instead, at last.[91] But at present *le peuple* tends to speak the only language it knows, the language in which it has been trained by this solidarity of regimes, the language of delegating decisions to others, of intransigence and discord, and of lingering nostalgia for a fundamental unity, which can be reached only at the level of feelings and dreams, or at the cost of ambiguity. In a substantive sense, France is not yet a political community, not because of merciless clashes of values (there are far fewer than before) but because of this common language.

I do not mean to say that a different language cannot be taught, or that the changes I have mentioned will not contribute to it, or that delegation and discord will necessarily be disastrous, once industrialism and France's new role in the world have been consolidated. But the questions today remain: how can they be consolidated while the old language is being spoken, and who will teach the new? One can argue that in the heavily fragmented stalemate society of yesterday, a political system such as that of the Third Republic, with its heavy mixture of an ideological component and of social immobilism, was exactly what was needed to maintain integration. One can argue that tomorrow's industrial society, less fragmented, less cramped, will be sufficiently integrated within a framework of pragmatic politics. But in the meantime, France is surrounded by the ruins of the old political system and does not know how to get to the new. The old integrating forces of politics have been *dis*integrated and the new integrating factors in society have not broken through. As the solidity and role of associations in French society have radically grown, parties have become weaker and even more like "delinquent peer groups." Indeed, all intermediate bodies in the political system—parties, bureaucracy, army—have been splintered by events into a chaos of small, conflicting factions. At present, on the domestic political scene, two moods alternate or coexist: apathy and rebellion. Complacency, bred by prosperous industrial societies, is encouraged by the spectacle of de Gaulle's often magnificent, often quixotic, often Machiavellian solo performance. And this complacency diverts many Frenchmen from the political wasteland and builds no transmission belt at all between the nation and its politics. During much of the period of the Third Republic, despite the clashing beliefs, symbols, and rituals of the left and the right, patriotism provided a common foundation, and the Republican faith, although it was a divisive one, supplied an inspiration and a focus. Today's largely renovated nation is far more paradoxical. The divisive and almost institutionalized and divisive old symbols are fading. Jeanne d'Arc now belongs to all—and we have seen to what extent the war has contributed to such a change. But if the nation now possesses shared memories, it no longer has any certitudes.

The decisive force which has destroyed the Republican synthesis and launched France's domestic transformation has been the pressure of the outside world. To use—for once—Toynbee's simplistic test, the French have responded to a challenge which seemed to threaten their very existence. But although *"la nature des choses,"* to use a Gaullist expression, seems to have drawn quite clearly the outlines of what France's new society and role in the world can be, as long as the political lag exists France's political genius slows down and at times threatens to disrupt this new distribution of her cards. To be sure, the answers to France's future are not all in France's hand. The degree of influence she will be able to preserve in Africa depends both on the evolution of Black Africa and on the ultimate policies of the Algerian nationalists; the amount of leadership she will be able to exert in Europe depends largely on the quirks of the cold war and on the solidarity of her neighbors. But there are also two purely French uncertainties which complicate France's response to the challenge. First, although the two responses—economic and social change, a new but still considerable role in the world—may be harnessed to the same objective—the "national ambition"—they do conflict because of the limits on

France's resources. Should this conflict worsen through a misman-agement of resources, or through domestic turmoil, and should any one of the two elements be sacrificed, then the "national ambition" itself may collapse. Secondly, even if the ambition persists, whether its goals are reached depends largely on the *way* in which they will be pursued. If the new society is still plagued by the residues of past tensions, if the path of development is constantly blocked by protests, if France's adaptation to the world brings with it a spirit of defeat and failure, then the whole long road may have been traveled in vain.

The paradox of authority

At this point, a second paradox stares us in the face. It can be called the paradox of authority. What France needs most is what she has always been least able to breed, and what she must discard is what has been most resilient. What is wanted is a new democratic style of authority, allowing for extended and powerful leadership and at the same time for participation.

In the past, France's fear of authority has severely curtailed the scope of authority and, in the political system, except during emer-gencies, the intensity of authority as well. These limits she cannot afford any more. None of those residues of the stalemate society which slow down economic growth and social mobility can be eliminated without strong authority. The bureaucracy cannot do it alone, so long as pressure groups—whether an alcohol lobby or a teachers' union—find through the parties a permanent access to veto power. Nor can the tensions of growth be managed by the bureaucracy alone. Nor can weak governments define a foreign policy and defend France's claims. One understands then why the need for powerful institutions, even though they are not the pana-cea which Gaullism once saw in them, nevertheless remains com-pelling. It is tempting to contrast *"le calme raisonné de la profon-deur française"* with the superficial agitation of politics. It is possible to point out that people's lives are only marginally affected by the political system, that in so far as people depend on the state the bureaucracy serves their needs. It is easy to show that just behind the distorting mirror of politics, old issues are being swept away and France is readjusting to the world. But the fact is that the mirror is what the people see, and the mirror itself becomes a major issue—far more real in people's minds, and just as real for the social scientist, as the growing consensus on substantive issues.

Only an adequate regime will be able to convince the French that the material sacrifices required by an ambitious new role in the world are not wasted, and to use the nation's resources so that no essential task will be neglected. Only an adequate regime will be able to heal old wounds, eliminate old habits, and pursue the "national ambition" without too many shocks. This is what de Gaulle has tried to do, and therein, as much as in his wartime role, or in his strength of character, or in his vision of history, lies the man's undeniable greatness. He has presented economic change as the condition of grandeur, he has described decolonization not only as a prerequisite for a new departure but as the crown of France's humanitarian traditions, and he has striven to offset the cruelty of the Algerian outcome with countervailing measures such as the effort to increase France's stature in NATO and the attempt to divert the army from imperial nostalgia to atomic reconversion. He has thus tried to project, on a reality which was often drab and all too often tragic, a ray of sunshine to make it glitter and glow. It is too early to say flatly that he will ultimately not succeed; but we see already that success, if it comes, will have been so dearly bought that it will not be complete—and that the next generation will have to do the job again, since France's new role ultimately depends on political leadership and since the present king has not groomed any successor. That the future of France in the world depends on France even more than on the world is a poignant truth that de Gaulle has always understood; but his leadership is only education through example and thus falls short of what would be needed to make the future safe.

The tragedy of de Gaulle is not merely that personal authority is never sure to strike roots deep enough to perpetuate itself. In order to be adequate, the future regime must not only be strong. It must be based on, and reflect in its institutions, the democratic pattern of authority. Otherwise, it will not be able to hasten the transformation of France's traditional authority relations in society.

This style is incompatible with *économie concertée*. It magnifies tensions between employers and employees and between civil servants and the public; it relies, for the removal of such tensions, on external crises and superior initiatives more than on procedures of cooperation. Nor will the old weakness of *"le peuple absent"*—and choosing to remain irresponsible—be remedied if this old style persists, nor will a new political class emerge now that the old notables are disappearing, nor will the blend of efficiency and representation which is the mark of mixed government ever be accomplished. It is in this area that the Fifth Republic has been most completely deficient.

That the two aspects of the problem—leadership and participation—are connected becomes obvious if one thinks of one of the major unsolved problems: the voting strength of the Communist Party. A weak regime will never be able to attract great numbers of Communist voters away from a party which has become the greatest collector of malcontents. Significantly the rise in the standard of living and the changes in the way of life have not weakened much the strength of the party in legislative elections; for many of its voters are precisely the men (workers or farmers) who feel left out, unconsulted, subordinated to higher authority without any other right than that of protest. And it is significant also that in order to preserve its strength the party has turned into a *"poujadisme de gauche,"* appealing to other protest groups, resisting the very changes which dismantle the old style of authority, and tirelessly defending the *petits*—in other words acting as the heir of Alain.[92]

The paradox of participation

But the question of participation shows yet another paradox. France, I have said, needs what she has never had. Could one not argue also that she now needs what she cannot have? It may well be that, once again, many Frenchmen who have felt alienated from the political system for so long now react by asking for far more participation than any democratic system can provide anywhere.

For unfortunately there are compelling reasons which prevent the leaders of democratic countries from exercising authority in the way which the democratic model would require.

In the first place, the questions with which states have to deal in their economic and social policies are becoming increasingly too technical to be handled by others than experts. Representatives of the public are simply not endowed with sufficient skills to be very helpful on credit policies, for instance, or decisions as to the "creation of new public or semipublic enterprises, the acceleration or slowing down of the movement of concentration of farms and of industrial or commercial enterprises." [93] It is therefore not surprising that trends appear in various governments toward less participation rather than more, and toward greater bureaucratic centralization—for instance in the management of France's social security system.

In the second place, even in countries with a much better tradition of "participation" than France, the nation's representatives and the delegates of large collective interests to consultative or decision-making organs tend to act as defenders of special interests and as the spokesmen for pressure groups; how to get such groups to agree on the distribution of the national income is such a headache that, almost inevitably, decisions to that effect are being taken by the "technocrats" of bureaucracy. Errors of fact and examples of inhumanity can easily be ascribed to those technocrats—for instance, in the handling of the 1961 Decazeville mine closing in France; but it is difficult to be convincing if one suggests, as Pierre Mendès-France did, that the cooperation of local civil servants, local enterprises, and local unions would necessarily succeed in reaching decisions compatible with both economic efficiency and social justice.

Thirdly, in no country can universal suffrage really be called a source of clear-cut decisions—precisely because people's desires are often incoherent, mutually exclusive, or totally unrealizable. The Rousseauistic model of total participation and of the general will is quite inapplicable to the national political system anywhere.[94] The best the electorate can do is turn to representatives who offer recognizable (if not necessarily detailed or widely diverging) alternatives and who, "without being endowed with special skills, know how to ask the voters questions that allow for an effective division of opinion." [95] The French electorate cannot do even that. Thus we are back once again where we came from—the bad condition of France's "intermediaries," and especially the parties, whose number, internal divisions, and traditions have ruled out such a role in the past.

Hence another set of obstacles to participation—this time obstacles peculiar to France. It is not only the nature of a technological society that tends to divert authority from the potentially frustrating techniques of democracy. France's political lag seems to compel the leaders to do so. As long as the residues and the vacuum I have mentioned survive, even decisions on the distribution of a growing national income may become the occasions of history-ridden battles; and expansion itself might be the victim of conflicting claims which could easily—it has happened before—provoke inflation and a new balance-of-payments crisis. It is difficult anywhere to get the representatives of large private interests to subordinate the proliferation of consumer goods to the growth of collective equipment and public services. And what is difficult in the affluent but traditionally liberal society of America is even more monumentally troublesome in a society unused to compromise and seething with long-repressed grievances. The temptation of authority by fiat is therefore greater than ever.

True, the absence of participation perpetuates the political vacuum and irresponsibility; but is participation going to provide solutions? Without participation, the only political consensus that can be reached is neither one on substance nor one on democratic procedures: it is merely a general agreement to leave all problems to a popular leader. But with participation, can any consensus be reached at all? The reluctance of political and civil service leaders to decentralize, and to multiply committees in which all interests would be represented, is quite explainable by the fact that certain of those interests—such as the Communist labor confederation (CGT)—would behave as a Trojan horse, and by the peculiarly French inability to compromise. Nor is there any guarantee that the entry of the new men into the party system would not resurrect the same old parliamentary game, both byzantine and distant from the people. The experience of 1945 has shown that an influx of new men is no panacea, especially if they bring into politics all the traditional ideas, reflexes, myths, and suspicions which have accumulated throughout French political history and outlived the circumstances of their birth precisely because the weakness of each political system has carefully nursed and preserved them for future use. Thus, although the very nature of the new society seems to make a much higher level of participation necessary, this goal may be impossible to reach without excessive damage to the political community.

Many recent studies, which take as a principle the need for participation, reflect unwittingly the old quest for unity, for a harmonious and reconciled polity without conflicts—as if the absence of legitimate institutions and the perilous state of the transmission belts could be dreamed away. The authors of such schemes assume that the problem is already solved—that France can have *both* strong authority and maximum participation. Most of them suggest pluralistic solutions—committees representing all major interests and committees of state agents for "democratic planning." In my opinion, this kind of thing is hardly a full solution; it is a recurrence of the 1944 dream of "economic and social democracy," and, as such, is based not only on a distrust of parties, but also on an undervaluation of their role in a political system. If the great political choices, including the choices about the allocation of resources, are not made by political leaders, they will be made by bureaucracy alone—or else the pluralistic state will become a kind of corporatist jungle. A nation which is being industralized undoubtedly needs to consult the representatives of the various interests, but in well-functioning democracies it is still the parties which provide the leadership and the control of the democracy. Too many democrats tend to see in participation a substitute for politics. Ruling saviors tend to see themselves as substitutes for both politics and participation. But the only real alternatives are politics without participation, and participation with politics, i.e., conflicts, alliances, programs, and debates.

The paradox of political community

For all the reasons I have listed, the tendency of authority in the short run is to go against participation. The Fifth Republic has demonstrated this well. The question thus becomes: how can one gradually introduce into the French political community measures and habits which will not only change the style of authority but make participation constructive instead of destructive? Here we find our final paradox. Even though, as we have seen, it is today the *political system* which is lagging behind, reforms in the political system alone will not be enough to bridge the gap. The gap will not be bridged unless reforms are introduced at all levels of the political community.

This does not mean that constitutional reform is unimportant. The need to devise institutions which will stabilize the political system somewhere between the extremes of the pendulum is great indeed. It may well be that this cannot be done within a parliamentary framework, which is always threatened with a return to "game politics" (even the remaining parliamentary aspects of the constitution of 1958 will be so threatened once de Gaulle has removed his overwhelming presence). It may well be that only a presidential system which fully preserves Parliament's law-making powers will give the electorate meaningful choices at last, by obliging parties to form new alignments for the election of the president. It may well be that provisions for joint emergency elections to both the presidency and Parliament would provide a safety valve in case of deadlocks, which otherwise might wreck a presidential system in a nation less prepared than the United States to take deadlock in stride or to reach compromises. And it may well be that the use of the referendum (not plebiscites) could be a way of avoiding too many crisis elections, and of preventing the president and Parliament from "confiscating" politics again.

Even so, those reforms could be only part of the answer. Such a system might gradually compel the parties to pragmatism and reasonableness, but this is far from certain. Everything will still depend on intangibles: the weight of the problems, the personalities of the first presidents. If the beginnings are smooth, the rest will

follow. If they are not, the drama will continue. In the present condition of the political system, it is not only hard to predict that
they would be smooth; it is also hard to envision such a new framework emerging.

Thus we have to turn to forms of participation more concrete
and detailed than general elections: i.e., local government and economic and social planning, so thoroughly discussed in France at
present. Despite the risks I have mentioned, measures to increase
participation in those respects strike me as essential, even if at first
le pouvoir reserves its right of final decision or veto. For the
poverty of local self-government maintains the irresponsibility of
the notables and the exile of party militants condemned to argue
about global abstractions.[96] Centralization dries up all of France's
intermediate bodies—parties, civil service, education system, army
—and keeps them segregated from one another.[97] In the long run
it is better to gamble on participation than on exclusion—at least
after the sequels of the Algerian War have been dealt with. One
may hope that, gradually at least, the disappearance of the old
ideological issues will make divisions less explosive. As for the survival of traditional attitudes, it is precisely the absence of participation that perpetuates them. The experience of those areas of
French life in which some participation exists, such as municipal
government, is far from discouraging. Also, as economic and social
change proceeds, the state may find that there are fewer risks than
advantages in calling on the representatives of the various groups
of the population in order to get its objectives approved and its
policies carried out. After all, the task of political leadership is to
transform a vicious circle into an ascending spiral.

Constitutional changes, and especially territorial and economic
decentralization, could go a long way toward creating a new political class, as broadly representative as possible of France's new
society. In other words, it could go a long way toward giving the
"new notables" a role within the political system and an incentive
to escape both from the temptation to cultivate their own gardens
and from the itch to behave as angry creditors of a bureaucratic
state.

Thus the solution of the problem of participation is the complicated one of seeking decisions from the nation directly on certain key issues through the referendum and the election of the chief executive; of organizing the consultation and cooperation of local and specialized interests on a more regular basis than in the past; and of seeing to it that a regular flow of "new notables" from the various groups in society into the parties becomes possible. Ultimately, too, there is still another reform, one which strikes me as the most vital of all, that of education.

For what the French system of education has fostered is precisely the kind of individual who tends to be an island—who has been provided with a mind so sharp and critical that he can push arguments until any relation to reality is a coincidence, and any chance of accommodation with other people's arguments a miracle. No area is more delicate; for this same system has produced a unique intellectual tradition and a civilization which even in the midst of a revolution of affluence is far more aware of problems of quality and culture than any other industrial society. How to preserve such gifts, while discarding traditions of "obedience without love," resistance without solidarity, and myth-making without compromise is a task which can be neither easy nor swift. But if a democratic style of authority is not taught at school, and through school, it is not going to spread in society, and the problems of participation, mixed government, and political lag will remain unsolved.

To say that such changes are needed is not to say that they will occur. Should they be introduced, the political lag would be eliminated much faster than otherwise. Should they remain in the centuries-long catalogue of dead suggestions for French reform, the centuries-long story of a political system that always seems on the verge of collapse while society appears solid and unconcerned would continue. But maladjustment comes in all sizes; the Third Republic, for all its defects, was more of a synthesis than any other system. To the question whether a new synthesis is in sight, my answer would have to be no. But to the question whether a new synthesis is more possible than at any time since the fall of the Republican one, I would give a very cautious yes. Yes because the measures I suggest are not utopian, cautious because all the negative factors I have listed indicate that their adoption is not very probable.

Meanwhile, the real drama will continue to be, as it has been for so long, that of France's relation to herself, the endless dialogue of the French with their mirrors—the mirror of history, the mirror which their leaders provide, and the mirror which the behavior of other nations toward France supplies to the French.

THE POSTWAR RESURGENCE OF
THE FRENCH ECONOMY

Charles P. Kindleberger

THE postwar economic revival of France has perhaps been slighted in economic literature. It is easy to see why this might be so. The recovery of neighboring Germany seems more remarkable in the light of wartime destruction and postwar settlement; and attention in France has focused primarily on political problems. But the recovery of France is no mean feat: industrial production rose about as much as German from prewar, though from a lower level in relation to capacity. And though France suffered less destruction and escaped the problem of refugees, its peculiar handicaps of war abroad and political crisis at home were severe enough.

The postwar economic vitality of France after about 1952 contrasts sharply with its miserable performance in the 1930's and the hesitant start in the early postwar period. Those delays produced a substantial literature on French economic backwardness, attempting to explain the country's incapacity to develop at rates equal to those of its neighbors. Some of this literature in fact appeared after the tide of recovery had definitely turned.

Even without the evidence of the present economic vitality, however, it is a mistake to regard France as a perennially backward developer. This essay, which will review the changes in the French economy, polity, and society accounting for the postwar resurgence, starts from a catalogue of explanations of French backwardness. But it should not be forgotten, despite the authors of these explanations, that French growth was rapid in at least three other extended periods in the last century or so—under the Second Empire from 1851 to about 1870; then from 1896 to 1913; and again in the 1920's. Some explanations for retardation imply that the French economy can never grow, others only that the growth will be sporadic and interrupted by the necessity to find new strengths. And it may be that the present period is due for interruption on similar grounds. In any case, interest in the current French recovery is heightened by past or current change in many of the alleged causes of retardation. French postwar experience commands attention on a more general basis than the history of the particular country, important as it is, insofar as that experience can illuminate the interrelations between a country's underlying characteristics and its economic growth.

The alleged causes of French economic backwardness must be analyzed with attention to what, if any, changes in underlying circumstances have supervened. One wants to know particularly whether the significant obstacles to growth have been removed— how, and when. I present the list of alleged causes first in brief summary, and then at greater length. The order is arbitrary.

The major explanations for French economic backwardness since about 1850 have been as follows.

On the side of production:
(1) lack of natural resources, especially of coking coal in an age of steel (Jean Chardonnet, Alexander Gerschenkron);

(2) lack of plentiful labor, not alone from the low rate of population growth but mainly from the slow release of manpower to the city by the agricultural sector with its love of the land and system of equal inheritance (W. A. Lewis, H. J. Habakkuk);

(3) diversion of savings from domestic capital formation to foreign political loans which "starved French industry of capital" (Maurice Lévy, Jean Weiller, A. K. Cairncross);

(4) the organization of enterprise into family firms which resisted market competition (David S. Landes) and followed inefficient practices in financing, recruitment, and promotion of technical change (Jesse R. Pitts);

Charles P. Kindleberger

On the side of demand:

(5) the slow rate of population growth, depriving France of an outlet for savings and a regular margin of expansion within which to effect technological change (Alfred Sauvy, Joseph J. Spengler);

(6) the French national character, which favored high-quality rather than mass consumption (Bert F. Hoselitz, Rondo E. Cameron);

(7) deep fissures in French society, preventing adjustment from traditional to modern patterns of social organization, exacerbating divisions among classes and sectors of society, promoting inflation, and diverting attention from growth to stability (John E. Sawyer);

On institutions:

(8) "Malthusian" market organization with firms too small and markets highly cartellized (Charles Bettelheim, Herbert Luethy);

(9) governmental intervention, whether to maintain social stability, to direct resource allocation, or to carry out unduly ambitious national designs, and entailing contradictory policies, over-centralization, and economic incompetence (Warren C. Baum, Jean Gravier).

Though differing in emphasis, these explanations overlap and are not mutually exclusive. The importance which attaches to each factor will differ among observers, depending on one's view of the process of economic growth, the relative weight of economic and noneconomic factors, and the tolerable limits of governmental economic activity. Thus if one adheres to a Harrod-Domar view of economic growth in which capital formation by the process of compound interest is the central engine of expansion, the major foci of attention become the export of capital, the weakness of the family firm as a device for investing in industry, and the slow rate of population growth. But one who believes that the prime force for growth is technological advance, raising output per unit of factor inputs, will attach greater significance to the resistance to change of family firm, family farm, and government, and the organization of markets to limit competition.

What has happened since World War II to produce rapid economic growth in France can be seen in perspective, if at all, only after an examination of the separate factors which had supposedly held it back and the extent of the change in them.

I

ON THE SIDE OF PRODUCTION

NATURAL RESOURCES

The complaint that France has been handicapped by lack of natural resources, and particularly of coal, has been recurrent almost since the invention of the steam engine. From at least J. A. Chaptal in 1819 to Jean Chardonnet in 1960, French economists, occasionally supported by foreign observers, have singled out the limited amounts and poor quality of French coal as a major obstacle to industrialization as rapid as in Britain or Germany. More subtle commentators have suggested that the difficulty lay elsewhere— for example, that French natural resources, including iron ore, were too distant from industrial centers and ports; that the internally "balanced" nature of the separate regions of France limited the gains from specialization once the country had been joined by railroad interconnection; that France, unlike Britain and Germany, had difficulties in achieving cheap natural transportation because of the scarcity of navigable rivers and the rough terrain; or that France never developed the widespread trade in coal which, as an indirect consequence, would have thickened the transport network and, as a by-product, would have cheapened freight rates for other commodities, thus stimulating their interchange and their use as inputs by industry.

But examination of the case against natural resources raises doubts. Coal production grew substantially in the first two periods of rapid growth, during the Second Empire in the Nord, and in 1896–1913 in Lorraine. The latter period also saw a great expansion in coal imports. During most of this time there was a tariff, which could have been reduced to cheapen coal for industry. A canal from the Nord to Lorraine, which would have increased the availability of iron ore to the Nord and coal to Lorraine, was declared a public utility in 1881 but never constructed. Only after World War II was its purpose carried out by the double-tracking and electrification of the railroad from Valenciennes to Thionville. And even without the canal, French steel production grew at a rate of 8 percent per annum from 1880 to 1913, very close to the 10 percent rate of Germany and Belgium, and much in advance of the British performance.

Albert Hirschman holds that economic growth produces resources, rather than resources growth. This view seems to be borne out by the economic history of France prior to 1945, especially if one believes that the availability of resources is largely a problem of transport facilities, which are man-made. It is clearly borne out postwar. The nationalized coal industry, Charbonnages de France, has performed with technical brilliance, consolidating small pits into efficient units, mechanizing mines above and below ground, raising output per man-shift faster than Germany or Britain. (There may be more of a question about its economic performance—for example, whether it invested too many resources in coal, and whether its pricing policies did not unduly penalize efficient and subsidize inefficient mines.) French hydroelectric sites on the Rhône, in the Alps, and in the Pyrenees have been exploited on a rapidly widening scale. The discovery of oil in Algiers, and of natural gas at Lacq (made usable by the development of new techniques to separate the sulphur from the gas, which incidentally create new competition for the United States sulphur industry) also testify in Hirschman's behalf. A long-run question has been raised whether Algerian oil is cheap or dear, compared to the resources which France would have had to give up to get an equal amount of oil from other areas through trade. If the Algerian War was justified in part by the riches of the Sahara, the calculation must be altered to include an allowance for an appropriate portion of the cost of the war. It is said to be a close question even without war costs.

Finally, note that at no time has there been any complaint about lack of resources in agriculture. On the contrary, the emphasis in all discussion is on France's varied and rich endowment of land. Blame for backwardness in agriculture is ascribed, instead, to lack of social-overhead capital such as roads, lack of education and technological instruction, the system of inheritance, inordinate love of land, and other flaws in administration or social values.

It seems clear that the alteration of France's resource base since the war has been a result rather than a cause of economic growth. As earlier in French history, resources have responded to the stimulus of industrial expansion. In this, as in much that follows, there is an inescapable element of interaction; growth begets resources and resources permit further growth. But the main point is that natural resources are not the controlling factor. In France it was not a lack of resources that held down the economy in its stagnant periods, nor an abundance of resources that prodded it forward in the 1950's.

LABOR SUPPLY

Chaptal in 1819 believed that France suffered compared to Britain from dear coal and cheap labor. The analysis evidently differed as between the two factors. Dear coal inhibited the plentiful use of an efficient fuel in static terms. The handicap of cheap labor was dynamic: it encouraged the abundant use of this input, maintaining the country in antiquated labor-intensive practices, and depriving entrepreneurs of an incentive to substitute machinery for labor.

There are traces of this view of labor through the nineteenth-century discussion. The present prevailing view, however, is diametrically opposite. It is believed that French industrial growth has been handicapped by stagnation in agriculture. This stagnation, arising from lack of education, French traditional love of the soil, and the Napoleonic system of equal inheritance, has limited the supply of savings for industry and the supply of agricultural raw materials used in industry, and has held down the demand for industrial products. Its major effect, however, is thought to have been its failure to release labor to industry rapidly enough. Industrial expansion has been frustrated not by too cheap labor, but by too expensive. Expansions have been brought to a halt by rising wages.

Space does not permit a thorough treatment of this problem in these pages, but a few conclusions may be in order.

French agriculture has been less technologically frozen than is generally believed. In the Paris basin, and in the North especially, but to a lesser degree everywhere, French agricultural practice advanced during the nineteenth century. The advances in agricultural rationalization were particularly rapid during the periods of industrial expansion under the Second Empire and before World War I. The agricultural advances were forced by the movement of labor into industry. But this movement was largely local in character. In France, as in Britain, agricultural workers did not move long distances to urban employment, except to the metropolis. There was this difference: redundant farm hands in Southern England who did not go to London emigrated abroad. In France, the rural surplus from the Southwest was recruited by Paris into the national services as gendarmes, railroad workers, postmen, and employees of the tobacco monopoly. Those from Brittany, however, would move neither to Paris nor abroad. And elsewhere in France, while the industrial economic historians were complaining of lack of labor supply, agricultural observers bewailed the rural exodus.

There is little evidence that the halting of French industrial expansion in 1870, 1913, or 1929 was due to inadequate labor supply. It is true that wages rose sharply in the 1850's and 1860's, and that prior to World War I the labor requirements of the North and East had to be met by immigration because of the unwillingness of French labor (which in most cases had already been drawn off local farms) to move the requisite long distances. It is also true that in some areas—Clermont-Ferrand, Sochaux in the Franche-Comté, and Bas-Rhin—industry and agriculture inhibited one another through the operation of isolated rural factories which used workers who continued part-time farming; here the recruiting of industrial laborers was hampered by the lack of small part-time farms available to them and farming continued by archaic methods because it remained a marginal contributor to family income, rather than a main support. But these factories were exceptional; they were not found in Paris or the North nor even in every part of

Lorraine. Moreover, the pressure of industrial expansion around 1910 was beginning to result in rapid agricultural reorganization when war intervened. Industry would have benefited from a willingness of French agricultural labor to move longer distances into industrial employment, rather than insist on limited local moves (frequently into the independence of *petit bourgeois* occupations). But on the other hand more persistent industrial expansion would have favored greater mobility.

Since World War II, there have been a rapid movement of labor off the farm and a rapid increase in French agricultural productivity. In the five years from 1949 to 1954, the active population engaged in agriculture, fishing and forestry—largely agriculture—fell by 30 percent, from 7.5 million to 5.2 million, or from 36.6 percent of the active population to 27.4 percent. The decline in men was only 19 percent, from 4.2 to 3.4 million, while the number of women dropped by 44 percent from 3.3 to 1.8 million. Productivity increased per worker and per acre, since the output rose while land tilled declined along with manpower.

This movement was partly motivated from the supply side. Mobility of the farm worker increased, with the spread of the motor-bike, scooter, and automobile. Young women refused to continue to bury themselves in the village. But the major change came from the demand for workers in industry, the pull of jobs rather than the push of labor off the farm. If there had been a greater demand for unskilled workers in industry, or greater education and skill among the agricultural population, the movement would have been still larger.

The backwardness of French agriculture at the beginning of the postwar period actually provided a force which sustained the subsequent growth, and in two ways. In the first place, it provided a reservoir of manpower for industry, just as German industry was helped by the influx of refugees which kept down wage rates, and Italian industry by the two millions of unemployed. Secondly, the movement off the farm led in turn to the necessity to rationalize agriculture, which contributed to the higher over-all rate of growth in a way which is not possible in a country which already has an efficient agricultural sector.

There are some independent sources of improvement in farming in France. Some returning Tunisian settlers have taken over deserted farms in Aquitaine, built up the land with modern techniques, and farmed it by machine on a substantial scale with the liberal use of capital. The local peasants—those who had not abandoned the region—were at first skeptical but then became interested and sought to follow the pattern. This proved difficult because of their lack of access to capital.

The improvement of agricultural efficiency created new problems at the same time that it helped solve old ones. Efficiency, improving faster than labor moved out of the sector, gave rise to surpluses in grain, meat, milk, butter, and vegetables, to add to the traditional burdens of excess supplies in sugar and wine. The new surpluses have helped to color French attitudes toward the European Common Market, and especially toward British entry into it and toward the access to European markets of traditional overseas suppliers.

On the whole, it is difficult to maintain the case that the family farm held back French industrial growth before 1939, or that its breakdown after 1946 has been responsible for the recent economic expansion. By and large, and though there is interaction, agricultural rationalization, like the discovery of natural resources, is a dependent not an independent variable in the equation of economic growth.

CAPITAL FORMATION

In many formulations, economic growth is a result primarily of capital accumulation. According to them, the retardation in both the 1880's and the 1930's was due to lack of the capital which would have raised capacity and output. In the 1880's the lack is ascribed to capital exports—loans to the Balkans and tsarist Russia funneled through a financial community in Paris which corrupted the press and misled the public to earn its commissions on bond flotations. In the 1930's some capital, escaping Laval deflation and the Blum Popular Front, sought refuge in Switzerland and New York as hot money, while domestic business capital, on strike against the government of the Left, refused to undertake productive investment.

Like any unitary-valued explanation, this is too simple. Capital exports took place not only during the 1880's but during periods of growth as well—in the 1850's and 1860's, between 1896 and 1913, and again in the 1920's. That Harry D. White's book on French capital exports contains the dates 1881–1913 in the title does not mean that capital exports began then, as Cameron has shown in great detail.[1] The notion that French industry was starved for capital in the period before World War I is clearly exaggerated; and though the rate of expansion in the 1920's was greater after 1926 when capital was returning than during the period of flight, it was still possible for capital exports and expansion to take place simultaneously. In the 1930's, French business had little reason to invest at home, either under Laval deflation or Popular Front inflation. Capital export was an induced rather than an independent and causal phenomenon.

One could make a case, perhaps, that it was not the over-all amount of saving which determined the rate of French industrial expansion, but only those funds available for industry. Under the Second Empire, capital for industry was furnished by the industrial banks, associated with the names of the Pereire brothers and the Crédit Mobilier. When these were destroyed or tamed, stagnation set in. In the period before World War I, there was lending by regional banks in Lorraine and Haute-Savoie, plus liberal rediscounting of industrial credits by the Bank of France, despite its rules and traditions limiting the rediscount facility to commercial acceptances. In the 1920's, government credit for reconstruction was the source of capital formation. After World War II there was a variety of methods: self-financing by companies to the extent of nearly 50 percent of all industrial investment; government deficits; special governmental funds derived partly from the counterpart of foreign aid; inflationary finance through Bank of France rediscounting. In these operations the traditional Paris capital market continued to play a minimal role. On this showing, the critical variable for economic growth was not the over-all supply of capital, but the mechanism for channeling savings into domestic investment. Capital exports were less a subtraction from the supply of capital available to industry than a means of mopping up the pool of savings which industry could not or would not use.

Blaming the barriers to capital flow into industry makes more historical sense than concentrating on the factors making for capital exports. But here too there is a problem of identifying cause and effect. Was it the barriers that restrained the demand, or the low demand that permitted the barriers to stand? Where demand for industrial capital is insistent enough, it can be said, institutional arrangements will adapt themselves to it and continue to channel savings into industry.

In any case, whether capital formation was deficient because of lack of demand or because of institutional blocks to industrial and governmental investment, it seems reasonable to exonerate the *supply* of capital. True, it is difficult to separate the demand and supply curves over time, because of their interdependence. On almost any showing, however, the supply of capital has moved in the wrong direction to explain France's postwar economic revival. Abundant during the period up to World War I, it was extremely scarce after World War II; yet this later period saw a larger expansion of domestic investment than the earlier. Postwar developments affecting the supply of savings—the discouragement to savers from inflation, the slight redistribution of real income to lower income groups, and the growth of appetite for real income in the lower middle and working classes—have reduced rather than expanded the supply. It is perhaps fair to say that foreign-exchange control after World War II prevented the diversion of capital to hoarding in Geneva, London, and New York on the scale that had taken place in the interwar period. But this is a small difference compared with the postwar change in demand. The Monnet, Hirsch, and Massé plans, the renewal of construction, the need for roads, schools and other social-overhead capital, and, above all, the expansion of investment by nationalized industry, private enterprise, and even artisans, shopkeepers, and farmers, have put perhaps the severest strain on the capital supply that France has known since 1856. Bank credit has been tight; dividends have been limited;

capital markets and Plan authorizations have served to ration the tight supply of savings.

The *supply* of capital is an economic concept which is clear in itself. There is the behavior of domestic savers—corporate, private, and governmental—and of foreign investors, and the competition of foreign borrowers for savings. But the domestic demand for capital is a less coherent aggregate. Back of it stand other factors with more basic explanatory force. It is to these factors—the character of entrepreneurship, the growth of population, functions assumed by the government, and so on—that we must turn.

THE FAMILY FIRM

An important body of thought holds that French economic retardation has been due to the dominance of industry by the family firm. On this theory, family enterprises have slowed France's growth relative to other countries by various forms of behavior. Landes emphasizes their support of monopolistic or imperfectly competitive forms of market organization.[2] The wider-ranging Jesse Pitts version of the theory contains a multiple indictment.[3] For one thing, family enterprises refuse to grow beyond the size at which they can be dominated by the family; in particular they refuse to dilute the family ownership by selling equity shares on the securities market. They minimize risks rather than maximize profits, and hence save in liquid form as insurance against adversity rather than invest in product or process innovation. They produce to fill orders rather than for stock. They are characterized by secrecy and mistrust; they fear banks, government, and even the consuming public. They hold prices high. Turnover is permitted to languish as the larger firms refrain from expanding output and sales in ways which would embarrass the small-scale inefficient producers at the margin.

The narrower Landes and wider Pitts theses are not universally accepted. Some scholars who do research on the origins of large-scale French industry insist that the theses overlook vast and significant fields of French entrepreneurial endeavor such as railroads, mines, iron and steel, automobiles, banks, and department stores. Some hold that family enterprise can function efficiently, as it has done in Britain. Some regard the family firm as a transitional form of enterprise in every country which happens to have lasted a little longer in France than in some other countries. It is generally agreed that family enterprise has characterized the French textile industry; but, even here, in various localities there have been examples of speculator firms which were interested in making money rapidly and selling out, rather than founding a conservative industrial dynasty as an extension of the bourgeois family. Family firms of a progressive nature can be found in iron and steel, tires, automobiles, locomotives, department stores, and so on. And when technological considerations require it, the pattern of many small-scale family-size units is replaced by concentration—despite the reluctance to dilute—by means of mergers, bankruptcy, or voluntary withdrawal after the sale of assets. Finally the French economic expansions of the 1850's and 1860's, of the period 1896–1913, and of the 1920's add to the doubts as the responsibility of the family firm for French economic stagnation.

But whatever its responsibility for stagnation, one would be hard pressed indeed to attribute the current French dynamism to changes in the structure of the family firm. A certain number of private mergers have taken place, especially in steel, and including some urged by the Planning Commission—though in Sollac, the new firm merely joins elements of the deWendel family empire which had worked together earlier as an entente. Nationalization of coal, electricity, gas, and the Renault automobile firm has consolidated some small-scale family units into large organizations, or replaced family organizations by those recruited on universal rather than particularist lines. These changes are much less significant, however, than the change in attitudes of the family firms themselves. Landes was bold enough to say in 1957 that three years of expansion did not make an industrial revolution. Presumably he believed that the institutional bonds of the family firm would bring the recovery to a halt. What appears to have happened, on the contrary, is that the expansion in the economy altered the attitude, outlook, and hence the behavior of the family firm.

This result can be seen nowhere more sharply than in the automobile industry where it is difficult and maybe impossible to judge from the behavior of the four major firms the nature of their ownership and direction.[4] The two family firms (Peugeot and Citroën, which is owned by the Michelin family) are respectively the most and the least profitable, respectively the most efficient producer and the most daring product innovator. The limited liability company—Simca—has perhaps the least distinguished manufacturing record, though it has participated in the growth of output of the industry by means of aggressive domestic marketing. The nationalized concern, Renault, has innovated brilliantly in production and in foreign sales. But all have been helped by a demand which grew at the rate of 25 to 35 percent a year and provided a margin within which risks of innovation could be undertaken.

I am not then disposed to attribute any great responsibility for the periods of slow growth to the family firm, nor to attribute the present resurgence to changes in this institution. There is, of course, some interaction between growth and the family firm in the postwar period of rapid technological change and increasing domestic investment. Inhibitions on the dilution of ownership through issuance of equity securities may slow down capital formation, just as the competition of public companies may have forced family firms to alter their policies on technical change. But basic causes of change cannot be found in the nature of the family enterprise.

II

ON THE SIDE OF DEMAND

◇◇

POPULATION

It is a paradox that too little population growth is thought to have slowed economic growth in France—and in the 1930's in the United States—whereas too much population growth is inhibiting development in underdeveloped countries. But the reconciliation of the apparent conflict is fairly straightforward. When a country starts on the road to development, increases in income stimulate the net birth rate, generally by reducing disease through improvement of sanitation and medical care. The survival of additional young and old people lowers output per capita, reduces income available for investment, and slows the rate of growth on a Harrod-Domar model (compound interest based on increased savings). But in countries beyond the early stages of development, population growth may have a different effect. A static population may mean an excess of intended savings over intended investment, with unemployment, a reduced level of capital formation, and slower growth of capacity. Limiting children to a boy and a girl per family lessens pressure for mobility because children can follow parental occupation. Restricting investment to the level which will maintain the ratio of capital stock to a fixed population narrows the opportunity to incorporate technological improvements in the economy's assets. It is principally for these reasons, largely concerned with demand, that economic activity in a developed country is stimulated by expanding population—especially if the expansion results from the immigration of able-bodied workers or from the maturing of a new crop of babies to fifteen years of age and more, rather than from an increase in the numbers of old people.

Since World War II both the economy and the population have grown at rapid rates. It is conceivable that the economic growth led to the population expansion, as occurs in underdeveloped countries, where development is accompanied by a reduction in infant mortality and improvements in public health which reduce the death rate. But in France the causation almost certainly did not run in this direction. The net reproduction rate, which indicates the extent to which a population is reproducing itself, turned sharply upward from 1945 to 1946, well in advance of the rise in output. The accompanying table shows the net reproduction rate over a period of nearly fifty years. A rate of less than 100 means that, under the conditions of female mortality and fecundity of the year given, the current generation will be replaced by a generation less numerous, and a rate higher than 100 means it will be replaced by a generation more numerous. The rate rose suddenly after both world wars, but in the second case it shot above 100 and stayed there, reaching the highest ground in at least a century and a half.

Net Reproduction Rate in France, 1911–1959
(100 means population is reproducing itself)

1911......87	1921......98	1931......93	1941...... 77	1951......126
1912......94	1922......97	1932......92	1942...... 85	1952......125
1913......92	1923......94	1933......88	1943...... 90	1953......124
1914......88	1924......93	1934......90	1944...... 94	1954......125
1915......57	1925......94	1935......87	1945...... 93	1955......124
1916......45	1926......92	1936......88	1946......126	1956......125
1917......48	1927......93	1937......89	1947......131	1957......126
1918......46	1928......92	1938......91	1948......133	1958......126
1919......58	1929......89	1939......93	1949......133	1959......128
1920......98	1930......93	1940......82	1950......132	

Illustration: The rate of 128 for 1959 means that under the conditions of mortality observed for all females in that year and under the conditions of fecundity observed for all child-bearing women in that year, 100 women of child-bearing age would be replaced by 128 females. This corresponds to a 28 percent increase from one generation to the next.

Source: Annuaire Statistique de la France, Rétrospectif (*Paris, 1961*), *p. 51, tableau VIII.*

The question follows as to what *was* the cause of the population upturn—whether a simple (or complex) independent change of taste or a result of efforts of French demographers (especially Adolphe Landry) translated into the *Code de la Famille* of July 1939. The answer must be sought in timing, and, to the limited extent possible, in the differences in fecundity in different groups as affected by the family allowances.

On the first point—timing—it is generally believed that French interest in larger families took hold during the war.[5] In the bourgeois quarter of Vienne, baptisms had been rising since 1936;[6] and this would square with the very slight rise in the net reproduction rate from 1935 to 1939. But those observers, like Sauvy, who see the origin of the change as the adoption of family allowances at the insistence of the demographers can hardly be refuted by the fact that the upturn did not coincide exactly with the *Code de la Famille*. The Code itself had its forerunners, and significant effects were of course overwhelmed by the war and postponed until its end.

There is, however, a limited amount of evidence—and considerable opinion—to suggest that the change in attitude toward family size was not contingent upon subsidy. It would be desirable to have data by income group on the size of families formed since 1945. If such data showed that the lower income groups, to which the allowances provided a more substantial proportionate increase in over-all income, had experienced a larger increase in family size than higher income groups, we would be entitled to say that the family allowances stimulated the increase in fecundity. The available census data are of little use because they relate to existing families formed almost entirely before 1946.[7] Data on net birth rates by French departments are misleading because of interdepartmental migration. More young people migrate than old, and this results in higher birth rates in departments of immigration and lower in those of emigration, without regard to birth rates by income groups.[8] But there is evidence to suggest that the pre-World War II demographic pattern has changed drastically. In Vienne in the postwar period, bourgeois couples have had the largest families; the number of children per household was: bourgeois 1.46; workers 1.06; lower middle class (employees and small shopkeepers) 0.98.[9] In a small sample of independent businessmen Pitts found that the number of children per family was well above the French average.[10] And it is reported that in the poorest agricultural part of France the third child is always a mistake for which the "family allowances and premiums are never more than a consolation." [11]

One can conclude, then, that the claim of Sauvy and the other French demographers that the family allowances produced the dramatic change in birth rates is not established. These allowances have doubtless had other significant effects in promoting child welfare and health. But the change in birth rate must be regarded as an independent change in taste. The question remains whether the change in birth rate has produced the French recovery.

It is certainly possible to regard it as an important remote cause, if not the proximate cause. The rising tide of youth has impressed on the French—government and public alike—the necessity to bestir themselves to achieve growth. This was by no means the only such stimulus; the humiliation of France in 1940 after the sorry record of the 1930's could equally produce a resolve for more effective economic performance. Nor did the birth rate provide the mechanism for growth. But the wave of children has modified French attitudes toward family life and toward social, regional, and occupational mobility; has led to an insistence on more housing and schools; and has reduced the resistance to economic growth of static elements in the society. The change in population growth rates contributed to economic growth but was not the sole basis for it.

SOCIAL CHANGES

The discontinuous change in population growth calls attention to the possibility that the change in the rate of economic growth may be attributable to wider social changes of which the step-up in the net reproduction rate is only one aspect. The social changes that have occurred in France are discussed in detail elsewhere in this volume by Laurence Wylie and Jesse Pitts. The economist is in no position to evaluate the quantitative importance of this sort of change. The purpose here is only to show how social attitudes and circumstances may have inhibited economic growth in the past, and, having undergone change, how they contribute to it at the present. Only two aspects will be discussed: values and social tension among classes.

It has long been observed that demand for mass products has been held back in France by French interest in elegance in consumption. Handwork was preferred to the output of machinery. The intense interest in individuality in consumption have kept Sèvres porcelain and Gobelin tapestries going today. In less durable goods the Paris dress industry provides the classic example, unless it be the French interest in good food and wine, which not only diverts demand to labor-intensive output but at the same time slows production for several hours in the middle of the day.

Pitts attributes the French interest in quality to the long survival of aristocratic values, in particular the concern for prowess —the unreproducible act, whether of art, valor, sport, or craftsmanship. To these values were added the dynastic interests of the bourgeois classes, anxious to perpetuate the "extended family" and hence to amass savings; and the coexistence of quality consumption and a high propensity to save left little room for broad markets for consumers' goods. It is significant that in 1913 when

France was the leading automobile producer in Europe, with a production of 45,000 cars, most of them were built to customer specifications and half the output was sold abroad, mainly in Britain. The country which originated the department store failed to adopt it as widely as did the United States, Britain, and Germany, or to accompany it with the chain store or multiple shop.

The lack of demand for large-scale production is also partly explicable in class terms. With wide social barriers, one saved if one were ambitious to become a bourgeois, but the great mass of workers and peasants had little interest in owning durable goods, beautifying their houses, educating their children. Peasants saved to buy more land. The rise in workers' incomes went into meat and wine to give France the highest per capita consumption of these products in Europe.

Postwar recovery has been caused—or at least accompanied—by widespread interest in consumption of durable goods. The phenomenon is by no means restricted to France; it affects all of Western Europe. But it is perhaps most striking in France, where it is intimately linked to the change in the family from the "extended" to the "nuclear," and the change in the reproductive pattern. Instead of living for the future of the dynasty, French people today seek enjoyment, including enjoyment in children. Rudimentary facilities for consumer credit have developed to assist in these gratifications. In bourgeois circles, there is probably less personal saving than before.

Along with the revaluation of mass consumption, France has undergone a change in attitude toward work. Partly this involved an abandonment of the aristocratic value system which disdained work in general, and particularly accorded an inferior status to selling, which would involve submitting one's worth to the whim of a customer. More generally perhaps it may have grown out of changed attitudes inside and outside the family. To refer again to the views of Pitts, the tensions of the extended family induced a polar change in behavior when men escaped from the family scene into business. There they constituted a "delinquent peer group," defiant not only toward home but also toward customers, potential competitors, and especially toward government. (By contrast, in the United States the tensions of school and business produce—in the home—the immoderate behavior of children and the relaxed attitude of breadwinners.) But with a change in the family structure to the nuclear unit created for enjoyment rather than dynastic continuity, there is said to have been room for converting the business enterprise from a delinquent community into an outlet for creative energy and accomplishment.

As for social tensions, the uneven economic development of France in the past has been explained by a number of observers in terms of the inability of the French to resolve deep divisions which extend beyond the politics of, say, the Dreyfus affair and embroil important economic interests. "The history of the Second Empire is in good part illustrated by the struggles of rival financiers." [12] France had two capitalisms, one producer-oriented, family-oriented, Catholic; the other financial, speculative, Jewish or Protestant. The speculative group appeared to oppose the family-oriented group's values and structure, but used them for its own ends.[13] The economic history of France from 1830 to 1880 can be written as a struggle between the Grande and the Petite Bourgeoisie.[14] Or the period from 1850 to 1939 was characterized by successive wars between the traditional economy and industrial society, with the petty bourgeoisie first on one side, then the other. In this combat there was insufficient pressure from population, from foreign trade, from the new national market, and from spectacular and sudden rates of growth, permanently to alter the patterns of traditional and petty bourgeois resistance.[15]

These views tend to be rather vague on the mechanism by which growth is held back. Some observers point to the family firm, which we have discussed. In a few cases the mechanism is said to be inflation, caused by distributional difficulties coupled with economic and political power. It is therefore appropriate to examine the theory that social divisions have caused inflation and that inflation has had a decisive effect on growth.

It is true that a small burden laid upon a society can cause inflation and inhibit investment and growth if there is difficulty in agreeing on how the burden should be shared among income groups and if each income group has some power to resist an undue portion of the burden being imposed upon it. If labor has power to raise wages and industry to increase prices, and if agriculture is prepared to withhold supplies when its prices rise slower than the prices at which it is buying, inflation is inevitable. This inflation will continue until the whole burden has been imposed on the pensioners, civil servants, rentiers, and other classes with fixed incomes. The power to resist burdens need not be narrowly economic. If police and civil servants go on 24-hour strikes when the cost of living rises precipitously in advance of their pay scales, or wine growers blockade Route Nationale 117 as a response to higher costs, higher taxes, or lower subsidies, the spiral mounts. Monetary theorists insist that a condition of inflation is that the money supply expand, and that inflation could be stopped if the central bank willed it. But this assumes away the problem created by the fact that the separate classes have enough power to prevent the burden from falling on them; industrial loans expand when wages rise as a result of strikes which in turn stem from the increase in the cost of living. To say that loans should not expand is to change the condition of the problem which arises from the capacity of industry, through its social and political power, to overcome any tendency to restraint which would force the weight of the burden on it, just as the threat or actuality of strikes prevents it from falling on industrial labor. On occasion the social struggle to fend off a share of the burden will take the form of a budget deficit as laboring and agricultural classes insist on governmental spending and all classes refuse to vote taxes, and industrial owners and professional classes refuse to pay those direct taxes which are levied on them.

But the main vehicle of inflation is the market, and inflation came to an end not so much through a change in monetary or fiscal policy as from a change in market power. When a good harvest and foreign aid destroy the capacity of farmers to raise prices by withholding supplies, the inflation comes to an end with a part of the burdens saddled on the farm sector. Thus the bumper crop of 1950 and the subsequent agricultural expansion broke the back of French inflation, and reduced agriculture's share of national income from 25 percent in 1949 to 14 percent in 1952.

But although inflation in France has been a symptom of social disharmony, revealed in persistent deficits and monetary expansion, it has not been harmful to growth. Nor, probably, has it helped. The growth of the 1850's and that of the 1920's were both accompanied by inflation, just as that of the late 1940's and early 1950's up to 1953.

Some of the deep social fissures in the nineteenth century are thought to have slowed growth in specific ways other than inflation; the *hautes banques* pulled down the Crédit Mobilier in 1868 and the Union Générale in 1882, and killed the Freycinet plan of 1879 for investment in feeder railroads, canals, and roads. In the 1930's, the economy was crippled by the clash between the extremes of left and right, culminating in the Stavisky riots, the sit-down strikes, and the Matignon agreement which humiliated industry. But there was also little social cohesion in the postwar period; yet growth began anyhow. Business groups emerged from the Vichy period in national disgrace.[16] Small businessmen and tradesmen fought against the collectivity in the Poujade movement. Peasants' dissatisfaction with their economic lot, expressed especially in the demonstrations and riots of 1961, has been continuous since 1952. The Algerian question has divided the country as nothing has since Dreyfus. All this without halting expansion. For in the postwar period the concern for expansion—stimulated by technocrats in government—has been dominant.

There is some evidence that economic growth has helped to narrow social divisions, but not much. The Frenchman is said to feel himself still disfavored, despite a 43 percent increase in per capita income between 1949 and 1958; and people are not happy.[17] The working classes have more material comfort, but their condition of life remains sharply differentiated from that of the bourgeois —except perhaps in the size of their automobiles. Tradesmen, farmers, and to some degree the petty bureaucrats have not done as well as the bourgeoisie and the industrial worker. They do not oppose the rise in the standard of living but are disgruntled that they do not fully share it. Particularly disaffected is the progressive farmer, who has changed his way of life as a producer, only to find, with falling agricultural prices on a saturated market, that he has taken on fixed service charges for his machinery which his enlarged output cannot help him to discharge because of the inelastic demand.

On the whole, then, France has adopted new attitudes toward the family and toward production and consumption, but without fundamentally altering class divisions and the mistrust felt by the individual for other classes, for other individuals, and for government as the embodiment of others. That the change in values was important in producing economic growth is likely but impossible rigorously to demonstrate. The unimportance of class antagonism as a general inhibition on growth—so long as all classes agree on the desirability of expansion—would appear to be established.

III
ON INSTITUTIONS

◇◇◇

When one turns from factors of supply and demand to the institutional arrangements governing the organization of production, he must acknowledge that the distinction is trivial. Institutions are outgrowths of underlying facts. The view that French economic growth has been held back by monopoly and monopolistic behavior is closely related to the view that it has been held back by the family firm.

The institutions that need close examination here are, first, the organization of the market, and second, the government.

MARKET ORGANIZATION

Two schools of thought may be distinguished in the field of market organization. The first is an outgrowth of the argument about the family firm; it holds that industry was small-scale and noncompetitive, or that such large-scale industry as existed held back from competing with small firms in the interest of high profits and social stability. The other school holds that industry was dominated by large-scale monopolies which restricted production and held up prices. In both cases the emphasis is on the structure of the market rather than on that of the firm. The first version, however, would expect an improvement in competition and productivity from bigger units. The second would not.

The version that better fits the facts is the one that rests primarily on the existence of inefficient small units protected by the unwillingness of the large to compete. Industries dominated by large firms have done better on the whole than those in which the average size was smaller.[18] Much of the French economic literature falsely identifies large firms with concentration and small with competition, whereas it is possible for big firms to compete, as the automobile industry reveals, and for small-scale industry to maintain prices or standard markups, with resultant overcapacity and waste where entry is free. But even where this identification is correct, as it may sometimes be, the monopoly embodied in large-scale industry has not held back growth since 1945, whatever its prewar record.

Price maintenance by agreement (open or tacit), refusal to compete through innovation, insistence on protection in the home market—these are the earmarks of what the French call "Malthusianism."

Malthusianism is the principal cause of the lag of the French economy. Industrialists and agriculturalists have always been haunted by the specter of overproduction and have feared a collapse of prices. To protect their interests they are organized into coalitions. These have as their purpose to maintain production at a relatively low level and to assure high prices for sales. They thus assure survival of the least profitable units . . . and occasionally even require the state to finance activities which have no interest for the national community . . . Mechanization and rationalization are held back; investment is limited . . . Prices are no longer competitive with foreign prices . . . Since the national market is limited, the forecasts of overproduction become justified along with the Malthusian measures which the industrialists and the agriculturalists demand.[19]

There has been an increase in the readiness of French industry to compete. This new attitude has appeared primarily in large-scale industry and reflects partly a change in attitude toward small

French business. Rather than restrict production and hold a price umbrella over the heads of small firms in the interest of social stability, large-scale business now believes that its interests lie in lower prices, expanded output, and wider markets. Reduced profits per unit of sales will be more than made up, it is thought, by enlarged sales. And the Common Market provides a convenient cover for this change in attitude by large firms toward their inefficient compatriots. If small business succumbs to competition when tariffs are eliminated within the European Economic Community, it will look as though foreign enterprise, not French, wielded the weapons that destroyed it.

But the change in attitude goes wider. French business has lost its inferiority complex vis-à-vis foreign competition. Experience in steel in the European Coal and Steel Community, and in the metal, automobile, chemical, electrical and even the textile industry has persuaded efficient French firms that they can hold their own in competition with the best that the rest of the Common Market has to offer. It is sometimes suggested that the acceptance of the Common Market by French industry is no indication of self-confidence, because tariff barriers are going to be replaced with cartel agreements. There have indeed been numerous business agreements, mainly with a view to settling on different specialties for large-scale production by long factory runs. But European business is too well versed in the history of these agreements to depend on the forbearance of foreign rivals; such agreements are not respected unless they are between equals. Despite the industrial agreements, therefore, French entry into the Common Market signifies willingness to compete at home, and capacity to compete abroad.

Malthusianism has gone, or been very much reduced. But what has produced this result? Not an independent change in the size of firm, not capital investment, not an increase in domestic and foreign competition, though these changes are associated and related to one another and in sum represent the end of Malthusianism. A major change occurred in technology, including innovations in both process and product. And this technological change, latent in French technical capacities, was the outcome of deep-seated social and value changes.

GOVERNMENT

Intimately related to social cohesion and division on the one hand, and to market organization, on the other, has been government, the focus of myriad French forces and ambivalent attitudes. Although government has occasionally taken a positive role, as under the Second Empire, its normal function has been to operate to maintain social stability in the face of divisive forces. Individuals, firms, social groups curse the government for its favoritism to others and appeal to it for assistance to themselves.

Warren C. Baum has studied the postwar record of government and found it poor.[20] He particularly attacks the inconsistencies and contradictions in policy. Government tried to improve efficiency and yet to maintain inefficient small firms and small farms. In providing security it discouraged output. In taxing sales on the *forfait* system, it encouraged high markups on low turnover with bad effects on the price level and efficient distribution. Rent controls inhibited building and limited labor mobility. The regressive system of social security taxes both raised manufacturing costs and had the effect of making the laboring classes pay for their own security.

An effective case can be made that French tax reforms have consistently been in the direction of encouraging private modernization, expansion, concentration, and adaptation.[21] Much of this occurred after the period covered by Baum, and during or after the strong upsurge of recovery from 1953 to 1958. Baum's book suggesting that the state has made it impossible for France to grow (most of it written in 1953) appeared in 1958 when the rate of growth was very high. Its more important weakness, however, is that government seems to be viewed as an independent organization outside the economy, whereas government is really a reflection, direct or distorted, of the contradictions embedded in the social fabric. French tariff history in recent years has reflected the same unresolved conflicts in that there have been tariffs for all

—on foodstuffs and home-grown raw materials, for farmers, and on industrial products, for manufacturers. As already indicated, inflation is an escape from the dilemmas implicit in sharing a burden, not a result of ignorance of monetary or fiscal policy.

Not only does government intervene internally. It is the instrument of foreign policy. Government and the country may make a success or failure abroad through ineptitude or excessive ambition. Here the postwar record is not distinguished, whether in Indochina or Algeria, or in France's share of NATO's defense of Europe. Large sacrifices have been imposed on the country and French allies alike, without substantial achievement, as concern for French greatness has outstripped capacity. But these failures have not had disastrous consequences for economic growth.

Two important discontinuities have occurred in government policy, one a decision to resist further centralization of control and activity in Paris, and the other a return to an ancient practice of government planning and investment.

All the French literature—produced partly by economists but mainly by geographers—has denounced the centripetal pull of Paris. Because of Louis XIV, or Napoleon I, or the layout of the railroads, or whatever factors, Paris is thought to have drained the rest of the country of vigor, capital, and opportunity. The Bank of France is stated to have taken steps as late as 1930 to centralize bank credit in Paris.

During the last quarter of a century this centralizing tendency has altered. In the late 1930's, the program of dispersal of aircraft manufacture helped; the transfer of more than one plant to the provinces (for example that of a Renault parts plant to Le Mans) may have been due to an urge to escape the Popular Front. But the real discontinuity occurred during the war. The division of France into the Occupied and Unoccupied Zones required initiative outside Paris. Moreover, a series of studies by geographers [22] formed the basis, after their publication in 1945, for a vigorous program of government support for investment outside Paris, especially after 1953. The attraction of Paris for economic vitality and brains has by no means been destroyed; local talent is still being

seduced to the capital, and certain regions of France continue un-
attractive for private investment. Nevertheless, expansion is most
rapid in a few towns of great tourist attraction, like Annécy; and
Lorraine, the Nord, and the Dauphiné are leading French economic growth.

There remains, however, a large question how much of the
growth of economic vitality outside Paris is the result of government policies, and how much of it is spontaneous. Separate influences are of course impossible to disentangle. Policy changed,
and the facts changed, but whether the policy change was responsible for the alteration of the facts is impossible to say with
any finality. Both may have depended upon the rise in economic
energy throughout France. In the 1920's, it was easy to identify
the expansion of the North with the governmental policies of reconstruction in that devastated area. After World War II, the
most that can be said is that the conscious decision of government
to reverse the concentration of economic decision-making and
vitality in Paris either produced the geographic decentralization or
was the product, along with that decentralization, of the revival
of economic energy in France.

Government planning and investment were a new departure,
at least since the defeat of the Freycinet plan in 1882. Their roots,
however, lay deep in French culture in Saint-Simonism, the technocratic view which found favor with Napoleon III. In the emperor's
view, government was not an ulcer, but a motor, and his early
support for the construction of railroads, canals, telegraph facilities, ports, and roads, and for the rebuilding of Paris, Marseilles,
and Le Havre, set the stage for the period of rapid growth from
1851 to 1857 and even to 1870. His letter to the Minister of Commerce published in the *Moniteur Industriel* of January 15, 1860,
outlined a plan for the economic development of France eight
days prior to the unpopular Anglo-French treaty for tariff reduction, imposed by decree in opposition to the majority of the French
Parliament. The Freycinet plan represented similar Saint-Simonian
tendencies under the Third Republic, though it was defeated by
the bankers; and Michel Augé-Laribé insists that "everyone knew

what needed to be done for agriculture in 1880—better methods, fertilizer, seed selection, irrigation, drains, roads, cheaper transport and education—but it did not get done, even slowly." [23]

Although the Monnet plan thus represented an ancient tradition, the vigor with which it was carried out and followed up by the Hirsch plan and subsequent ones was new in French governmental annals. I shall explore presently the forces that gave rise to this burst of energy, which was felt earliest in the nationalized coal, electricity, gas and railroad industries, in the nationalized Renault automobile firm, and also in steel. The Monnet plan with its variety of controls and financing techniques has been said to have raised the level of investment without overexpanding basic capacity. But the level of investment which France could maintain was much higher than it would have been in the absence of the Marshall plan and other aid from the United States, such as the Export-Import Bank loan of 1946. Of course the possibility exists that this aid supported France's overseas wars rather than recovery, and that without it defense expenditure would have been cut back rather than investment.

Government, apart from its intervention in investment, may have made some contribution to economic recovery after the war by means of economic policies in other lines—but this is more questionable. The monetary theorist may contrast the Laval deflation with the Rueff stabilization plan of December 1958, or the forty-hour week under Blum with the policy of forced mergers under the Monnet plan. It is dangerous to push the contrast too far. The French economy began to pick up after Munich when the Reynaud government took office. This was partly attributable to defense spending, though mainly to the removal of unwise policies which held back production. On the other hand, it is hard to find sound governmental policies in the early postwar recovery period, except on investment. Monetary flaccidity, along with the policy of a prize for every group, permitted inflation. The devaluation of 1946 was unsuccessful. Inflation was halted more by foreign aid and a bumper harvest than by Pinay's policies. And with all respect to the Rueff plan, which was a model of its kind, the devaluation and stabilization of 1958 were successful because of the recovery that had taken place rather than responsible for it. There is no justification for attributing great significance for French recovery to these monetary policies, which tidied up but did not build.

In brief, governmental policy is an expression of social and political consensus or its absence. It is naive to blame contradictory, muddled, or inept policies on the intelligence of members of the government rather than the political matrix in which the government operates. With his superior vision Paul Reynaud may have advocated policies which hindsight rates as far superior to those adopted. But it is almost as much of an error to be in advance of the times as behind them. And few are the Churchills with the luck and leadership to have the bankruptcy of other views demontrated in time.

IV

FRENCH RECOVERY

This recital of alleged causes of economic backwardness has dismissed lack of resources, labor, and capital as causes of French economic backwardness, and has found no profound independent change in the French family firm which would account for the postwar revival (or for the earlier periods of rapid expansion). More interest attaches to the demand side—to the independent change in rates of population growth which occurred during the Second World War and to the change in French attitude toward levels of living. Market organization was found to be a dependent rather than an autonomously changing variable, and government too was largely dependent since it and its policies reflected the national consensus in the economic field or, as under the Second Empire, reflected the seizing of power by a strain of French thought normally in the minority. It remains to examine how French attitudes toward growth changed, whose hands carried out the new consensus, and what modalities were used. But before we get to these topics it is important to address one significant ingredient of growth which has not been blamed for French economic backwardness—technical capacity. Economists are increasingly persuaded that economic growth is a process less of accretions of capital, labor, and new resources in a given state of the arts than of technological change.

TECHNOLOGICAL CHANGE

It was the insight of Joseph Schumpeter that focused attention on the role of the entrepreneur as the introducer of new techniques. But after the Schumpeterian view of development had given way to the Harrod-Domar view that growth was the result of substituting capital for labor, a number of statistical investigations found much more growth than could be accounted for by the expansion of capital, and attributed it once more to technical advance.

As Schumpeter pointed out, technical change requires invention and innovation, the latter consisting of transforming new processes or new products from ideas to economic realities. Frenchmen claim that they are more effective at invention than at innovation. William N. Parker goes further and suggests that French intellectuality in the Cartesian tradition produced inventions of wide adaptability, whereas British empiricism and especially German method yielded industrial secrets of immediate *local* usefulness.[24]

This is evidently too complex a subject to be dealt with summarily. It is fair to say, however, that France was technologically very backward at the beginning of the nineteenth century. At this time French technical progress was clearly differentiated from British, being inspired by government rather than spontaneous and private, and it was in response to the British example and the competition it provided. After the Napoleonic wars, French businessmen flocked to England and undertook a mass imitation of British methods, assisted after 1828 by the removal of the British embargo on machinery exports.

The British technological lead over the world was at its biggest at the time of London's Great Exhibition of 1851, and was especially pronounced in textiles, iron, and railroading. It did not exist in all fields, however, nor was it maintained long. The major competition came from Germany and the United States; but even in France, by the 1880's, successes in industrial technology were being achieved in locomotives, glass, jute, shipbuilding, chemicals, and, of greatest importance, steel.

Even so, French technology was not distinguished on the whole, either prior to 1914 or in the interwar period. Believers in the family firm as the cause of economic retardation are persuaded that this institution is notoriously slow to take the risks involved in innovation. French business was riddled with secrecy, which provides exactly the wrong atmosphere for technical progress. Innovating firms must exhibit a willingness to absorb a large quantity of technical information, survey potential ideas, be willing to share knowledge, to look outside the firm, and so on.[25] The distrustful family firm hardly fits this picture. Pitts has gone further: "To change the industrial secrets of the firm which have been taught to a few is like withdrawing the sacraments from a communicant." [26]

Postwar has brought significant change in the French technological performance. The success in solving the desulphurization problem at Lacq has been mentioned, as have the innovations in the automobile field from the DS19 and the 2CV to the Dauphine and 404. Renault developed its own machine-tool production in an effort to acquire modern automatic machinery for automobile production, and in so doing created a new machine-tool industry in France. The Caravelle is well known in aircraft, as is the Mystère. A brand new firm, Bulle, has risen to international prominence in computers. French railroads have set new technical standards for the world, including the feeding of electric current into locomotives at 20,000 volts, so as to eliminate the need for stationary transformers. Electricité de France, in placing orders for power-generating equipment, has continuously raised the technological standards until by 1958 it was generating power and transmitting it to Paris from Genissiat at 380,000 volts.

Cameron exaggerates when he claims that French industry played a large role in spreading economic development to the rest of Europe in the nineteenth century.[27] The technical contribution was almost entirely limited to civil engineering and mining, two fields in which French education at the Ecole Polytechnique and the Ecole des Mines was particularly distinguished. Today, however, French engineers are spread all over the globe on a variety of technical tasks. In the short space of fifteen years, French engineering has risen from a European substandard to the equivalent of the world's best.

French technical virtuosity in the postwar period has been largely overlooked. British economists, for example, were disposed to attribute the fact that France's economic growth was faster than Britain's to the forced-draft investment by the "secret government" represented by the permanent civil service, which investment could be undertaken because all mistakes were underwritten by United States aid. German monetary theorists, and their sympathizers, considered that French economic recovery was achieved by the Pinay and Rueff policies of deflation. But technical change is to a considerable degree independent of the level of investment, as demonstrated by British experience of investment without technical flair; and expanding in technically advanced lines may be said to have made deflation possible, rather than the other way round. The discontinuity in French technical performance is an important causal factor which, like the changes in population growth and in social values, can be traced back to the war.

WAR AND ECONOMIC CHANGE

One economic theorem holds that war on a considerable scale reinforces economic trends already under way. A growing country will grow faster, as the United States did during and after World War I. And a stagnant economy will continue to stagnate, as Britain's did in the 1920's. But the postwar French recovery on top of the spreading collapse of the economy in the 1930's provides a contrary case where the direction of economic change was reversed.

There are also other cases. German interest in nationalism, and indirectly in national economic development, dates from the defeats inflicted on Prussia by Napoleon. In turn the German victory over Denmark assisted that country in transforming itself from a grain producer to a major exporter of animal products. Even the French economic expansion after 1896 is linked to the defeat at Sedan and the 1871 Treaty of Frankfort—for one leading industry, woolens, was developed at Elbeuf by refugees from Alsace; [28] the discovery of new iron deposits was the result of exploration undertaken to compensate for war losses; and the growth of Lorraine, and the steel industry there, was stimulated by the pressure of refugees and the need to make up national losses. The time lag was long, until the Gilchrist Thomas process was developed and the technological difficulties at Briey were overcome. But the association of this expansion with defeat in 1870 is not altogether far-fetched. The classic example, however, is Germany's economic revival after World War II. More ambiguous cases are furnished by Italy, which was and was not a defeated country, and by France, whose war was even more anomalous.

On this showing, defeat may be a greater stimulant to economic expansion than victory. The case is not clear-cut, as the example of the United States after World War I demonstrates. Nor is the stimulant of defeat a simple phenomenon. Part of the explanation is the purging effect of war's destruction, which assists development by making it possible to build new plants embodying the most modern techniques.[29] But this is not all; the humiliation of defeat—and in the French case, defeat without the satisfaction of having made an effective stand—may destroy old values and induce a country to sublimate in ways which are conducive to economic growth. Refugees who have lost their possessions are particularly ambitious in these respects, as suggested by the Alsatian migration and the more recent influx of East Germans into West Germany. But even without a particular class which seeks to compensate for its losses through economic success, a country may undergo in defeat a change of values which releases its energies for economic advance.

There were of course contributing factors which turned French interest after 1940 to economic expansion. Ideas were contributed by the success of the Russian experiment, the New Deal in the United States, and even Swedish Socialism. Pierre Lalumière believes that the most important intellectual change was the discovery of Keynes by the Inspection des Finances.[30] It is necessary to point out that Keynes was concerned not with growth but with stability. On the other hand, the "discovery of Keynes" can be taken to mean the change of attention from problems of monetary stabilization—

which had occupied Aftalion, Rist, and Rueff—to concern for real output. The point is well made.

The ancient formula of social stability made no sense in a world of French defeat and possible nuclear holocaust. Living for the future led nowhere. It was time that France turned from balancing social forces to expansion which would hopefully spill over to all groups.

THE NEW MEN

Who were the new men called for by the Schumpeterian system to lead the expansion? A number of different answers have been hazarded. In one view they had existed all along, buried in the business staffs of 1935–1940. Or they emerged from the experience of Vichy, which developed efficient business administrators like Pucheu, or from German occupation. The difficulty here is that business finished the war thoroughly discredited in French public opinion from its opposition to the Popular Front, its support of Vichy, and its failure to participate fully in the Resistance. Or they thrust themselves forward from government, not from the ranks of politicians but from the civil service.

One thesis is that the Inspection des Finances was the focus of change. Great numbers of the men in the Inspection left government for industry. These civil servants, who are said to have admired businessmen but not politicians, went largely into finance— either into banking and insurance, where their financial training was particularly useful, or into the financial side of large industry like automobiles and chemicals. Moreover, most of the members of the Inspection who remained in government had long since given up the narrow auditing function for general administration, and operated not in the Inspection but throughout the government. By 1955, approximately 170 members remained in the agency, and 109 of them were on detached service: 26 in the nationalized banks, 11 in other nationalized industry, 26 in international organizations, 30 in the regular ministries, and 16 in other governmental jobs.[31] (Those in noneconomic international organizations were able to contribute only marginally to French economic development, and many of those in the ministries were concerned with noneconomic problems of foreign policy or defense.) Lalumière regards the Inspection des Finances as "alone or almost alone" as an active group, in the middle of general French inertia.[32]

But this view attributes too much credit to the Inspection des Finances and underestimates the change which occurred elsewhere in the economy. Assume that there were 50 or 60 inspectors inside the government and concerned neither with auditing nor with non-economic administration, plus an equal number of alumni outside. To ascribe the vigor of the French postwar recovery to these men alone is excessive. The French civil service as a whole, or at least that portion of it which had not followed de Gaulle abroad, emerged from the war rested, fresh, ready for a fast start, in contrast to British governmental employees, who reached V-E day fairly exhausted from almost six years of overtime. The entire French civil service, and not only the Inspection des Finances, had time and opportunity to reflect on the deficiencies of French economic and social life prior to 1940.

But more than the civil service was involved. The change in attitude toward economic expansion was universal in France. The proof is that the net reproduction rate moved in a big jump in violation of normal causation as recognized in social science. There was vigor in many sections of society: in the resistance leaders themselves; in the Communist Party which organized the revival of coal production; in the neo-Catholic Centre des Jeunes Patrons; and among geographers. Economists organized the Institut Scientifique d'Economie Appliquée with its focus on national-income accounting. The Confédération National de Patrons Français gradually abandoned its protective attitude toward little business. The family firm looked for outside help. One significant index: the demand for youth in business expanded rapidly. The Ministry of Labor stated in 1951 that the top hiring age for middle-rank executives (*cadres*) declined from sixty in 1898 to fifty in 1945, forty-five in 1950, and forty in 1951.[33]

NATIONALIZED INDUSTRY AND PLANNING

It remains to evaluate the role in French economic recovery of the "planning" carried on by the Planning Commission under the initial direction of Jean Monnet and later under Messrs. Hirsch and Massé. A certain mystique has collected about this effort; in particular the British, conscious of the wide gap in postwar expansion between their country and France, have sought to find in planning the force responsible for French success.

There can be no doubt that the French government has controlled a large proportion of the French economy. Approximately 30 percent of national income has gone through government hands in the form of taxes. Nationalized industry was responsible for half of total investment. But the scope within which government operated to direct the economy was much wider than that implied by its tax receipts and the income of nationalized enterprises. The Planning Commission affected the operations of private enterprise in ways which were almost as pervasive as those of nationalized industry, and in some cases equally so.

Nationalization may have been necessary to French postwar economic recovery, though this is dubious in the light of the general public interest in expansion. Alone it certainly was insufficient to bring the recovery about. The British experience is relevant as a touchstone. Productivity increased much more in the nationalized French coal, electricity, and railroad industries than in the similar nationalized industries in the United Kingdom. Nationalization need not spark technological change.

Moreover, the extent of control over industry deriving from governmental ownership is debatable. The first five-year plan called for expansion in six key sectors: coal, electricity, transport, steel, cement, and agricultural machinery. Only the first three were nationalized. And the government contributed finance to private industry through the various funds for modernization and equipment, as well as underwriting the large deficits of the railway system and providing huge capital sums for electrical construction. Ultimately, to be sure, Electricité de France sold its obligations in the capital market much like a private company, although it had a state guarantee. And Pierre Lefaucheux, the dynamic leader of the Régie Renault, "recalled unceasingly as much by his action as by his intervention and speeches that if the Régie belongs to the state, it is in fact administered in the same fashion as a private enterprise." [34] The quality of leaders—Massé in electricity and Armoud in railroads, along with Lefaucheux—was more important than state ownership.

If not nationalization, then what about planning? In 1961 the British suddenly awakened to an interest in French planning, hoping to find in the techniques a secret of growth that could be applied to the sluggish British economy.[35] The hope, unfortunately, is doomed to frustration. French planning is in some important respects the opposite of planning. Knowledge of income and industry projections and faith in the inevitability of expansion are communicated to firms at intra- and inter-industry meetings. This is perhaps the most powerful effect, and one which has a faint resemblance to a revivalist prayer meeting. In addition, and importantly, the Planning Commission uses a series of controls— powers to fix prices, adjust taxes, control credit, lend governmental capital, and authorize construction—to encourage firms to expand.[36] There is far more stimulation than restraint. But levels of output are decided by the individual entrepreneur, not by planners; and profit anticipations have ultimate power of decision. Industry projections are fitted into national-income accounts as a check against their logical consistency, and even measured against input-output tables. These operations, however, have exhortatory rather than regulatory results, unless they imply an absence of stimulation.

The fact is that French planning is empiricism. The total polity is bent on expansion. This fact is communicated to all corners of the economy, expressed, so far as possible, in terms of numbers. Given the underlying faith in expansion, the numbers tend to confirm themselves, within limits. Where a sector or industry falls short, one weapon or another may be employed to help. The French insist that their *planification* is flexible *(souple)*. This comes close to a contradiction in terms. There is little *dirigisme* in the system, and much readiness to proceed by whatever paths lie open. The roles have been reversed from the nineteenth century when the British were the pragmatists and the French were doctrinaire.

Much is made in the recent French literature of the "technocratic" character of the expansion. In some quarters this spirit is identified with James Burnham's "managerial revolution" in which the bureaucratic employees have interests different from those of the owners, the workers, and the consumers.[37] This hardly fits today in France. To the extent, however, that the term can be taken to refer to a society in which all groups are interested in expansion, partly by capital investment but primarily through technological change and increased total productivity, the characterization is apt.

The technological character of French expansion is one further proof of the unimportance of planning as such in French postwar expansion. Immediately after the war, planning referred primarily to investment planning, with implicit Harrod-Domar models of capital output ratios and the like. The growth of output was estimated from the growth of investment. The strong element of technological change in the expansion was unplanned. It emerged, unexpectedly, from the French intellectual tradition and the nation-wide consensus on the need for economic expansion.

v

CONCLUSION

The economic recovery of France after the war is due to the restaffing of the economy with new men and to new French attitudes.

The opportunity for hiring new staff came from the discrediting of many of the existing leaders of the economy (whether in the prewar government or in Vichy), the passage of time with little constructive work taking place, and the upthrust of new energetic people in the Resistance and in the invading French army. Unlike World War I, the 1940's brought no widespread loss of youth which made it necessary to retain the prewar generation in economic command. The new men were found in private as well as nationalized industry, in family firms as well as corporate enterprises, in administrative positions as well as technical ones. Some of them had a "passion for innovation," some for expansion, all for efficiency of one sort or another, whether economic, engineering, administrative, or in terms of profit maximization. Dissatisfaction with the past led them to substitute change for stability as the operating guide.

New attitudes followed from the change in leading economic personnel. But the new attitudes went far wider. Not only did firms want to expand, but workers and consumers became willing that they should. The movement from the extended to the nuclear family, and to increased numbers of children, has been referred to. The causal connections between these sociological phenomena and the new staffing are not easily comprehended, but doubtless exist. And these new attitudes on the part of the public—at least in the social field though perhaps not in the political—seem to have had their origin in the frustration of the 1930's and the war and the occupation. Workers have become less revolutionary, more practical. The individual, or his parents on his behalf, has begun to be seized with more ambition for education and opportunities, and less for holding on to place, position, acquired rights.

To conclude that the basic change in the French economy is one of people and attitudes is frustrating to the economist. *Natura non facit saltum* (Nature doesn't make a jump) was Alfred Marshall's motto in the *Principles of Economics*. Marginal analysis, compound interest, growth as a function of fixed resources, evolving technology, and growing capital are more compatible with the economist's modes of reasoning. It is true that capital has grown, and technical progress has been made, but these are accompaniments of a more far-reaching process, rather than exogenous variables.

Nor have the sociologists and economic historians furnished much in the way of explanation. The family firm and deep-seated fissures in the social structure fail to explain the rate of progress of the past, and exist even today when growth is again rapid.

The interest in progress is not new in France. Saint-Simon was a technocrat, and Napoleon III, Michel Chevalier, Eugène Rouher, and Charles de Freycinet continued in the tradition. When there was a clear view of the need to expand, whether responding to the destruction of World War I or taking advantage of the railroad, the Thomas process in steel, or the discovery of Briey iron mines, expansion followed. The present demand for economic growth at all levels in French society is different only in the extent to which various groups in society share in it. It has not been accompanied by a similar consensus in political matters. Whether its continuance into the future for a decade or a score of years will be self-perpetuating, as it has not been in the past, remains to be seen.

SOCIAL CHANGE AT THE GRASS ROOTS

Laurence Wylie

Americans have often traveled to France in search of a refuge from the pressures of life in the United States. During a two-hour lunch an American tourist could forget what it meant to grab a sandwich during a twenty-minute noon break. Visiting Mont Saint-Michel and Chartres he was refreshed by the evidence of a culture that seemed oriented toward the permanent and the beautiful rather than the temporary and the expedient. If his car broke down in the country the American tourist might not find the needed spare part, but he was sure that the village blacksmith would have the will and inventiveness to fashion a substitute piece. While waiting for the car to be repaired the visitor savored village life. He even enjoyed the discomforts one had to tolerate—the antiquated plumbing, the scolding of the innkeeper, the lack of cool, pasteurized milk—for these inconveniences only added to the zest of recounting the experience and to the pleasure of returning to the twentieth century after a foray into the past.

Today visitors seeking escape into tradition may return from France disappointed. In Yugoslavia and Greece they may find what they once sought in France, but the France of today has lost much of its quaintness. The corner bistro is still there, but there are also milk bars where one may even buy a hot dog. Every restaurant still has wine, but the visitor says it is no longer the "little wine" carefully chosen by the restaurant owner from vintages produced by his friends in the wine country; rather the same mediocre

Algerian wine is served as *vin ordinaire* in most restaurants as well as most French homes. Through-traffic stalls in villages lying along the highways. The visitor complains that there is not even the thrill of being scolded by hotel owners, cursed by taxi drivers and snubbed when one asks the way; returning tourists now report as often as not that the French have become polite and hospitable to foreigners. France they think has been transformed.

There is no doubt that France has changed, and changed dramatically in the last ten years. The question is how deep these changes lie beneath the superficial observations of the tourists. Has the very structure of French society been transformed? Has France become "Americanized," as the French have long feared that it might be? Which forces have made for change, and which have retarded it? What continuity is there between the France of the past, the France of today, and the France of tomorrow?

These are the questions that naturally arise when we speak of a transformed France. Before I am through I shall consider in general terms the social structure of France as a whole and point out some of the features that inhibit change or model it in such a way that much of the basic structure is preserved. But first, in order to seek partial answers to our questions, I should like to lean heavily on the remarkable changes I have observed since the Second World War in two rural communities, Chanzeaux and Roussillon.

There are some advantages in going to rural communities to view the process of French change. In the first place, the villages are the most conservative elements in French society, not conservative in a political sense necessarily, but in the sense of being the most resistant to change. If we observe change there, we may assume that the transformation is not simply a city phenomenon but one which has taken place in all of France. Furthermore, in studying these microcosms we can see the interrelationship of various aspects of the social structure. I shall not concentrate on political evolution or economic change or technological transformation but shall try to clarify how these and other processes function together, sometimes reinforcing, sometimes retarding one another. An understanding of this perhaps may be approached through the human aspects of social change—through an "inside view" of how transformations affect individual people and how these people in turn act to speed or inhibit the process.

Chanzeaux is a commune of about 1100 people in the department of Maine-et-Loire, some fifteen miles southwest of Angers. Like most of the communities in this part of western France it is politically conservative and religiously devout. The commune of Roussillon is in the department of Vaucluse in southern France, thirty-five miles west of Avignon. It has about 700 inhabitants. Politically the Roussillonnais are either middle-of-the-road or far to the left. Although nearly all of them are baptized and married and buried by the Church, few of them go regularly to Mass. Politically and ideologically, then, these two communities represent complementary aspects of French culture. Economically they are similar in that the people are neither rich nor poor but lead a comfortable though modest existence from the cultivation of a variety of crops. Each commune has at its center a village of the same name, in which live the artisans, merchants, government employees, and retired farmers, most of whom are supported indirectly by the farmers living in hamlets and on isolated farms in the surrounding countryside. Since there is nothing abnormal about either of these communes, they may serve as examples of the traditional French community.

I

FRENCH SOCIETY ACCEPTS CHANGE

The most remarkable change between the Roussillon I first knew in 1950 and the village as it is today is psychological. In 1951 the Roussillonnais seemed haunted by despair. They had a dream of what life should be and were frustrated because it seemed less and less possible to realize. They spent a great deal of energy trying to conserve the remnants of the days before the First World War when they believed their dream had been fulfilled. In 1961 I found that the despair they had felt in 1950 had at length killed the dream.

The nostalgic yearning for an outdated ideal had all but disappeared, and the energy formerly devoted to preserving it was being used for other purposes.

What had the dream been? It was largely a conception of the family and its relationship to other families, to society, and to the government. The family was seen ideally as a strong, independent unit, father, mother, and children all working together for the common good. It was a biological unit, a sentimental unit, an economic unit, and a social unit. It functioned apart from other families, but since all were supposedly motivated by a common ideal there was theoretically little friction among them. Their common efforts gave strength to the greater unit of which they were a part, *la patrie*. The metaphor traditionally used to describe this relationship was the bee hive; the strength of the whole (France) depended on the strength of its cells (individual families) and the function of the government was primarily to strengthen the family cells and regulate relationships among them.

PUBLIC CATASTROPHES

The twentieth century was cruel to this dream. It was shattered by a series of catastrophes beginning in July 1914. On the Monument aux Morts which stands at the entrance to the village of Roussillon are the names of thirty-eight men, many of them fathers of families, who were killed in the First World War. The inflation that followed the war destroyed the savings of many families. From 1918 to 1939 the attempt to return to the days before 1914 was continually frustrated. World conflict, technological change, social unrest, political squabbles seemed all to work against the fulfillment of the dream. Then came the Second World War.

The disruptive force of the war made the dream more appealing than ever. Whether one was on the side of the Vichy government or of the Resistance there was a common yearning for the old France. Vichy put the family in its motto— Work, Family, Nation —and enacted legislation designed to bolster the shattered family cell, so that when the war ended the ideal might finally be fulfilled. In the Resistance, Communists and Catholics, Freemasons and clericals worked together. The feeling was that France itself had become one great family and that after the Germans had been driven out and Vichy dissolved, the different parties would continue to work for the common good. France had learned its lesson, it was thought, and with Liberation would come the fulfillment of the national dream.

Liberation brought only disillusion, however. Party strife became more bitter than before the war. Inflation once more destroyed family savings. Even the value of gold dipped to a new low in 1950, so that those families who had placed their confidence in this most dependable of all commodities felt there was nothing more to be trusted. Housing was wretched, and efforts to solve the problem were deadlocked. The Korean crisis made it seem that the United States and Russia were spoiling for a fight. The French, with the experience of two world wars behind them, believed themselves fated to have their land become again the battleground of forces over which they had no control. For individual families there seemed less possibility than ever of returning to the days before the war. The walls of the family cell seemed to be crumbling from the impact of technological change. Even government policies designed to strengthen the family were either futile or actually reinforced the changes that were taking place.

By 1950 the feelings of helplessness and despair were strong in France. The people of Roussillon, traditionally inclined to accept the worst with a fatalistic shrug and the words "C'est comme ça!" found little to hope for in the gloomy future. "Pauvre France!" they said, "On est foutu!" (We're done for!)

The agricultural experts of the region agreed that probably the most profitable crop for the farmers of Roussillon was fruit, but obviously this would mean planting trees and waiting for them to bear. The farmers' reaction to this advice was skeptical. "Why should I plant fruit trees?" said Jacques Baudot. "So the Russians and the Americans can use my orchard for a battleground? No, thanks. *Pas si bête!* I'm not that stupid!" His father had been killed in the First World War, and as soon as Jacques was old enough he left school to work the farm and support his mother and grandmother. By the end of the 1930's he had established himself and was about to marry. Then came World War II. Jacques was captured by the Germans in June 1940 and spent five years as a prisoner. He returned home in 1945, and it took another five years to put his farm back in shape. In 1950 Baudot had no more thought of marrying than of planting fruit trees. What was the use? The ideal life he had been brought up to work for was obviously impossible to attain.

In 1960, however, Baudot took me to see the apple and apricot trees he had planted. He had even planted olive trees, to replace those that had been killed by the great freeze of 1956, and it would be twenty years before their fruit could be marketed. In the whole community, spirits had revived. There was no more talk about being "done for." The basic change that seemed to have taken place was that the old ideal had finally been cast off. Released from the burden of yearning and working for the impossible, the people were able to utilize their energy more constructively. I had observed Roussillon in 1950 at one of the low points in its morale. By 1960, morale had to a large extent been recovered. The Roussillonnais were not exactly cheerful, for despite the impression created by their southern exuberance they are not a sanguine people. They simply had more confidence in the ability of themselves and their children to face the future. A consequence of this was an increase in the size of families. The same thing has happened in most other French communities.

Another manifestation of the new confidence was a different attitude toward credit. In 1950, Baudot had a mule and a twenty-year-old car he had rigged to serve as a truck. In 1960, he had a new car, a tractor, and a television set, all of them bought on the installment plan. In the old days buying on credit was taboo. It was understood in the well-managed family that goods should be bought only when there was cash to pay for them and no purchase should be made unless it could be justified as strengthening the family cell. In principle, spending weakened the family; saving strengthened it; going into debt threatened the security of all. The national catastrophes that took place between 1914 and 1950 changed this attitude. By 1960 it was obvious that the people who had prospered were not those who held back but were those who took risks. By buying on credit Baudot and the people of Roussillon were following a new family code.

The same idea is taking hold in Chanzeaux. Georges Davy, the blacksmith in a neighboring hamlet, gave up shoeing horses and began repairing cars. Now he has a prosperous garage in Chanzeaux. The blacksmith in the town itself failed to follow the trend. As the local farmers replaced their horses with tractors, he lost much of his trade and now spends most of his time sharpening plowshares and doing miscellaneous small jobs. One of the two cartwrights in the village gave up mending wagons to manufacture the light-weight baskets in which fruit and vegetables are packed. Now he has a factory and employs thirty people. André Auffret, the other cartwright, made a poor living from his trade. In the summer of 1961 I learned, however, that Auffret, too, had hired several workers to help him make baskets. The common phrase in the village, expressed by the *garde-champêtre*, was: "Those who took a chance have all succeeded. Now the others have caught on." (Ceux qui se sont lancés au début ont tous réussi. Maintenant les autres ont compris qu'il ne faut plus hésiter.) Of course capital is needed for a new undertaking, but the old fear of being in debt seems to have died with the traditional image of the ideal family.

Sitting around a table at the town clerk's home in the village of Saint-Lambert, we were discussing this matter of credit and debts. A surveyor who had been spending weeks in the commune, remaking the cadastral maps of the area, leaned over to the mayor and said: "Pardon me for saying so, Monsieur le Maire, but you and I are idiots if we aren't in debt!" When the mayor recovered from the shock of being called an idiot, for he obviously did not have debts, he admitted that those who had bought on credit or borrowed money to expand their operations had done well. He said he was too old to change his habits and would have to remain idiotic, but he could see that the surveyor was right. If he were younger he might join the game.

To expand, to venture forth, to take chances, these seem to be actions implicit in the new French ideal. The despair of 1950 killed the ideal of the family cell with its shell of conservatism. The younger people saw that by saving, their parents had not succeeded in achieving their ideal. The new injunction is not to "eat, drink, and be merry," but for the modern world, buying on credit seems practical as well as "idealistic."

Laurence Wylie

In the summer of 1961 two vacuum cleaner salesmen descended on Chanzeaux and had spectacular success in selling their wares. Before they arrived almost no one had a vacuum cleaner, and within a few days dozens of households had one. The mayor of Saint-Lambert told me that in one of his hamlets the men sold twenty-eight cleaners in one day! In Chanzeaux, their success had been as great. According to the town clerk the salesmen had come to the town hall hoping to sell a cleaner to the municipality for use in the public buildings. They not only made that sale, but they sold a cleaner each to the mayor, the assistant mayor, the town clerk and the constable, all of whom had gathered to see the demonstration. This wave of enthusiasm is an illustration of the technological transformation which is taking place in the traditionally conservative French countryside. The implications and ramifications of the change are numerous and varied; some of the results are obviously beneficial while others have had side effects which are harder to evaluate.

The most publicized transformation of rural France is the replacement of horses by tractors. Many French city people became very aware of this change in the summer of 1961 when farmers blocked traffic with their tractors in the peasant strikes—*manifestations paysannes*. Yet only a small proportion of the tractors in France were used in the strikes. When the men of Chanzeaux went to Angers they were told to leave their tractors at home, that there were already enough machines nearer Angers for the demonstration. If all the tractors of France had been used the effect would have been colossal, because their number is so great.[1]

This growth in the use of tractors is reflected specifically in the statistics of the villages of Chanzeaux and Roussillon. In Chanzeaux the first tractor was bought in 1946 by Monsieur Georgin with Marshall Plan aid. By the summer of 1961 there were thirty-four. During the year 1950–51 when I lived in Roussillon, tractors seemed so insignificant a part of the culture that I neglected to note their number; certainly it was very small. The Tractor Cooperative had just been formed but had only one machine, which was used to pull a heavy plow for a kind of deep plowing that cannot be done with horses. By the summer of 1961 fifty-seven farmers had their own tractors, and of these thirty-three were modern diesels. The Tractor Cooperative in 1961 owned sixteen pieces of basic equipment, including a diesel bulldozer, a special caterpillar tractor for use in the vineyards, another for general plowing, and a wide assortment of specialized equipment such as two asparagus earthing machines, a forage press, and a harvester. It also owns an assortment of plows for different types of soil and crops.

The advantages of using tractors on a farm are too obvious to describe here, and most of the farmers who have invested in them are satisfied. However, in order to utilize a tractor efficiently a farmer must have relatively large fields. Because so many French farms consist of separated, small fields, some of the new tractor owners are now finding that the machines are not *rentables*, that is, they do not "pay their way." An official in the farmers' union thought that 50 to 80 percent of the tractors bought on credit could not be profitably operated. This estimate is obviously broad and certainly seems exaggerated; but it is true that many farmers were too easily persuaded by the government campaign or were all but forced to buy a tractor by sons who threatened to go to the city unless the farm was modernized. Now the farmers who invested unwisely are bitter about it. The reasons for the farmers' strikes in 1961 are numerous and reveal a number of facets of modern France; but not the least among these reasons was the embittered farmers' claim that the government had set agricultural prices so low that the farmers could not make enough money to pay for the new equipment they had purchased.

Another innovation in rural life which has many ramifications is the use of bottled gas. In 1950–51 when we lived in the town of Roussillon our only heat was from the fireplace where we burned oak logs and from the kitchen stove and two salamanders in which we burned small pieces of wood and pressed coal briquets. In 1957–58 when we lived in Chanzeaux we found the situation very different. Although the houses in Roussillon and Chanzeaux were basically the same, thanks to bottled gas our year in Chanzeaux was much less colored by the problem of heat—or rather lack of heat!

We had hot running water. We had a gas range with an oven. We had a heater on wheels that could be taken from room to room as the need arose. At the end of the year when we left Chanzeaux we had no problem in selling the equipment to neighbors who were eager to acquire modern conveniences whether second-hand or new.

On the farms in Chanzeaux the effects of using bottled **gas** are much deeper than simply increased comfort. Chanzeaux is in the *bocage* country, where each field is surrounded by a thick hedge of bushes and trees which for centuries have been harvested about every ten years for the wood. Curiously enough, bottled gas has made the hedges all but obsolete. The farmer used to spend a substantial amount of his time in the winter sawing wood and making bundles of faggots, for the family depended completely on wood for fuel. Now on many farms piles of faggots and logs are accumulating, for there is less and less need for fire wood. Cooking is most often done with gas. Open fireplaces are no longer the only way to heat a house. Big wood fires are built when animals are slaughtered, although home slaughtering is done less and less. And a quantity of wood is used when the laundry is boiled in a great cauldron, although with the advent of the electric washing machine laundry is seldom bleached this way. Therefore the most immediate practical purpose the hedges now fill is to fence in the livestock, but even this they do inefficiently since they not only take the nourishment from the fields but make it impossible to alter the size and shape of the holdings. So farmers are beginning to uproot the hedges, these relics of the past, and replace them with wire fences. When the size and shape of fields may be altered easily, it will become possible to attack the problem of regrouping the widely dispersed landholdings of Chanzeaux's farms, and with redistribution, the farms of Chanzeaux could be worked more efficiently with tractors. So the little matter of cooking on a bottled gas range instead of with wood has important but unsuspected consequences.

Fifteen years ago several farms in Chanzeaux and Roussillon did not have electricity; today there is not a single farm without it. It is usual for farms to have an electric pump; thus, with a bottled gas heater, hot running water is available. Electric refrigerators are not uncommon. When I called on some of my wine-growing friends on a hot July day in 1961, they did not need to go to the cool wine cellar; there were bottles of *rosé* in the refrigerator.

Traditionally one of the heaviest jobs for farm women was milking, but today many of the farms have electric milking machines. With this and other labor-saving appliances already mentioned, the farmer's wife now does most of her work without the help of one or more hired girls. It is important to remember, though, that the farm woman is now more tied to the farm. In the past she could easily enough arrange to leave the work for her hired help. Now a farm wife can do without help, but she must be at home to run the machines.

Finally radio and television have made their impact on life in rural France. In Chanzeaux there could be no television sets before December 1960, when the first transmitter was built in the area, but by June 1961, there were already a half-dozen sets in the commune. One of the first was bought for the public room in the rectory, where the people of Chanzeaux, 85 percent of whom attend Mass regularly, may see the programs which are announced on the bulletin board in front of the church. As people buy their own television sets, however, they will be more independent in deciding what programs to watch.

In Roussillon television was introduced a few years earlier. By the summer of 1961 there were twenty-three sets in the village itself and seventeen on the farms in the surrounding country. Some of my friends who used to come regularly to the café for a game of cards now own a television set and rarely go out in the evenings. One Sunday afternoon when there was a *boules* tournament, I met Jean Casal walking in what seemed to me the wrong direction. Since he had always been one of the most active *boulistes* of the village, I asked him where he was bound. He replied, "There's a swimming meet in Paris I want to watch on television. It's more interesting than *boules*." Most of the people in the *boules* tournament that afternoon were not the Roussillonnais who used to play, but city people spending their vacation in the village.

In Roussillon where almost no one goes to church there are

few enough opportunities for people to get together, but the *boules* and *belote* tournaments used to bring a large group of the men together every week. Television breaks up this pattern. However, Jean Casal and the several dozen Roussillonnais who watched the swimming meet in Paris were sharing an experience with thousands of other people in France who were looking at the same program. Social contacts at home may be weakened, but it would seem that national ties are strengthened with the spread of television.

Some of these technological innovations which have appeared on the French scene in recent years have either directly or indirectly deprived certain of the villagers of their livelihood. It is easy to see how modernization on the farms has reduced the number of hands which are needed. Milking machines and other conveniences have obviated the need for hired girls to help the farmer's wife. Less manpower is needed to run a farm with a tractor than with horses. But the village artisans, too, have been affected. Monsieur Bonnerot, by trade a harnessmaker, was ready to retire when he was seventy years old. In the past an older man would gradually have let his son or an apprentice take over. Unfortunately Monsieur Bonnerot could find no one to take his place in Chanzeaux. Who wants to be a harnessmaker in a community where the number of tractors has increased from one to thirty-four in fifteen years and where horses are fast disappearing? Eventually Monsieur Bonnerot's shop will be closed and the farmers who still have horses will have to go to the city to find a harnessmaker—or they will follow the trend and buy a tractor.

Our neighbor across the street had already retired when we came. He was a sabot maker. It was actually because of failing eyesight that Monsieur Uzureau had stopped working, but there was almost no business for him anyway. Rubber boots or black plastic "sabots" have replaced wooden shoes in France. In 1958 Monsieur Uzureau had a few pairs of sabots to sell but by the summer of 1961 they were all gone. His tools, rusting in his old shop, would be of interest only to a folklore museum. Ironically, Madame Uzureau earns a bit of money by taking orders for a factory in the city for the plastic "sabots," which are modeled exactly after the sort of wooden shoes her husband formerly made.

The introduction of plastic goods also ruined the business of another neighbor, Monsieur Nougier, the tinsmith. He used to spend a large part of his time mending milk pails, but now everyone uses pails made of plastic. Monsieur Nougier accepted this philosophically and explained to me that plastic pails last longer than metal ones and they seem easier to keep clean; so people naturally prefer them. The same thing is true of other housewares which in the past were always made of metal. Madame Nougier tries to make up for the loss in her husband's business by selling plastic utensils of all sorts, but this is not a real solution since she cannot compete successfully with the city stores where the farmers do their shopping on market day.

The only successful artisans today are those who have been able to adapt their businesses to meet the new demands and pressures. We have already seen how the blacksmith Davy became an auto mechanic and a Chanzeaux cartwright started a basket factory. Monsieur Bertrand, whose father was a blacksmith before him, long ago began to follow the new trends. He turned his smithy first into a bicycle repair shop and more recently into a motorbike station. He also sells bottled gas and installs electric and gas appliances. One of his sons is studying electronics in the army and when he returns home will without doubt be the first television repair man in Chanzeaux.

Some of the artisans who have lost their trade are bitter, and Pierre Poujade made the most of this bitterness. Nevertheless they seem to share the pride the French feel in the technological advance of their country. When I called on Monsieur Uzureau he was always eager to ask questions about America but he never failed to show me in what ways France was outdoing us. He liked to point out that the Caravelle airplane was the best in the world, that Dauphines were selling well in Detroit, and that the 2cv Citroën was the most practical car on the market. Uzureau knew very little about the French cultural empire founded in the seventeenth and eighteenth centuries, but he knew a good deal about the exploitation of the Sahara, the discovery and utilization of gas and oil in France, the tunnel under Mont Blanc. He was excited by these new French technological achievements.

DEMOGRAPHIC EVOLUTION

When I first went to the village of Roussillon in September 1950, I was struck by the fact that it was a community of elderly people. The man who drove the bus from Apt to Roussillon was in his late sixties. Monsieur Baume, a blacksmith and the first man I saw in the village, was seventy. The owner of the horse being shod was Baume's contemporary. There were elderly women in black sitting in groups knitting and talking while they kept an eye on the few little children playing nearby. In 1961 when I returned the scene had changed. The bus driver had died. Monsieur Baume had retired, and his smithy was closed. A large number of children were playing about the streets and young women in colorful dresses had replaced the older women of the gossip groups.

These impressions are based in fact. As in all of France the demographic change in Roussillon since the end of the Second World War has been radical. To understand the importance of the effects implicit in the change, one must first be aware of three basic facts in the recent demographic history of Roussillon.

The first is that like most French rural communities, Roussillon is a much smaller community now than it was a hundred years ago. Today there are about seven hundred inhabitants; in 1860 there were over fourteen hundred. The drop in the population was gradual, but most of it occurred in the first half of this century. Because of this, in 1950 a large proportion of the villagers—one out of four—had been born in the nineteenth century. Ten years later, in 1960, many of these older people had died. Because the life expectancy is greater today there is still a considerable number of old people in the community, but they no longer dominate the scene.

The second fact is that between 1914 and 1945 the birth rate in France was low. Beginning in 1914, when many of the men went to war, the birth rate quite naturally declined. There was a temporary rise immediately after the war, but the rate remained low throughout the 1920's and 1930's. Those women whose husbands or fiancés had been killed in the war were not having children, and for the remaining couples the insecurity of life made it seem safer for the prosperity of the family cell to limit the number of children to one or two.

The third fact is that since the Second World War the birth rate has been high. An increase was expected after the war, as it is after every war, but to the surprise of everyone, the rate remained high through the 1950's and into the 1960's. The ideal size of the family has changed in France as it has in the United States. More and more families are having three, four, and five children instead of one or two, which had been the style between the wars.

In communities like Roussillon and Chanzeaux one of the results of these demographic trends is an intensification of the conflict between generations. In 1950 the older people were in control in these communes and approached the problem of town government from a nineteenth-century point of view. The mayor and town council were concerned with keeping taxes down and limiting the encroachment of government as much as possible. In the last ten years the atmosphere has changed. The few members of the older generation who remain in power are challenged by the younger men who see the function of government as something much broader than their elders did. They see it as an agent for many different services for the community; they want more public facilities—sewage disposal, waterworks, public laundry and showers, education and recreational opportunities for the young. The young men are impatient with the older people who feel they have done their duty if the roads are kept passable and the schools are open.

The same conflict between generations that we see on a public level is present in family life. Young adults continually ask: what shall we do with the old people? and what shall we do with the children? The middle generation feels caught between the two. Traditionally the three generations lived together in a patriarchical household which was both a sentimental and an economic unit. Today younger parents feel they should live alone with their children and without interference from the grandparents. Whenever possible in Roussillon and Chanzeaux the older people are persuaded to move into separate quarters. Sometimes they leave the farm and move into the village. If they remain on the farm a partition is often built actually to divide the two ménages. Usually the older people accept this new arrangement saying that it is wiser that way, but sometimes there is trouble.

In the summer of 1961 in Chanzeaux a farmer's wife and her three children were living in the village. She had been on her husband's family farm but his parents insisted on keeping the two big rooms of the three-and-a-half-room house for themselves. Because the old man could no longer work, the young couple had tried to persuade the grandparents to move to the village, but they had refused. Finally, the young woman, desperate at trying to bring up three children in a room and a half, had moved to the village herself. Her husband came to town late every night but at dawn he roared back up the hill on his motorcycle to the farm. This solution was not typical in the community, but the basic problem was.

The question of what the children will do is even more difficult to solve than the one about their grandparents. The first children born after the war are now leaving school and are ready to go to work. What will they do? Traditionally there was plenty of work at home, on the farm or in the father's shop, for both boys and girls. If there was not and a young man wanted to become a farmer, he could find odd jobs or even a steady job working as a farm laborer. When he married and had a family he could look for a suitable farm of his own to manage. In the past this was the usual course of events, but sometimes, if nothing could be found, as a last resort the would-be farmer went to the city.

The fate of these people who had to go to the city to work frightens the parents of today's young people who are looking for jobs. They know that if the fruitless search for a farm had lasted until the would-be farmer was thirty-five or even more, it meant that the country man went to the city untrained for any special work and had to take a job as a common laborer. An alternative to having a menial job was to try to establish a little store, but competition and inexperience meant that at best the venture would barely remain alive.[2] The suspicion that country people have for city life has decreased with the urbanization of France, but they still dread the temptations of the city, the anonymity and degradation of a factory job where one is not one's own boss, the poor housing and living conditions, and the existence of values which alienate children from their parents and their past. Today's rural parents still prefer keeping their children at home.

But how can all of the young people who grow up in the country remain there and make a living? Technological developments have all but obviated the need for agricultural laborers except during the harvest season. Twenty-five years ago in Chanzeaux on the Avelin farm five men were needed to do the work—Avelin, his son, and three hired men. Madame Avelin had a hired girl. Now with a tractor Avelin and his eldest son can do the plowing in one day which used to take four men five days to do with horses. None of Avelin's younger sons will be needed on his farm when they finish school. There are no jobs with artisans and shopkeepers of the village, for we have seen that their businesses are dying, too. What can the young Avelins do?

One solution is being tried by the Association Nationale des Migrations Rurales, which finds abandoned farms in less attractive regions of France in the hope that young men seeking farm work may bring them back into use. To persuade someone to rehabilitate a farm that has already been abandoned because a decent living could not be made from it is not easy, however, and the Association Nationale has not been startlingly successful in its efforts.

Another solution is increasingly possible. City entrepreneurs have traditionally taken advantage of the cheap labor available from country people who need work but do not want to leave home. In the eighteenth century, country people were able to make a living by weaving at home for the cloth manufacturers of the city. The modern version of the putting-out system is for industries to establish branch factories in rural areas. Within a few miles of Chanzeaux there are several shoe factories; there is a factory manufacturing electric light bulbs and another corkscrews, a canning plant and a radio assembly plant. All of them are located in villages and take advantage of the cheap labor available in the community. The basket factory started in Chanzeaux by the man who used to be a cartwright not only gives work to four of his five sons (the fifth is a priest), but to four other young men and twenty-five girls in the community. The future of all these factories is dubious, however. As the rural areas become increasingly urbanized, it seems doubtful that labor will remain so cheap, and it is only cheap labor that enables these village operations to compete with larger, more efficient factories.

Another possibility formerly not available to the farm youth seeking employment is that of working in the city but living at home. With the development of transportation facilities in the last ten years several young people living in Chanzeaux now work in the neighboring city of Chemillé, eight miles away, and a few of them even commute to Angers, some fifteen miles away. On a scooter or even on a *mobilette* it takes only forty-five minutes for the trip. Some young people commute by bus, but in this Catholic area parents are worried by their children's spending two hours on a bus with the chance acquaintances one makes there. In one village, the commune of Saint-Lézin, whose mayor was formerly national president of the Catholic Agricultural Youth, many of the young people live at home but work in the city of Chalonnes. The municipal council has arranged for a town bus to take the young people to and from work so that they will not lack supervision.

A final solution of the problem of how rural youths can find their proper roles in the adult world is to help them stay in school longer to prepare more adequately for specific jobs. This solution is one that country people are taking more and more seriously, so that in Roussillon and Chanzeaux, interest in education is an important concern.

EDUCATION

To understand this recent awakening of interest in education among the people of Roussillon and Chanzeaux, we must first see what their attitude has been in the past. Traditionally they gave full support to the primary system of education. They felt it was important for their children to learn to read and write and figure and to learn about the history and geography of France. The parents complained of the program in the village school only if they felt the children were not having to work hard enough. But rural parents believed that when a child reached the age of fourteen he ought to start to work.

As early as 1941 an official attempt was made to persuade families to give their children something more than a primary educa-tion. *Classes post-scolaires* were opened in the village schools for farm children aged fifteen and sixteen who had finished their regu-lar schooling; the boys were given a chance to study farm methods and the girls home economics, one day a week. In order to be assured of the parents' cooperation, the government offered to pro-long the "family allowances" (*allocations familiales*) for children who attended these classes. In theory the idea was sound but in practice in the villages I know, it was a joke. The classes were taught by the regular school teachers on their free day, which they gave up mostly because they so desperately needed every bit of extra income. Generally they knew too little about the specialized material they had to teach, and the young people, forced by their parents to attend the classes, did not take the work seriously. As members of a small generation born during a time of low birth rate, they thought they needed no extra training to compete for jobs, and this day in school seemed a complete waste of time.

Governmental attempts to arouse more interest in technical or advanced education were also ignored. Only those children who did not seem fit for farm work and who at the same time seemed to have an aptitude for academic studies were encouraged to con-tinue their education. In Chanzeaux, Monsieur Delay explained to me why he had a son studying mathematics at the Faculté de Poitiers: "Henri is too small to do farm work. He's like a doll (*Il fait poupée*) compared to his brothers; so he might as well go on to school." Delay was proud of the son's success but he felt it neces-sary to explain why the boy had not stayed on the farm.

This lack of interest in the opportunities for advanced educa-tion has been typical of the farming and laboring classes of France. An amazingly small proportion of children from the families of farmers, workers, and artisans is enrolled in the faculties of the French universities, although these families represent the over-whelming majority of the population.[3] Monsieur Delay's attitude toward Henri's preparing for a teaching career in mathematics is a traditional one; it is more typical of the old than of the new France. The attitude of the farming and laboring classes is chang-ing rapidly.

As the great numbers of children born since the war reach the

177

age when they must start to work, their parents are becoming more than ever aware of the seriousness of the problem. If they had only one or two children, the future would not be so perplexing, but now many French families have a number of children. What will the younger children, especially, do? The Catholic Agricultural Youth have undertaken several research projects on the prospects of youth. They have also made a movie which has been very widely shown. "La Route Barrée" dramatizes the problem of a farmer's young son who finds the traditional road in life closed to him. In Chanzeaux the community leaders have done their best to make everyone more aware of this problem of the future of the young and of some of the ways a solution may be found.

One result of such worries has been a widespread awakening to the possibilities of the "complementary courses" (*cours complémentaires*), a three-year extension of the primary educational system. These added grades were instituted in France as long ago as 1886 but attracted little interest in the rural areas until after the Second World War. No commune was legally obliged to create and pay for these extra classes, and they existed mainly in big cities. The exact nature of a "complementary course" can vary enormously; it may provide for general studies not very different from those given in the *lycée*, or it may in specific localities give needed training in technical studies. The flexibility makes the system extremely useful now. It lacks the awesome formality and standards of the *lycée* and therefore does not frighten country people. That the growth of the complementary courses does not simply reflect the rise in the birth rate and growth of the French population as a whole may be seen if we compare two sets of figures. From 1945–46 to 1960–61 the enrollment of children in French primary schools, which does directly reflect the increase in population, increased by 57 percent (from 3,869,000 to 6,076,867). But in the same fifteen-year period the enrollment in complementary courses increased by 240 percent (from 162,000 to 551,522).[4]

This movement is just beginning to touch communities like Chanzeaux. Rural communes cannot usually afford to set up complementary courses, and until 1959 there was no way for a child to live at home and attend classes in the city. In that year, however, some of the parents in Chanzeaux formed an organization in order to participate in the new system of school buses operating in the area—the *ramassage scolaire.* By the summer of 1961 four boys and two girls were taking the school bus to the city of Chemillé every day to attend a complementary course, and another girl took a bus into Angers. The first four children who had taken advantage of this opportunity were children of artisans living in the village itself. The three additional children who signed up were from farm families; it would seem that farmers are beginning to send their children in increasing numbers to school in the city. Yet I had been told as recently as 1958 that it was not feasible to send children into the cities by bus because parents would not want their children to go regularly into that environment.

Still other children from rural communes have left home to become boarders in technical schools. The number of pupils in such schools in France increased from 230,000 in 1947 to 378,000 in 1959.[5] Agricultural schools, especially, are becoming more popular in France, because the farmers are becoming increasingly aware that the future lies in technical skill. There used to be a general feeling of contempt for the expert who had "learned farming from books," but now there is a growing realization among farmers that they cannot compete in the European market unless they modernize their operations. This they know not only from reading their newspapers and farm journals but from having to work every day with modern chemical fertilizers, sprays, and mechanical equipment and from having to interpret market quotations and government regulations. Today's farmers know the importance of a technical education and encourage their children to acquire one.

The emphasis on technical training and on developing the complementary courses within the primary system has caused concern, however, because it seemed to perpetuate the sharp social distinction that has traditionally existed in the French educational system. There has always been a clear division between the primary branch, in which the great mass of French children were trained, and the secondary branch, which trained the elite and through which one had to go for admission to institutions of advanced training. An effort was made to help exceptional children in the primary branch move over (*faire le pont*) into the secondary branch, but only notable exceptions were recognized. Many French people have been disturbed because the development of the complementary courses is perpetuating and even intensifying social inequalities.[6]

A desire to democratize the school system, combined with pressure to increase school facilities and bring them more into harmony with modern needs eventually led the French government to make sweeping reforms of the educational system by a series of decrees, *circulaires*, and *arrêtés*, beginning with de Gaulle's decree of January 6, 1959. Acknowledging the need for advanced training, the state now says that all children entering the *classe de sixième* (roughly equivalent to the sixth grade) in 1959 or later must attend school to the age of sixteen, instead of fourteen, which was formerly the required age. The distinction between primary and secondary education has been abolished: all children will share the same educational program until they are thirteen. The last two years of this elementary period is called the *cycle d'observation*, during which time the capacity of each child to profit from further education will be evaluated. Four courses will then be available: short and long technical training and short and long programs in general education. A child will be given a later opportunity to transfer from one kind of school to another, but on the whole it is expected that the children will remain in the program to which they have been assigned.

The law provides for other changes in the educational system, but those mentioned are the main ones that will affect people in rural areas. Since there is always a wide margin between a principle as it is enacted into law and its realization, the system may not in reality be so completely reformed as the law states. There has already been considerable criticism of the *cycle d'observation* on the ground that its development may be different from what was anticipated. Furthermore some of the changes are primarily changes in labels. Thus the *cours complémentaire* is retained but will henceforth be dignified with the title *collège d'enseignement général*. The present *centres d'apprentissage* will be called *collèges d'enseignement technique*.

However the new plan for educational reorganization works out, one thing is certain. Technological development and new demographic patterns have created a need for education which people cannot afford to ignore. Education will play an increasing role and have important indirect effects in hastening both the urbanization and the democratization of France.

URBANIZATION

During recent years the differences between country and city life which have traditionally existed in France have markedly lessened. Peasants and villagers go more and more to the city and the bourgeois have increasingly extended their activities to the countryside.

The village used to be the focal point of a farmer's life; it was his administrative center, spiritual center, cultural center, and economic center. With the development of transportation facilities the farmer now finds the city a better place to satisfy many of his needs. The village remains the administrative center where he must vote, declare his wine production, and register the birth of his child, but in economic matters the village has largely lost its function.

No farmer would think of bringing his produce to the village to sell. In Roussillon the old market was long ago walled in and converted to a recreation hall. In Chanzeaux one man sells flowers and cress in the town square on Sunday mornings, but he is not from the commune. The Chanzeaux farmers take their produce either to the market center of Chemillé five or ten miles away or to Angers, the provincial capital. Here they also sell their cattle and pigs, and farm wives sell their butter and eggs and rabbits. Modern transportation has made the larger market centers easily accessible to everyone.

Going to a city hospital was once dreaded, but now it is taken for granted, and doctors have no compunction in sending a patient from the country to a hospital (*clinique*) in the city where more services are available. Few rural mothers now have their babies at home. In Chanzeaux itself there is no longer a resident doctor. Again modern transportation has made the difference; not only can the patients themselves get to the city, but without too much inconvenience their relatives can visit them. Formerly a trip to the city would have meant the loss of a whole day's work.

The city now attracts people for more frivolous reasons, too. Young people may drive in for a movie or to go to a dance. Frequently a group of Chanzéens go to Angers on Sunday afternoon to watch the Angers soccer team play in the national league. One summer evening in 1961, Michel Jabeau, a young farmer, was standing on the corner of the public square in Chanzeaux dressed in his best clothes. When I asked where he was going he said, "A bunch of us got tickets for the play tonight. You know, they're giving an outdoor performance of Shakespeare's *Othello* in the courtyard of the Angers château." Traditionally in Chanzeaux, parish theatricals were the most popular entertainment, but people now willingly drive miles to see a good play. Even children now depend on the city for some of their entertainment; every Chanzeaux child is taken to Angers on some Thursday before Christmas to see the decorations and to visit Santa Claus at the big Angers department store.

People go even beyond the regional cities for entertainment. Every year a carload of young men drive to Le Mans for the automobile races. One time I heard the young man whose father owned the bicycle repair shop across the street from our house in Chanzeaux start his car in what seemed like the middle of the night. The next day I found out that he had driven to Angers to take a train for the one-day excursion to the automobile show in Paris.

Meanwhile with increasing frequency city dwellers turn to the country. We have already seen the two vacuum cleaner salesmen who in a day sold twenty-eight cleaners in one town. This incident shows the growing importance of rural outlets for city merchants and salesmen. For centuries in France there have been peddlers going from village to village, but these men who stocked up in the city and then wandered through the countryside, sleeping in farmhouses and village inns, were a different race from the men who nowadays leave the city every morning in trucks stocked with goods for the farmers. Country people, besides having fresh meat and oysters,

Algerian oranges, clothing and kitchen utensils brought to the door, now have a daily exchange of opinion and gossip with someone with a city point of view.

As the villagers turn more and more to the cities for their needs and as city merchants push out into rural areas with their wares, the services offered by the villages decrease both in number and in quality. As we have seen, there is no longer a doctor in Chanzeaux and certain of the village artisans and shopkeepers are also disappearing. In the past, Monsieur Longuet, a cabinetmaker, made a large part of the furniture that was bought in Chanzeaux. When a couple married, they traditionally asked him to make a bed and a dresser and whatever else they could afford. Especially since the Second World War, Longuet's business has largely disappeared; young couples prefer to buy their furniture in city stores where it is both more up-to-date and cheaper. Monsieur Forget, the tailor, still makes suits for some men in the commune, but his son and he have to fill in their spare time doing work for the city tailors who send things out to them.

The countermovement from city to country is not only for profits but also for pleasure. From June to September there are actually city people living in the villages. In Chanzeaux in the past the owners of the château were always there for their vacations, but there was very little real exchange between them and their village neighbors. Essentially it was only from their contacts with the local people hired as domestics that the *châtelains* had the illusion that they knew and understood rural life. Today the contacts between city and country dwellers which take place in the villages are much less superficial. With paid vacations for factory workers and with government allowances for families that will take their children a certain distance from home, Paris and all the big cities empty their populations into the country. Thanks to these inducements as well as changes in means of travel, city people in summertime fill the villages and farms of France. In August the invasion of the countryside reaches its peak.

People with enough money go to the mountain or seashore, but resorts there are crowded and expensive. Villages like Chanzeaux and Roussillon, with little beside the country atmosphere to offer, suit the budget of a lower-class family. There are walks to take. One may fish in the brook and play *boules* and sit in front of the house in the evenings gossiping with the neighbors. The house where we lived in Chanzeaux had seven rooms. During the summer it is rented to city families; three families are sometimes there at one time. The landlord makes a solid profit on the operation; he not only collects the rent, but he and his wife sell wine, eggs, and vegetables to the tenants. They also become friendly with these summer visitors from the city. The children watch Monsieur Bonnerot at work in his harness shop and in the evenings Madame Bonnerot and he have a chance to chat with these city people. Sometimes in the winter the Bonnerots go to the city to visit their former tenants who have now become their friends.

Roussillon is in a singularly picturesque corner of Provence, and the influx of summer people there is even greater than in Chanzeaux. Because of the invasion real estate prices have rocketed. In 1951 when the village had lost its economic function as well as a substantial part of its population, I could have bought a windmill and the hill on which it stood near Roussillon for ninety dollars; the present owner is a city person, and in 1959 refused an offer of two thousand dollars for the property. During the winter Roussillon is rather sad, since one third of the houses now belong to summer people, but during the season it is crawling with life.

DEMOCRATIZATION

Just as the differences between country and city people are lessening in France, so class distinctions have lost something of their former sharpness. There is still far more awareness of class differences in the minds of the French people than in the minds of Americans, but shifts have taken place and certain extremes have been reduced in the last twenty years. In the urban situation, where this question has received more attention by both the press and by scholars, the traditional distinction between proletariat and bourgeoisie has lessened in the last few decades, so that it is now often not so easy to distinguish at a glance between a laborer and a middle-class person.

Social stratification exists in rural communities, too. The extremes are obvious to anyone—no one confuses the owner of the château with the villagers. Other differences are less glaring but still obvious, the difference between village people and farm people, between the government employees (*fonctionnaires*) of the village and the artisans and shopkeepers. There are also subtle differences among types of farmers—the landowning farmer; the *fermier*, who rents a farm from someone else; the *métayer*, who works shares with the owner; the *ouvrier agricole*, a farm laborer with a steady job; and the *journalier*, a farm laborer who is hired only from day to day. In Chanzeaux one is reminded of the difference between vintners and dairy farmers: "wine people" consider themselves superior to "cow people," and the latter resent the distinction. There is something of the same sort of distinction between the farmers who live near the national highway and feel more abreast of the current of life, and those who live in rather in-grown hamlets off the highway.

In certain cases especially the lines marking these differences have changed radically in the last few years. The *statuts du fermage* (legislation governing the renting of farms), which we shall study in a later section, have given the *fermier*, or land-renting farmer, advantages that place him above the small landowning farmer with small, dispersed fields which cannot be worked efficiently by modern methods. The *métayers*, or crop-share farmers, formerly a large group, have dwindled in number and at the same time have risen in status because most of those remaining are "wine people."

The story of the role which the owner of the principal château in Chanzeaux has played in the life of the village in this century will illuminate our consideration of the recent changes in class structure in France. From the beginning of the century until the Second World War the *châtelain* of Chanzeaux was Monsieur de Kerdouec, a career army officer who was so outraged at the separation of the Church and State in 1905 that it is said he broke his sword over his knee. He retired from the army and then settled on his country property which consisted of twenty-four farms in the commune as well as the large park of the château. M. de Kerdouec was soon elected mayor of the commune and was the patriarch of the community until his death thirty-five years later. It was he who maintained the huge church that had been built, mostly with Kerdouec money, in 1900. It was he who paid most of the salaries of the teachers in the parochial schools, which had also been built by the *châtelain* before him. Monsieur de Kerdouec oversaw the construction of a parish recreation hall, the *patronage,* where his wife directed dramatic productions and he himself sponsored the gymnastic team and the drum-and-bugle corps. The villagers liked him because he had the reputation of being fair and kind, even an easy mark in some ways, but there was no doubt where the ultimate power in the community lay. In modern corporation terms Monsieur de Kerdouec was chairman of the board; the priest was president and general manager.

Monsieur de Kerdouec died in 1939 and the priest, who had been curate of Chanzeaux since 1919, retired shortly afterwards. The twenty-four farms of the Kerdouec family were divided among several heirs. Traditionally the landed gentry in France made a great effort to maintain the unity of their domain, but conditions have changed. Monsieur de Kerdouec's eldest daughter, Madame Delbosc, who inherited the château, could neither afford to buy out her brothers and sisters nor maintain the château properly. She now has only two farms and one of them is the park of the château where a *fermier* grazes his cattle.

The two-mile wall that enclosed the château grounds has fallen into a worse and worse state of repair. A hundred years ago this wall was built by the *fermiers* who lived on the Kerdouec farms; they quarried and carted the stones from the Kerdouec stone quarry. Today the Delboscs cannot afford to spend a million francs to have the wall repaired by the village masons. Besides, since the Delboscs spend most of their time in Paris and come to Chanzeaux only for the holidays, they have little interest in keeping up the château and less interest in the welfare of the community. Most of the year the château is closed and empty.

When Monsieur de Kerdouec died and the old priest retired, there were no leaders in the community prepared to take their places, but economic, social, and educational developments made it possible for men of the village eventually to assume the responsibilities formerly borne by the two patriarchs. It was not an easy transition but finally the cartwright who had stopped mending wagons to start a basket factory became mayor and has held the office ever since. Leadership and financial support for the parochial schools had to be financed principally by the people themselves. This task was accepted by the most active members of the community—farmers, artisans, and merchants—many of whom had received leadership training in the JAC and JACF, the Catholic Agricultural Youth Movements. These people have taken on the imposing responsibility of raising enough money to support both a large church and the church schools which nine tenths of the children of the community attend. The most active, most prosperous, and best prepared laymen have taken over running the community. The priest even complains privately that he is not consulted sufficiently on how things should be done, and as Professor Duroselle has said in commenting on this development: "L'insuffisance des prêtres est compensée par la suffisance des laïcs!" (The lack of priests is made up for by the *suffisance*—meaning both ample supply and conceit—of the layman.)

The system which has evolved for the selection of the most important community leaders is democratic in the extreme. There are no formal nominations for the thirteen-man council; voters simply write on their ballots the names of the thirteen people they want, and any person appearing on a majority of the ballots is elected a councilman. In a recent Chanzeaux election, on the first ballot about forty names were written in and nine councilmen were elected. The other four members were elected on the second ballot. Monsieur Delbosc, incidentally, was elected to the council, but he received the fewest votes of any of the thirteen; the man who received most was his *fermier*! For the Catholic school board the same procedure is used except that each family has an extra vote for every child it has in the schools. The twenty-five people on the board are in charge of raising the money for the schools, hiring teachers, seeing that the buildings are kept in repair and handling all the other problems of running the schools.

Several new committees have been formed recently in Chanzeaux: the committee which organized the school bus service, a committee in charge of maintaining a social worker in the commune, and a group concerned with agricultural education and experimentation (a branch of CETA—Centre d'Etudes Techniques Agricoles). There are conflicts among the leaders of these community activities: the mayor represents the older, more conservative people; the JACistes (the Catholic Agricultural Youth) are more active and more progressive. But the important thing to see is that Chanzeaux now is a democratic community, quite different from the Chanzeaux before the war.

The process of democratization has also extended to many other aspects of life in the community. We have seen the effect of increased educational opportunities for the farmers' and artisans' children. We have seen how technological developments have brought modern conveniences to the farmhouses, so that many farmers now in some ways actually live more comfortably than the people of the château. The château's staff of servants has been replaced by one part-time cleaning woman; its stables are empty except for the farmer's horses. Monsieur Delbosc has a Peugeot just as many of the farmers do.

Though there is still an important difference between the extremes of the social hierarchy, it is increasingly restricted to a difference in values and attitudes. Two marriages, taking place in Chanzeaux within a few days of each other, illustrate the narrowing of the gap. The granddaughter of one of the local gentry was marrying a wealthy young nobleman from the city, and the baker's daughter was marrying the new postman in the village. Between the two ceremonies and following festivities there was a tremendous difference, but it was a difference in degree, not in essence, and many aspects of the two marriages were precisely the same. Formerly the marriage of humble people in a village was organized around a series of local customs that differentiated it from marriages in other social classes or in other parts of France. Now everyone seems to have the same model in mind. The baker's daughter no doubt would have had the elaborate wedding the other girl had, if her means had permitted. The same photographer from the city of Angers was hired to take informal pictures of both weddings. The album which the postman's bride later showed me must have been very like that exhibited by the bride of the nobleman.

True, for the baker's daughter there was one wedding banquet and for the other bride there were two—one for the invited guests and one for the farmers, servants, and local artisans who had helped prepare the old château for the wedding. The two banquets at the latter wedding were held simultaneously, and each had a printed menu—although the menus were not the same. The custom of having an extra dinner for the farmers and retainers is an old one, but now the separation of the two groups is thought of primarily as a sensible and convenient arrangement to make guests with different circles of friends more comfortable. This still represents a sharp class division, of course.

"Still, times have changed," the carpenter told me when we were talking about this division. "When I was a boy, the children of Monsieur de Kerdouec used to come into the shop and speak of my grandparents as *le père Charbonnier* and *la mère Charbonnier* ["old man and old woman Charbonnier"]. I wanted to crawl under the counter with shame. Now the Delbosc children wouldn't think of addressing my mother and father as anything but Madame and Monsieur."

STATE INTERVENTION

The first time I heard of the proposal to establish the *cycle d'observation* within the education system was at a Catholic school teachers' meeting in a small town near Chanzeaux. The primary inspector of the schools of the diocese, in reporting on a number of developments that might be of interest to the teachers, warned them that the state might push through a school reform bill which would have far-reaching effects in their communities. The teachers were advised to do all they could to prevent the passage of the bill. It must be remembered, he said, that the Church was not against the democratization of the educational system, for, as they all knew, the Church was concerned that all people have equal opportunities. The *cycle d'observation* could have nefarious side-effects, however, the most important being the possible increase in the power of the state to determine what every French child should make of his life. In the opinion of the diocesan authorities this danger outweighed the advantages of democratizing French education. The *cycle d'observation* has in fact, as we have seen, been incorporated in the educational law. It will be interesting to see what side-effects the new system will actually have on the lives of the people of Chanzeaux.

Often government policies, planned for the good of the country as a whole, have had unexpected consequences. In considering French social change, therefore, one must always consider not only the intentions with which governmental policies are formulated but the unintentional and unexpected effects of these policies, too. The fact that these effects are often varied, indirect, and difficult to define makes them no less important.

After the Second World War, legislation was enacted to establish a housing program designed to protect the family, that all-important cell, from profiteering landlords. The original notion was that public housing would be built to fill an obvious and pressing need; it was assumed that, with housing in abundance, competition would hold down rents and wartime rent controls could be removed. However, the public housing program was not sufficiently implemented; rent controls had to be kept, and these discouraged private capital from building more houses. Because the law forbade the eviction of tenants except for unusual circumstances and because the rents were often not high enough to cover expenses on the upkeep of the property, people who had houses and apartments often preferred to keep them empty. As a consequence, in a village like Roussillon about one third of the houses were vacant in the fall of 1950 when we arrived there. Still, young married people sought housing in vain. Frequently they lived with parents, a most unhealthy situation for a young French couple trying to establish a new home. The effect of the housing law, therefore, was quite the opposite of what was intended: the French family was weakened rather than strengthened by the program.

The way in which the elaborate system of social security has worked out proves again the necessity of looking at the forces making for social change in France today from the point of view of both intent and practice. Although the principle underlying the social security program is not stated explicitly in the constitution of the Fifth Republic, it was defined as follows in the preamble of the constitution of the Fourth Republic and remains basic to French social legislation:

The Nation guarantees the conditions necessary for the development of the individual and the family. It guarantees every individual, especially the child, the mother and the old worker, the protection of health, material security, rest and leisure. Every human being who because of his age, mental or physical condition or economic situation is incapable of working has the right to obtain from society (*la collectivité*) suitable means of existence.

The program as it is being worked out by the French government naturally affects all persons living in France and affects them in a myriad of ways—both predictable and unexpected.

The best example of devious and unpredictable effects of the social security program can be seen in its most publicized feature: the *allocations familiales,* or family allowances, paid monthly to families with two or more children. The main purpose of this program as it was worked out in the 1940's and 1950's was to strengthen the family. If parents could be encouraged to have a large family, bring up their children well, keep them in school and prepare them for a life of industrious citizenship, then society as a whole would benefit from the change.[7]

Because the birth rate has risen noticeably since the social security program was instituted, it has often been assumed that the rise was due to the help families received for having more children. This assumption seems to me unjustified, though it would be difficult to prove either side of the question. What is clear, however, is that family allowances have in some ways undermined the traditional family structure. The mechanism operates as follows. Technically the money is paid to the father as head of the family, and this principle is written into the law. Basically, however, it is work the mother does which is being compensated. The law also recognizes that the main responsibility for bringing up the children ought to remain with the mother; so it offers additional payments if she refuses to take outside employment and if she stays at home to care for her family. Frequently, therefore, the *de facto* income of the wife is equal to or greater than the wages received by her husband. This is true, for instance, in the family of an agricultural day worker with four children; the amount the mother receives as a family allowance makes her in effect the head of the family. Furthermore, since the children are the justification for the allowances, their role seems more important than it was in the traditional French family in which the father was the real as well as the titular head. Thus instead of strengthening the structure of the family, as was intended by those who elaborated the social security system, the family allowances have actually weakened the structure.[8]

One of the incidental purposes of social security was to help redistribute the wealth of the French people.[9] Recent studies, however, tend to show that the social security system is having the opposite effect and is strengthening existing economic and social divisions.[10] Although the upper classes complain that they are asked to share their wealth with the poor, they are actually receiving proportionately more benefits from the system and contributing less to it than the wage earners.

In Chanzeaux one of the effects of the social security system that is most obvious to anyone studying the professional structure of the commune is the distortion which now exists in official listings of professional categories. Normally an adult son and his father would have worked a farm cooperatively, but because the self-employed farmer could not share in the benefits of social security, the father officially hired his son as an agricultural laborer so he would not be self-employed. Thus, in Chanzeaux, Joseph Brée in fact manages the farm shared by him and his father (who also owns a café), but officially Joseph is only a paid laborer. What their financial arrangements actually are I do not know, but it is certain that they are not what they are officially stated to be. Joseph Brée is not alone in adopting this fictional relationship with his father. Of the fifty *ouvriers agricoles* recorded in the commune, twenty are sons sharing the income of the farm with their fathers. Whether this shift in official status actually transforms the relationship of father and son and creates the kind of strain that exists between employer and employee is a question. However, it illustrates a small way in which national policy may have unintentional and indirect effects on the structure of a society.

Agricultural policies of the Third, Fourth, and Fifth Republics offer further and important illustrations of my point. Through the Méline tariff of 1892 and subsequent legislation, the French government sought further to protect what was considered the basic unit of French society, the traditional farm family. Independent farm families seemed threatened on the one hand by competition from huge new agricultural regions like the United States and Canada and on the other hand by French factories which, it was thought, were enticing farm youth away from the country. To counteract these forces and make the life of the farmer more attractive, a high tariff was erected. In the course of the years, legislation continued to support the farmers, protecting them from still-growing competition, giving them tax advantages and in general trying to ensure their security in an increasingly industrial world.

Meanwhile, decade after decade, the farmers of France slipped down the economic ladder. It was not only that the number of people in agriculture decreased while that in industry, services, and government expanded. Those who remained in agriculture, even though they turned more and more to modern techniques, could not increase their incomes as fast as other workers did. Professor J. Milhau reports that in a hundred years the average income in the nation as a whole, in constant francs, rose to an index of 221 while the income per person active in agriculture reached only 144. In the 1860's, farmers towered high above other workers and salaried people in income per producer, but by the 1950's they had fallen considerably behind the other groups.[11]

There is a tremendous variation among the farmers of France, and the great mechanized latifundia in the Beauce and Normandy prospered under the protection of the government, but the independent farmers whom the government had intended to nurture ceased to evolve with the times. The real effect of the protective legislation was to encourage much of rural France to remain as it had been in 1892. Seemingly, the French farmer was not challenged to adapt to changing conditions and became less and less fit to take his place in the twentieth century.[12]

At the end of the Second World War in both Chanzeaux and Roussillon wheat remained the preferred crop, along with grapes and beets, although a changing world demanded a change in agricultural products. Neither commune is well adapted for raising wheat, but, in 1950, 14 percent of the arable land of Roussillon and 20 percent of the arable land of Chanzeaux were still planted to wheat. Equipment was out of date. The Perron family in Chanzeaux was still threshing with flails in 1945 and no one in either community owned a tractor. Living conditions were poor. It was rare for a farmer to have been to agricultural school. In a word, the protection afforded the French farmer had in a way preserved his traditions but he was increasingly unable to function in the world.

Additional unpredicted effects have come from the farm tenancy legislation passed after the Second World War. The purpose of the *statuts du fermage* was threefold: agriculture in France was to be further democratized; it was to be made easier for the tenant farmer to own the land he worked; and encouragement was to be given for the continuing modernization of agriculture. As the law has worked out, it is only in the area of democratization that the intent of the legislation seems to have been realized. In the two other areas unexpected developments quite contrary to the primary purpose of the legislation can be seen.

The *statuts du fermage* guarantee a tenant farmer *(fermier)* first option should an absentee landowner wish to sell his land, and special courts assure a fair purchase price. An owner may not take over land worked by tenants unless he or his son will continue to keep the land under cultivation and live on the premises. Contracts run for nine years, but when a tenant leaves at the expiration of his lease, he has a right to an indemnity for improvements he has made on the property.

The area in which the intention and the result of the legislation have most nearly coincided is that of democratization, for certainly the legal protection given the tenant farmer has assured him more independence from, and nearer equality with, his landlord than he had before. In the past an owner could threaten not to renew a tenant's lease for the most arbitrary reason. In Chanzeaux the story is told of a tenant who in the past was threatened because his son not only had poached in the château woods but did not have a perfect record for attendance at Sunday Mass! The recent election results in both Chanzeaux and the neighboring town of La Jumellière give concrete evidence of the status the tenant now enjoys; in both towns the owners of the châteaux received only enough votes to be elected as the thirteenth members of the town councils and in both cases the two men's tenants led the ballots.

The slogan which was used in popularizing the section of the *statuts du fermage* which was designed to increase the opportunity of a tenant to become a landowner was "the land to him who tills it." Curiously enough this opportunity has become increasingly less attractive, for just because of the legal protection given a tenant farmer he now has in many ways a more favorable position than the landowner. It is commonly said in the villages that the *fermier* is lucky because he pays no land tax, doesn't have to worry about putting a new roof on the house, often has his capital in more fluid form, and is able to leave his descendants some cash and equipment rather than plague them with problems of dividing up the farm. Usually, when a landowner dies, each child receives a share of the land but since only one is needed to work the property, he must find a way to acquire the portions inherited by his brothers and sisters. If he does not have cash he must borrow, or else work shares in the hope of accumulating the necessary money. Whatever the solution his situation is difficult; owning the land one tills is not necessarily an enviable position.

If a landowner rents out his land and has the misfortune to have an inefficient tenant, he has very little chance of getting a better one. It is true that he can go to court to have his tenant evicted but the off-chance of winning in the face of the protection given a tenant by the *statuts du fermage* may well be outweighed by considerations of the expense of the legal action.

Under the *statuts du fermage* another possibility for the landowner saddled with an undesirable tenant is one that a businessman from Nantes has availed himself of in Chanzeaux. His property there had belonged to his mother's family and for sentimental reasons he wished to keep it. It was also a pleasant place for his family to vacation. M. Delattre was tired of the complaints and demands of his farmer, however—a new roof for the house, a larger barn, crushed stone for the road. Because the owner of a farm is obliged by the *statuts du fermage* to keep the property in good condition and make all but very minor repairs (by law 25 percent of the rent must be put aside for this purpose each year), M. Delattre was not able to overlook the demands of his tenant. Perhaps because of the inadequacy of this tenant, perhaps for other reasons, on expiration of the lease M. Delattre asserted his right to take over and work the property himself.

Obviously a prosperous man from Nantes is not actually going to establish himself permanently 100 kilometers from his business in the city on a property of doubtful economic value. Without doing anything so extreme, M. Delattre has been able to comply with the law, however. He spends the minimum of time in the big old family house. The fields have been let go to grass, on which graze a flock of sheep. By hiring a shepherd, M. Delattre not only has someone to keep an eye on his property but, far more important, he has the excuse he needs in the eyes of the law to justify not having renewed his tenant's lease. In this case, although the oc-cupancy of the land has changed, one more farm has been taken from crop production and one less farm is available to a young would-be Chanzeaux farmer.

After the Second World War when the government shifted its focus and abandoned the protective policy in favor of the European market, the farmers were assured that they would profit by the change. If only they would "tool up," modernize their operations, abandon the traditional pattern of subsistence farming and produce for the market, they could prosper as they never had before. Relatively easy credit was made available; they were encouraged to take advantage of it—and they did. The great extent to which the French farmers were willing to go into debt to buy new tractors and equipment is seen in the huge increase between 1955 and 1958 in loans made by the Crédit Agricole Mutuel, a semiofficial bank, which had existed for years but became important only after the war as the farmers overcame their traditional reluctance to go into debt.[13]

But once again, government action has not had the intended effect. As we have seen, farming in France today has indeed been modernized. Certainly in many cases giving the farmer this chance to improve his operation has strengthened his position and increased his productivity. Still, a good many farmers working small farms have not profited from modernization. Tractors are practical on large farms with big fields but since so many French farms consist of small, dispersed fields, mechanized operations are often inefficient. Farmers working such land who took advantage of the easy credit extended by the government in order to improve their condition have in fact often found themselves in a still more vulnerable position. They have overextended their credit and they own equipment which does not increase their earning power. One more facet of the *manifestations paysannes* was the expression of the disappointment and bitterness these men feel; they are still pressed by a fear that they may indeed be doomed to extinction (*appelés à disparaître*).

SOCIAL INTEGRATION

A sense of being integrated within the larger framework of the country is not new in France, of course. At the cultural level, a Frenchman feels his identification with the many manifestations of French civilization. He knows that along with every other Frenchman he is an integral part of *la patrie* which everyone must help defend in case of need. He shares the feeling of being *administré*, of being governed by the state in many ways. In the last fifteen years, however, a new sense of solidarity and cooperation has developed among the French. With lessening of a number of barriers which have traditionally separated the French from one another—regional differences, class distinctions, the conflict between rural and urban points of view, and religious divisions—France has become socially much more tightly integrated.

Traditionally the aspects of life which most forcefully reminded the foreigner of the lack of integration in France were the regional differences he so easily saw. A hundred years ago one could tell the regional origins of a French person by his accent, his dress, and even, it is traditionally maintained, by his way of thinking and feeling. At the turn of the century the government began to discourage these regional differences but now serious efforts are being made to preserve or revive traditions before they become extinct. It used to be a punishable offense for children in the school in

Roussillon to speak *provençal;* now their teacher is encouraged to teach it formally. Folk dancing in traditional costumes has become more and more popular as the regional differences have disappeared. Regional museums are founded and endowed. In 1958 the only part of the proposed national budget that was not cut by the government was that of the national folklore museum—the Musée des Arts et Traditions Populaires. This attempt to preserve the French subcultures is direct—and ironic!—evidence that the subcultures themselves are dying.

Obstacles formerly set up by the Church to prevent the integration of the French people have been removed too. The priest of Chanzeaux, a vigorous man in his thirties, and l'abbé Caillaux, the elderly retired priest who had returned to the village for a visit, were discussing a problem in the relationship between the Catholic and the state school. Caillaux was surprised at the willingness of the younger priests to work with the government to find a solution to their differences: "The difference between you and us is that you didn't go through 1905. You don't know what it's like to feel that you're standing alone against the whole country. You seem to think that you can get along together!" Certainly the old quarrel between the clericals and anticlericals has lost its vitality. And the younger generation's feeling that today there are more vital issues than the quarrel between Church and State is strengthened by the official attitude in Rome. In the encyclical "Mater et Magistra," July 14, 1961, the sons of the Church are specifically called on to cooperate with non-Catholics in working for the general advancement of their communities. Unlike the "Rerum Novarum" issued seventy years earlier, this encyclical caused no great stir in France, because it introduced no revolutionary ideas for that country. *Le Monde* commented that times have changed—customs too— and the religious controversy is not what it used to be.[14]

Just as regional and religious differences have lessened in France in the years since the war, so the extremes of political thought seem less marked. In the rural areas I know, the Communists appear to be a much weaker force than they used to be. In the past the farmers were easily split by political leaders who appealed to their feeling of identity with various religious, regional, or social factions. But in 1961, Catholic JACiste farmers of Chanzeaux took part in the same movement with Communist farmers from Roussillon. They were united by a professional organization, the FNSEA, the Fédération Nationale des Syndicats d'Exploitants Agricoles, which included farmers of all political shades, and their ideological differences seemed to have little importance in their common protest.

The French farmer has been increasingly integrated into the economy whether he wanted to be or not. The production of tobacco has always been controlled by the state. Before the Second World War the cultivation of vines was regulated. The postwar economic programs have speeded the process of integration. The Renault factory is government owned. Many banks, insurance companies, and credit agencies are closely controlled or even operated by the state. Radio and television are state owned and operated. Perhaps it was because of this history of increasing integration and the farmers' realization of its benefits that, in the summer of 1961, I found the farmers in both Chanzeaux and Roussillon eager to be even more closely integrated into the national economy.

In Chanzeaux their feeling was expressed in their attitude toward two rumors which were current that summer. Everyone knew both were false, yet everyone seriously considered the questions which were raised.

One rumor was that in the future all farmers would have to pass a special examination testing their professional aptitude before they would be allowed to sign a lease to operate a farm. The general reaction to the idea was expressed in the phrase "Remarquez que ce ne serait que juste!" Since farms are scarce it seemed not only fair but desirable that the government should see that the best farmers be given a chance to farm.

The other rumor was that for efficiency all the land of Chanzeaux was to be divided into four large farms. Perhaps this rumor had its origin in the many proposals for forming land cooperatives or "agricultural workshops" or "rural centers" as an intermediate stage between the traditional French farm and the Russian kolkhoz.[15] At any rate, no one even began to take this seriously, but the fact that the rumor circulated at all indicates that farmers are aware of the criticism that their operation is inefficient and that it can eventually be improved only through radical governmental intervention.

The way in which integration affects people at the local level is a measure of the fundamental change which greater social integration has made in France. It also points to the possibility of still further integration on the national level; for, as individuals become accustomed to participating in a joint venture, their reliance on cooperation increases.

Traditionally, rural families liked to keep to themselves as much as possible. In an unpublished novel about life in a mountain town of Provence, Raymond Caizac caricatures this attitude. "In the village they didn't even like to read the same newspaper. Every family had a car, but each family had a different kind of car. Rouget had a Peugeot, Paul had a Fiat, Féli had a Citroën, and Jacques had a Ford. That way there was no possibility of lending one another spare parts." There is still some of this feeling in Chanzeaux and Roussillon, but experience in, as well as a need for, cooperation has substantially helped people overcome their fear of becoming involved with neighbors.

In both Chanzeaux and Roussillon there has been a transformation in the lives of the people in the last fifteen years that can be seen in many little ways. For example, one day I saw M. Clément, a teacher in Chanzeaux, trundling a washing machine through town. When I asked him about it, he explained that three families had pooled their resources to buy this piece of equipment which they all wanted but which none could afford to buy alone. Since each family would need the machine only one day a week, a joint investment seemed logical.

Families in Chanzeaux work together in more formal ways, too. The Association de l'Aide Familiale is a group organized four or five years ago to bring the community a trained social worker licensed by the state who can temporarily take the place of a mother in a family. This association is directed by the townspeople themselves and has worked out very successfully just as it has elsewhere in France. Other group projects—a local unit of the Crédit Agricole, a group fire insurance plan, and a prepaid surgical plan affiliated with the regional system—are going well. Since the present owner of the château has neither a fortune nor an all-consuming interest in the community, the people themselves have had to shoulder the burden of supporting and helping direct the Catholic schools which all but a few children attend. As already described, a new group sponsors the school bus system permitting the older children to attend the complementary courses in the city.

The farmers in Chanzeaux are not content to read the farm page of the newspaper to find out what is happening in other parts of rural France. In 1961 the men were considering organizing a unit of CETA (Centre d'Etudes Techniques Agricoles) which would be a cooperative study group, affiliated with the national organization. It would be supported in part by state funds but mostly by members' dues. Through the CETA the men pool their knowledge and experience and if necessary hire an agricultural engineer to guide them. Once a year the Chanzeaux farmers also organize an outing to visit farms in some other part of France. Buses are chartered; wives are invited. The trip is an expedition for pleasure as well as for learning.

In Chanzeaux the leaders of these cooperative efforts are often members or former members of the JAC, the Catholic Agricultural Youth Movement, which is seeking to form an active elite among farmers to further agricultural progress.[16] They are frequently criticized by the older, more traditionalist people of Chanzeaux who say that the young men are trying to run the community by imposing new ways of doing things and meddling in the affairs of other people. In spite of such criticism the trend toward cooperation grows.

It should not be thought that this phenomenon of ever-increasing cooperation is characteristic only of regions of France where the Catholic Church is strong enough to encourage and sponsor group activities. We have seen the amazing development in the last fifteen years of the tractor cooperative in Roussillon, which is in a region where the Church actually sends missionaries (*pères missionnaires*) to care for the few religious demands of the community. Even among the poorest class of industrial workers living in furnished hotels in Paris, we find the same trend toward cooperative behavior based on need born of circumstances.[17]

The farm tractor manifestations of July 1961 can be seen as a symbol of the increased solidarity of French farmers. The demonstrators united to act directly on the government rather than through their elected political representatives. One of the traditional griefs of the people of both Chanzeaux and Roussillon, regardless of party or belief, is that they cannot trust their political representative. He will promise anything to be elected, and when he gets to Paris and is part of the Chamber of Deputies or Senate they believe he is basically indifferent to the interests of the people whom he represents and does only enough to be reelected. The farmers feel that their professional organizations represent them more faithfully than the politicians. The French people have always known that the strength of government lay in its administrative branch, but the political branch always before overshadowed this real source of authority. In 1961, however, the target for the protest of the farmers in all parts of the country was invariably the symbol of government in France today: the prefecture in which the administration of the *département* is housed.

The French people now are better prepared to act jointly than they used to be. Their sense of organization and responsibility has developed through the associations in which they actively participate at the local and regional level.

II

FRENCH SOCIETY RESISTS CHANGE

◇◇

To understand the behavior of the French people and their social system, one must be aware of three basic assumptions concerning existence that are shared by most Frenchmen—assumptions concerning *reality, man,* and *time*. It is especially important for Americans to understand these principles, for Americans operate on very different ones concerning the same entities.

For the French people, reality is inevitably dual. There is a reality which is hidden to man, mysterious, not directly perceptible through the rational instruments at his disposal. This reality may represent a meaningless chaos, inert matter, or a mysteriously ordered world; there is no common agreement among Frenchmen as to that. However, the fact that this level of reality exists is commonly accepted. Meanwhile a person must live, and the French have acknowledged a second level of reality designed to answer practical needs. It is the world of law, of rules, of practical social restraints, a world the French see as full of injustice to the individual. There is nothing sacred about these social rules; they are thought of as unavoidable necessities that could easily be improved and would be—if they were not made and carried out by men. To live, man must adapt himself to the social reality, but he does not confuse it with the other reality.

As for the assumption about man, the French feel that in a sense mankind is great because from chaos it has fashioned society and even art, but that individual men are on the whole unworthy. Individuals must be fashioned by human intelligence into reasonable beings capable of living in society. Since the individual is so resistant to the civilizing force of a process of education which can never be perfect, no individual is ever completely socialized. Children eventually accept the limits that society imposes on them, but their acceptance remains superficial. Furthermore, since all individuals are on the whole malicious and since society never tames the deeper self, every individual is actually motivated by hidden forces which are probably hostile. The irony of this principle is that the French feel that although society must mold the individual, society, too, is corrupt because it is man-made and consequently society corrupts the individual it seeks to form.

But the French also feel that the situation has not always been that way. And this is the third basic assumption underlying the French value system. There was a period in the past—exactly which period in history is a source of disagreement—when life was better organized, society more just, and people more virtuous. Unfortunately men corrupted this more-nearly perfect life. The French believe there is no likelihood that the future will improve unless careful plans based on past experience are made. Indeed the future cannot be planned without reference to the past because the present is the product of the past. The only assertion the French feel can be made definitely about the future is that things will not naturally work out for the best if left to themselves.

In brief, then, the three basic assumptions about human existence are that men must accept two levels of reality; that people can be expected to be hostile; and that the present is not so good as the past and the future will not improve unless we plan it carefully. These assumptions are basically different from the usual American point of view that there should be only one level of reality, that people are likely to be friendly to us, and that everything will work out for the best in a future which will be superior to the past.

In a sense it is surprising that a people so bent on analyzing and clarifying the phenomena of human experience as the French has not successfully analyzed and described its value system. The nearest thing to such an analytical description is the *Code Civil*, but the French would be the first to point out that this is on the official level of reality and is in no way a compendium of the values of that other deeper reality. The need the French feel to impose a rational construction on existence has led to clear delineations and descriptions of differences; the French emphasize the variety of values within the social system rather than the unity of these values.

Even though no acceptable analysis of the French value system exists, it is obvious that there must be startling contradictions within the system and many subtle connections and shades of distinction that escape the observer. We know that this system constantly shifts and changes, but we also know that the change is slow and that aspects of the value system are sufficiently stable to give unity to French culture. It is because of this unity that French individuals and groups from many varying backgrounds can understand one another and agree on certain essentials. It is because of this unity that we can see similarities among such a wide range of French individuals as Calvin, Voltaire, de Gaulle, and Brigitte Bardot.

In order to understand the way social change takes place in France we must place it in the context of this indefinable value system to see how it either accelerates or impedes the forces for change as they make their impact on French culture. In this way we will succeed in understanding how France is changing and at the same time remaining the same. One can repeat aptly at this point the worn French aphorism: "The more things change, the more they stay the same."

I have said that the French assume that basic reality cannot be known but only intuited. They have, however, created a rational framework for existence to expedite the workings of everyday life. For example, French children are taught that France is a geometrical form. Although they know it is not actually a hexagon, they learn to think of their country in this way. They are taught that history is the rational unfolding of the personality of France as a nation. It is expected that the individual child will grow up in the same rational manner, step by step, developing a distinct personality but at the same time fitting neatly into the rational scheme of society. The traditional French garden is one in which man has imposed rational forms on nature. The value, then, for which man should strive in society is the rational organization of that society. Good government, like the balanced individual, the strong family, the attractive garden, is one which is rationally organized.

Because the French feel that the future is a realm of flux and uncertainty, rational planning seems of particular importance. Parents should plan a child's life, a writer should follow a plan worked out concretely in advance, a traveler should carefully consult his *Guide Michelin*. Paul Valéry summed up the principle that men should conduct their lives with as much *prévision* as possible by saying that

the mental process of foresight is one of the essential bases of civilization. It is both the source and the means of all undertakings, whether they be large or small; it is also the assumed basis of politics.[18]

In a sense the concepts of reality and time lead the French to place great value on attitudes that are favorable to the factors of social change studied in the first half of this essay. Because rational foresight is essential to the technological development of a country and to the integration of the various sectors of the economy into one efficient whole, and because the state is the proper agent for planning this development, the French attitudes toward reality and time make change seem both possible and desirable. In a most revealing article in the review *Prospective*, Pierre Massé, in charge of economic planning for France, speaks of state planning (*planification*) as a game against nature (*jeu contre la nature*). The function of the state is to study the possibilities for development and select those which are most likely to create the kind of future man wants.

Every agency in charge of making decisions must avoid two dangers. One is to put too much trust in mechanical projections based on the past; the other is to accept too eagerly anticipated situations which lack date, substance, and definition. Prospective [i.e., both the review *Prospective* and the whole system of state planning] must avoid both dangers. With an attitude of scientific doubt it must examine hypotheses critically and accept no assertion as true before it is carefully checked by a team of workers representing different and extensive special fields. The evidence of the laboratory technician is not that of the public health worker; the evidence of the economist is not that of the sociologist. They have a common denominator that must be found.

But when this process of questioning is ended, Prospective must reestablish order. Provided with a temporal radar which scans the ramifications of what is possible, its role is to sketch with a light but sure touch the shape of the future.[19]

There are other attitudes, stemming from the same fundamental assumptions concerning *reality*, *man*, and *time*, that act in a contradictory way and retard social change. One is a corollary of the concept of nature. Man fears losing the rational control over nature that he has achieved with so much effort. Since only man is endowed with reason, rational control means human control, but there is always the danger that man may devise mechanical controls that will function without heed to human needs. If this were to happen the individual would become the slave of the machine and forfeit rational control to an irrational force of his own creation.

A recurrent theme in modern French literature and French movies is this fear of excessive mechanization and organization. The classic expression is found in René Clair's *A Nous la Liberté* but the same moral is drawn in more specific and modern terms in Robert Dhéry's *La Belle Américaine* and in Tati's *Mon Oncle:* the happiest and truly healthiest people are the ones who stick to the old ways and do not become slaves to machinery.

Mass production, known as *américanisation*, is equated with the loss of human will and makes a fool of the man ensnared by it. The Four-Year Economic Plan published in the fall of 1961 contains a reassurance to the French people that French values will be preserved and not deteriorate into the American *civilisation du gadget*, but one must also note that in the issue of *Le Monde* in which the summary of the Economic Plan was published, the article on the facing page concerned an exhibition in Paris of new business machines! The fear of *américanisation* does not prevent technological advance in France, but it does slow it until it can be translated into French terms.

Another deterrent to social change springs from the French assumption that men are naturally hostile and selfish, frequently motivated by considerations for their personal welfare and not by considerations for the good of other individuals or society in general. In France the social system would be better integrated if each individual were not fearful of the hostility of others. He is likely to blame *les autres*—other individuals and other groups in society—for any trouble he has, and he is especially suspicious when *les autres* have power over other human beings. Thus an individual may accept economic planning in principle but in practice he is suspicious of it; he fears the hidden motives of the planners. The farmers believe that *les autres* keep them from gaining their rightful share of the profits of the economy. Artisans and shopkeepers are temporarily taken in by Poujade when he succeeds in confirming their suspicions that they are being persecuted. Workers in the public sector go on strike because employees in the private economy are being favored by the government. There is no doubt that in assuming the hostility of *les autres* the French act in a way which impedes a closer integration of the social system.

The French often say that this hostility is a result of jealousy. An individual or group which complains of being persecuted is accused of being jealous of another's good fortune. As a consequence one must be careful not to make other people jealous. To avoid the attacks and suspicion of *les autres* it is also important not to display the signs of success. Obviously mass production cannot succeed when the potential consumers are afraid to buy new articles!

The contrast that existed until recently between the pace of modernization in the American economy and that of the French reflects this fundamental difference. Traditionally in America an individual wanted to keep up with the Joneses, while in France the individual wanted to appear to be *behind* his neighbors. This attitude has changed considerably in France, as we have seen; gradually as more people buy cars and television sets and vacuum cleaners the individual purchase does not stand out. The attitude persists, however, and has been a deterring factor to social and economic change. The feeling is still expressed that it is better to pass unnoticed, "forgotten by God" as the characters in Jean Giono's *Moulin de Pologne* long to be, because by calling attention to ourselves we are only inviting disaster. This does not mean that the individual does not want to be rich and powerful; it means that he dreams of being *secretly* rich and powerful.

Because the French assume that men are hostile, they have protected themselves from *les autres* by a complicated network of legality quite in keeping with the French tendency to limit and define carefully all aspects of man's existence. The resultant legal straitjacket quite naturally inhibits change. Of course, citizens of all modern states are plagued by red tape and forms, but the elaboration of the French system is famous. It exists in all government offices as well as in private businesses both large and small. A man, or more often than not his wife *(la patronne)*, sitting at the cashbox *(la caisse)*, guarding the treasure and surveying with suspicion the behavior of everyone in a store, is a monument to French suspicion and formalism. The amount of time and energy spent to preserve society from the dishonesty of *les autres* is hardly a force for progress in a modern economy.

On the other hand, we must note here that in France it is never forgotten that these official rules are only man-made and therefore not worthy of the respect ostensibly given rules in the United States. In France one accomplishes the impossible by relying on personal contacts. On the unofficial level, where personal relations and not social regulations guide behavior, the rules which so often strangle business deals and in general inhibit change are minimal and may even be successfully by-passed. The existence of this "*Système D*" (the art of wangling) favors social change in France by permitting individuals to accomplish things which would have been impossible were the paralyzing formalities of the official world respected.

It is this which helps account for the fact that the private sector of the French economy has outstripped the public sector in technological progress and prosperity. It explains the phenomenon many visitors have found striking in France: the country has obviously experienced a real economic boom since the war but its collective and official personality, the state, has suffered from difficulties of all sorts. Attempts to persuade the individual to accept austerity programs so the government can solve its basic problems have fallen on deaf ears. Each individual knows that he must look out for himself and not play the role of the *poire* (sucker), for he has seen that all his fellow citizens put their own interests before those of the commonweal. This hierarchy of loyalties in France obviously lessens the success of government planning. Any plan would have a better chance of success if people were to work for it in fact rather than giving it open approval but secretly disregarding it.

The prosperity of private enterprise has been a source of conflict in the greatly expanded activities of the government. The government is the largest employer in France and must compete for the services of its personnel with private industry. The organizations representing government workers complain that they are not receiving their share of the benefits of a prosperous economy, but de Gaulle has complained that private companies have raised wages unreasonably high. Like the farmers, and like the miners of Decazeville, government workers feel persecuted by *les autres* and neglected by their employer.

The government, however, has the responsibility of trying to keep each faction of society satisfied at the same time it enforces the official rules. In order to accomplish this, the government makes each faction in turn an exception in the total situation. This satisfies one faction but irritates the others, who believe the exceptions are made at their expense.

To adhere to the rules and still enable life to move on—this is the impossible task of the government. A cartoon in the *Canard Enchaîné* (November 29, 1961) concerning de Gaulle's efforts to accomplish this task shows several de Gaulles dressed in the garbs of the various favored factions. He is made to say: "The law is the law, and no exceptions can be made—except for peasants, members of parliament, business men, gas and light workers, subway workers, students, railroad workers, and out-of-work lamplighters and street sweepers . . . !"

The value the French place on delineation and definition intensifies the feeling of individuality of every person and every group. The resultant rivalry, even jealousy, among them increases the need for social equality and thus accelerates the trend toward the rise of the lower classes. On the other hand, their sense of individuality combines with the feeling that *les autres* are hostile—and with the belief that present factions are the product of past events —to work against the integration of the parts of society into an efficient whole.

This sense of differentiation may create a further important but subtle obstacle to economic planning and national integration. Pierre Massé, in the article already cited, points out that successful national planning is based on game theory and that one of the essential elements in successful strategy is the ability of the player to identify with his opponent in order to outguess him. The great stress the French place on individuation prevents the planner from identifying successfully with people in groups and classes and associations different from his own; so he cannot predict accurately how his plan will work. When this inability to empathize with individuals in other groups is combined with the Frenchman's tendency to attribute unworthy motives to them and with his explanation of present conflicts in terms of past social divisions, it undoubtedly helps explain the many unexpected and undesirable effects of state planning.

In studying rural France, I have always been amazed that French administrators base their generalizations concerning the rural population on so slight and indirect an acquaintance with it. Because an administrator has a house in the country and a peasant girl to cook, he too often assumes he "knows" rural life. A typical reaction to rural people was that of a sub-prefect who learned that I, a professor, was actually spending a year in the village of Chanzeaux. "But why should you go there?" he asked. "There's no one but peasants!" Naturally, I knew this and was not even surprised that the sub-prefect should have reacted this way. But later when we discussed agricultural matters and his arguments in every case were based on indirect evidence—he even quoted Balzac as an authority on peasant mentality today!—the unwillingness and inability of the sub-prefect to understand the motivation of the people within his administrative district seemed both surprising and important to me. His ignorance seemed particularly unfortunate since he was unaware of it.

HOW CHILDREN ARE BROUGHT UP

Many aspects of child training in France reinforce and hasten social change. The training in analytical thought and the stress given to the importance of logical planning help the course of orderly social *planification*. The emphasis on equality, the conception of the state as the good head of the house who wisely plans the economy of his family, the insistence on an individual's persisting in an effort despite lack of official encouragement, are all parts of the French process of socialization which help promote social change. But there are other aspects of the way children are brought up which impede change, and those aspects are the ones that concern us here.

In every society, both in the family and in the school, children are taught the values and attitudes by which the society lives, and they learn to think and to act by means of a system of symbols representing features of the existing social system. Moreover, because children learn as much by imitating the behavior of their parents as from instructions given by their parents, the home training of a child of necessity acts as a brake on his adapting to the future. Children grow up to function as their parents have; much of what they learn is more relevant to an earlier situation than to the present.

Laurence Wylie

France is notable for the importance attached to the training that children receive in the home and the education they receive in school. Children are not considered naturally good: they are born the product of nature, and it is the obligation of parents to train them (*dresser*) to be *civilisés*. Parents feel this obligation strongly, and one of the traditional reasons given by French couples for not having more children is that if there are too many they cannot be properly trained. In the minds of French parents there is little of the doubt which many American parents feel about the right way to bring up children; so the conservative features of child-rearing are especially strong.

A great deal of affection is given infants and little children, for the French love babies. This love, however, does not keep parents from punishing a child when he resists the training being given him. When he is still very young he therefore learns that there are strict limits for his own behavior. He learns both at home and later at school exactly what is expected of him.

As a child's world expands, he encounters new limits to which he must conform. The teacher enforces school discipline; friends have their own group code; family and neighbors emphasize still other aspects of behavior. These limits are all different but all are enforced by the same means—ridicule, isolation from society, deprivation of pleasures, or added chores. It is only as a last resort that physical punishment is used.

Normally the French child openly accepts the restraints put on him—the elaborate code of etiquette, patterns of eating and cleanliness, the substitution of verbal for physical aggression, the stress on working hard in life ("the point of life is not just to have fun"). Since little effort is made to control the feelings and private thoughts of an individual, however, he can observe official tasks and loyalties and still withdraw from group responsibilities ("so they'll leave me alone"). He respects the limits imposed on him but at the same time he escapes them by retreating to the world within himself. As a result of this, the individualism of every Frenchman is intensified.[20]

This individualism has often been an obstacle to the success of those social reforms which depend on individuals' accepting the responsibility of working together for a common cause.

Another conservative force in the process of French social-ization is the emphasis which is put on deductive reasoning. The assumption of the validity of this method permeates the French educational system. A child is first taught the principles and then shown how to apply them. He is never allowed to experiment and then to draw conclusions from his experience. This theory that a child cannot know the truth by himself but must learn it from the experience of adults is obviously a conservative one. Of course, a great deal of learning in all cultures necessarily relies on the ex-perience of the older generation, but when a culture actually stresses the impossibility of learning from one's own experimenta-tion and experience, the inhibitive effect on social change is espe-cially marked.

There have been remarkable changes in French education in the last few years. Textbooks have been modernized, filled with illus-trations, brought up-to-date with historical and scientific develop-ments. Schools themselves have been modernized. Children are given more physical training and are required to do less homework. Other changes we have already noted. The fundamental principle of learning remains the same, however. As in the past, the teachers and the authors of textbooks still present the children with a body of knowledge which is organized and cut into digestible morsels for the students. "Learning" consists of fitting all these bits into an established scheme, the "truth" of any body of knowledge. The emphasis in the curriculum on history and geography bolsters the conservative force of French education. Foreign observers are par-ticularly struck by the amount of information on French national and local history and geography that children are required to learn. The reason for these requirements is the French insistence that the child must learn what formed him and his world in order to be able to act in accordance with it.

The introduction to one of the most popular history textbooks, insisting on the virtues of the study of history, shows the value of impartiality, modesty, and tolerance and the importance of feeling a sense of solidarity with one's ancestors and one's past.[21] This is illustrated by a drawing spread over two pages showing the "chain of generations"; representatives of all generations from the time of

Louis XIV to the present are in a long line holding hands. Today's representative, a little boy, stands under the smiling gaze of his father and contemplates the line of ancestors to which he is linked. The student using this book is shown the direct relationship with even his remote forebears, not just with his grandparents and great-grandparents whose graves he visits on All Souls Day. The child may grow up to worship this long past and feel that France must live up to its former glories or he may grow up to believe that everything is wrong with this past and sing with his Socialist and Communist comrades the words of the *Internationale:*

"No more tradition's chains shall bind us!"

In either case he knows that the past is something that binds him. He will be bewildered when he learns that for Americans the future begins now; for a Frenchman the future begins in the past.

The way in which geography is taught in French schools also gives the student a sense of the inevitability of the course his life must follow. In France geography is an important subject from elementary school through the university. After the details of physical geography have been drilled into the student, human geography is emphasized. The underlying principle is that man is the product of his environment; he may succeed in adapting his physical environment to his needs, but he cannot alter it fundamentally nor can he alter the fact of his relationship to it. In a geography class, children might learn, for example, that their town came into being because it lay at the junction of two paths of migration which primitive travelers had been forced to take because of the topography, natural resources, and vegetation of the area. The child is taught that the type of house he lives in, the slant of the roof, the stones with which the walls are made, the crops grown in the fields beyond, are all determined by elements of nature to which his ancestors adapted. Thus a French child grows up believing that he is the product of geographical forces which he cannot alter but can only adapt to his needs.

Of course, a Frenchman would point out that man *is* the product of his environment and of his antecedents and since only through an understanding of these two forces can he understand himself, the study of history and geography is essential. I shall not attempt to quarrel with this point of view. My argument is simply that a child growing up to think of himself primarily as a product of his historic past and of the geographical forces around him will feel less able to control his future than a child who is not so aware of these forces.

HOW SOCIETY IS ORGANIZED

In the context of this study, social organization means the network of rules and institutions that pattern human relationships, both those which are formally recognized and those which are not explicitly defined. Thus it includes not only the constitution of the Fifth Republic, the Civil Code, and the traffic laws, but also the relationship of a child to his teacher, the code that unites a group of adolescents in a clique, and the patterned behavior of a lawyer with his client. It includes institutions like the family, the Church and the State, and also the *bachot*, the "*Système D*," and the sidewalk café. The social organization is the manifest expression of the value system by which people live; it is the practical framework of the social structure.

In this wide sense, the social organization of France, like the value system which it represents, has never been described and undoubtedly never can be, for quite obviously it is a complicated mass of constantly changing and often conflicting elements. Descriptive studies are usually limited to a consideration of recognized and relatively stable aspects of the structure—written constitutions, industrial organizations, tax systems, codes of etiquette, literary movements, schools of art. To define completely the organization of even a limited part of the French social structure—a Paris suburb, a *département*, even one family—is a formidable task, and to relate all the elements of French society at a given moment in history is obviously impossible. This study will be limited to a consideration of the inhibiting force in certain features of the social structure, features either peculiarly French or particularly important to the French. Four of these are: the importance the French place on their relationship to the past, the clarity with which each element in the social structure is defined, the rigidity of the political structure, and finally the effects of the French concept of *égalité*.

The first feature is the weight of the past. By its very existence, the social organization is a conservative element blocking social change. We have already considered a number of changes which have taken place in France in the last fifteen years, and in every case the structure of that portion of the social organization in which the change has been observed has itself limited the rate and the extent of the change. Today the farmer in France has the opportunity to modernize his operation, but the way in which a French farm is traditionally cut into many dismembered bits notably limits the usefulness of modernization.

Once rules and habits and relationships are established, inertia if nothing else would tend to preserve them. But besides this force there are others. The fear many people have who identify the values for which they live with the social organization through which those values are expressed tends to maintain the *status quo*. It also takes time for social change to assume a form that is in harmony with the existing value system. A state-planned economy may be generally resisted if it is thought of as the result of *dirigisme*, or of the manipulations of the privileged group called the "two hundred families," but it becomes acceptable if it is thought of as *planification* carried out by trained functionaries trying to improve the whole social system. The planners of the new French economy seem less alarmingly revolutionary if they are called "neo-Colbertists" or Saint-Simonists.

An example of the conservative effect of an existing organization is the obsolete political structure of the *départements* in France. Their present boundaries were established in the eighteenth century so that a citizen could travel from his home on the periphery of the *département* to the capital and back in one day. Now the round trip can be made in two hours at the most. The same general problem exists for every commune. The village of Chanzeaux was at one time a social, economic, and political entity. With the transformation of communication facilities and the consequent integration of

Chanzeaux into a wider regional unit, the original function of the village as an economic and cultural necessity has disappeared. Administratively, however, Chanzeaux remains a relatively autonomous entity; and its functions could certainly be carried out more efficiently if the village were officially integrated into the larger area.

The ways in which the past impinges on the present in France may be either real or imaginary. In the case of the administrative organization of the departments and communes the effect is concrete. So is it concrete in the school system in Chanzeaux, where two hundred children crowd the two Catholic schools and are taught by teachers who can barely live on the funds raised by the community. In the same village a public school with a well-trained teacher stands almost empty; only the seventeen children of social deviants of the community attend it. The age-old argument between Church and State continues to exert its divisive influence.

In national politics particularly, the past encroaches on the present in less specific but no less important ways. Every political leader seeks a tie with the past to gain strength for his cause. Poujade shouts that his movement is a continuation of the Revolution: "The sacred breath of the French Revolution is felt by the nation which once more comes to its senses and rises again." [22] De Gaulle explains the need for social change and appeals for support on the basis of past situations:

France, throughout her existence, has passed through periods in which the general process of evolution demanded a regeneration on her part, under penalty of decline and death. This was the case, for example, at the beginning of the seventeenth century, when our monarchy succeeded in bringing a definite end to feudalism, for both internal and external conditions demanded a centralized state and national unity.

This was the case with the Revolution, which brought about liberty and equality within our nation and intervention outside, because democracy, competition and proselytism corresponded to the political, economic and social character of the period that was beginning. And this is certainly the case today, for the age in which we are living— marked as it is by the acceleration of scientific and technological progress, the need for social betterment, the emergence of a host of new states, the ideological rivalry between empires—demands a vast regeneration both within ourselves and in our relations with others. The problem is to accomplish this without France ceasing to be France.[23]

The second feature of French social organization that hampers change is the sharp way in which all of its elements are defined. Every function, attribute, responsibility, right, or relationship of the individual has been spelled out in either legal or official terms, or in tacit but clearly understood codes. The individual knows exactly how society expects him to behave in any situation. To a degree, of course, this is true in any culture, but it is particularly characteristic of France. The manner in which a criminal is punished, the way children ought to spend their time in recess, the specific responsibility one has for the material welfare of his parents, the procedure *boules* players should follow in the rare event a *boule* should split during a game, and the correct complimentary close to use in a letter to one's prospective mother-in-law—all these contingencies are foreseen by an item in some code or other.

These clearly stated definitions may well follow from the stress which in French education is put on the necessity for detailed and rational planning. They are perhaps also an outgrowth—or corollary—of the emphasis the French place upon limiting human behavior to protect an individual from hostile action by other people. In that case rules governing behavior would be intended as limits to unexpected actions, but in restricting human initiative they also inhibit social change.

The notion of the family as a clearly-defined cell remains powerful in France. A friend from Roussillon often comments that going into another person's house is like "crossing an invisible frontier." Another French friend once told me that in spite of the fact that he had played all during his childhood with the children living next door, as far as he could remember his playmates were never once in his house, and it was only for a single emergency during the war that he had ever been inside their house. "We preferred neutral ground, the street in front of the houses."

The clear definition of the family cell is formally strengthened by law. The Civil Code defines exactly what constitutes the family, what its relationship to society is, and the rights and duties of its members to each other. Little by little the definition has been altered but the extent of the alterations has been bound by the very clarity and formality of the original definitions in the Civil Code. The *Code de la Famille*, the social security system, the *statuts du fermage* have all been justified mainly on the ground that they help preserve the traditional family cell. Legal changes come slowly and, as often as not, only give official sanction to a transformation that has already taken place.

A third feature of the social organization in France that hinders change is the rigidity of the political structure. This may come as a surprise to those who see France as a land of political chaos, with new constitutions and a succession of governments. These phenomena are not to be denied, but their spectacular character and the common ignorance of the way the government of France really works often blind us to one of the most conservative institutions in the French social system: the vast, well-organized, and hierarchically controlled corps of government employees who are in charge of public services. The cabinet officers and elected officials come and go, but the corps of *fonctionnaires* remains. The members of the *Conseil d'Etat*, of the *Inspection des Finances*, of the prefectorial system, of the national police, and so on, are the men who actually govern France.

At every level in the political hierarchy there are appointed counterparts for the elected officials. The elected officer is considered temporary; the *fonctionnaire* has tenure. The elected officer has official responsibility as well as the right, in principle, to make policy; he is well-known to the public and takes the praise or blame for turns of events. But his counterpart, the *fonctionnaire*, has actual responsibility. He is not well-known to the public but his power is real. Since in principle and by definition the *fonctionnaire* is not responsible for policy, he is neither praised nor blamed, but it is thanks to him that government goes on even when governments continually fall.

This double authority is obvious in certain sections of the government—for example, a cabinet minister and his personal aides versus the permanent staff of the ministry—but in other political areas the division is not so widely known.

In Roussillon, for example, as in all the communes of France, the government consists of an elected municipal council, which chooses a mayor from among their members. The council also appoints the town clerk when a vacancy occurs, but he is not chosen from among the councilmen and by law he is guaranteed tenure. He is chosen from a list of applicants whose training and interests would seem to qualify them for the position. As a matter of fact the present mayor of Roussillon lives in Paris and usually comes to Roussillon only for the council meetings. It is there that public issues are debated and official decisions made. These decisions, however, are made largely on the basis of information and advice furnished by M. Rivet, the town clerk. He attends all the council meetings and his voice is often the most important in the group since the mayor knows little about what is going on in the community and relies heavily on Rivet's advice. In effect, therefore, Roussillon comes close to being governed by M. Rivet.

In every election in Roussillon there is a vigorous campaign among the town's factions and political parties. Heated discussion revolves around questions concerning candidates for mayor and council, but as likely as not, no mention is ever made of the town clerk. The outcome of the election actually will have relatively little effect on how the commune is governed afterwards though; it is Rivet who will have the responsibility of carrying out the decisions which are made, and few will be made unless he favors them. Of course, the fact that the mayor of Roussillon lives in Paris adds to Rivet's responsibilities; but even in communes like Chanzeaux, where the mayor is a resident, the situation is not much different.

The real check on Rivet's power is indicated by the visits he makes every week to the sub-prefecture in Apt or the prefecture in Avignon, for a large part of a town clerk's job is to carry out—through the intermediary of the prefectural staff in the *département*—the official duties required by officials in Paris. Although the commune of Roussillon, like all other communes in France, enjoys a certain autonomy, it is officially under the guardianship of the national government. Its budget must be submitted to the officials of the prefecture for their approval. By national law, a school must be maintained and the teacher paid. The town government may support the Church or church organizations only in ways explicitly permitted by the government.

These responsibilities as well as others are Rivet's. Wine production must be declared. Social security applications must be filled out. Statistics must be sent to a government office in Marseille. The national census must be taken. Arrangements must be made for the tax commission to meet with the tax collector, and the taxes must be assigned and collected. So we see that the town council by whom Rivet was chosen is not in effect his boss: Rivet is his own boss although the many responsibilities, both explicit and implicit, which he has to the national government limit his freedom. Since a town clerk has so many responsibilities which are national business, Rivet is in a sense the ultimate extension of the central power in Paris. When one has a knowledge of this network and a feeling for the way it functions, one is left with no doubt that the hierarchical structure of the political organization in France is a strong conservative factor.

The illustration chosen to show the hierarchical organization of French society is in the area of government, but it could have been taken from almost any other segment of the social structure—economy, education, transportation, religion, literary production. In most activities there is a line of authority and interest that runs from the local community through the *département* and the regional center to Paris. This form of organization can be a force for change if, as in the case of *planification*, the hierarchical authorities transmit orders calling for change. In the nineteenth century the provinces saw the strength of the hierarchy and complained that all the revolutions took place in Paris and were then imposed on the rest of France. Today, however, the usual effect of the domination of France by its many hierarchies is strongly conservative. The long lines of command are filled by *fonctionnaires* who have an established interest in keeping things as they are. Initiative comes from the top and deadens initiative at the lower levels. People cannot act without orders from above; so unless they can exert influence at the top they must resign themselves to complaining about a situation without hope of changing it.

It should be pointed out that the hierarchical structure of French society is also an example of my earlier point that because the elements of the French social organization are so clearly defined, social change is limited. French officials are notorious for their awareness of the precise limits of their responsibility and for their consequent reluctance to take even the slightest chance of doing something which does not lie within the precise limits of their duty. Every visitor to France has come away with at least one story of the *fonctionnaire* behind his grill whose only reaction to a repeated plea was: "The law is the law . . . This is not my responsibility . . . You'll have to go to some other office . . . How should I know which one? . . . I can do nothing about your case . . . Go talk to my superior if you like."

Every person in the hierarchy must avoid understanding too much about the individual problems of the public, for, according to the old French proverb, "tout comprendre, c'est tout pardonner" ("to understand is to excuse"). The public official must remain aloof, on a level at which "ne pas comprendre, c'est tout condamner" ("not to understand permits one to condemn everything"). Only thus can the hierarchy be preserved. An official of a prefecture once said to me: "Si le public dit du mal de moi, je l'emmerde sereinement. Cela ne fait que prouver la valeur de ma section et de mes méthodes. Plus le public est emmerdé, mieux l'Etat est servi." [24] The incivility and sometimes tyranny displayed by its "public servants," the French seem to accept as natural and inevitable manifestations of an effective civil service.

The French have not completely given in to the power of the hierarchy and its civil servants, however. Officially and ostensibly there is acceptance, which indeed limits the possibilities for progress in the development of the social organization. Unofficially and not quite openly a whole system of escape hatches has been worked out. Just as the individual escapes the limits placed on his personal behavior by openly accepting various codes but privately living in the world of his imagination, so society has found an escape from the limitations placed on it by a too-rigid hierarchy.

The *Système D* consists of any devious and usually ill-defined means by which an individual can take initiative in spite of the restrictions imposed on him by society. Earlier in discussing the French attitude toward the reality of man-made rules, we saw how the *Système D* favored social change by allowing the individual to by-pass the strangling mass of official red tape. In avoiding these entanglements of hierarchical red tape, however—for essentially this is the aim and accomplishment of the *Système D*—time and energy are wasted and the social organization itself is kept from evolving. Ironically, the rigidity of the political structure is increased because its rules are ignored at the same time they are accepted.

The French acceptance of hierarchy—even though the acceptance may be punctuated with cries of outrage or an escape into the devious paths of the *Système D*—points to a further characteristic of the French social organization which acts as a brake on social change. Each clearly defined unit within a hierarchy is aware of its rights and responsibilities in relation to other units in the system, and it is generally understood that one of the important functions of any superior authority is to protect the rights of his subordinates. Assured of this protection from above, every group barricades itself behind its "acquired rights" (*droits acquis*) and resists all movements for change; at the suggestion of a threat an organization is formed which invariably takes the name "Association for the defense of the rights of the . . ." In the blank space one may substitute the name of any group which feels its rights are under attack—"peasants," "middle classes," "savings bank investors," "taxpayers," "independent distillers," and on and on.[25]

This phenomenon is not uniquely French, of course, but it is acutely French. The authors of the Armand-Rueff Report, in their effort to discover the causes of "inhibitions, des blocages, des scléroses, des déséquilibres ou des contradictions qu'il convient d'éliminer" from the French economy, again and again point to the evil arising from the *droits acquis*, the *positions acquises*, of corporate groups of French people. They point out that the government has difficulty in correcting this fault because the government itself shares in the fault.[26]

Many examples, both spectacular and trivial, could be given to illustrate how the belief in the necessity to protect the rights of a group has kept social change from taking place in France in recent years. Poujade's principal appeal was that little merchants and artisans had a "right to exist" in French society. The most forceful argument of the Algerian Europeans is their claim that they have a "right to remain Frenchmen." The farmers blocked the roads with their tractors to call attention to the threat they face of losing their "rightful place in French society." The butchers of Paris resort to strikes and plastic explosives to protect themselves against what they consider discriminatory action. The government is frustrated in its attempt to dislodge the wine dealers from their *position acquise* along the Seine to make room for seriously needed expansion of educational facilities. The *bouilleurs de cru* (small independent distillers) have again and again insisted on their right to produce cheap alcohol even though the health of the nation is at stake.

A corollary to the existence of *droits acquis* in French society is the necessity which is felt to give equal treatment to parallel elements within the social organization. Within a hierarchy a responsibility of every member is to respect and preserve equality among subordinates belonging to the same rank. This is a concept which permeates most of French life. The principle of equality was a motivating force of the Revolution, one ideal of which was to suppress legal privileges of favored sections of the population such as first-born children who were favored by primogeniture. Many of the elaborate plans for the modernization and economic encouragement of the less favored regions of France have been justified by the principle of giving equal opportunities and thus establishing a more harmonious equilibrium of the country. The second and third terms of the national motto, *liberté, égalité, fraternité,* consecrate the principle of equal rights for similar elements within the social organization.

The necessity which the government feels, and which we have

already noted, to regroup (*remembrer*) the holdings of the French farmer into more efficient units is a direct result of this insistence in France on the principle of equality. In Chanzeaux, I was shown a small field that quite obviously used to be much larger than it is now. Originally it had been part of the farm which belonged to the grandfather of the present owner's wife. Because the old man had wanted to treat his two children with scrupulous equality, he did not simply divide his property into two parts when he died. Since no two fields are exactly the same, he left half of each field to each child, except in one instance. A particular field was on a slight slope, and the soil was better on the lower side than the upper. Accordingly this field was divided into four strips so that each heir might have one of good soil and one of bad.

Over the generations the principle of equality has brought about the division of much of France's agricultural land into these morsels that are inefficient to work, especially with modern equipment. The progress made in regrouping the morsels is slow and hardly keeps pace with the continual division of land which takes place from generation to generation.

Between December 19, 1961, and February 20, 1962, there was a strike in France in the coal mines of Decazeville. Its story is long, complicated, and intriguing. It illustrates the depth of the French concern for equality and for the protection of *droits acquis*.

The French coal industry has suffered the fate of mining elsewhere in the world. The government, which owns the mining industry in France, was said to be losing about thirty New Francs a ton on the extraction of coal in the Decazeville field. Clearly this situation could not go on indefinitely; therefore the government decided to abandon all the mines at Decazeville except the open-pit mines which could be run more economically. The closing was to take place gradually. Plans were made to protect and help the miners as the pits were closed.

When the first eight miners received notice in 1961 that they were being released from their jobs, eight hundred of their colleagues carried out a sit-down strike in the mines. Exactly what did the miners seek? They wanted the right to retire at the age of 55, ten years earlier than they would retire if they went into other work. They wanted the right to the social and medical benefits that government employees enjoy and which the miners would lose on going to work in private industry. Most of all, though, they did not want to move. They had a *right* to their place in society and would not give it up without consenting.[27]

The cause of the miners at Decazeville immediately captured the imagination of all France. The time was just before Christmas, and the nation was touched by the fate of these men who refused to be deprived of their rights. Every group tried to identify itself with them; it was just as though Frenchmen, by sponsoring the cause of the miners, were strengthening their own claims to one right or another.

But the government held firm. If it recognized the *droits acquis* of these miners, it would have to assure equal treatment to thousands of other workers in industry and commerce who might be dislocated by the economic change in France.

Meanwhile, the cause of the miners had become so popular that it became the driving force of a larger movement. The southeastern portion of the Massif Central, where Decazeville is located, had never participated fully in the prosperity of France because of its natural poverty; regional organizations had demanded government aid so this part of France should not be denied its "rightful share" of the nation's wealth. The cause of the miners now was identified with the cause of the region because their grievances were parallel. Each claimed rights equal to those of any other group on the same level in the hierarchy.[28]

The movement supporting the strikers continued to grow. Both moral support and money were sent to the miners. On January 22 two hundred representatives of organizations from the surrounding seventeen departments met in Rodez and made a statement supporting the miners: "Their fight is everyone's fight; their defeat would sound the death knell of the underdeveloped regions." [29]

Finally, however, the heat of the movement began to cool. After everyone had acknowledged the right of a group and a region to insist on their share of the nation's wealth, it came to be recognized that the cause of the miners was lost. Obviously, people said, coal could not be mined at a loss of thirty francs a ton.

After all, the miners' *droits acquis* were not the rights of a privileged caste which could be perpetuated forever.[30]

The strike at Decazeville did not prevent social change from taking place but social change was slowed by the determination of many groups to maintain the *status quo*. In France popular support is easily rallied, hours of time and a great deal of energy are spent when an association is formed for the "defense of the rights of . . . who do not wish to die." In the blank is written the name of any individual or group whose rights would seem to be in jeopardy.

THE SYMBOLS PEOPLE LIVE BY

The system of symbols the French have evolved to express their basic values is, like the social organization, a force working against change. As we have seen, the French attach great importance to defining and classifying observable units of existence. One result of the creation of these well-defined compartments has been the need for the further creation of labels by which the compartments might be easily identified; symbolic expression in France is, therefore, more elaborately and more subtly developed than in most cultures.

There is no segment of French life in which these symbols cannot be found and where their effect on social change cannot be seen. The symbol which has been developed to represent France itself is a perfect hexagon. With imagination one can see a similarity of the geographic form to the geometric figure. Generations of French school children from 1871 to 1914 saw every day a map of France with a corner (Alsace-Lorraine) split from the hexagon. More recently, the fact that Algeria was outside the hexagon may have helped console the French for the loss of this territory. Conversely, Algerian French refugees have a contemptuous epithet for metropolitan Frenchmen—"hexagons."

A homely example of the importance of a symbol was seen recently when a poll was taken in France to find out why dehydrated soups were not selling. It had been shown that presumably most people cannot tell a dehydrated soup from a home-made one and it had also been shown that it takes from one to three hours to make the evening soup for the average French *ménage*. Fifty-two percent of the women polled recognized that powdered soup was convenient but said they preferred not to buy it. Obviously they seldom did, for although 96 percent of the French eat soup once a day, the average consumption of powdered soup is only 10 bowls a year per Frenchman. "Madame Express" explained this phenomenon by pointing out the importance of the steaming soup tureen as a family symbol.

In truth, the use of dehydrated soups is blocked by an obstacle that lies deep in the personality of most women, and many of them are not even aware of it: the stereotyped image of the steaming soup tureen on the family table. *It is the symbol of the family.* Just like the father's bedroom slippers or the comfortable chair by the fireplace. The simmering soup with its suggestive aroma awaits the return of the husband and children just as the wife who has remained at home waits for them. To take away the wife's soup tureen is to deprive her of a considerable part of her prestige and authority.[31]

These symbols, the *signes extérieurs*, often come to be mistaken for the things themselves. To be sure, it is acknowledged that external appearances are deceptive; the gap between appearance and reality—and the consequences, either comic or tragic, of one's being mistaken for the other—is a frequent theme in French literature and movies. Nevertheless there is general acceptance among the French of *signes extérieurs* as criteria for judging existence.

A caricature of this acceptance is in Jules Romains' play *Topaze*. A seasoned teacher in the Muche Boarding School explains his method of keeping order in the classroom. One boy in the room is always held responsible for a particular kind of misdemeanor; there is never any need to look for the real culprit. The boy responsible for that particular kind of crime is punished when it occurs and the affair is settled; no one complains and order is kept. Besides, adds the teacher, nine times out of ten the chosen boy is actually the one who commits the misdeed—"parce qu'il a une tête à ça"— because he looks like the kind of boy who would do it!

The acceptance of the *signe extérieur* for the thing itself underlies the French tax system, too. The village tax commission decides from the nature of a field how much income a farmer should receive from it; whether he does or not is not taken into account. At the other extreme of the social gamut, the income of the very rich may also be judged by their visible possessions and expenditures. If there is a "marked disproportion" between their income as they officially report it and their income as it is suggested by their standard of living, the *signes extérieurs* are taken to be a more accurate indication of the real income. A definite scale is therefore set up by the government to translate the symbols into money. For example, it is assumed that if a man has a personal airplane he has 150 New Francs income for each horsepower of its motors. It is assumed that if he has a race horse he has an income of 6,000 New Francs—unless the horse is stabled outside the four departments of the Parisian area in which case the assumed income is reduced to 4,000 New Francs.

More than three-quarters of French businessmen and artisans never file an estimate of their income with tax authorities. Instead, under the system known as the *régime forfaitaire*, they simply supply information concerning sales, purchases, inventory, wages, and general expenses, and on the basis of these facts the authorities decide what the income of the taxpayer probably was and what taxes he should pay. If the taxpayer thinks the figure is unjust, he has the right to have his real income calculated, but in practice this almost never happens. Appearances are a sufficient indication of reality for practical purposes; it is on the symbols of a man's wealth that his actual wealth is measured.[32]

This system of symbols, which permeates all aspects of life in France, is a force inhibiting social change primarily because by definition a symbol has its roots in the past and can never presage new developments. The French, with their awareness of two levels of reality, realize that a symbol is only a superficial representation of the thing itself, but there is inevitably a tendency to overlook this distinction in making a judgment. People and situations are identified, thought about, and judged by their symbols. A problem arises when situations change; since the symbols remain the same, the stereotypes on the basis of which people think and act are outmoded and have only a tenuous relationship with reality.

In 1793 Chanzeaux along with the other communities in the "Vendée angevine" revolted against the new Republican government. The reasons for this revolt are obscure and complex, but in the nineteenth century a myth grew, explaining and justifying the rebellion. It is the explanation generally accepted in the Vendée today and is the basis for the symbols which motivate its political life. According to the myth, the Vendée revolt was a spontaneous uprising of the people trying to protect their religion, their king, and their nobles from attacks by a hostile government.

On the stained glass windows in the church at Chanzeaux are the names of the villagers who died in the Vendée war—"pour la religion et pour la patrie." This "patrie" is, of course, not the "patrie" of the *Marseillaise;* it is the "patrie" of the kings who ruled France before the Revolution. For many years the people of the Vendée rejected Republican France and thereby alienated themselves from the rest of the country. Their political representatives in Paris were frequently of the nobility and consistently sat to the far right in the chamber.

Sitting on the left and opposing the deputies elected by the people of Chanzeaux were the representatives of the Vaucluse, for whom the people of Roussillon had voted. Roussillon, since its history was different, has a set of symbols very different from those in Chanzeaux. In the Revolution, because the Vauclusiens in order to become citizens of France had had to revolt against the Pope (who was their sovereign), their revolutionary hero, the young Viala, was a man who gave his life to prevent Catholic and Royalist troops from crossing the Durance River.

These two sets of symbols are still powerful today and, through the representatives in Paris, separate the people of Chanzeaux from those of Roussillon. Since I know both communities and feel how much they have in common, I see the irony of this separation. They have no real quarrel with each other, but the symbols the two communities have inherited keep them apart.

The religious behavior of the two communities also seems very different. The huge church in Chanzeaux is almost filled twice every Sunday. Roussillon has a small church which, however, is too large for even the handful of people who regularly attend Mass; it is filled only for funerals. The people in Chanzeaux sacrifice to maintain two Catholic schools, although the state offers a free education.

In Roussillon the only school is the state school. Still, priests living in both areas feel that in each community the majority of the people simply follow the religious traditions established by historical accident in their region, so that even religious belief in the two communities is not, in the opinion of those who know the problem best, really so different as it seems. Most of the people of Chanzeaux go to Mass because in Chanzeaux one goes to Mass; in Roussillon the custom is not to go to Mass. Religiously as well as politically Chanzeaux and Roussillon have far more in common than they think. Yet, when their leaders brandish the slogans representing 1793 and 1905, the continuing power of the symbols acts as a deterrent to the process of national integration.

Just as the people of Chanzeaux and the people of Roussillon are alienated from each other by the disparity of symbols which motivate them, so many communities and groups within communities are separated from each other because of their symbols. Growing up, a child learns with what symbols his family identifies itself. Beyond the limits of the family he becomes aware of groups of people, of *cercles*, with which he and his family are either associated or not. He recognizes the associations through many symbols, some small, some important, some obvious, some hidden from all but the initiate. Clothing, food, dress, language, education, profession, all reveal membership in one circle or another.

Within the totality of French culture, these circles are fused into still larger groups, *familles d'esprit* (ideological families). They exist in every area of French life, although they have scarcely been studied except in their political manifestations. Thus Albert Thibaudet describes the six political families of France as the Traditionalist, the Liberal, the Industrialist, the Christian, the Jacobin, and the Socialist.[33] At any moment in French history we can pick out these *familles d'esprit*. Their problems change, the goals change, but the attitude of each family to the others remains the same. Each thinks that it represents the best in France, and that all would be well if "the others" would either reform or desist. Each says, "Pauvre France," how she is put upon by "les autres" who ought to be supporting her! Only very occasionally has a consensus been achieved among all these *familles*, and most often there has been a compromise satisfactory to none or else the stalemate that Stanley Hoffmann describes.

During the First World War a working agreement was achieved among the various members of the national family. The *Union Sacrée* is one of the few instances when *les familles d'esprit* sacrificed their own interests for what seemed the good of all France. Increasingly during the Second World War and again in 1958 it looked as though a *Union Sacrée* could be achieved again through the appeal of one individual.

De Gaulle has appealed to each of the spiritual families without seeming to favor any one over the others. Like a good head of the household, playing favorites with no child—but satisfying no one completely—he seemed to be motivated primarily by a desire to preserve the identity and to work for the welfare of the national family as a whole. He addressed his appeal to all the political families in ways which were significant and meaningful for their particular sets of symbols. De Gaulle was himself a member of the Traditionalist family and spoke easily in its terms. His rejection of extremists of both the right and the left gave reassurance to the Liberal family. To the state planners of the Industrialist family that sought to renovate economic France, he gave full rein. His religious devotion appealed to the Christian family. His direct appeal to the people in 1940, 1944, 1958, and 1961 related him to the Jacobin family. His preoccupation with building a better future made him acceptable to many within the Socialist family. "Besides," an old French Socialist said to justify his support of de Gaulle, "what other political leader has earned public gratitude by actually putting generals in prison?"

The most serious opponents of de Gaulle have been the most partisan elements within each *famille d'esprit*. He has attempted to demonstrate that like Louis IX and Henri IV he seeks not to favor any one group but to work for the welfare of the French people as a whole. He leads his audiences, *les enfants de la patrie,* in singing *la Marseillaise,* and at the same time he insists that the French should rise above partisan slogans, above the Republican slogan *liberté, égalité, fraternité,* above the Vichy slogan *travail, famille, patrie.* Instead, to reduce the effect of partisan symbols which inhibit constructive change, he has coined a new slogan, well anchored in the past, in the name of which he hopes all Frenchmen may unite in a common effort for the sake of *la patrie*. This new slogan is: *puissance, fraternité, grandeur*—power, fraternity, grandeur. General de Gaulle told the nation:

The condition which dominates the whole future of France is that her children unite in a great national task. Today, as always, it is through collective ambition that we will conquer our divisions and find hope and faith. What task, what ambition? Those which are dictated to us simultaneously by the nature of our times and of the world in which we live, the necessities of life for our people, the great impetus which is already making itself felt and which will be swelled as the great number of our young people join the ranks. The development of France—that is the vast undertaking which offers us power, fraternity, grandeur.[34]

Beyond *la patrie* there is another France which certain people in the world embrace as the symbol of man's ability to rise above the chaos of matter—*la civilisation française*. French art, architecture, music, literature, cuisine, etiquette, and fashion are woven into an image which over a long period of time has appealed to the need for refinement felt by a few people in many countries. This devotion is strengthened by a feeling that only in France can the individual live the fullest expression of his personality.

For these Francophiles the recent changes in French society are alarming. They see the same forces impinging on France as elsewhere in the world, because the forces for change which we have observed are not peculiar to France. Other societies have felt the impact of massive catastrophes in the last twenty years. The effects of technological progress are universal. France's demographic expansion is a part of the world population explosion. Everywhere rural communities are being urbanized, social barriers are being lowered, cultures are being integrated into larger entities. Everywhere the state is intervening more in the lives of individuals and of smaller groups within the state. The Francophiles assume that "their" France is rapidly losing its characteristic qualities.

I hope that with a clearer understanding of the ways in which change has always been a part of the French scene and the ways in which the French social structure itself has acted as a brake to this change, the lovers of French civilization will not find the developments in France so distressing. They may be reassured by the fact that the essential values in French culture change relatively little. The basic French conceptions of reality, man, and time have evolved much more slowly over the last hundreds of years than the rate of social change might have led us to expect. French culture does change, but it still gives expression to the values which we intimately associate with the French.

The late Gaston Berger coined a slogan which he thought might express a France in which the old values could coexist with new technological forms: *culture, qualité, liberté*. This is a slogan which can be accepted by the people of Chanzeaux and Roussillon as well as by people elsewhere in the world who feel themselves at one with *la civilisation française*.

CONTINUITY AND CHANGE IN BOURGEOIS FRANCE

Jesse R. Pitts

THE problems that France has encountered in developing new economic and political structures for the twentieth century can scarcely be understood without studying the traditional values of the French society. My purpose is to offer a scheme for a better understanding of France's learning problems, not just since the cataclysm of the 1940's but during the last sixty years or so. My approach is to analyze the society through the values of its culture and through the basic groups and institutions forming the warp and woof of its social structure. Values will be described on the basis of known historical manifestations of class behavior—especially the behavior of the aristocracy and the bourgeoisie.

The analysis of a total society is a dangerous endeavor; our theoretical tools are limited, our knowledge of the relevant data is poor, and there is always a risk of calling something "French" that is found generally in European societies. But the intellectual attempt must be made, for it is only through such attempts that our theories and our identification of the strategic facts will improve. The importance of values in such a study has long been recognized by learned travelers and essayists such as Ernst Curtius, Friedrich Sieburg, and Count Keyserling.[1] They speak in terms of French personality or French character which, when confronted with the choices of life, produces decisions different from those that would be made by a German or an Englishman. No doubt my approach owes much to these insights. In any case I go on the assumption that the terms of adaptation to conditions are not automatically given by some sort of hedonistic or *Realpolitik* utilitarianism; that one of the major elements of this adaptation is what a society wants, how it defines the good life; and that this varies from one nation to another depending on their values. Hence the emphasis on values and their institutional incarnations, rather than on other factors such as the presence or absence of coal, the climate, the birth rate, predatory neighbors, or simply the weight of past history.

I shall try to construct a model of the traditional French value system and some of its crucial incarnations. Some salient features of the model are the French concept of *prowess*, which stems from aristocratic attitudes and which is highly individualistic but at the same time rooted in authoritative principles of order; the French *bourgeois family* with its many implications for social behavior; and a special kind of comradeship, the *delinquent community*, which is closely linked to the "peer group" of pupils in the traditional French school. Formulation of the value model will be followed by an attempt to show how recent forces of change have modified aristocratic and bourgeois values and have affected French society.

The aristocracy and the bourgeoisie, of course, make up only a small fraction of the French population, perhaps 3 or 4 percent. Their great importance resides in their having provided a model for those below them in the social hierarchy. Each of them is found in what are commonly called, in English, the "upper class" and the "upper-middle class." The aristocrats make up perhaps 15 percent of the two classes combined, the situation being complicated by the fact that "passing" from the bourgeoisie to the aristrocracy is fairly easy; at least half the aristocratic-sounding names in the French social register are not legitimate. The other 85 percent consists of the true bourgeoisie, with the *haute bourgeoisie* being in the upper class and the *bonne bourgeoisie* in the upper-middle class. To be a bourgeois, strictly speaking, requires at least one previous generation in a bourgeois occupation, such as industrialist, high civil servant, doctor. Hence many people in bourgeois occupations must endure the ambiguous status of one who is in the process of "passing." Below the upper and upper-middle classes are the *classes moyennes*—a term which covers two middle-class groups that will be encountered again later, one being the so-called "middle-middle" class (people who may be upper-middle in education but not in occupation or style of life), the other being the "lower-middle" class, otherwise known as the *petite bourgeoisie*, or petty-bourgeoisie. Down through these levels to the broader masses of the people has flowed the influence of aristocratic and bourgeois values.

I

THE TRADITIONAL FRENCH VALUE SYSTEM

CATHOLICISM AND PROWESS

In analyzing the value system of any Western society one must refer to Christianity. In studying France we must look at Roman Catholicism. All religious systems contain internal tensions, contradictions, and ambiguities; and how these are resolved depends in part upon cultural tradition and social structure. Hence one may speak of a French Catholicism as against a Spanish or an Italian or an Irish Catholicism. For example, in French Catholicism one does not find the emphasis on death and the dangers of damnation found in Spanish Catholicism, nor the puritanism found in Irish Catholicism. Although these differences seem to be important to the understanding of national cultures, we know very little about them. We do know, however, that Catholicism in general, as compared with Protestantism, especially of the Calvinist variety, is not interested in building the City of God upon this earth through the application of science (a combination of human reason and will) to Nature. In the eyes of Rome this is Protestant pride. Catholicism is more interested in increasing the power of the Church, which acts as the apostle of Christ on earth. Through sacraments and dogma a contact with the Divine is maintained which transcends human reason, human utility, and the sins of church members. It is as church members that human beings reach their highest level of value achievement. *It is the organization that is divine,* and no salvation can be gained outside this organization.

The power of the Church has a material aspect which involves it in the world, and an even more important spiritual aspect which is strengthened by every act of faith accomplished by man. And this is where we meet one of the main tensions in the Catholic value and idea system: acts of faith derive their meaning from man's freedom of choice in the face of temptation. This is the individualistic strain in Catholicism. The Church recognizes the possibility, even the desirability, of any Catholic's sharing contact with God directly through prayer, ecstasy, and special signs. But it is only through membership in the Church that the individual has qualified for this special grace, and he is supposed to use it to strengthen the Church rather than strike out for salvation on his own, as the Puritan of "Pilgrim's Progress" would be expected to do. This is the collectivistic strain in Catholicism. Since the Church's wisdom is greater than that of man, the act of faith will mean the choice to obey the commands of the Church, a genuine contrition for sins, and a commitment to greater effort to defeat the tempter. The Church prevents any individual from harming the Church through sinful or uninformed action. The Church represents the spiritual capital of mankind in a world of sin, and is the intercessor, the helper, the defender, the protector of the sinner who shows a true desire to be saved, even if his flesh be too weak. The supreme value of free choice and the sanctity of the *Church qua organization* create the crucial Catholic dilemma.

Faced with this basic tension in Catholicism, French culture has stressed the inner cohesion and perfection of doctrine rather than the discipline of organization. In this doctrinaire direction the free will of man has been interpreted more in the reflexive sense of reason and comprehension than as a force for systematic action upon the world. The result has been to put upon the Church the burden of remaining intellectually meaningful on a sophisticated basis. The stress on doctrine and upon rationalization has produced a remarkable array of theologians and dissenting movements which have given Rome many difficult moments.

Nevertheless there has been an effective commitment to the Church's unity since the Church was a body that had a theological (doctrinaire) and sacramental continuity with Christ. The effort is to influence the consensus—the Church's doctrine—toward one's point of view, rather than divide it.

We find here, in what could be called the "doctrinaire-hierarchical" aspect of French Catholicism, a trait that seems fairly specific to French culture. This trait is a commitment to a nexus of authoritative ideas which incarnate the highest spirituality. In religious terms the nexus is the Church, in secular terms the Nation. There is a conviction that all behavior should have a clear deductive connection to this spirituality through rules, principles, regulations which insure inherent value to the action. It is not necessary that the action be effective, or even altogether moral, as long as it demonstrates the link of the individual to the sacred tradition. Here we find the roots of French formalism, the demand for deductive chains of reasoning and hierarchy, the insistence upon the unity of the power center, and formulations where everything and everybody is *à sa place* (in its place). Individuality here means finding one's position in the hierarchy and using it as an anchor for one's thoughts and even for one's deviance. Aspects of French social structure that seem to implement this doctrinaire-hierarchical theme are the centralizing and formalistic features of the civil service, and its technocratic tradition.

Another aspect of French Catholicism is the "aesthetic-individualistic" theme, which was strongly reinforced by the humanist "reform" of the Renaissance. Here the whole of Nature—which includes society—assumes a divine quality. The proper goal of man is to reveal this divine quality through understanding and aesthetic appreciation. He must become attuned to the spirituality that is incarnated in Nature. *In this process he is his own authority.*

This approach is still compatible with Catholic allegiance, although it is more sensitive to the artistic and supportive nature of the Holy Mother, the Church, than to the rigor of its doctrine. It sees in pleasure of aesthetic experience, of ecstasy, the clearest signs of grace. Yet this grace is not accessible without a long period of preparation, realized usually, though not necessarily, by an exacting education and thorough familiarity with the basic principles and organic realities of one's existence such as family and community. This is *enracinement* (rootedness) which replaces the logical connection to the sacred body of ideas, so essential to the "doctrinaire-hierarchical" theme described above. *Enracinement* puts one in harmony with God's creation. Here the action of the individual is to reveal the sacred content of the world, rather than disturb the equilibrium of the world. This aesthetic-individualistic polarity in French Catholicism exists in atheistic, deistic, or even orthodox Catholic varieties: in the latter case we have a sort of anti-clerical Catholicism. If the doctrinaire-hierarchical polarity corresponds to the centralizing and logico-deductive aspects of French life, the aesthetic-individualistic polarity corresponds to its humanist and aristocratic tendencies.

Although there is a certain tension between the two polarities, they also complement each other. The aesthetic-individualistic polarity needs the framework of principles and the security of membership provided by the Church if its individualism is to be compatible with the order necessary for the maintenance of society. The doctrinaire-hierarchical polarity cannot but recognize the ethical value of the individual's freedom of choice and—on its own hierarchical grounds—the fact that the individual soul is closest to the problems of implementation raised by the Church's commands. Both stress communion with the Harmony of Ideas that defines the City of God. In one view this communion is reached by the aesthetic-intuitive methods of the autonomous individual, in the other by rational deductive methods within a holy organization (Church, State). But, in both views, communion with the Harmony of Ideas is the way to salvation, and both have been represented in either of the Right or Left ideologies which have divided Frenchmen.

The search for salvation—in secular terms the search for success—is pressed in different ways according to whether the search is made in the hierarchical-doctrinaire direction or in the aesthetic-individualistic direction. In the first case we have the attempt to reach the higher levels of the hierarchy through encyclopedic knowledge, the discovery of universal solutions, and disciplined service to a valued organization. In the second case we have the phenomenon of *prouesse* (prowess). Of course none of the structures nor any complex pattern of action will ever be a pure and exclusive expression of either one of these two value polarities. They will be syntheses where one or the other dominates. Prowess deserves special attention because it is a type of action which is less understood and yet it is a greater component of behavior in France than in other European countries.

Prowess is a conspicuous act by which an individual signals his success in reaching, within particular circumstances, the highest possible level of value achievement attainable by man. What matters in prowess, though, is not success in terms of increased power or wealth for the community or for oneself. Prowess does not concern itself with utility. "Do what you must, happen what may" is an expression typical of the spirit of prowess. Another one is "All is lost but honor." Historically, *faire des prouesses* meant to perform a noteworthy act of valor, to perform it spontaneously and unpredictably although the principles governing and limiting the act were clearly defined and well known. At Roncevaux, Roland by an act of faith in the principles of chivalry seized an opportunity to turn adverse circumstances into an occasion for the triumph of the spirit. Today, as earlier, prowess must be spontaneous: it is not a tormented surmounting of oneself, but rather the discovery and demonstration of a harmony between the self and the environment in the service of the divine. Here Nature provides man with the occasion of honoring God through demonstrating the primacy of the spirit. Man becomes leader of a rite in which Nature reveals the design of God.

Prowess depends for its formulation and evaluation upon canons of value which are given to it by the Church—or by the traditions of the Nation-State. These are he *principes*. Prowess consists in the application of these *principes* to particular situations that result in elegant solutions where the immutability of principles, their sacred character, and the talent (grace) of the individual are clearly revealed. It is an "act of faith" and reinforces the commitment of its author and of his witnesses to the true faith.

The application of the principle is an element of individual decision, not reducible to rational components available to all. Rather it is a question of instinct, of intuition, and contingent opportunity. When knowledge intervenes as a variable, it is not so much systematic knowledge as it is insight.

Although the concept of prowess evokes the notion of an elite, prowess in fact is theoretically available to anyone who has deep enough roots in the locale of his action (*enracinement*), or, more generally, in the field of his prowess. For prowess is not a perfect solution for any problem at any time, but rather the concept of the conspicuously perfect—miraculous—solution by which one person triumphs over a unique situation. What can be imitated is the skill in finding the occasion when the individual can demonstrate his capacity. And prowess can be found at all levels. The creation of a piece of jewelry by a Parisian craftsman, the peasant's careful distillation of a liqueur, the civilian's stoicism in the face of Gestapo torture, Marcel Proust's suave gallantry in the salon of Madame de Guermantes—all are examples of prowess in modern France.

Prowess depends upon an opportunity and a capacity which cannot be predicted. It depends upon a gift of grace which can be withheld. The concept of prowess is not the Judaic-Protestant concept of election, which implies a commitment of God to the individual and which makes him "saved" forever. In French prowess there is little of the Protestant "calling" with its rationalization, systematization, and reliability of individual behavior.

In any society with an individualistic value system—whether of the aesthetic or puritan type—personalities are bound to have a problem of self-validation which is not raised so acutely by collectivistic value systems. In a society with puritan values this self-validation will be achieved through pragmatic success that is objectively measured: profit, buildings, discoveries, and so on. In the aesthetic-individualistic value system, self-validation cannot claim such objective tokens because the personal component of the actions is so important. Hence validation has to bear on the total personality. Is this a man of taste? Is this a man of honor? These questions are answered in the affirmative when the author of prowess wins unconditional support through some form of love. His act is validated in his own eyes when the spectator to it acknowledges the irresistible appeal of both the man and the deed. Thus the spectator of prowess is "seduced" by its author. In turn, the spectator shares the values the deed represents.

To illustrate this point let us take the example of the military. It is commonly said of a successful French officer that "his men adored him; they would do anything for him." The ideal group under these conditions is *la bande*, a group with minimum organization, where all members are equal in their common subordination to the leader and where the *bande* shares the superiority of the leader by protecting him. The relation between superior and inferior in this context has many of the aspects of romantic love. The leader seduces. The *bande* reciprocates with unconditional support. The gratuitousness of the support is all the more evident if the leader goes against generally recognized authority or traditional practice. Love in the context of prowess leadership must be gratuitous. Since there is no other aim in the relationship but to be with the leader, there is no uncertainty about the hero's validation.

The support the *bande* gives the leader is necessary to validate his action, but this support also validates the *bande*'s own behavior. In this type of leadership the author of prowess requires either enthusiastic passivity (the spectator's role) or an imitation of his goal for prowess. The leader's action lifts his followers beyond themselves. They partake of his essence; there is no more inequality. This is one of the major paradoxes of the aesthetic-individualistic value system and of its cult of prowess: it promotes a very jealous equalitarianism. First, everybody is capable of prowess, and second, prowess is created by the recognition of the spectator as much as by the actions of the hero.

A consequence of the stress upon prowess, with its equalitarianism and its contingencies, is that it raises very acutely the problem of order. This is solved in France by: (1) the existence of a state that is immune to seduction because it follows a logic that is not of this world, this fact explaining all at once its strength, its legitimacy, and its unrealism; (2) the respect for any stable system of rights and duties such as the *positions acquises;* and (3) above all, the strong demand that is made upon individuals by that sense of proportion and appropriateness which is expressed in the familiar French ideal of *mesure*.

Mesure is an important ingredient in French classical thought, derived from the Greek idea that the unforgivable sin was defying the natural order according to which each man must keep to his proper place and function. *Mesure* requires that every author of prowess should avoid damaging the fabric of society and its network of *positions acquises*. *Mesure* is reason applied to human action, the result being that certain areas are considered legitimate and suitable for acts of prowess. In a relatively stable society the best fields for prowess must be those where unpredictability of performance can be high without endangering social order—for example, limited warfare (preferably in colonial lands); conspiracies that never succeed; contemplative religion; missionary activities; gratuitous personal relationships (love, friendship, *politesse*); craftsmanship; and elegant selection and use of consumer goods.

Thus, although prowess is intuitive, intensely individual, and unpredictable, the limitations necessary to maintain the stability of the social order are built into the *principes* on which prowess itself is based. The French do not have the cult of the tragic surmounting of self that is characteristic of the Germans. Prowess is above all the discovery of the predetermined harmony, rather than the imposition of a personal will.

ARISTOCRATIC PRESTIGE AND THE FRENCH ECONOMY

The prestige of the aristocracy in classical France was based on its dedication to the values of aesthetic individualism and in particular to its expression of the concept of prowess. Because traditionally the aristocrat was free from the responsibility of saving money and earning a living, he could devote his full attention to performing deeds of prowess. Limited only by the necessity to act *comme il faut* and challenged to exhibit spontaneity and individuality, the French aristocrat developed models of elegance and taste. In matters of love, war, dress, housing, and conversation he showed the world how the application of the principle of prowess could affect these everyday concerns.

Though the aristocracy provided—and provides—a model, it is not a caste forever out of reach of the rest of French families. For the French, all children are barbarians who must be tamed and molded ruthlessly to adult standards. The aristocratic family believes that it has an inherent capacity to provide good education. Since it claims universality—that is, that its culture can and should be assimilated by anyone lucky enough to be within its reach—it must accept the consequence that training can be accomplished successfully by families which have accepted this culture, even though they are not related by blood with the originators. Being *bien né* (well born) gives an advantage; the aristocrat's traditions and rootedness in elegance and taste give him naturally what others can reach only through effort. But he also believes that one can become *bien élevé* (well brought up) and *distingué* (refined) without necessarily being *bien né*.

Thus the advantages of aristocratic traditions and rootedness are not beyond the reach of persons from outside the aristocracy, and this is especially true where prowess deals with consumption. Money, whatever its original source, opens up a possibility for prowess which is not as easily accessible when prowess depends upon specialized training or organizational support, such as prowess in war or in political administration. It is easier to show oneself a man of taste than to show oneself to be a brilliant officer, a clever diplomat, a saintly monk, or a dedicated Jesuit. Good taste means doing particularly well what must be done anyway; it is an art of everyday living and theoretically accessible to anyone. It is also a mode of living that is very expensive and thus creates in the French aristocracy a continuing demand for money. By the same token, when a non-aristocrat has wealth the possibilities for prowess are greatly increased. Because of the aristocracy's emphasis on education and talent rather than on the superiority of its blood, there is competition within its own circles and from those in other strata of society who accept aristocratic standards of taste. And because of its emphasis on elegant consumption the aristocracy has maintained close contacts with the professionals of the crafts that are most closely involved in problems of taste of universal reference: literature, fine arts, music. Almost anybody who could compete successfully with the aristocracy in conspicuous and tasteful expenditure or the creation of acceptable new fashions has been entertained by it. Money also opened the *salons* to those willing to subsidize the aristocrats by giving their own daughters big dowries and to follow aristocratic patterns. This has permitted many bourgeois families to attach themselves to the aristocracy through marriage, and through the addition to their names of the particle "de."

The paradox of the aristocratic values of prowess is that they turn out to be the most democratic, because in one's little sphere where one has roots, it is always possible to reach the unique and perfect solution of prowess. The broad diffusion of aristocratic-aesthetic-individualistic values in French society is due to this, and also to the essential role played by the spectator to the aristocrat's deeds of prowess. As in the case of the officer and his soldiers, the aristocrat has been successful in exhibiting his prowess only when others have acknowledged it and thus shared in it. A further reason for the general acceptance of French aristocratic values is the strength of the bond the aristocracy has had to the literary world. Descriptions of upper-class behavior gave the bourgeoisie and middle classes the same vicarious pleasures they now find in the movies. Moreover the assumption of aristocratic symbols by bourgeois families eager to climb socially is not considered a heinous crime. Indeed, because of the universality and relative accessibility of the aristocratic values of consumption prowess, an intense current of upward mobility exists through all the French society.

What were some of the consequences of these values for the French economy, prior to the Second World War?

As the industrial revolution gained headway in France, certain characteristics essential to its growth were seen to be incompatible with the aristocratic concept of the role of the consumer. In a bourgeois capitalist economy, economic action must be governed by the encouragement of sales, a concern for consumer demands, an acceptance of the need for specialization, and the necessity to keep costs as low as possible in order to increase profits. The aristocrat's tradition of devoting his life to proving himself through his prowess could not fit into this framework.

The aristocrat had traditionally been a consumer *par excellence* but there was no possibility of his becoming a salesman. Offering something for sale implies that it can be rejected; and this contradicts the theoretical irrelevance of the public in the realm of prowess (although in fact acceptance and recognition by the spectator were basic to the success of each individual's acts of prowess). In a way the aristocrat was a salesman, selling himself and his values while pretending not to care; but commercial selling would have violated the requirement for prowess both by subordinating the seller to the *random customer* and by denying the aristocrat's generalized superiority. To encourage sales, one must subject the value of the product to the judgment of anyone.

The value of goods produced for the market is determined by society's needs and wishes rather than by their value to the producer. Theoretically the reverse was true for the aristocrat; to *faire des prouesses* was its own reward. The aristocratic tradition was rather to direct craftsmen in the creation of objects according to individual taste and specifications.

Specialization implies the necessity of focusing on a limited area of problem-solving and is therefore contrary to the aristocratic belief in a man's capacity for top performance in any area he may choose. The refusal to specialize is a favored theme in French education, which aims to create cultured gentlemen—the *honnêtes hommes* of the seventeenth and eighteenth centuries. In refusing to specialize, the aristocrat also refused the dependency which goes with specialization.

Finally, the aristocrat could not accept the economic necessity of keeping down costs because for him perfection and not price was the measure of the worth of an object or a deed. Costs were irrelevant; even the value of his own expended time could not be considered. To use economic terms, the aristocrat felt he must act as if the expenditure of his energy always produced the highest marginal utility.

These incompatibilities, of course, did not make the French nobility indifferent to the process of industrialization. But some activities were more acceptable than others. The aristocrat could enter an economic organization which had a political dimension as conspicuous as its purely economic one. Organizations which centralize savings and create credit fall in that category. Besides, the man wanting to buy banking credit usually comes as a solicitor; thus there is no problem of being judged by inferiors. Firms which produce basic raw materials or which produce essential services such as railway transportation are in a position where the individual customer exercises little sanction power over them. In steel and mining the economic organization assumes the posture of a sort of benevolent purveyor to the nation or a direct retainer of the state. In fact, as David Landes [2] points out, the prestige of industries varies in direct proportion to their distance from the random customer.

Once the economic organization was defined as a retainer of the state it was entitled to favored treatment from the state, which guaranteed opportunities for profit through monopolies, selective immunity for the violations of regulations, blocking of entry into the field, discouragement of foreign competition, and other props characteristic of what Max Weber calls "politically oriented capitalism." The history of French railroad building under the sponsorship of the state-financed Freycinet plan is a good example of political capitalism. [3]

The man of aristocratic values, bringing to industry the attitudes which elsewhere win him prestige and power, is not primarily interested in the applied-science aspects of production or in the problems of adding value to the goods or services produced. He will visualize the firm as being superior to its customers, inferior to the state, and hostile toward the rest of the world. His executive function will be—through shrewd diplomacy—to neutralize the threats of competitors, the greed of the random customers, and the fickleness of the government. He will think of his remuneration more as tribute than as payment for a performance objectively measured. He assumes that "the world owes him a living." He represents for the whole society the rewards that must accrue to the exercise of certain virtues regardless of their contribution to the wealth of the nation.

The importance of this aristocratic point of view was the marked influence it had upon those groups which aspired to identify themselves with the aristocracy. Bourgeois families tried to assume as soon as possible a *rentier* relationship with the economy. Both capital and executive ability were therefore withdrawn from business pursuits, and the economic growth of France was slower than one would have expected from the human and material resources that existed.

I have been emphasizing the aesthetic-individualistic values held by the aristocracy and those groups which accepted its social leadership. The aristocracy, in its pattern of living, shows a higher concentration of aesthetic-individualistic values than of doctrinaire-hierarchical ones. On the other hand, the classical French bourgeoisie, whose center of gravity was to be found more among lawyers and civil servants than among merchants, showed a higher concentration of doctrinaire-hierarchical values. During the nineteenth century the two great value streams were combined in new creative forms. This could be seen during the first Napoleonic period; and later the Saint-Simonian movement tried to give to the economy a prowess interpretation and yet at the same time to fit private enterprise into a general plan of social organization. But the two sets of values have been adapted and combined most successfully in institutions where there is a common attitude toward property, authority, and the terms under which a group is organized. The existence of these syntheses is responsible for the fact that industrialization did not fundamentally alter the social pattern inherited from the *ancien régime:* the industrialists merely became another set of notables combining many of the functions of the old rural aristocracy and of the traditional burgher. Two such institutional syntheses are the bourgeois family and what I shall call the "delinquent community." Although these two institutions have declined in strength in the last twenty years or so, a knowledge of them is still indispensable for the understanding of contemporary France.

THE BOURGEOIS FAMILY

The French bourgeois family traditionally stressed emotional dependency between the members of the family rather than the formalism and detachment often affected in the "pure" aristocratic family. It is precisely because many aristocratic families in the eighteenth and nineteenth centuries did in fact adopt this emotionality that the bourgeois family became a true integrative institution for French society. The climate of emotionality between the parents and their children was a factor in the abandonment of primogeniture; it became difficult to discriminate in the giving of property, since one did not discriminate in the giving of affection.

Another factor working against primogeniture is the way the "nuclear family" (parents-children) is embedded in the "extended family" (grandparents, uncles, aunts, cousins, great uncles, second cousins, etc.). In France the dominance of the paternal line was not maintained as strongly as in Italy or Germany. We have in France true bilaterality. Both lines of kinship—the father's and mother's—are equally important to the nuclear family. For this reason problems often arise from conflicting loyalties, making it hard for the nuclear family to act as a united group. The French bourgeois family has partially solved this problem by supporting some strong personality in the larger family group who carves out a "patronage" empire and presents an overriding claim for the loyalty of his relatives. Such leaders are usually the richest and most successful members of the kin group; hence the nuclear family which attaches itself to each leader is likely to benefit from its associations. Conflicting claims within the extended family may cause a nuclear family temporarily to suspend a relationship through the device of the family quarrel. The seat of authority in the extended bourgeois family is never permanently fixed. Some branch is sure to challenge it.

Within the nuclear family, however, the parents try to be omnipresent and undisputed. The child is allowed little initiative—officially. The proper forms of behavior, the *principes*, exist once and for all, and parents require perfect performance before the child is allowed to make his own decisions.

Although parental authority and particularly the father's authority are theoretically unquestioned, the child of six and over soon perceives that there are possibilities for evasion and relief. In the kin group of which the nuclear family is a part there are relatives whose prestige may equal, if not exceed, that of the father's. When these relatives offer the child preferential treatment, he can find oases of relaxation and security from the exacting pres-

sures, particularly those of his father. These preferential relationships are one of the child's main sources of spontaneous and sensual
pleasure in a society which prizes pleasure highly. The child is
taught both implicitly and explicitly that without knowing how to
please (*savoir plaire*) one is not *distingué* (refined).

The French child continually attempts, in face-to-face encounters, to create these preferential relationships with extended kin
(and sometimes even within his own nuclear family), although he
realizes that these demands are somewhat illegitimate. In terms of
the aesthetic-individualistic tradition which makes every man the
priest of Nature's truth, he has a right to these preferences. In terms
of the doctrinaire-hierarchical values upon which paternal authority
is based, his demands are illegitimate because they bypass parental
authority and because the preferential relationship is part of the
power struggle within the extended family. A grandmother seeks
a new protégé; an uncle wants an admirer. For the child the new
relationship implies guilty secrets and betrayal of his parents. On
the other hand, the nuclear family encourages these preferential
relationships in the hope that they will lead to increased prestige
or property. Thus a strain is felt in the preferential relationship.
It is love but also interest, and a change in the interest aspect can
challenge the justification for continuing the relationship, for the
individual owes his first allegiance to the nuclear family and the
second to his own pleasure.

When face-to-face encounters do not result in the formation of
a preferential relationship, hostility is likely to follow; the other
person is *pas juste* (unjust) and gives a preference to someone else.
"Who is not with me is likely to be against me." An elaborate
politeness pattern will permit holding down the expression of this
hostility and will make it possible to preserve a future in which the
rejected of today may become the favorite.

Within the nuclear family, the authority of the father depends
on his aloofness. By avoiding intimacy, he can embody justice; he
is immune to the attempts a child makes to seduce other members
of the family. Only the mother can be intimate with all her children and not be accused of having succumbed to persuasion or
wiles. In the formal relationship, especially between the child and

his father, the child's need for pleasure cannot be satisfied. Compliance with the rules testifies to the child's respect for authority while he finds pleasure under the secrecy and protection of a preferential relationship. The child realizes that each member of the family is equal on the formalized and authoritarian level; but he also knows that each member is expected to satisfy his needs for pleasure by paying only lip-service to this concept of equality. Thus the French child learns to expect that his need for love will be gratified by some illicit relationship.

We may now ask what are the consequences of these family roles for the future citizen roles the child will be called upon to play. First, the child constructs in his mind two sacred extra-familial collectivities: the state and the motherland. Though the bourgeois child is very early made aware of God and the Church, these categories tend to dissolve into the two secular collectivities, state and motherland. They correspond to the ideal parental couple. The state is the arbiter, the judge, the source of the *principes* (unconditional rules of conduct) which must govern behavior. The motherland is the *Madone*, loving all equally, that de Gaulle speaks about.[4] Second, the child sees that in the constant struggle for supremacy among the various branches of the family his duty in the struggle is to serve his own nuclear family to the best of his ability. There is not, as in classical Germany, a status order which is immutable. Third, although rules and regulations are sacred, they may be easily bypassed if one has a preferential relationship and a zone of secrecy.

This type of family system allows for much individuality. A French child develops a considerable subtlety and a realistic sense of the intermingling of interest and affection in preferential relationships. Although the same person can represent quite different values depending upon the context in which he or she is viewed, what happens within one context must not be allowed to interfere with what happens in another. The family network of sometimes contradictory objectives and emotions prevents any one obligation or feeling from being pursued to a deadly ultimate. This is an important source of the famous French *mesure*.

At the same time that it respects the individuality of all its members, the French bourgeois family gives them all a high degree of emotional and financial security. For the aristocrat, ownership of property is not crucial; an aristocrat ruined is still an aristocrat. But a bourgeois without property is no longer a bourgeois. Property for him is a symbol of family relationships, but it is also the proof of the family's rootedness and the guarantee of its status. Therefore, traditionally, it has been kept safe from the fluctuations of the market. Savings are in gold, land, government bonds, and certain very safe stocks which are usually backed by the state. Everything possible is done to preserve the continuity of the bourgeois family by maintaining it as an island of integrity and order in a disorganized and unprincipled world. The family respects and depends upon the older members to link the generations by bonds of affection and tradition. The bourgeois further protects himself from the threats of the world by favoring those careers where safe revenue is assured. A family firm is managed so as to minimize market risk. A bourgeois investor feels a great responsibility not to lose money, for this would be a crime against his family. If the French bourgeois seems often obsessed with saving, it is because he wants to be freed from the economy just as his aristocratic neighbor appears to be.

Given the high valuation of the family, the destruction of one family by another is considered a heinous offense. The thought that mere business failure, the result of market mechanisms, could wipe out a family, is most distressing to the classical French bourgeois. That an essentially moral force, the family, should be destroyed by events which concern exclusively the material, seems illegitimate. It will happen, but few families will want the blood on their hands. Hence the competition among families, inevitable in the drive to maintain or better one's family position, is moved to the *salon*, where the wounds are not mortal, and to marriage, where the wounds are mortal but where the wounded take a long time to die.

The bourgeois marriage is the great test of the family. This is the moment when all the efforts of one generation can receive their reward. A "poor marriage" is almost a confession of failure, and the family finds it difficult to maintain its social relationships. But if the family has been thrifty and has worked hard, if its representative behavior has been better than average without being showy, it can hope for a good marriage, perhaps even a "brilliant" one. And with the marriage and the new allies, an introduction into a new milieu can be made, more often for the brothers or sisters of the bride or bridegroom, but often also for the parents. Thus we may explain the paradox of the desire of the bourgeois to move up on the social-economic ladder and the respect with which he acknowledges a fixed position on the same ladder (*positions acquises*). Once an improved position is obtained it becomes family property and is therefore regarded as sacred.

The French bourgeois family has been admired by many people for many reasons. It is the source of a rich literary and artistic culture. It is an organizational *tour de force*. Despite its strains and weaknesses, in the pantheon of organizations it takes its place next to the Catholic Church, the Roman army, the American corporation, the German general staff, and the British Commonwealth as a great creation of the human mind.

THE DELINQUENT COMMUNITY

In school, the French child gets more of what he has gotten at home. We have seen how the French bourgeois family teaches the child basic attitudes toward authority. He learns to accept an aloof father as the primary source of authority; he expects protector-protégé relationships; he knows the importance of *savoir-plaire*; and he recognizes the fact that in order to protect his individuality he must resort to secrecy and political manipulation. The school experience reinforces these attitudes toward authority and elaborates the ways in which a Frenchman will join with others in formal and informal organizations.

In dealing with the teacher the child will meet a typical implementation of the doctrinare-hierarchical tendencies in French culture. On the one hand the teacher uses magisterial methods exclusively: there are definite standards of excellence, standards of what a cultured Frenchman should know, how he should express himself. The teacher makes relatively few allowances for the interests and fantasies of youth. Typically, he ignores his students' needs as children. He often talks to pupils of eleven and twelve years old on a level which supposes an intellectual maturity that they are far from having reached. On the other hand the teacher defines the world into a set of clearly delineated principles, and what he wants from the students is easily apprehended by them. In his relationships with students the teacher attempts to maintain aloofness and impartiality. The child will respond by trying to "seduce" the teacher. This can be done by playing on the teacher's pet peeves, his political or stylistic preferences. The child is very sensitive to cues which indicate what the teacher—as a man—wants to hear or read beyond the requirements of the curriculum, and the child will try to please the teacher, to break down his commitment to impartiality by playing on these preferences.

The peer group, like the teacher, is a crucial force for the socialization of the child. However, contrarily to what happens in England or in America, the peer group receives no official recognition and no legitimacy from the school authorities or the student's family. For that matter the family will not encourage attachments to teachers, to peer groups, or to the school as a corporate body. The school is seen as a *facility* where the child must procure the knowledge without which one cannot become a cultured personality. It is a facility to be used, but it is not supposed to compete with the family as a center of loyalty. Though the parochial schools have an enhanced prestige with the bourgeoisie because of the spiritual standing of the priestly staff, even they do not receive from their students (boarders included) the loyalty and attachment that are common among the alumni of English or American schools. In fact the ideal among the French upper classes was to have children tutored at home by private instructors, or even by their mothers; and even in the early 1950's one could find bourgeois mothers who made it a point to teach their children at home the equivalent of the elementary school curriculum.

Hence the peer group operates *sub rosa*. Games and sports are too minor an aspect of French classical school life to provide a legitimate outlet for peer group activities. Every student *as a student* has to recognize the legitimacy of the teacher's demands in homework and formal perfection. On the other hand the teacher's classroom administrative authority will not be taken for granted. On the contrary the teacher will find the peer group engaging in a continual battle against him, a battle which he can never win. The best he can get is a truce; and he gets it by his capacity to punish without pity and without argument. Authority, to be effective, has to be aloof and immune to seduction. A few teachers rule by charisma, but the great majority find aloofness and unilateral decisions the best guarantees of order. Every time they let down the barriers of hierarchy they find the peer group ready to abuse the situation. The teacher who tries to appeal to reason, who attempts to win the responsible cooperation of the peer group in the preservation of order, and who finds the use of arbitrary power difficult and fraught with remorse, will be heckled mercilessly.

The peer group thus is in a perpetual stance of delinquency. True, the occasions to realize this delinquent potential do not occur very often, because the administration, taking this stance for granted, attempts to exercise the most rigid supervision of student groups at all times. What is crucial to the peer group, then, is the delinquent potential, rather than immediate success in delinquent actions. And this delinquent potential not only covers the possibility of transforming the *class situation* into occasions for entertainment or for cheating, but also creates a friendly public for the expression of all sorts of deviant fantasies on the part of the individual members. Aggression against parents or teachers, sexual fantasies sometimes close to the "abnormal," smut, slang, make up the essence of the peer group activities. To a certain extent this is true of all student peer groups everywhere, but the French peer group has a much stronger delinquent characteristic than the British or the American. It operates above all as an organization for defending the interests of the individual member—the integrity of his personality in its entirety and particularly in those aspects of the self which find no outlet in the roles encompassed by the legitimate group activities.

On the other hand the peer group, lacking a collective legitimacy of its own (which it might gain through a connection to some adult value), finds it difficult to ask for sacrifices in its own name. Its function is centered on guaranteeing each member the maximum enjoyment of his private interest, which, in the school context, is mainly the freedom to express delinquent feelings through fantasy and verbalization. There is the defense against the school authorities, useful to all, and there are the *copains* (pals) who provide the supportive audience for spontaneity and for the search for forbidden pleasures—the spectators for the delinquent version of prowess.[5] Since the basis of the peer group is supremacy of individual interests, one cannot expect from the members the type of loyalty that the American and especially the British or the German peer group can ask as its due. First, there are the claims of the family which override all others. Second, the systematic delinquent posture of the peer group debunks all official morality, which includes the heroic mandate to suffer for the group's welfare. The peer group understands that the member cannot prejudice his interest position for the sake of the group, since the *raison d'être* of the group is to protect his interest position. There is a general expectation that members will not *cafarder* (play stoolie) on one another; but if the school administration starts putting pressure on an innocent, which it might do out of plan or out of the inevitable arbitrariness of its unilateral decisions, the innocent is unlikely to take punishment for someone else very long. The delinquent "task force" of the moment will collapse, without, however, threatening the peer group in its fundamental structure, since this structure depends more upon a compact of delinquent motivation than upon the achievement of any specific goal.

An interesting aspect of this delinquent community is that it accepts the legitimacy of the teacher's demands for school performance. It is his business to make these demands just as it is the business of the peer group to facilitate formal compliance or evasion, as the opportunities may be. Even though certain teachers have a sort of permanent revolution on their hands, the work will somehow proceed. The peer group does not develop an anti-intellectual culture. The teacher thus benefits from a basic legitimacy as bearer of the sacred models. In his priestly quality he is invulnerable. The peer group tries to prevent him from utilizing this priestly quality too often against its own interest, and against the unofficial self— "the flesh," as it were, of each of its members. In this defense the peer group has a sort of "second-order legitimacy," but it is vulnerable at any moment to the teacher's charisma.

The teacher, taking advantage of this vulnerability, can manipulate ridicule as a powerful sanction. If a student makes a crass mistake or an unintentionally humorous one (this will happen frequently in Latin or in French essay writing), the teacher may expose the culprit to the whole class. What happens then is somewhat unexpected (though not altogether unknown) by American or English standards: the peer group will respond to the teacher's action by deserting its own hapless member and siding with the teacher, thus demonstrating its commitment to the teacher's values. The student stands completely alone. To be sure, in this betrayal there may be a good deal of unspoken sympathy, but the victim becomes the *lampiste* (scapegoat), whose sacrifice gives a breathing spell to the peer group. Few experiences can be more devastating to the child. It will help him remember forever the great rule of French life: *faut se méfier*. ("Be on your guard" would probably be a better translation than "don't trust anyone.") One can never predict when the authority figure will be able to call upon the prestige of his connection with ultimate values, or when the balance of individual interests and costs will lead the *copains* to abandon a member who finds himself in an exposed position.

In some ways this process continues the complex game of shifting family coalitions. The family provides a much higher level of personal protection but does not preclude the insecurity of exploitation. The peer group provides a higher level of acceptance to the most idiosyncratic of feelings, so that the individual feels encouraged to search for his uniqueness as long as it does not affect the interest position of other members. The peer group is more sincere, and yet creates the insecurity of abandonment of the individual. It is very efficient in defending the *status quo* where the interest reference of each member is obvious and immediate; in such a situation the intensity of interaction, the flexibility of roles, will be very high. The French peer group, more perhaps than the peer group of other Western societies, requires the cement of opposition to the "outgroup," but an opposition that would be embarrassed by a complete victory. The peer group is more in its element as a consensus of delinquent motivation than as an organization. It has developed a great technique for establishing this consensus and excluding the non-initiates who are insensitive to the passwords, the nuances, the implicit. It gives respect and prestige to the communicators, the articulate ones who deepen the consensus and who elaborate new refinements which quickly make a stranger of the non-participator.

The school peer group is the prototype of the solidary groups which exist in France beyond the nuclear and extended family. They are characterized by jealous equalitarianism among the members, difficulty in admitting newcomers, and conspiracy of silence against superior authority. They do not deny authority, however. Indeed they are incapable of taking initiative except in interpreting the directives of superior authority and accommodating themselves to those interpretations. In an effort to create for each member a zone of autonomy, of caprice, of creativity, these peer groups thrive on the unrealism of the authority's directives. The directives testify to the authority's connection to a superior world, and create greater zones of *debrouillardise* (make do). On the other hand any change that is apt to create new ambiguities of status, or restrict the individual zones of autonomy in favor of a systematic and rationalized approach to the problem, will be resisted with all the strength the group can muster.[6]

ROLES OF THE CITIZEN

The roles taken by the Frenchman *as citizen* are shaped by the roles taken by him as a member of the nuclear family, the extended family, and the student peer group.

In relation to the motherland, which gives without counting or discriminating, the Frenchman *takes the role of the motherland* by offering his life. This is the romantic and heroic aspect of French citizenship, and Frenchmen have always responded well to any leader who could define the situation in these terms.

But when the citizen, still in relation to the motherland, wants to take the role of the state, he acts out the conception of the good authority that he had formed as a child and student. Putting himself in the place of the father and teacher, he offers a systematic ideology, a set of principles which insure the welfare of the country. This ideological commitment is the one major collective representation, beyond families and peer groups, which gathers Frenchmen into warring parties; nevertheless it sustains a strong interest in the over-all invisible collectivity.

With a Parliament representing opposite ideologies, France might seem vulnerable to violent factional struggles. What happens most of the time, however, is that the Parliamentary deputy in relation to his partisan electorate does what the child did in relation to his father and his dogmatic teacher. He compromises, betrays here and there, and creates what has been described as the "République des Camarades"—the Peer Group Republic—which transforms dogmas into speeches, programs into legislation (some of it dead-letter legislation), and unrealistic principles into working compromises.

To this government, which does not and can never represent his ideology, the citizen refuses the dignity of statecraft. To him this is the negative symbol of authority. The government is made of incompetents, swindlers, or fools, who are usurping the function of the state. The government is that which prefers someone else. The government is that which threatens the family property through taxes. The government is that which threatens the established order through partisan legislation. The government is that authority which must be checkmated or exploited through seduction, silence, and systematic obstruction. The government replies in kind through police spying, blackmail, bribery, and undercover deals with citizens who threaten to be difficult. The government is the political branch of the state, and in the minds of the public it is the Parliament, the tax officials, and the police.

The state, on the other hand, is the middle and higher echelon of the civil service, invisible, aloof, inflexible, which sees to it that the families and the delinquent communities of interest groups do not go to extremes in their competition and that the basic framework of order is not threatened by their opportunism. Without this civil service there would be, many Frenchmen are convinced, a dog-eat-dog existence replete with Red and White terrors. The ideological support of this higher civil service resides in the intellectual prowess of its members certified by diplomas, and in the need for an effective umpire.

This system, with the citizen roles which make it possible, has been efficacious in maintaining order in a society which aimed to derive the greatest possible enjoyment from industry while remaining faithful to eighteenth-century aristocratic values. It results in an equilibrium of private interests, in providing a framework where a Frenchman's life can evolve without too many surprises. It replaces the government of men, which Frenchmen tolerate only in terms of serious crises, with the government of things. Acceptance of the accomplished fact and the force of things is easier than obedience to a decision made by someone with a concept of the good which the citizen does not share.

The family and the school peer group, where the future adult learns to cope with authority, provide the pattern for much of French organization, including the French family firm. In that institution the accepted attitudes toward authority result in certain problems which make it harder to maintain economic rationality. Some of the problems of the family firm are similar throughout the world—for example the problem of succession, the hiring on the basis of kinship rather than competence, and the confusion between executive and family roles. In France there is a special difficulty: once the great entrepreneur—the father figure—has disappeared, *there is no clear-cut principle of authority*. For sentimental reasons the sons and daughters (and consequently the sons-in-law) are likely to have been taken into the firm; there is no primogeniture, and there is little likelihood that any one of the branch families will abandon the struggle for supremacy. As a result the French family firm is more vulnerable than most to rule by groups of elders on the basis of tradition. Agreement is often based on a stalemate among some of the contending forces, a stalemate that is not compatible with effective cost control and central quality control; for these controls would permit a fairly definite evaluation of the performance of the family executives. The firm thus tends to be fragmented into family fiefs, and engineers are blocked by the elders' reliance on natural methods and experience.

The political consequences of the combination of bourgeois family and delinquent community produced localities which were split between impermeable milieux made of families, their retainers, and family friends. The intermediary groups between the state and the family are "delinquent communities," and it is they that have preserved the *status quo*. Many observers of France from Tocqueville to Arnold Rose have argued that France suffered from a weakness of intermediary organizations between state and family. William Kornhauser has been led by this common belief to speak of a vulnerability of Frenchmen to mass movements, which endanger the basis of democratic government.[7] It seems that the extensiveness and strength of the informal organizations have been overlooked because they lack the clear references of name, headquarters, formal officers, and the like.

Although the "delinquent communities" may facilitate protest actions they do not allow sufficient availability of French citizens for supporting effective reform movements. Hence France has suffered more from her stability (*immobilisme*) than from the vulnerability of her supposedly atomized individuals to mass appeals. This stability may be well-nigh proof against tyranny, since the capacity of the state to alter the social equilibrium is smaller than in any other Western nation.

II

THE FORCES OF CHANGE *

The system I have outlined was a workable equilibrium; its social elite had top standing in international society, and its writers and artists were supreme. Nevertheless, forces had been at work which were bound to disrupt this equilibrium. Some of these forces were acting upon the whole Western world, such as the increasing penetration of rural areas by urban cultural patterns, the increasing levels of education, the lengthening of life expectancy, the com-

* Some of the material used in writing this section was gathered on a trip to France (1959) financed by a grant-in-aid from the Social Science Research Council, whose assistance is here gratefully acknowledged.

plexity of industrial technology, the improvement of the standard of living of the peasantry and the working class, and more important, the rising expectation of these two groups. After the world depression came a World War which saw most of Europe subjugated to Nazi Germany before being liberated by the Allied armies; and after the war the world discovered that the dominant military forces in Europe were in the hands of two powers peripheral to Europe: the United States and Soviet Russia. Such are some of the major facts of life for all Western societies. We shall see how these forces altered French society—first, in terms of its basic values which remained comparatively stable and, second, in terms of its social structure which showed more or less resiliency depending upon the institutions that were affected.

THE DECLINE OF THE STATE AS AN INCARNATION OF THE DOCTRINAIRE-HIERARCHICAL ASPECT OF FRENCH CULTURE

The history of the French state after the Versailles treaty points to the progressive weakening of its sacred character. Several factors are responsible for the process. First the victory of 1918 deprives the French state of any long-range goal. Instead of being a source of *idées-forces*, the state loses some of its intellectual prestige as against the League of Nations, as against the idea of a European civilization threatened by the eastern ideology of Communism or the "materialism" of the United States. The sentimental internationalism of the Socialist parties is replaced by the disciplined internationalism of the Communist parties. The *Marseillaise*, which used to be the revolutionary song *par excellence* for the intellectuals and trade unionists of North and South America, of Russia, of the Balkans, is replaced by the *Internationale*—only a small symptom, among many, that French culture is losing some of its universality. And the French state, based on this prestigious culture, is bound to lose some of its magic.

The reaction to this stress is a frenetic attempt to maintain the old equilibrium. The government becomes more than ever the scapegoat for all the financial losses contingent upon the waging of the war—the default of Russian and Balkan bonds, the devaluation of the franc—and the struggle to seize a state power reputed

omnipotent becomes more exasperated. Yet this state power reveals itself well-nigh impotent to cope with any of the problems
faced by French society because these problems are sufficiently
pressing to create a *malaise* and some anxiety but never pressing
enough to create a desperate need for action that would break
through the infinite resistance of the delinquent communities.

The world depression hit France later and with less impact than
in other industrial nations. The family firms which set the tone to
the various industries used their cash reserves (often maintained
at the cost of insufficient depreciation reserves) to remain open,
though economic rationality would have dictated the closing of
many of them. As a result they preserved their workers from the
worst hardships of unemployment. The rural contacts of many
French workers, either through their gardens or their families,
softened the impact that short work weeks or unemployment had
upon the standard of living; so did the use of factory-owned housing. Furthermore a relatively high percentage of the industrial labor
force was made up of foreigners. In 1931 the census listed 2,715,000
foreigners in France, and this was very likely an underestimation.
They must have constituted some 10 percent of the labor force,
concentrated in the lowest-paid employment. As the depression
struck, many of these foreigners were denied labor permits and
about half a million went back home. Native French workers kept
their jobs while foreigners were laid off. The point here is that
the pressures upon France were strong enough to create dissatisfaction both among bourgeois and workers but they were not
strong enough to force *learning*, that is, the development of new
structures.

The aborted movements of both February 1934 and June 1936
left many with a feeling of helplessness and drift. The state was
paralyzed. It could not even fulfill its old function of protection:
the bourgeois had seen their factories, or the factories of their
friends, occupied by workers who often raised the red flag over
the buildings. The workers and employees saw the state unable to
stop inflation or fulfill the hopes of the Popular Front. For the
bourgeois families the loss in *felt* security was probably even
greater than for the working class: they felt betrayed by the sit-

down strikes, betrayed by their workers, and betrayed by the state—and even betrayed by their representatives in the Matignon Agreement of 1936, which signaled the capitulation of the employers to the sit-down strikes that followed the victory of the Popular Front at the polls. The disappointment, the rancor, the apathy which existed in many circles in 1939 had damaged much of the sacred commitment of the citizen to the couple—state and motherland—as embodied in the citizenship contract typical of the Third Republic.

Among the salaried managers of the large corporations a strong internationalistic current had developed. Extrapolating from their experience with European and even global cartels, some of the more brilliant managerial minds had visions of economic and political planning on a European scale, with a reinforced dominion over Africa and much of Asia. These ideas led some to collaboration with the New Europe proposed by the Nazis. They were the ideological complex behind the myth of the *Synarchie*,[8] and one of the forces behind the abandonment of nationalism à la Maurice Barrès by an important sector of the political Right. Among the Left there were groups which thought along similar lines: the group which included Daniel Halévy and Robert Aron, and many of the *Socialistes de France*, a splinter group expelled from the Socialist Party.

Not only did nationalism become intellectually deficient but from 1940 onward France ceased to have an effectively autonomous sphere of decision in the world arena. The Liberation did not change this situation appreciably; it replaced German control by financial and military dependence upon the United States. The impact of such a situation upon Frenchmen, who were used to thinking of France as one of the great powers, if not the greatest, is bound to be quite different from the impact it might have on Belgians, for instance. French nationalism, deprived of its crusading and universalistic features, becomes a nationalism of self-deception, of humiliation, of xenophobia.

Self-deception was fostered by the various Liberation governments to create the fiction of unanimous resistance to the Germans; in return for support they offered a general whitewash and Pétain and Laval as scapegoats. Since the self-deception could never be complete it became another source of humiliation, added to the crushing defeat of 1940, the continued presence of American troops, the colonial rebellions, the defeats in Indochina, the fund-raising trips which took Prime Ministers to Washington, the scandals affecting the faith the French had had in the justice and impartiality of the state apparatus.

The xenophobia was mainly directed at the Germans and Americans, and was encouraged by the Communist Party and its intellectual fellow travelers. It is likely that this tactic undid some of the work done by the old Socialist movement, which had seen to it that the authoritarianism and xenophobic tendencies inherent in the low status of the working class had been unable to find an ideological manifestation.

Thus nationalism becomes associated, at best, with narrow protectionism and a fixation upon the past, and at worst, with defeat and decline. Even though the Resistance had attempted to save the honor of the country, it only succeeded in saving the honor of individuals; the fact that fighting was the voluntary choice of a minority emphasized the abstention of the majority. Furthermore one of the consequences of the Resistance was the duality of sovereignty created by the coexistence of the de Gaulle and Pétain regimes during World War II. Although great efforts were made by the Liberation governments (even while prisoners of their anti-Vichy ideology) to recreate a continuity of state power which would include many of the acts of the Vichy government, they could not prevent a weakening of the links which tied the French state to the doctrinaire-hierarchical elements of French culture and made it the defender of the true faith.

The negative kind of nationalism, which reached its zenith in November 1956 with the ill-fated invasion of Egypt, has been considerably abated by the growth of the French economy, the return of de Gaulle to power, and the end of reliance on American aid. Such events undid the humiliation of the past. But the state has yet to recover its unity and autonomy in the eyes of many citizens. As a result the use of the government as a scapegoat to maintain the sacrosanct character of the state-motherland image has been less and less effective. The search for an inspiring collectivity takes the citizen beyond the frontiers of France, to a combination Catholicism-and-Europe. For some, Catholicism is replaced by the bureaucratic-humanitarianism of Socialistic ideology.

This diagnosis of a decay of the state as a sacred institution, correlated with a loss of meaning of France as the protective mother to all her sons, may warrant the conclusion that the French state will no more be able to mobilize its citizens for a life-or-death struggle to defend either its frontiers, its colonial possessions, or the integrity of its constitutional regime.

PROWESS REVISITED: HEROES AND PRODUCERS

This does not mean that individual Frenchmen are less willing or capable to die to express their commitment to values. It does mean that this death will be more private, less available for organizational purposes than is a broad acceptance by the masses of citizens that the state incarnates the right and the just. We are back to the notion of prowess discussed in the first part of this essay. The Resistance, the Free French Forces, the Indochina war, the Algerian war have offered many chances for individual prowess, since to die or to risk dying has become in the main an increasingly personal choice. This is prowess à la Bournazel,[9] à la Malraux, à la Saint-Exupéry. The decay of the state has created a new opportunity for Don Quixotism, or d'Artagnanism.

In the confusion created by the decay of the state, heroes organize around themselves bands of worshipers, who live a life practically outside social structure. *The Centurions*, by Jean Lartéguy, depicts what could be called "sociological throwbacks" who, however, have a very powerful fascination upon the French, precisely because they represent the image of life as an aesthetic venture without structural costs. Leclerc de Hautecloque, Lionel de Marmier, Schloessing, Rémy, Corniglion-Molinier, La Porte des Vaux, Monclar, Gilles, Lalande, Bigeard, are some of the names that come to mind.[10] Leaders of that type constitute the hard core of the present French army, with its relatively low stress on spit and polish and its high personal initiative, cult of physical fitness and heroic dash. A substantial portion of the provincial aristocracy continues to provide officers for the armed forces which are abandoned by the bourgeoisie. Aristocrats and officers from the old lower-middle class (petty civil servants, career noncommissioned officers, shopkeepers, sons of the artisans) will build one of the best "obsolete" armies the world has ever known. However, this army elite has little or no understanding of political realities, both national and international. It becomes a refuge for those who cannot adjust to a changing society. The army may have had the ambition to seize power and return the nation to goals of glory and domination, but very likely its capacities and its desires were satisfied more effectively by existence as a delinquent community camping in Algeria.

As against those who cannot adjust, there have been those who have switched the grounds of aristocratic-type prowess from consumption to production. The threats of Communism, the acceptance of a more solidarist type of Catholicism have pushed those aristocrats who were not interested in the useless wars of the Fourth Republic to try in earnest their chance in the civil service and in business. It became the fashionable thing to do. They bring to the economy a prowess orientation in which problems of cost are secondary in comparison with the novel, the grandiose, the ingenious. They adopt machines as their fathers and grandfathers adopted cars and airplanes. Some have taken to cultivating their ancestral lands as scientific farmers, and drive their own tractors. Others join the traditional fields of steel, insurance, and banking, and the not so traditional ones of advertising and public relations. They swim with the tide and find a general popularity in the nation that their fathers had not known in the period between the two wars. They have found a way to be true to their tradition of prowess and seduction in the middle of the twentieth century, and the state is there to channel their economic activity into the fields of greatest urgency.

THE NEW PRAGMATIC CONCEPTION OF THE STATE

If the political and romantic goals of the state have disappeared, and with them much of the state's sacred character, on the other hand its economic goals have been clarified and extended, and are being pursued with efficiency.

The aftermath of the Second World War found the French state considerably enmeshed in the economic living of its citizens. It pledged 100 percent compensation for war losses, and a high percentage of French families became claimants. It broadened the categories of veterans entitled to pensions, however nominal. Social security benefits were extended and covered up to 80 percent of medical expenditures. Implementing the *Code de la Famille*, voted in 1939, the state began allocating family subsidies to wage and salary earners. For a father of four children, these might mean a sum equal to his factory earnings. Although these measures did not seem to result in an effective redistribution of income among social classes, they increased the number of people who had a vested interest in the permanence of the state. At the same time that the Communist Party was consolidating its voting bloc to about 25 percent of the electorate, its supporters felt tied to the state by rights which had been in the past the privileges of civil servants or of rich families engaged in subsidized industry or farming. The doctrinaire-hierarchical tradition, blocked in its traditional paths, finds a new incarnation in the economic sphere. The providential state offers its shelter to all its children. This shelter, however, is meager. The state is going to strengthen it, at first by using its usual dirigist and doctrinaire reflexes.

At the end of the war the belief had been widespread that the major cause of the 1940 defeat had been France's inferiority in armaments, itself due to her inferiority in industrial production. The remnants of old-fashioned patriotism and the imperatives of peacetime reconstruction, combined with the Colbertist and Saint-Simonian tradition of the French state, made possible the initiation of the Monnet plan, backed by the Fonds de Modernisation et d'Equipement, replaced since 1955 by the Fonds de Développement Economique et Social. American aid provided so much of the capital required that the executive branch was able to set the plan in motion without special debate by Parliament. Priority was given to the industries that had been nationalized—electricity, coal, gas, and railways. It is even possible that there was some excess investment in these activities to the detriment of oil prospecting and the retooling of major capital goods industries. Hydroelectricity may have been favored over thermal units for reasons which were aesthetic rather than economic.

The *Plan Monnet* was largely inspired by a definition of French economic retardation as the result of energy shortages, such as coal. Its achievements did facilitate the economic expansion of the middle fifties. The great advantage of this neo–Saint-Simonian state is that it has means for credit creation which it never possessed when investment banking was in the hands of a few family dynasties. La Caisse des Dépots et Consignations, the Crédit National, La Caisse des Marchés and similar credit agencies have increased considerably the power of the state to promote the development of production potential. Controlling the nationalized banks and insurance companies, developing postal savings, administering the social security funds, and systematically using inflation, the state now oversees about half of the national income. It makes between 20 and 25 percent of the investments, and exercises a large measure of control over another 25 percent.[11] As a result of the availability of funds, many plans which had been slumbering for decades in the files were pulled out by the *Polytechniciens* in charge of civil engineering and put into operation. The dam at Donzère-Mondragon, built by the state-controlled Compagnie Nationale du Rhône, is an example.[12] It is only one of the major works in a French version of TVA, destined to make the Rhône navigable throughout its length, to harness its power, and to irrigate the relatively dry areas on both sides of the river bed. The concept behind these works is still that of the *jardin à la française*, where the application of will transforms the disorder of nature into a monument to human reason. From a pragmatic standpoint some aspects of the project can be debated. The navigability of the Rhône will be more useful when Marseilles becomes a European port rather than a purely French one. These grand works weaken the intellectual justification for the nation. Aesthetically they suffice unto themselves today as they did sixty years ago when they were first conceived; economically they require the integration of Europe.

These technocratic conceptions of economic action, which start from a preconceived notion of what deserves to be built instead of letting the market determine it, represent essentially a traditional response to stress.

A more novel reaction has been the development of a new type of association between the state and the citizens and their interest groups. It is best exemplified by the nationalized industries and the type of organization (*commissariat*) that elaborates the various plans that have followed the original *Plan Monnet*.

Theoretically the mixed companies which have been created by the nationalizations of 1936 and 1945–46 are supposed to be largely autonomous under the ultimate control and subsidy of the state. At the beginning there was a tendency to use them as political rewards and well-paying plums, which, in fact, called for reliance on the judgment of the state engineers who supervised operations. Eventually these mixed companies developed a style of their own, with generally better-than-average personnel and customer relations. This is partly because their boards give statutory representation to the public and to the various regional interests affected by their operations. Civil servants detached to these national companies learn economic and political realities; businessmen learn governmental realities. The criticisms made toward the nationalized industries have often been made from a dogmatic political standpoint. These companies have been affected by few scandals. And considering the fact that the state will at times set prices on the basis of political considerations rather than economic ones, their performance seems to have been competitive with that of private firms.[13] Where monopolies exist in railway and air transportation, and coal mining, their performance seems to have been superior to that of the old state monopolies such as tobacco, the post office, and telegraph and telephone.

The type of leadership in which communication is only downward and which offers only the accommodation of the delinquent community does not work so well where customers' tastes and preferences have to be taken into account. The growth in the standard of living provides customers with more choices and substitutes even when the state holds a monopoly.

The greatest innovation in the French state's relation to the economy has been the creation of a Planning Commission (*Commissariat au Plan*).[14] Around a central staff of about sixty officials of variable background, allegiances, and training, twenty-five modernization committees were formed, each representing a particular economic activity and consisting of some thirty to fifty persons— business leaders, officials of trade associations and trade unions, civil servants, and leading citizens. These people have served with no more remuneration than the appreciable prestige of being chosen by the national figure who leads the Planning Commission.

Each of these committees—within the framework of a basic consensus on the aim of increasing the production of the French economy—must arrive at some recommendation for action that will guide its particular activity for four years. Eventually the recommendations of the various committees are harmonized by the central offices of the Planning Commission and ratified by the Economic and Social Council and by Parliament.

The Planning Commission has been a creative synthesis between the doctrinaire-hierarchical and the aesthetic-individualistic tendencies of French culture. On the doctrinaire-hierarchical side it does not challenge the final authority of the state vested in the Ministry of Finance, to which the Commission is attached in a special semi-autonomous "staff fashion." By themselves the Commission and its committees have no power. They deal with ideas. An initial push comes from above: build a stronger nation, increase the welfare of the citizenry. But here the delinquent community is not working to dilute the initial directive. Instead, the reverse occurs: it works to develop and specify the directive on the private level where each of its members is the sole authority. The members of the modernization committees feel themselves to be a select group at war against the conservative tendencies of the Ministry of Finance and of their own interest groups. They are in a prowess situation acting as individuals, participating in the building of the France of tomorrow, in direct contact with the truth, and they are also vested with the dignity of statecraft. Dealing with ideas instead of immediate interests, they avoid many of the temptations of special pleading. Committed to their committees as "delinquent communities" they build a consensus which remains a recognizable framework of the final plan directives, but the directives are not binding like an order. They do not arouse the defense mechanisms of the private interest groups. Though the state will promote the plan through its own business activities, and by offering various incentives that make higher production and productivity the profitable thing to do, the plan is not a rigid prescription. It is a pact of mutual assistance between economic agents and the state. This is far from the blind subsidies of the past or the narrow self-seeking of the family firm. The state, in a sense demystified, is more approachable by the citizens. The relationships are more pragmatic, more reasonable, and less emotionally charged.

That this style of relationship is becoming more characteristic of industrial matters is further evidenced by the creation of regional committees of economic expansion, centered around the prefect, which originate local plans to be eventually implemented after several reviews by state agencies. Another step toward decentralization has been the giving of various state subsidies (decree of June 1955) supporting the creation of corporations for regional development. Nevertheless these regional corporations have been slow in developing their financial base through appeals to local savings; hence they have not yet remedied the weakness of the locally rooted banks, few of which survived the depression of the 1930's. The family firms are often reluctant to accept loans and even subsidies to modernize and expand, because this destroys the secret of the firm and the exclusive control of the family dynasty.

The state administrative apparatus which is supposed to assist the implementation of the national Plan throughout the country is not well geared to its task. The departmental basis is too small and often does not correspond to the realities of economic geography. Some progress has been made by reinforcing the authority of the prefects over the departmental echelons of the Parisian ministries and by increasing the range of decisions which need not be forwarded to Paris.[15] Serious efforts have been made to translate the industry-wide programs of the national Plan into effective regional programs; inventories and statistics are now available which go beyond the "keyhole" type of information that the prefect formerly obtained from his many informers. But the efforts to date are not sufficient.

The French state, in trying to decentralize industry away from the Parisian region, finds itself in a dilemma. On the one hand its normal tendency is to insure for all its citizens a means of making a living, wherever they may live. It recognizes the importance of the citizen's geographical roots, his reluctance to move once he has married. This is one of the rationales behind the policy of decentralization: bring work to where the workers already are. On the other hand, decentralization also means working with businessmen who are guided in their decisions by profit considerations and by preference for regions where an industrial "culture" already exists. The result has been a tendency for new businesses to establish themselves close to active industrial centers. The Parisian region, instead of losing ground, has gained it, spreading outward to cover a greater area of France but still, essentially, the Parisian region.[16] A massive approach to the problems of decaying regions would require long-range investments of large magnitude, and this would disrupt the balance of the interests which the state has pledged to cooperate with. Furthermore the map of France which is being considered in the efforts to decentralize may not perfectly comport with the map of the Common Market.

Hence we must not overestimate the part of state action in the new prosperity of France. True enough, the state has never possessed more effective powers over the economy than it does today, and at the same time it never has more successfully associated the citizens to its policies. The latter phenomenon has been rendered possible by some changes in the structure of the trade association.

FROM THE DELINQUENT COMMUNITY TO THE VOLUNTARY ORGANIZATION

The reinforcement of state authority in economic matters has been accompanied by a regrouping and development of trade associations. Until 1936 these associations were mainly delinquent communities; they had very little capacity to promote productive change because they had little basis of consensus except the sacredness of established positions. They systematically went about the promotion of privileges, customs barriers, and subsidies, and the allocation of sales quotas. Their leaders were often seen as mere straw men or mouthpieces. Their offices were frequently staffed by business failures, for whom it was a graceful way of retiring from the field. In the major industries like steel and coal, trade associations had better levels of talent because much of their work centered around high-level price negotiations with the state or with international cartels.

As a result of their successes in the old economic structure, some of the trade associations in the basic industries will be the last ones to adjust to the new economic order. Steel seems a case in point. Henry W. Ehrmann has described these organizations very aptly,[17] though it would seem that the description of what, for an American observer, must have been economic dinosaurs may have led him to underplay the real changes that were taking place in the functions and structure of the trade association. In this connection a crucial experience was the decision of the Vichy government to link the trade associations to the Administration in order to allocate scarce raw materials, to prevent unemployment, and to preserve French machinery and labor from German requisition. These were the famous *comités d'organisation* which legitimized the trade associations on a national level and forced them to take responsibility for the welfare of the total society. The *comités* robbed the trade associations of their legitimacy as delinquent communities in opposition to a state noble in intent but ignorant of economic realities.

After the war the formula of the *comités* was retained (law of April 1946) because the problems of allocating raw materials and machinery still existed. There were abuses, to be sure, and Ehrmann has pointed them out. Nevertheless many of the trade representatives did not wish to think of themselves as mere spokesmen for narrow industry interests. Such men do not accept as final the isolation of the working-class organizations.[18] They want a general European federation with an organized, if not planned, economy.

In 1950–1952 many of the officers of local trade associations to whom I talked were bitter, indignant men, who complained of the insincerity of the employers, of their lack of true concern for the public welfare of their workers. In 1959 this note was sounded more rarely. There was less feeling of frustration, more talking about plans for future growth, more feeling of pride within the industry one served.

Trade associations have established schools for employers (Lille and Rheims, for instance) and research laboratories. They have been able to reorganize whole industries, such as cotton, by closing down marginal plants. They have sponsored market studies. They have carried on these activities in addition to their negotiations about wages and hours with the government, which was acting as the effective representative of the working class. In short, without yet coming to the level of organization of the German *Verein*, the French trade association movement is much stronger than it was twenty-five years ago when it signed the Matignon Agreement only to have the chief signer dismissed from his post a few months afterwards.

In the last few years the trade associations have been able to alleviate the fears of their marginal members over the possible consequences of higher productivity and European competition. The comparatively painless way in which the reorganization of the cotton industry was accomplished is a guarantee that economic growth can go hand in hand with more security than is offered by stagnation.

More and more the focus—the "charter"—of the trade association is economic growth rather than mutual defense. There is more membership participation in the various committees and in the executive training sessions which have been initiated by many organizations. As the trade association develops doctrine, and gives effective authority to its officers, it partakes of the doctrinaire-hierarchical tradition of French culture. Besides the delinquent community dimension—which still can be found although it is no longer the main dimension of the organization—there now exist many points of permanent contact with the national master plan of economic expansion. In many ways the trade association, the mixed companies, and the regional expansion committees have linked industrial activity to the state in a manner which reassures the French because the unknowns of movement seem to be neutralized by conforming action to great principles. Change is accepted because it is clear that change is unlikely to threaten social status or to conflict with order.

This is the paradox of a society where weakening of the state in the political field has gone hand in hand with its reinforcement in the economic. The doctrinaire-hierarchical and the aesthetic-individualistic traditions maintain their strength, but a creative impulse has combined them into new institutional incarnations.

Along with the development of the trade associations there has been an increase in the number of pressure groups. Before World War II the few pressure groups that existed in France kept their activities as secret as possible. Many a Frenchman brought pressure in the interest of his own family, and the "delinquent community" acted to neutralize government directives, but the pressure group as known in the United States was not much in evidence. It is interesting that there was no French expression for "pressure group" before French social scientists introduced a translation of the everyday American expression—*groupes de pression*.

French pressure groups now have become more open and more widespread; one might say "more democratic," since they are no more the privilege of a few. Being more open, they are bound to become less particularistic in their arguments. They have to accept the rule of the general interest and try to fit their particular interests into that. Their leaders deal with civil servants who know economics [19] and have plans of their own. Once the pressure groups have placed themselves on the terrain of the national interest, they cannot act or argue in terms of the delinquent community (seduction or blackmail) or in terms of the sacredness of the *positions acquises*. The national interest becomes the legitimate basis for a decision jointly made; the pressure group has the duty to make its desires and views known to the administrator who, in turn, like the British judge, convinces the loser that he had to lose in terms of the common values. In this framework there is no more need for the romantic conception of the state as superman or of the government as a slut.

Good examples of the new pressure groups are those concerned with housing. The Confédération Générale du Logement, an offshoot of the Abbé Pierre campaign in the winter of 1952, promotes the access of its membership to home ownership. It might be described as a voluntary do-good association, though it has been capable of dramatic gestures in order to put a sort of Gandhist pressure upon governmental authorities. Working in another direction is the Centre National pour l'Amélioration de l'Habitat (CNAH), which informs and advises employers, who, under law, pay one percent of the payroll to the Centre Interprofessionnel du Logement (CIL). There is also a pressure group known as the Union de la Propriété Bâtie de France (UPBF), which presents the more classic landlord point of view. Jean Meynaud, the French student of pressure groups, says of the CNAH: "It does not present itself as a deprived victim but as a source of ideas aiming to promote efficient action. In the same way the UBPF tries to put itself under the sign of the general interest." [20]

A weakness of this system of government by civil service and pressure groups is the tendency to overlook the working class and peasant organizations, which, then, must resort to the device of the *baroud d'honneur*—in this case a strike or demonstration—in order to get a hearing.[21] This weakness is partly due to the refusal of the Communist trade unions to cooperate with bourgeois government in bourgeois organizations. There are indications, however, that some prefects and employers' groups such as the Centre des Jeunes Patrons are trying to include the working class in their programs. In 1961 when the prefect of the Isère demanded that all trade union groups should be represented in the regional expansion council there, the experiment was apparently successful.[22]

We have seen how, under the pressures from inside and outside French society, there has been a decay of the classical concept of the state-motherland couple, and a development of a new style of relationship between the state and the citizen, and between the state and the "delinquent communities" which constitute such a large aspect of French associations. How far have these changes affected the basic pattern of French politics? At the present time there are two possible interpretations of the de Gaulle regime. One is that this regime is a prelude to a presidential system with a stable political executive. The other is that the de Gaulle regime is one of those periodic authoritarian shake-ups between the long periods in which bureaucratic stability is coupled with ministerial instability—a combination best suited to French values and social structure. Both conceptions are compatible with a growing commitment of the French citizen to the supranational structures of a United Europe. In twenty-five years a United Europe should have advanced so far that the interpretation of what the de Gaulle regime now represents becomes academic. It seems unlikely that the decay of the national state as the central locus of loyalty can be reversed, especially when a renewed Catholicism seems to have taken the place of the motherland as the exalting image of the good.

THE NEO-CATHOLIC MOVEMENT

Indeed a crucial event which parallels in importance the decay of the state as a sacred institution is the revival of the Catholic faith among the middle and upper classes, and its easy appeal to the ambitious family on the fringes of the white-collar world. The French Revolution and the nineteenth century had seen the return, first of the aristocracy and then of the bourgeoisie, to the Catholic faith. Before 1914, however, one could still point, in the neighborhood of Lille and Roubaix, to a "red bourgeoisie," that is, an anticlerical and atheistic bourgeoisie. After 1914 this was no longer true.

Nineteenth-century Catholicism assumed that the bourgeois families were the surest ally of the Church in its holding operation against the growth of "free thinking" and Republicanism in the bulk of the population (peasants, working class, and petty bourgeoisie). The Church backed up the authority of the paterfamilias, controlled the women, and used its remaining influence on the peasantry and working class to reinforce the power and prestige of the château and of the family firm. The Church was not monolithic, however, and was concerned over the growing disaffection of the masses. Adrien Dansette draws our attention to the two major tendencies in the Catholic Church which tried to cope with this problem.[23] One tendency, at once doctrinaire and authoritarian, resulted in the creation, in 1886, of the Action Catholique de la Jeunesse Française, which sponsored the creation of workers' "circles." The second tendency, more democratic, resulted in the creation of an intellectual group around Marc Sangnier, which edited a periodical called *Le Sillon*, a sort of forerunner of *Esprit*. This group was condemned by Rome. The most lasting expression of left-wing Catholicism was the founding in 1919 of the Catholic Trade Union movement (CFTC). Thus we have the constituting elements of social Catholicism, which founded between the two wars the Jeunesse Ouvrière Catholique (JOC) and the Jeunesse Agricole Catholique (JAC). After the JOC congress of 1937, membership in the Catholic workers' youth sections climbed to 65,000, a figure very likely equal if not superior to the membership of the Communist Youth.

The rapid success of all these Catholic organizations led members of the hierarchy to believe that the battle for the rechristianization of the masses was on the verge of being won. Such was not the case. What these movements accomplished was a regrouping of the Catholic families that already existed in the working class and peasantry. They also slowed down the process by which a young boy, once having accomplished his first communion and done with catechism, found adult society and embraced the anticlerical subculture which ruled the local peasantry, working class, and shopkeepers. The JOC and JAC centers were often the only places for adolescent recreation in village or working-class settlements. They provided girls with a measure of supervised freedom from the chores of home and school. They created opportunities for social mobility by exposing their members to a more varied world. But, as in all youth movements, the percentage that continues active in the adult organization is comparatively small. Sometimes the "graduate" does not find a comparable adult organization in which to be active. Often the requirements of family and job leave comparatively little time for the type of commitment the free adolescent had made. Furthermore the youth organizations are full of a do-good spirit which used to contrast greatly with the somewhat cynical and competitive climate of adult life.

Nevertheless, in the 1930's a change took place in the temper of the Catholic laity in the working class, and especially in the lower-middle class—and not just among the youth. The morale of these Catholics rose. Instead of being on the defensive, they showed pride in their faith and attracted elite minds to their groups. And this new temper was of great importance in its implications for the future.

After the Second World War great efforts were made to develop Catholic movements among the rapidly expanding group of university students. The Chartres pilgrimage attracted every year some 25,000 students from Paris. The Centre Richelieu of the Abbé Charles was successful in encouraging the missionary activities of middle-class students in spite of their bourgeois-type reserve and fear of ridicule. Catholic Action groups for adults have been developed all over France, whether under that name or under the name of Les Cercles Notre Dame, which attempt to involve married couples in active implementation of the Church's teachings.

A common characteristic of these adult organizations is that they give much more initiative to the Catholic layman. The most active of the lay workers for the new Catholicism are mainly middle-class white-collar employees, nonpropertied, who owe their status to their intellectual skills and moral discipline. The Church now finds itself in more intimate contact with its faithful, who express their religious problems in new terms. They are less interested than past Catholics in the retreats, the relics, and the medals, and more in the application of Catholic principles to their professional and civic problems. Certain changes in the rituals of the mass have been made to satisfy them; French is used more often in the services, the priest faces the parish when officiating, there is congregational singing, and there is greater concern with economic and political sin and less with sexual sins, which are not a crucial problem for this group.[24]

True enough, concern with economic and political sin can be a way to reassert an ethical superiority over those propertied groups, shopkeepers, and industrialists who have more opportunities for white-collar crime than are possessed by salaried employees. This middle class is in fact interested in promoting Catholic groups not only for valid religious reasons but also for reasons of leadership over their class superiors. Although the Church does not expect to break down class barriers, it cannot avoid mixing bourgeois milieux that might not have come together otherwise. Catholic Action groups have been active in housing developments, hospital work, and adult education movements, besides the usual charitable activities.

Compared with the "delinquent communities" these are, of course, "do-good communities." Their prototype is the bourgeois Boy Scout movement. Nevertheless they share with the classical delinquent community the same reliance on improvisation and the same tendency to spend much time in developing their own particular consensus. This can lead to a delinquent stance toward the central office; and therefore the Catholic hierarchy, while applauding the enthusiasm of its adult action groups, has worried lest they become too intellectually independent. In fact recently the central organization of the Action Catholique de la Jeunesse Française was dissolved, and a brake has been put on the development of lay activities concerning which the Church has not had the time to think through its doctrine and its strategy.

Has the Catholic movement been able to rechristianize the working class? The answer must be "no." The failure of the Church's worker-priest experiment was largely caused by a failure to understand the proletarian milieu. Catholic organization among the young workers never reached beyond the areas of traditional Catholic implantation. Against a systematic campaign of neutralization and absorption by the revolutionary Marxist "church" the isolated worker-priest was largely defenseless.

It is possible that the number of Catholics is not very different from what it was twenty-five years ago.[25] Nevertheless the quality is different. Traditional Catholicism, as represented best in Brittany, has continued to lose ground, but a new Catholicism, more deeply rooted in the individual will and more concerned with building the City of God on earth, has been replacing it. The clergy has not declined in numbers as much as was feared in the 1940's, and its quality has more than kept pace with the greater depth and sophistication of the faithful. Certainly it now exercises a real influence upon the middle and upper classes and does not shy away from challenging the selfish interests of these groups. The traditional Church, through its school system and monasteries for surplus girls, was a bulwark for the bourgeois family, but the modern Church becomes more and more concerned about the excessive subordination of the individual to family imperatives. It encourages marriages based on mutual love. It drops Victorian puritanism (the mixed discussions on sex during the Chartres pilgrimage are quite a surprise for one who has known the prewar attitudes), but encourages chastity as a free and personal choice. It frowns on excessive attention to dowries and property. It demands an application of Christian principles to all phases of life.

Thus the Church has weakened the values of rootedness, extended family, and family property. Even future heirs of family firms were taken by the new church spirit and when, after graduation, they came to work for their parents, they found the Centre des Jeunes Patrons ready to welcome them.

In many respects the Catholic Church has replaced the state-motherland as the effective locus of the sacred. Often it is the only organization that demands real sacrifices from the bourgeois. The old Catholicism had become a sort of family cult with features of ancestor worship; the new Catholicism has been working for a greater Christian community in Europe. René Rémond cites with approval a declaration by the Gaullist leader Terrenoire: "With the disaffection of the Catholics toward the notion of Motherland, a key support of French patriotism has collapsed." [26]

Thus the Church has benefited from the decline of the sacredness of the state and has also accelerated it. Furthermore neo-Catholicism has had a direct influence upon the economy, especially through its impact upon the motivation of the patrimonial employers.

THE CENTRE DES JEUNES PATRONS

The growth of the Centre des Jeunes Patrons—the Committee of Young Employers—is an example of the influence the new Catholicism has in French industry. Inspired by the paternalistic Catholic thinkers, Albert de Mun and La Tour de Pin, the CJP was founded shortly before World War II to encourage employers to feel a greater responsibility for both the community and their workers. Employers, through too much hedonism and too much preoccupation with financial security, were thought to have failed in their duties as business leaders. The CJP provided a doctrine to help recover the moral standing of the employer as head of the enterprise. Classical management thinking in France had emphasized unity of command. However, there was some feeling that in order to give effective leadership in the firm, one should not stress the subordination of employees as much as in the past, but should encourage them to take more initiative. The CJP leaders shared this belief. They were persuaded that the American "human relations" approach might be the answer to their concern. American capitalists seemed to be capitalists with a good conscience. In the new perspective the firm is seen less as a family-oriented operation than as a servant of the region where the plant is located; and profit loses the aspect of tribute or of illicit gain characteristic of the aristocratic frame of mind and becomes rather an indication of how well the businessman is doing his job of producing more value than he burns in the process of production. The Centre des Jeunes Patrons, with its clubs in all industrial regions of France, organizes numerous conferences; and its members take seriously their obligation to learn scientific methods rather than rely upon "natural methods."

There are other expressions of this reinterpretation of the employer's role. For example, in 1952 the Catholic university in Lille organized a course in management, given by a graduate of the Harvard Business School to local employers. Between 1948 and 1951, in the Lille-Roubaix-Tourcoing region, the Moral Rearmament movement had a vogue and promoted some soul-searching on worker-management relations. Classical paternalism was shown to be in disfavor when Albert Prouvost started a building program for workers' housing paid by a volunteer payroll tax. He made it quite clear that this should be done on a regional basis rather than through individual firms; his idea was adopted by the government and made into a national policy.

Nevertheless, as François Bourricaud well points out, a *malaise* remains within the progressive employers' group.[27] The Catholic Church, a force more important than ever in the minds of the progressive employers, finds it difficult to accept the legitimacy of the market as a provider of cues for action. To promote a vigorous attack upon the degradation of the worker's condition it believes in paternalism, self-sacrificing and Church-inspired but still, fundamentally, paternalism. In many cases where plants ought to be shut down for reasons of inefficiency the Church is in the forefront of those who demand that the plants be kept going to avoid the demoralization of the work force.

Mass production of consumer goods, changing the style of life of the French workers and white-collar employees, has achieved a higher prestige among industrialists. The employer has to submit to the control of the market, and this means that stability of employment, both for him and his work force, depends upon whether the public accepts or rejects his products and prices. Such dependence conflicts with the feelings of the Church. The CJP has tried to solve this dilemma by offering the employer as a sacrifice in order to save the workers' jobs; for example one speaker at the CJP Congress at Cannes in 1960 declared that if the family is not capable of making the firm grow and produce for the community, it has the moral duty to abandon management and delegate it to competent hands! Many Americans and, in fact, many Europeans might take this statement as a matter of course (without the moral overtone); but in a French organization where the heads of family firms provide the basic leadership, this declaration is an eye-opener. Property, instead of being the tabernacle of the family, the incarnation of its hard work and virtue, becomes a means to the end of serving the community by the production of wealth. Control over property must be put into the most competent hands regardless of family origin. Of course few are the families that will take this literally. But the very notion gives a weapon to those who want to weed out from the firm the most notoriously defective of their brothers or cousins. It gnaws at the automatic right to leadership of the elders.

For the CJP the proof of the pudding would be to abolish in its membership the *de facto* distinction between *patrons*, who are the owners, and *cadres*, who are hired executives. At the beginning the organization was overwhelmingly made up of patrimonial employers. Executives have been admitted, however, and their numbers have been increasing.

Many cynical predictions were made about the Jeunes Patrons in the late 1940's. It was commonly said: "When they are young they are not *patrons;* when they are *patrons* they are no more young." As a matter of fact the organization now has members in their fifties who have kept the faith. The general likemindedness of the members may have slowed their numerical growth but it has increased the depth and durability of their ideological commitment. That is why I believe that their importance is out of proportion to their comparatively small numbers (they employ about 10 percent of the labor force occupied in middle-sized firms).[28] Through their periodical, *Jeune Patron,* they reach a broader public. Not the least of their accomplishments has been their contribution to the breaking down of the intellectual isolation of the provincial entrepreneurs. The Jeunes Patrons outside Paris show no feeling of intellectual inferiority toward the big city; on the contrary, they believe that they are the ones who are located where things happen. In fact it is not too much to say that the Centre des Jeunes Patrons has become the vanguard of the business bourgeoisie in France.

Other expressions of neo-Catholicism in French industry have been the profit-sharing experiments of the Télémécanique Electrique (Migeon) and of Alexandre Dubois. Their concept of the firm—which goes back to a tradition at least as early as 1848—is one happy family, working as a sort of production cooperative. The Dubois plant and especially the Télémécanique are examples of a selected work force and of leadership which, by foregoing most of the personal benefits of entrepreneurship, has been able to combine very high wages with plant expansion. As in the traditional family, there is no question as to where the effective authority lies, but the respect and self-interest of the subordinates create a spontaneous cooperation which denies the problem of power. Another example, at the utopian extreme, is the Boismondeau community, with its equalitarian (Rousseauist) social structure. The CJP has been sympathetic to these experiments. Their significance is that they are attempts to find a religious legitimacy for profit-making.

These various forms of organization are manifestations of the growing awareness that one does not order the twentieth-century worker, acting in a complex scheme of the division of labor, as one ordered the ignorant and insecure worker of yesterday. Modern industry requires a high amount of communication and initiative on the part of the worker. This realization does not come easy to the patrimonial employer. But he can arrive there with less pain than before. A sort of broader, more humble Catholic paternalism provides his guide line. He could fall into line behind the *Plan Monnet* because it alleviated many of the uncertainties of the market. Without changing his values very much he could bring his capital out of hiding places and start investing it because the frontiers in Europe seemed to be stabilized and, in fact, Europe might be target number 2 rather than target number 1 in an atomic war. Besides, maybe the age of the great depressions had finally ended. With an economic courage not necessarily superior to that of his father, the present-day employer can try more innovations without risking such heavy penalties for failure. Today firms often end by mergers, which are not the same as failures. The world is less dangerous to the family firm.

Certainly the French economy has not become transformed as if by a magic wand from a creaky old car into a sleek sports model. In many large concerns, modern cost-accounting has just begun. The comptroller does not have the place in top management that he should have. A mere thirty-day delay in securing cost figures is conceived to be an achievement. The number of certified public accountants is sadly inadequate to the needs of a modern economy. In general, the administrative aspect of the large French firm is rigid and cumbersome. Secretarial techniques and materials are antiquated. Many large firms literally do not have a table of organization. French enterprise, whether an anonymous corporation or a family firm, grants more freely than in Germany—but less than in Japan—a *right to the job* which compels it to carry executives who should have found their level elsewhere. Those misfits or incompetents hang on to their positions, making of bureaucratic ritualism a religion and an insurance policy.

French industry still suffers from a serious weakness in wholesale and retail trade. This is changing, and may change still faster in the next few years. Modern, centralized commercial outlets are needed. Because so many shopkeepers lack business know-how, and because retail careers are still in low repute with French university students, certain fields, especially in wholesale food marketing, have become dominated by delinquent communities, which exact high fees for mediocre service.

Finally, in manufacturing the separation between the engineers and the shop is still far too great. This is a major problem handed down from the past. The weakness in the staffing between the engineer and the worker is due to the structure of French education which leaves little opportunity for the creation of a career line between the two. Important efforts are being made to remedy this weakness.

EDUCATION

The people who now dominate French politics and the economy are largely people who received their secondary education before World War II and their university education in the forties at the latest. Depression, defeat, occupation, liberation, and inflation have been their postgraduate courses. The youngsters now finishing their university studies were not exposed to these shocks in a way that would have been meaningful for the development of their attitudes; on the other hand they have experienced new conditions in the family, in the school system, and in their extra-curricular activities. What have been *adjustments* to the older generations have become *expectations* to the younger; and thus some changes in French political and economic structure have become changes in the motivational structures of the new cohorts of Frenchmen.

French primary and secondary education has been conducted by two systems, the parochial and the public. The parochial schools cater mainly to the bourgeoisie, but also to many peasants and workers, especially in areas where traditional Catholicism still has a strong hold over those classes. The public, or lay, schools cater to the "people" (*le peuple*), to the Protestant and Jewish minorities, and to the lower-middle and "middle-middle" classes.

Both parochial and public schools have stressed the same respect for formal perfection in speaking and writing the French language, the same respect for models of perfection set once and for all, through rote learning and copying. Individuality was to be expressed by stylistic variations on this model. The same religious fervor has been manifested in both the parochial and public school systems except that it took different directions. The parochial school has stressed God (even more the cult of the Virgin), nationalistic devotion to the motherland, opposition to the "godless" government. The public school has stressed the motherland, science, progress, humanity, and opposition to the forces of obscurantism; these forces of obscurantism were defined as composed of religion and of the higher estates which center around it—the Church, the aristocracy, and the bourgeoisie of hereditary wealth. The parochial school tended to find fault with the established order in the name of the royalist past and the "real France," the public school in the name of equality and progress.

What permits us to call the education "religious" in both systems is not only the "categorical imperative" aspect of the myths transmitted (and after all, any nation's elementary education has to transmit some myths), but the intensity and atmosphere of conflict in which they are taught. Imagine its American equivalent: private schools teaching the essential correctness of the loyalist position in the American Revolution, and public schools teaching that the loyalists were traitors and that George Washington partook of the divine.

To understand the traditional French process it is helpful to consider the personality types recruited into the teaching profession and the roles which the primary-school teacher played in the community. Most primary-school teachers were men, dedicated both to their creed and to their job, and fiercely patriotic (30 percent of the enlisted died in World War I). They were very well trained for a narrow task through the Ecole Normale d'Instituteurs, and remained all their lives in the primary schools. Many of these teachers (as in the secondary schools) had talents which could well be used in occupations of higher prestige and income. They usually derived from the elite of the peasantry, small shopkeepers, or working class. An *instituteur*, sent into a district other than his native one, inherited and carried on the struggle against the clerical forces led by the parish priest. In fact, the struggle permitted him to establish some leadership over the parents of the students. Furthermore, he often doubled as the mayor's assistant and this increased the willingness of the parents to support his discipline upon the children. On top of everything else, in the 1920's and 1930's many primary-school teachers adopted militant Socialist or Communist ideologies. The French child was taught in an atmosphere of struggle and dedication.

After the Second World War, however, the climate of opinion becomes much more moderate. An increasing percentage of primary-school teachers are women. Left-wing Catholicism competes successfully with the traditional radical ideologies. In many French centers and communes the most left-wing person may be the young priest. The *instituteur*, and even more the *institutrice*, in the public school has moved toward Catholicism and away from the radical extremes. The result of all this has been some notable changes in the atmosphere in which primary education takes place in France. The *instituteur* and the priests do not need to carry out the struggle against one another as they used to.[29] The basic myths of France are taught in a spirit of greater relaxation.

Soon after the Liberation the government introduced what are called the *new methods*—actually the types of "learning by doing" with which Americans have been familiar. They are much easier on the teacher in that they do not require as much talent. They require more empathy with the child, a closer relationship less bound by problems of discipline. They submit the child to fewer restrictions, and they promote the creation of peer groups which take responsibilities within the school.

This switch to the new methods was parallel with a decline in the specialized competency of the teacher. The regulation that the *instituteur* should get at least the first *baccalauréat* means that if a student has it in him to aspire to higher diplomas he is very likely to avoid the career of *instituteur*. At the present time, many of those who become *instituteurs* see in it a sort of stop-gap career (women tend to be in that category) or they are persons who failed the secondary cycle or the superior cycle. Furthermore, after the war an opportunity was given to the better *instituteurs* to switch over to the secondary cycle, and many of the most aggressive ones did so. Today in the primary cycle there is less talent, less dedication, less demand of formal perfection.

On the other hand it is quite possible that the amount of learning that is effectively assimilated by the child in the primary school is not smaller today than it was twenty-five years ago. There may be a decline of spelling competence and grammatical perfection. But there is very likely a greater familiarity with society as it is and a greater capacity to organize among students for limited and legitimate ends.

A similar process has taken place in the secondary schools. Immediately after the war the Communists were the major political group at the Ecole Normale Supérieure. From 1950 onward the progressive Catholics have tended to replace them as the elite group. It is not rare to find today among *lycée* professors Catholics who can propagate ideas that might be too bold for a Jesuit college.

Hence neither the primary nor the secondary schools are any longer feeding the Catholic-atheistic quarrel which had been a mainstay of local social structure and a particularly useful (because largely harmless) focus of national political struggle.

French secondary schooling is in a phase of crisis just now because it is not adapted to the demands of the public for mass education. The enormous amount of work required for absorbing the facts and models, and developing one's own style, works well only with students of relatively high IQ who receive constant reinforcement from their family milieu. It does not work well with a tidal wave of students of varying abilities and class backgrounds. And such a wave has arrived. The number of secondary students is several times what it was in the 1930's. The *baccalauréat* was devised for less than 20,000 candidates but in 1959 more than 110,000 presented themselves at the first part of the examinations alone. The number of girls in secondary schools has risen swiftly and is now equal to that of the boys. France spends more for the formal education of its women than any other European country. This fact has important repercussions for the structure of the nuclear family—of which more later.

Against this inundation of students the French educational system has attempted to maintain its standards. Large numbers are forced to drop out along the way toward the *baccalauréat*, and, of those who present themselves at the examinations, a large proportion fail. Such a failure, after long years of study, was bad enough for bourgeois students who could find easy employment in the family enterprises, but is an even greater deprivation for those from poorer classes.

Students have become more vocationally oriented. The classics, which were the core of French secondary education, have lost considerable ground to the sciences and modern languages. At the same time the professors have declined in caliber. As a result, manuals have become more important. Professors are more often content to control the reading of the manual and to stimulate class discussion. The manual is far from the austere compendium that was used before World War II; it has considerable eye appeal and is less loaded with detail.

In the student bodies of the secondary schools, the change of atmosphere is caused not only by the growing number who are poorly prepared and poorly equipped, and lack reinforcement at home. Other activities besides school have come to solicit the youth. One third of the *lycées* and *collèges* are now coeducational. Mixed parties begin at a much earlier age than in previous generations. Young French girls who used to dress in the most unglamorous attire until they were eighteen or nineteen are now putting on high heels at fifteen, and the sixteen-year-old imitations of Brigitte Bardot were quite obvious in the Paris of 1959–60. Even the provinces, always more conservative in these matters, are following suit, especially in the lower-middle and "middle-middle" class. Hence there is much more teen-age life than used to be the case in classical France, and especially more teen-age life that escapes supervision of the parents.

There is, furthermore, a greater interest in sports. Between love and soccer football the average adolescent is less willing to accept the grind of French secondary education. The protests against excessive homework become louder and louder, and since the Association des Parents d'Elèves has become more effective (after many decades as a paper organization), the means for putting pressure upon the school are stronger.

In line with the gradual moving away from the lecture form of teaching, the French *lycée* (secondary school) has been experimenting with student government.[30] France is still far from the American high school but the distant trend may well be in that direction. The trend already differentiates several possible avenues of school achievement besides the purely academic one—for example, excelling at sports, or being a success with the girls, or a connoisseur of jazz, vanguard literature, or cars, or being a great party promoter. The youth society that is fast developing around the schools provides more chances for the young to find their own levels and to develop ambitions suited to their inner selves.

The peer group, less constrained by the school and by family structure, does not have to resort so often to the patterns of the delinquent community. Having a legitimate autonomy of its own, it develops patterns of leadership and membership that teach the young Frenchman the skills of "competitive solidarity" indispensable to the creation of voluntary organizations for limited but positive ends.

Education in France, as in most of Europe, is so organized that an individual's wrong turning at an early point can commit him for life to a lower status than he would otherwise have attained. In one well-managed industrial plant, a review of workers who had become incapacitated through illness or accidents, and who had been shifted by the firm to white-collar work, showed that 40 percent of them were making remarkable careers once they secured a hold on the white-collar ladder. This is to be expected when artificial barriers reduce the opportunities of workers to upgrade themselves. In France, the failure of a worker's or peasant's son to enter the secondary cycle at the age of eleven used to be an almost unconquerable barrier to entry into a middle-class occupation. "Late bloomers" who had become sidetracked to vocational curricula had very little chance to rejoin the circuit of studies leading to the *baccalauréat*. Various reforms have been tried and proposed to make the structure less rigid and the early decisions less crucial, but without very much success so far, because they are resisted by the *agrégés* who control the curriculum sequence most likely to produce university students.

In the last ten years, however, under the initial impulse of a Socialist university professor named Esclangon, a group (Promotion

293

Supérieure du Travail) was started in Grenoble to help working-class promotion. The idea has been taken over by a group of Catholic professors who have turned the project into a sort of crusade for giving workers a second chance. The first problem is to help workers aged eighteen to fifty to obtain the *baccalauréat* or the equivalent which will permit them to accede to the university curriculum. From this they have been led to develop methods of teaching that are better integrated to a worker's life problems and perceptual system. Because of the many difficulties the night student has to surmount, the organization has developed an intense group life which separates the student from his "immobile" peers and reinforces his motivation. Wives are also involved in the process so that they can move up on the social level while their husbands are upgrading themselves in education. The organization has spread to other parts of France and claims a membership of 20,000 students. Recently the top student in the graduating class of the Institut Electro-chimique de Grenoble—one of the better engineering schools—was a worker who had been prepared through this new system.[31]

This organization has been watched with sympathy by the state. Its experience should provide important guide lines to those who wish to reform French education so that it can effectively train students of all social backgrounds and give late bloomers a second chance.

THE TRANSFORMATION OF THE FAMILY

I have mentioned the tendency for trade assocations and interest groups to develop into effective voluntary organizations instead of paper organizations covering delinquent communities. One of the factors behind this tendency is that the nuclear family—the couple and their children—has been reinforced to the detriment of the extended family.

The reasoning behind that statement is as follows. If the nuclear family increases its efficiency as a center of emotional security and "tension management" for the personality, the individual does not need to carry the search for this tension management into roles outside the family. To put it in terms that go beyond my thinking but which may suggest the situation, the world outside the family becomes to a greater extent "desexualized." Relations with others can be entered into on the basis of mutual cooperation for limited gains.

The nuclear family has indeed increased its efficiency, and one of the chief reasons for this is the greater intimacy of the couple. The bourgeois family has been buried by essayists many times since 1920, but it refused to stay dead. I shall be less ambitious and say that the *bourgeois marriage*, arranged or heavily oriented by the families, does seem dead, even in the provinces. Orientation by frowns or smiles upon suitors presented by the daughter is still the pattern in all the Western world; but that is quite different from the pattern in which much of the initial selection process was made by the families themselves. Even in the late 1940's this was still a common occurrence in the French upper class, and in the upper-middle class of the provinces. Today this is no longer true except in cases of desperation over the failure of the girl or boy to find a mate. There was a time when the Catholic Church would support the family in its attempts to force a marriage upon an unwilling girl. Today the Church would generally be hostile to any such pressure. The present stress is indeed upon the importance of free consent by each party, and by "free" is not meant a simple lack of coercion but a genuine gift of the self. In practice, romantic love becomes the basis for marriage choice.

The parents are reconciled to the situation by the obvious out-moding of some of their old prime criteria. Property has lost weight as compared with the earning power of executive work, and will continue to lose weight as professional management becomes able to grant itself expense accounts and stock bonuses. A dowry may not turn out to be as effective a contribution to the strength of a marriage as a good university education which may lead to a civil service rating. Actually, many bourgeois families, because of higher marriage rates and war losses, do not have those reserves of linen, furniture, and living space which they could give, besides cash, to the new couple. Dowries still exist but they become more nominal. Before World War I, when many a daughter got married her bourgeois father could expect to live only ten to fifteen more years.

His economic activity was beginning to slow down. Capital was relatively easy to free for a dowry, which was an advance on a forthcoming inheritance. At present the average French bourgeois who gives his daughter away in marriage can expect to live some twenty to twenty-seven additional years.[32] The demands of business are such that he is unlikely to have much free capital to give to a young couple. Furthermore, installment buying and more widespread use of the substantial mortgage has taken over some of the functions served by the dowry in making it easier for a young couple to get started.

The decline of the dowry parallels a change in the status of women in general. Frenchwomen have always had a high *de facto* status; nevertheless in bourgeois families girls were less valuable than boys because they represented greater prestige risks and their marriage required large divestment of property. Their sheltered education tended to promote at least an *official* infantilism which led to marriage with men easily ten years their senior in age and five or six years beyond them in formal education. Even in the early 1950's university education for girls was not the pattern for the upper-middle-class girl and certainly not for the upper-class girl. Even these classes have become converted to university education, which in fact removes many of the controls parents can exercise on their daughters' social life.

Marriage in the bourgeoisie takes place earlier than before. One reason is that the sexual exploitation of lower-class girls is no longer good form, and besides is more difficult to accomplish in the way in which it can still be done in Italy and Spain. Another is the fact that beginning salaries for junior executives are more nearly sufficient to permit a couple to live—especially when the wife can work until the first child is born. An upper-class girl graduating from Sciences Po wants to marry a young Jewish man who works in movie producing. Her parents offer her the alternative: stop seeing the young man or leave their home. She leaves their home and goes to work for 75,000 francs a month in an advertising agency. Before the war nobody would have employed her; ten or twelve years ago the job did not exist. In 1962 she can live her own life long enough for the parents to capitulate. In the upper, upper-middle, and middle-middle classes, marriage takes place in the early twenties, the age differential being usually not more than two or three years and the educational differential even smaller.

A young Frenchman is unlikely to think of the dowry when he falls in love with a girl of his milieu. His relationship to his wife, expressed by the term la femme-camarade, is more that of a true equal. The "peer group" dimension of marriage is much stronger. Having chosen each other in relative freedom, husband and wife cannot resort to the escape of extramarital affairs without "contradicting" themselves more than was the case for their parents and grandparents. An affair is no longer a right or a prowess. In many ways it is a confession of failure. People will work harder at making their marriage a success. Their communication system is better.

This does not mean that the French couple does not preserve its originality. It has to cope with greater extramarital pressures than are met in the United States. There is probably more hedonistic romanticism than is met in the United States or Great Britain, and this is marked by a higher valuation of sexual prowess and of the folie-à-deux type described in the movie "Hiroshima, Mon Amour." Although maid service is getting scarcer and less skillful, French husbands will not push togetherness to the point of partaking of the household chores, certainly not to the extent of their American counterparts. There still is more interest in family politicking than in civic activities, although the Catholic Action groups offer a form of transition between the two.

The form of man-and-wife relationship I have described is comparatively new in the upper and upper-middle classes. In the middle-middle class, where financial and family considerations played less part, this marriage pattern was already better known. What has happened is that this class has become larger and has increased its prestige, and, as this has occurred, the new-type marriage has gained in other classes. It is becoming more widespread in the petty-bourgeoisie and in the upper reaches of the working class.

In the old working-class family the wife controlled the purse strings. Her husband showed his dominance by certain masculine rituals such as "revolutionarism," wine drinking, and "acting tough." Common-law marriages were frequent. The present trend could be summarized as "from red flannel and blue collar to white coat." The husband has more voice in financial matters, since these now often imply the purchase of a house, an apartment, household appliances, or a used car. On the other hand, there is less verbal dominance.[33] The working-class family goes camping on the motorcycle or the tandem, and increasingly in its Dauphine. The patterns and prestige of the new family are spread and consolidated by the diffusion of women's magazines like *Elle,* whose readership goes all the way from the upper-middle class to the petty-bourgeoisie and skilled working class.

Finally, the married couple has been reinforced by the rise of a youth culture, which provides a transition between the childhood home and the home created by the marriage and helps to sever the ties to the parents.

Before World War II the only youth culture that existed was limited to the universities and especially to the University of Paris, around the Latin Quarter. Most French students lived at home. Youths of the upper-middle and upper classes indulged in a period of irresponsibility characterized by sexual license and extremist political opinions; but even much of this activity was under the control of maturer people through their control of the political and aesthetic movements. Much of a young man's social life was still guided by the *salon,* where again older men and women set the tone.

Since the war the "existentialist" movement, the swiftly growing number of female university students, the diffusion of the "surprise party" as the most common form of social activity for the teen-ager, the popularity of jazz—all these items have created a special language for the young and a special society from which the older age groups are kept apart.

The uncommitted relations between boys and girls of roughly the same milieu are a crucial armature of this youth society. It is not dating as known in the United States. Rather there are *bandes* of six or more boys and girls none of whom is specially committed to another and who, when they do become more involved, cultivate a sort of *amitié amoureuse* which usually avoids sex unless two people have decided that "this is it." The *bande* in fact derides couple formation within its ranks, though it does happen. The unit of social life is thus not the couple, as in the States, but the group. When dating does take place it will be more formal than in the States. Otherwise the French boy has one or more *copines* (pals), or *amies* [34] as they would be called in the upper status groups. They often split expenses. Sexual relations sometimes take place—by joint agreement—for "hygiene" or "freedom," but typically the relations remain more platonic and stable than in the usual American dating. Often enough, engagement and marriage will be with someone else with whom the relationship has been one of more distance and mystery.

This youth society is stratified but the stratification is less marked than in adult society, more open to personal charisma. Manners are simplified. There is greater stress upon "sincerity," *engagement* (commitment), and less upon the status of parents. Sports and Catholic activities as well as the old aesthetic interests create different hierarchies which cut across the hierarchy of the families.

This new style of life, noticeable among middle-class youth, is easily imitated by the young worker of today. Even if he does not "mix" with the student crowd, he goes to the same skating rinks and the same ski slopes; he dresses the same way; and his *copine* will be the same imitation of Brigitte Bardot as is the engineer's daughter. They all sit in the same café drinking identical Cokes. Indeed, the young worker may have a Vespa, whereas the young student who depends on his parents for his pocket money may not have one. The rock-and-roll tune hummed by the young worker has the legitimacy and prestige of an American import. If he lives in a province, and is handsome, he may be less an outsider to the youth society than the well-off bourgeois young man who is compelled to attend the elaborate affairs prepared by his uncles and aunts. The Communist Party organization seems terribly dull and "square" to such a young worker.

The style of the youth society is not lost by the young married couples. There are fewer of those great bourgeois ceremonies where the status groups renewed their solidarity and tested their boundaries, and where links were forged between young couples and older clan heads. Social life is generally more gratuitous—centered around a smaller circle where differences in age and interest are minimum and the career advantages to be derived from membership are small. And social life is increasingly organized around a civic or religious purpose. Even when the status groups are still closed and ritual is elaborate, as in the highest classes, there is a tendency toward simplification; but it is in the middle class—the "middle-middle"—that informality is most noticeable. This group, as we have seen, is growing in number; the 50 percent increase in civil-service employment and the multiplication of white-collar jobs in industry have contributed to this growth, and at the same time the classical petty-bourgeoisie of shopkeepers and independent craftsmen is declining. In the past, members of the middle-middle class were always held back by the disproportion between the standards they received from the upper-middle class and the financial means which were equivalent to those of the lower-middle class. But now they can have a more active social life, and, as a result, they have developed a greater consciousness of kind. They used to be a marginal group, of low biological fertility, hence "evaporating" in the laborious climb to the upper-middle-class status. But now we find there a source of manners, a style of life proud of itself, people who are convinced that the trends are with them and who have enough children to reproduce themselves.

The influence that this large and vital class exerts on groups of lower status is not confined to the new-type marriage already mentioned. More broadly, the emphasis on performance and on technical skills as against power and property—which is characteristic of the "middle-middle"—is highly acceptable to lower-status groups. The higher standard of living and leisure affords to the subordinate a broad range of activities in which there is no correlated inferiority of a clear-cut nature. As a result the subordination of the job can be more easily accepted. There is less need for the autonomy of secrecy and delinquency.

If these statements are correct, there should be in France a decline in the diffuse suspiciousness which marked the relationship between strangers. It is possible that the marked decline in automobile accidents per car may be an index of this greater trust and capacity for spontaneous cooperation between strangers. Automobile traffic is a school of citizenship where the penalties for failure can be very high.[35]

Finally there seems to have been developing a new sort of regional patriotism broader than the localism that used to exist. The region receives some of the loyalties that used to go to the nation-state. It is also a frame for cooperative action. The strengthening of the regional press since World War II has helped in this regard, although the city dailies need to be complemented by an effective network of neighborhood weeklies. In fact, for the more educated, this regional patriotism goes hand in hand with the beginnings of a commitment to a United Europe.

A SUMMING UP

The responses of French society to the challenges of history have been analyzed here with reference to two fundamental value themes in her culture, one being the doctrinaire-hierarchical and the other the aesthetic-individualistic. The first responses to any stress are often escapist fantasies and a repetition of procedures that were successful in the past. Examples of fantasies were the romanticism of the colonial fighters and the dreams of "grandeur" of de Gaulle I in the 1940's, and even, to a lesser extent, of de Gaulle II beginning in the late 1950's. The "repetitive" response could be seen in the initial "dirigist" impulses of the state in 1944–1947 and the counterreactions of the "delinquent communities"— whether made of industrial families, shopkeepers, peasants, workers, or civil servants. But, simultaneously with these habitual reactions, there have been creative outbursts resulting from new syntheses between the doctrinaire-hierarchical and aesthetic-individualistic trends of French culture, rooted in the dilemmas of Catholicism. The organization developing and implementing the Monnet plan and the plans which followed it is a good example of such a creative force.

I began with a description of the dominant strands in French culture and tried to show how these strands combined in making prestigeful models of action such as the aristocratic concept of prowess, the motherland-state-government complex, the bourgeois family, the delinquent community, the family firm. These aspects of France have not disappeared. They exist in the minds of Frenchmen, especially those aged fifty and above, and they are implemented in the behavior of many people.

Nevertheless, shifts have occurred which decrease the importance of those structures, so characteristic of prewar France. Some of the forces pressing in that direction have simply resulted from changes in the definition of the situation without any change in the basic attitudes; two good examples are the definition of business as a field of prowess and the decline in the uncertainty of the market. Other shifts that have affected the old structure seem to be responses to situational imperatives such as the need for greater two-way communication in modern technology, or the shriveling of national sovereignty under the protective umbrella of American power. Another factor of change is the discovery of new techniques, such as techniques for the management of the business cycle by government financing, and the use of computers for solving problems of economic planning. What *orients* change in a society, however, seems to be what its people want out of life, and this is determined by their values.

A good example of the new synthesis appears in the growth of a deeper commitment to a supranational Catholicism, in which the sanctity of the collectivity calls forth the initative and the responsibility of the individual member. It is a new Reformation, the importance of which is overlooked because it does not manifest itself in organizational schisms and passionate polemics noticeable by the outsider. This Reformation is not limited to the Catholics bearing allegiance to the Church; it affects all who partake of the living French culture. One of the main manifestations of this new synthesis is a change in the style of association; the delinquent community takes more of the aspects of a plot to do good; formal associations become more numerous, more specific, more intent upon creative goals, and less interested in the delights of a motivational consensus. Other manifestations are the more pragmatic relations between the state and the citizen, the attempt to find a fraternal meaning in the labor contract (Centre des Jeunes Patrons), the decline in formal doctrinaire education, the development of the couple to the detriment of the classical bourgeois family (a phenomenon which in turn influences the pattern of association), the loosening of class barriers, and a strengthening of the property-less middle-middle class. This neo-Catholicism (which has its atheistic equivalents) gives its individuality to the French version of a phenomenon which is affecting the whole Western world.

These creative drives, emerging from the conflict between different cultural strands, have enabled France to set its economy in order, to redefine its relations toward its old colonies, and to take some steps toward the integration of Europe.

Progress has not been without strains; indeed the strains are sometimes more apparent than the conditions that needed remedying. Progress has threatened the prestige and even the identity of some groups to which France owed much of her glory and stability —for example the officers and noncommissioned officers of the colonial wars, who need a complete reorientation for atomic warfare. There are also the excess peasants, the excess shopkeepers, and the type of wholesaler who derives a good part of his profit from a power relation to an ignorant and unorganized peasant. The Communist trade unions, based on the classical blue-collar status of rebellious subordination, are also likely to decline after long serving as one of three supports of the classical French economy (family firm, small store, and revolutionary syndicalism). So is the feudal-type family firm afraid of the Common Market. The professors of the secondary cycle, lamenting the end of the classical *lycée*, and the utopian intellectual who acts as a political sage are also likely to lose some of their clientele. A fortunate aspect of these results of social change is that these "obsolete" groups hate one another as much as they fear the present drift of events which is leaving them adjusted to a world that is no more. Hence I would hazard a prediction of continued civil peace intermixed with the usual strikes and demonstrations, and of continued economic progress. True enough the changes in political structures appear less thorough than the changes in economic structures, but changes in the expectations and responsibilities of citizens sometimes take place without any obvious change in the constitution or the name and number of political parties and administrative agencies. True enough, on the level of political and ideological representation there seems to have been much less reform than on the level of the state in its bureaucratic and doctrinaire-hierarchical aspects. The conflict between the simultaneous desire for impartial authority and for being the favorite, so characteristic of the French family, and the delinquent stance of the parliamentary *République des Camarades* —these may be too ingrained to permit the implementation of a true presidential regime in France.

On the other hand, if Europe, rather than remaining an American satellite, does become an autonomous economic and political unit, it will have to develop federal structures commensurate to its responsibilities as an atomic power. In that case it is likely that the French parliamentary theater will shrink in audience size and significance. In fact a weak *political* executive in France may facilitate rather than hinder the growth of a strong European executive. French politics may become more and more a game and a tension-reducing mechanism, while the bureaucracy integrates itself with the federal state.

Those of us who did research in France in the late 1940's and early 1950's created models in which the remarkable economic growth of the 1950's had no place. The present model may seem to some to be overoptimistic, perhaps as a reaction to a pessimism which I shared with David Landes, John Sawyer, Herbert Luethy, and Warren Baum.[36] This will only underline the fact that we know very little of what we would like to know about a total society and that our models are consequently, to use Auguste Comte's expression, in the metaphysical stage. However, science progresses by the making and undoing of models; the errors and insufficiencies of this one, when revealed, may increase our scientific potential.

CHANGES IN FRENCH
FOREIGN POLICY SINCE 1945

Jean-Baptiste Duroselle

Changes in the policies of a nation cannot properly be observed without determining what was stable over a relatively long period in the past. Therefore a study of the evolution of French foreign policy after the Second World War must begin with tradition. There is indeed a tradition of French foreign policy, prevailing from 1815 to 1940, in which a certain unity can be discerned amid the complexities of detail. The next essential step is to bring out the nature of the violent upset experienced by France in 1940 and the following years. In other words, after examining the "normal" we must examine the catastrophe. After the catastrophe came the effort to readapt, an effort that took two contradictory aspects: the movement toward "return to the normal" and the movement toward "radical innovation." In this essay I shall try to illuminate the tradition, the catastrophe, and most of all the adaptation.

I

THE TRADITION

The analysis of a tradition is necessarily complex. Tradition manifests itself in the acts of foreign policy, that is, in the conduct of governments; it also shows in the general and particular objectives pursued, that is, the conception—with varying degrees of confusion and precision—of the national interest. Furthermore, governmental acts and objectives exist in the general context of the questions: What does the public as a whole think? What are the attitudes of particular groups? A strong government can take certain liberties with opinion; the weaker a government is, the more closely it must follow opinion so as not to risk opposition—in France possibly its own existence. Governmental weakness makes it difficult to take initiative or launch innovations.

On the level of national goals, one might use Raymond Aron's distinction between abstract goals (such as power, glory, ideas) and concrete goals (such as space, people, souls). But this distinction seems to leave out the following types of goals: wealth, independent of any territorial ambition; the will to peace as the supreme value; a will to develop internal cohesion of the nation, or, on the contrary, a desire to favor the supremacy of one class over others. I would prefer to keep to a classification of "extroversive" and "introversive" goals. Extroversive goals result in the priority of foreign policy—power, security, glory and *grandeur*, the sense of a civilizing mission. Introversive goals result in the priority of internal matters with foreign policy serving as an instrument only. Where this type prevails, foreign policy must avoid risks that would interfere with the achievement of domestic goals. Wealth, peace, social cohesion or the domination of a particular class are goals of the introversive type.

If this distinction between extroversive and introversive goals is adopted, one must conclude that, since 1815, French public opinion has definitely chosen to give priority to introversive goals, and that only governments—which must act and take initiative—have sometimes asserted a positive foreign policy.

Since the usual foreign image is of a more "nationalistic" France, we should try to explain the point of view which justifies this statement, possibly surprising to the reader at first sight.

There have always been and still are minority groups in France, usually active and very vocal, who inject nationalistic claims into the political scene. Sometimes from the Right and sometimes from the Left, they take an arrogant tone, charged with aggression, which is distasteful and often incomprehensible to foreigners. These groups hailed Napoleon III when he destroyed the Second Republic, they supported General Boulanger, they predominated in the *Chambre-Bleu-Horizon* or national bloc of 1919–1924. They also supported the "revolution" by which de Gaulle came to power in May 1958. They always favor government action which takes risks and have often criticized governments for being too cautious; they urge the government to greater audacity without being responsibly aware of the possible consequences. In brief, there are always some who are ready to pull the trigger on every occasion.

My thesis, however, is that at least since 1815 public opinion in general has not approved this aggressive or extroversive attitude, and that when it had a chance, it has always exerted power in the direction of caution in foreign affairs, and finally, that it has been primarily concerned with internal problems. No doubt there have been brief periods when opinion has seemed temporarily to be carried away under the influence of these fanatical groups. There have been periods of nationalist fever—July 1870 and July 1914— but they were not to determine the substance of policy and very quickly they became absorbed in much more cautious, reasonable, or resigned attitudes. Furthermore, such excesses have never occurred except in one of two circumstances—either a threat from outside, as in July 1914, or at moments of national humiliation, as in July 1870, and in November 1956 during the Suez crisis. Public opinion in general has never *pushed* government to actions which were dazzling but dangerous. Almost always, on the contrary, public opinion has checked governments which had undertaken such actions, or, if it supported the government—as in the instances cited—it was because it had been conditioned by the government or aroused by the action of a foreign power. There have then occurred the moments of "sacred union" (*union sacré*). In the history of modern France, however, the moments of sacred union have never had any real follow-up or lasting effects. Two short texts from different periods will testify to this distinction.

François Guizot wrote to Lord Aberdeen on September 16, 1849: "You may count on the fact that foreign policy does not concern the French at all and will not be the cause of any important event. Governments can do what they please. If they make foolish mistakes they will not be supported; if they are stupid they will be hissed at without anger and without their being overthrown as a result. The only ones [governments] that are taken seriously are those that accomplish something in terms of domestic affairs of the country." [1]

Alfred Grosser has shown how an identical contrast existed between General de Gaulle and the parties in 1945. "For General de Gaulle the nation and its foreign power should be the center, the focus of all political thought. People often quote the well-known formula of his radio broadcast of November 17, 1945, in which he refused to give the Ministries of Foreign Policy, War, or Interior to the Communists: 'None of the three levers which control foreign policy, that is the diplomacy which expresses it, the army which supports it, the police which protects it.' What does this mean if not that the government is conceived of in terms of foreign policy? Even the social structure itself is considered in relation to it . . . On the other hand, looking at the programs which the parties and political groups presented to the voters in November 1945, one cannot help being struck by the almost total absence of foreign policy. It is specifically reconstruction and the standard of living which held first place." [2]

In all, between 1815 and 1940 one cannot discern in France a single occasion when public opinion had literally forced the government to adopt a policy involving risk. Collective nationalistic hysteria did exist in the French Revolution, especially in the spring of 1792 when the Jacobin Club as well as the court wanted war, but it later disappeared. Only certain groups had aggressive attitudes and each time that a test of strength was made these groups were shown to be a feeble minority of the nation. Well before the terrible bloodbath of 1914–1918, war had lost its "fresh, joyous" character in France. In 1830 no serious pressure was put on the government to try to conquer Belgium. In 1840 only small groups of Republicans and intellectuals encouraged Thiers to protest against the coalition of four great European powers against France. To Musset's incendiary poem, "We have had your German Rhine," Lamartine replied with his famous "Marseillaise de la Paix." The same Lamartine let Europe understand in 1848 that peace was the dearest wish of the French Republic, and when the clubs of the extreme Left organized a revolutionary movement to aid Poland, public opinion did not follow them. Napoleon III came to power with the slogan "The Empire is Peace." During the Crimean War in 1854 and the War of Italian Liberation in 1859, opinion was resigned rather than enthusiastic.

Collective hysteria appears again, perhaps, in July 1870 when the Legislative Corps, indignant over the notorious "Ems Dispatch," sincerely supported the decision of Napoleon III to unleash war. Despite Thiers, the Legislative Corps passed the military budget by 159 to 84 votes. But it was evident that this hysteria existed only in ruling circles and not in the country as a whole. A few months later, at the time of the defeat, when the highest-ranking Republicans wanted to continue the war, the country responded by electing (on February 8, 1871) a big monarchist majority, not that the country was monarchist, but because the monarchists were then pacifists. Thiers, the man of peace, was elected in twenty-six different *départements*.

Finally, after Alsace and Lorraine were lost, there was no popular movement of "revenge" until after 1914. Those who claimed revenge were always a minority group.

A penetrating remark of Jacques Bainville makes this same point in a different way: the warmongers, or at least the extreme nationalists, are to be found on the Left until about 1875 and on the Right since then. Significantly the Right was in power until 1875 (with the exception of a few months in 1848) and the Left (at least Left Center) since then. Extreme nationalism was always an emotional opposition to the usual moderate and prudent position of the government. Guizot defined his policy as an attitude "favoring peace without giving up anything of quiet pride." He stigmatized the warmongers as being governed by "a revolutionary spirit exploiting the national drive, pushing towards war without legitimate motives, or a reasonable chance of success—with revolution the only goal and hope."[3] If Guizot's analysis is correct, even this extroversive attitude of Leftist opinion is in reality introversive in its object, that is, the revolution itself.

If we look at *boulangisme* in 1889 we find an almost parallel situation in reverse. This time the nationalism for revenge came from a minority of the Right or rather a fraction of the Right which had rallied to Boulanger—"General Revenge"—with a very few Radicals. It was the nationalism of the famous League of Patriots, whose leader, Paul Déroulède, supported Boulanger to the hilt. The government, however, even if it was not reconciled to the loss of the eastern provinces, followed the rule, "Let us think of it always, but let us not speak of it." As Maurice Reclus, leading defender of the Third Republic, wrote, "The progress of democratic ideas in France could not help but be accompanied by a certain pacifism, at least in theory. Although their patriotism adapted itself easily to the prospect of a defensive war, the French still condemned war as such, theoretically as well as emotionally. The Regime, for its part, did not intend to assume the responsibility of a war-like policy in the eyes of all Europe." [4]

What are the ingredients of this dominant introversionism? The first and most important is *territorial satisfaction*. The frontiers of 1815—approximately the same as those of 1792—were considered satisfactory enough so that it was agreed that no war should be risked just in order to change them. The first "great debate" on this subject took place at the beginning of the Directory in 1796. We see three main tendencies emerging. The first was "revolutionary expansionism" advocated by the Director La Revellière-Lepeaux, who thought that the French army should conquer territory to create a zone of liberty. France was establishing around her a group of "sister republics" (today we would say "satellites"). Secondly, there was the doctrine of natural frontiers, that is, the aim to reach the Alps and the Rhine, "boundaries set by nature," as Danton had said in a famous speech on January 3, 1793. This thesis was supported by another director, Reubell, an Alsatian. Finally, there was the doctrine of moderation—to maintain the frontiers of 1792—which was supported by the wise Carnot. We know that in 1796 it was the doctrine of revolutionary expansionism which prevailed, because of the pressure exerted by a young general who saw in it a means to develop his ambitions, Napoleon Bonaparte. By 1815, however, twenty-five years of fighting had brought France around to content herself with Carnot's conception. That France had accepted these frontiers seems proven by the following examples:

First, no government in power since Louis XVIII has ever tried to go beyond these frontiers except that of Napoleon III, and even for him the goal of "destroying the shameful treaties of 1815" was only acceptable if pursued by pacific means. In this way Nice and Savoy were annexed in 1860, following treaties and plebiscites. Napoleon III renounced the Rhineland and Luxembourg in 1866 when he realized that to acquire them would mean a war against Prussia.

Next, the degree of territorial satisfaction was reflected in the profound shock caused in France by the loss of part of the 1815 territory—Alsace-Lorraine. By annexing them Germany really overstepped the intangible limits of the country. France resigned herself but never really accepted it—all the more so as her claim was based on rights stemming from the clear and frequently expressed will of the peoples of the "lost provinces," a fact which seemed much more significant to the French than the matter of language, so emphasized by the Germans.

Finally, in 1918, when France was one of the principal victors, her ambition was confined to the recovery of Alsace and Lorraine —with a temporary exception. Clemenceau and Tardieu, not satisfied to see "injustice wiped out"—to use Woodrow Wilson's expression—set forth the idea that the injustices done to France in 1815 (as compared with 1814) should be wiped out along with those of 1871. This implied a very small annexation, a little strip of territory on the left bank of the Saar, with Saarlouis and Saarbruck. We know that after heated discussions in the Supreme Allied Council, Wilson and Lloyd George obliged Clemenceau to abandon even this minimum claim. The important point is that it was just a minimum. Clemenceau had opposed "natural frontiers." Although he wished to detach the Rhineland from Germany and to occupy it with military forces to ensure French security, he never planned to annex it, despite the strong pressure of the nationalistic extreme Right. Jacques Bainville and Charles Maurras had suddenly rediscovered the theory of natural frontiers and were proclaiming it in *L'Action Française*. Clemenceau agreed that our ancestors of the Convention had taught us that we must reach the Rhine—but times had changed. "Is it my fault?" he asked, "that when I move towards the Rhine now I find German people in the way?" Briand was to say, "Reconstituted as we are by the recovery of the provinces which belonged to us and which were a part of our body, we do not think we have anything more to ask; we wish to live and work in peace and we consider that we pose no threat whatever to other nations." [5]

When analyzing territorial satisfaction as a national goal, one cannot stop with European territory. Another ingredient must be included. From 1815 to 1914 France had thought it useful to pursue colonial expansion. Only in the Restoration period had the government hesitated, contenting itself with the recovery of former colonies. That government had in fact made the first gesture of decolonization in the history of France in 1825, by renouncing officially its claims on San Domingo, which had become the Republic of Haiti. But Polignac launched the nation on the conquest of Algiers, the July Monarchy established itself in Algeria and in the Pacific, and the Second Empire extended French dominion in Senegal and in Southern Indochina. The Third Republic took part in the great European colonization movement and by 1912 had conquered a vast domain in Asia and Africa. Even the treaties of 1919 and 1920, through the mandate system, added to French colonial possessions which toward 1938 began to be called "The Empire."

How is this colonial expansion to be explained? Jules Ferry, who was chiefly responsible for it—although he was only converted to the colonial idea in 1881—showed that it resulted from complex motives. Economic interests, first of all.

A colonial policy is necessary for nations which have to resort to emigration, whether because of the poverty of their people or because of their excessive population. It [colonial policy] is no less necessary for nations which have either excess capital or excess goods, and this is its present form, the most widespread and the most fertile: France, which has always had large amounts of capital and exported considerable quantities of it abroad, must consider the colonial question from this point of view . . . But there is another aspect to the question which is much more important: for nations destined like ours to large exports by the very nature of their industry, the colonial question becomes the question of markets. When political domination exists, there is also domination of products, that is, economic domination.[6]

Paul Leroy-Beaulieu had already written that "the main purpose of colonies is to provide a great outlet for French commerce, to stimulate and support industry and to provide the people of the mother country with an increase in profits (industrialists), in wages (workers), and in comforts (consumers)." [7]

As it turned out, a difference between Britain's colonial empire and France's was that French colonization was not economically viable; France invested little capital in the colonies. In any case, colonialism had more than economic causes. Another cause was the will to power. Jules Ferry saw this perfectly. Gambetta, congratulating Ferry on the establishment of the Protectorate in Tunisia, wrote to him May 13, 1881, "France is resuming her rank as a great power." [8] Ferry never ceased to insist on the necessity of territories and bases for the navy. "To shine without acting," he said in 1885, "without taking part in world affairs . . . to regard all expansion in Africa or in the Orient as a trap or as an escapade, to live this way is, for a great nation, to abdicate, and, faster than you might believe, it is to descend from the first rank to the third or the fourth." [9]

Finally, for Ferry and for many others there was a clear notion of France's "civilizing mission": "Messieurs, we must speak louder and more truthfully—it must be openly stated that the superior races have rights in relation to the inferior races . . . I repeat that they have rights because they have obligations—the obligation to civilize the inferior races." [10]

In all, colonization, traditionally accepted in France (especially by the Third Republic), was combined with an economic tradition, and a civilizing and missionary tradition, but also with a will to power, a will to remain in the first rank.

This leads us to another element of the tradition in French foreign policy, one that can be called the *primacy of political factors over economic*. The desire to gain wealth, which exists everywhere, has generally been the supreme national interest for the British. Montesquieu already saw this when he wrote: "Above all jealous of her trade, England binds herself by few treaties and depends on her own laws alone. Other nations have subordinated the interests of commerce to political interests, while England has always made political interests cede to those of commerce." [11] Using this famous remark as a point of departure, Raymond Aron, in an analysis of the French and British methods of financing underdeveloped nations, shows that this contrast between British and French ideas is still true.[12] One could of course find many examples in the centuries between Montesquieu and Aron. The best example of all is that of the Russian State Bonds before 1917. While England invested her capital wherever economic profits would be greatest, the government of the Third Republic pushed Frenchmen with savings to buy Russian State Bonds. Why? Because the need of the Russian alliance and the consequent necessity to bolster the ally won out in the minds of French leaders over considerations of long-term profits. And the possessors of savings, ill-informed, allowed themselves to be easily convinced—all the more as the Russian financial adviser in Paris, Raffalovitch, "bought" a number of newspapers to spread propaganda which would increase the sale of the bonds.[13] Similarly, between the two World Wars, France thought it necessary to subsidize the small European allies, while England preferred the system of "splendid isolation."

We may conclude, then, that although opinion is generally introversive in France, governments sometimes take more positive attitudes, taking advantage of the public indifference mentioned by Guizot. In this sense, French tradition, in contrast to British and American tradition, allows for a great divergence between the actions of those responsible and the reaction of the people. More precisely, one can say that French governments oscillate between various policies more or less tolerated by opinion.

This tendency is also to be found in a more recent element of the French tradition, the *will to peace*. Everything said at the beginning of this section shows the slight interest of the French masses in foreign policy, but, up to 1914, basic pacifism had few adherents in France, except among the Socialists. Even the Socialists, with their backs to the wall and despite the tragic assassination of their leader, Jean Jaurès, rallied to the "sacred union" between

1914 and 1917. Pacifism is not the same thing as the desire for peace; it is rather the idea that peace is the supreme good. France, having lost 1,400,000 men between 1914 and 1918, became so enthusiastic about peace that this desire became one of her traditions. There were some precedents; the much lighter losses of the First Empire and the losses of 1870 and 1871 had increased hostility to the policy of risk.

The great new feature of the period after World War I was the widespread nature of the movement and its adoption in political circles. But how could one make the will to peace prevail? Between the two wars one can make out two methods: first, security through force, through the execution of the Treaty of Versailles, through pressure on Germany; and second, security through Franco-German *rapprochement*, through the League of Nations, through arbitration and disarmament. In general we could say that the first was the method of the Right, of Millerand, Poincaré, Barthou, and the second was the method of the Left, of Herriot and Blum and also of the man who wished to be the apostle of peace, Aristide Briand. "We must choose," said Herriot on October 26, 1921, "between the policy of M. Tardieu and that of M. le Président du Conseil [Briand]. We know M. Tardieu's policy well; it is one which takes the offensive every time . . . great questions of foreign policy arise . . . And, in contrast to this absolute policy, magnificent on paper . . . which promises all and which produces nothing, we have another policy, a liberal one; I declare it to be more concerned with the true interests of France . . . it also guarantees our rights but it is more human and thus more French. It is this one which I prefer." [14]

The two major elections which gave substantial majorities to the Left, that of the victory of the *Cartel des Gauches* in 1924 and that of the Popular Front in 1936, turned to a great extent—though indirectly—on the question of pacifism. In 1924 the voters demanded reduction of the military budget and of the term of military service, as well as the end of the occupation of the Ruhr undertaken by Poincaré. The election went against Poincaré and brought to power, with Herriot, men who believed in the League of Nations. The election of 1936 was the most "introversive" of all. The need of social reform and the hatred of deflation gave victory to the Popular Front at the very moment when the real question was the security of the country—for Hitler had just reoccupied the Rhineland. Despite the intelligence of the new leaders, public pressure made them follow a "waiting" foreign policy, whose chief symbol was nonintervention in Spain. Without a doubt it was a mistake, but our task is to analyze the tradition and nothing prevents tradition from being a source of mistakes.

The growth of the will to peace—even, for some, peace at any price—coincided with the decline of a traditional tendency which foreigners often seem to consider one of the major features of French national character: the *taste for glory*. As Raymond Aron interprets it, the French feel it necessary to be among the leaders, to shine, to win just for the sake of winning—"this general passion which the French nation has for glory," said Montesquieu.[15] On the superficial level this taste for glory corresponds to a taste for *panache*, that is, the outer trappings of glory. Although the subject deserves profound study, one can still outline it briefly as follows.

In the nineteenth century the Napoleonic legend not only maintained the cult of *la gloire*, but was a sort of clarion protest against the prudent moderation—one might say the eclipse—of foreign policy under the constitutional monarchy. "*La France s'ennuie*," it was said at the time of Guizot. Auguste Barbier wrote in his *Iambus* (1831):

> O Corse à cheveux plats, que ta France était belle
> Au grand soleil de Messidor.

And Victor Hugo in his "Ode to the Column" (1830), contrasting the pettiness of the deputies with the greatness of the Emperor, pities the Emperor:

> Qu'un jour à cet affront il te faudrait descendre
> Que trois cents avocats oseraient à ta cendre
> Chicaner ce tombeau!

All this was part of Romanticism and declined with the end of that movement, not without some brilliant last gasps, of which Edmond Rostand's *Cyrano de Bergerac* is the symbol. But the

Republican generation after 1848 rejected *panache,* in which it saw a way of deceiving the people. More and more the *tricolore* became a property of the nationalists—themselves more and more recruited from the Right. The Dreyfus case dealt a hard blow to the legend of the army's infallibility—France's last moral recourse. The poems of Déroulède on the flag did not inflame the whole country, and Gustave Hervé (before the war converted him to exalted patriotism) daily in the press scorned the symbols of a voracious Fatherland, avid for cannonfodder. The First World War, when its exalted mood had passed, proved the bitter truth that devotion to the flag had been paid for in more than a million lives.

The taste for patriotic jingoistic display became established in Rightist circles which saw in pacifism a sort of international treason —whence the attacks that Maurras made on Léon Blum, "naturalized German Jew," "*heimlos.*" After the Popular Front elections of 1936 the "nationalists"—that is the Rightist minority, displayed the *tricolore.* Their young men wore it in their buttonholes while the Communists and Socialists wore a rose or a red ribbon. It caused a scandal on the Right when Blum appointed as Minister of Education Jean Zay, who had published at the age of twenty a poem in which he spoke of the flag in really violent terms:

> Ils sont quinze cent mille qui sont morts pour
> cette saloperie-là.[16]

It need not be added that the Left was rejecting the surface symbols, not patriotism itself. The tragic events of 1940 would show strikingly that the cleavage followed quite different lines from those which separated Right and Left.

Furthermore, the Popular Front reacted in favor of the symbols stolen from the people by the Right. "We have been robbed three times," wrote Albert Bayet in *L'Oeuvre,* May 15, 1936, "because we have suffered three losses—we have allowed Jeanne d'Arc, the *tricolore* and the Unknown Soldier to be stolen from us." [17] And Jean Perrin said even more boldly: "They have stolen Jeanne d'Arc, that girl of the people abandoned by the King after the surge of the people had made her victorious—and burned by the priests, who have since made her a saint. They have tried to steal from us the flag of 1789, the noble *tricolore* of Republican victories, of Valmy, of Jemmapes, of Hohenlinden, of Verdun, this flag which soon will fly beside the red flag of the USSR, which symbolizes the hope of the unfortunate. They have, finally, tried to take from us the heroic *Marseillaise*, that fierce revolutionary song which made all the thrones of Europe tremble." [18] But the result of the debate, where the flag in its turn became the object of a desperate struggle, is one more confirmation of the introversive character of French attitudes in general. To a large body of opinion in 1939 *la gloire* meant war, and the French people wanted to avoid war.

II

THE CATASTROPHE

The oversimplified way of defining the catastrophe is to say that it was France's military defeat in 1940, but the phenomenon is in reality more complex. It includes all the factors which in a short time made France fall from the rank of a great power to a situation of extreme weakness.

One can list the signs that foretold it: the loss of life in World War I; the decline of the birth rate, especially in the 1930's; the decline of industrial expansion after the 1929 record; the increase of political strife because of economic crises, and consequently a substantial decline of that "national cohesion" which is an element in power; the decline, finally, in "administrative capacity"—the ability to make rapid shifts in the use of resources, which, according to Klaus Knorr, is the very condition necessary for using potential power. In all there was a decline in France's *élan vital.*[19] It is possible that these various factors might have inevitably led to a slow decline and that sooner or later France might have become as weak as she was in 1945 even without a dramatic upset; but for our purposes it is significant that the change came about by catastrophe and not by evolution.

Indeed, for anyone who studies change and adaptations to new realities, the psychological element has a basic importance. The very idea of catastrophe implies a psychological upset for its victims which would not exist in the case of slow erosion. It is therefore especially important to study what the catastrophe really was.

For the sake of clarity, we will distinguish four elements: the *war*, the *defeat*, the *occupation*, and the *slight share in the common victory*. On the psychological plane these elements can be translated thus: the war brought despair to France when she found herself fighting again after the bloody and triumphant victory of twenty years before; the defeat brought the stunning discovery of the real weakness of the country; the occupation brought the shame and anger of having lost independence; and the small share in the victory brought the humiliation of not having a really satisfactory revenge. On the material plane, the war brought home the inability of French diplomacy to defend the national interest; the defeat meant the annihilation of the nation's military potential; the occupation meant the inevitable exhaustion of economic resources, that is, ruin; and the small share in the victory meant the near-certainty of failure to attain national goals unless they happened to coincide with those of powerful allies.

Before analyzing each of these elements more in detail, it will be interesting to compare France briefly with the United Kingdom and Germany.

The United Kingdom had known the disillusion of not having been able to avoid war but none of the other three elements. Since only the other three imply that form of collective feeling that can be called "national humiliation," England came out of the war in a condition potentially similar to that of France but with the sentiment of legitimate pride that in basic matters she had not committed a fatal error as France had. She could regard recent history as continuous with the past. She had remained herself.

Germany knew that she was largely responsible for the outbreak of the war—although many Germans tended to rationalize it as a legitimate protest against the unjust treatment of the 1918 victors. In any case she did not bear the onus of having failed by following the path of pacifism, because this was never the German way, except for some very minor sections of public opinion. She had conducted the war by such means and with such decisiveness and effectiveness that it took the efforts of most of the world to defeat her. But there was no national humiliation here either. Her defeat was different from that of France in two essential ways: it was the result of an immense four-year effort and not a sudden collapse, and it was a defeat without hope, since it coincided with the end of the war, whereas France's defeat was near the beginning and left hope alive. As early as June 18, 1940, General de Gaulle had expressed this idea: "Has the last word been said? Should hope really be given up? Is the defeat final? No! Believe me, I speak to you knowing the situation and tell you that nothing is lost for France." [20] Germany was in a situation opposite to that of England with its continuity—she faced a total defeat, unconditional surrender, total destruction of the state, which implied that a new Germany would be built, totally different from the old. The realization—greatly delayed and really terrifying for the majority of Germans—of the systematic extermination of the Jews by the Nazis added fuel to this desire to make a new Germany, to break with the past. "The collapse of 1945," says Alfred Grosser, "divided the history of contemporary Germany neatly into two periods, 'before' and 'after.' " [21]

For England, continuity; for Germany, discontinuity; for France, semicontinuity. Nothing shows this better than the first question in the French referendum of October 21, 1945: "Do you want the Assembly elected today to be a constituent assembly?" This meant that if one replied "no," one wanted a return to the Third Republic; if one replied "yes," one expected something new. Germany could not avoid starting anew when her state machinery was reconstituted in 1949 and England had nothing essential to change.

Let us now take up the four elements of the catastrophe and see how they worked out in France.

1. *The war*. The outbreak of the war was proof of the failure of a diplomatic policy sincerely devoted to peace. The dominant idea in September 1939 was, "the First World War accomplished nothing." To this were added other types of commentary. Some people accused the government of taking too weak a stand, of constant concessions to pre-Hitler Germany (about occupation and reparations), and of a passive policy when faced with Hitler's successive attacks. The Right asked: was not this the fault of the Popular Front, which in 1936 sidetracked attention from the one important thing—the reoccupation of the Rhineland—to sow domestic disorder through its social reforms and to encourage inertia by the forty-hour week? To this the Left could instantly reply that foreign policy and national defense had always been in the hands of men of the Right and conservatives (sometimes represented by the Radicals), except for brief periods in 1924 and 1932. The Quai d'Orsay was largely recruited from conservative circles, the General Staff even more so.

But the schism was less between Right and Left than between the men of Munich and those opposed to Munich, or between appeasers and those who advocated counter-thrusts which would risk war. Furthermore, the extremists played a separate game. All of a sudden *L'Action Française* showed itself hostile to France's going to war, and the Communists, faced with the Nazi-Soviet Pact, were opposed to war against the "friend of the USSR." There were small groups who agreed with Marcel Déat that Frenchmen did not want to "die for Danzig."

In general, every effort to blame one's political enemies for not avoiding the war was futile. Objectively, the mistakes of French foreign policy as a whole were responsible. Since similar errors had been made by Great Britain and the United States, it makes it all the easier to assess French conduct impartially.

The point of departure had been the Treaty of Versailles, a treaty which was perhaps, according to Jacques Bainville, "too soft, for all that it was too hard," but which in any case had the merit of being in existence, and of assuring what Clemenceau had considered essential—French security.[22] It was a compromise between French principles and those of the Allies. Could one have done better? "No," replied Clemenceau, "all these people crying murder, playing the bully, displaying such vanity, such intransigence . . . such foolishness, as if we, all by ourselves, with no aid, no support, no effort had broken Germany's neck!" [23]

The treaty allowed for two possible policies: strict execution or reconciliation with Germany. The second was undoubtedly more moral, but, on the realistic level, the effectiveness of either of the two if consistently followed was probable. What happened was that the governments between the wars oscillated continually between the two. Once Hitler was in power, when a firm policy was needed, there occurred a disintegration of the political will and, so to speak, a profound misunderstanding of Hitler's thought among Frenchmen in public life. Who had read and reflected upon *Mein Kampf?* Finally, it was found convenient to place France in the wake of England, which in 1938 was following deliberately one principle, the policy of appeasement. Daladier, who did not believe in this policy, followed England, and France abandoned her Czech ally. When Neville Chamberlain finally discovered after March 1939 that "Hitler was not a gentleman" and adopted the policy of guarantee, France again followed England and went to war.

One can thus judge that the outbreak of war, twenty years after Versailles, proved the inability of French governments to secure lasting peace for the nation. The outbreak of war raised the question of the effectiveness of the Third Republic in time of trouble. It made the French look at the world situation in a new perspective—the dilemma of a "have" nation which was satisfied, but which was faced with the growing ambition of an aggressor. For the first time it brought up the problem of adaptation.

2. *The defeat* made the problem still more pressing. On the social level it created the most dramatic situation France had ever known in modern times: millions of refugees on the roads, an army assumed to be invincible in full disintegration after a few days of smashing blows from the enemy, 1,500,000 prisoners of war. The main impression of the French when the Armistice became known on June 25, 1940, was of amazement. How could this have hap-

pened? Of course we cannot analyze the French defeat here, but we must examine the possible explanations and especially the interpretations which the French have given it. Materiel, morale, treason, strategy—these are the essential themes on which the French have been searching their souls since 1940.

Materiel? Certainly France was handicapped by inferiority in the air. "The number of planes at the disposal of the state in 1937 was 450 for France as opposed to 4,320 for Germany." [24] In other respects, however, the French supply of arms as compared to that of the Germans was respectable, notably in tanks, cannon, and munitions. More and more the French have asked themselves whether the enemy's superiority in numbers and in munitions could by itself explain the defeat.

Morale? It is evident that Marshal Pétain's colleagues saw the principal cause of the disaster in the low morale of the army and of the country. From this stemmed the conclusion that everything must be begun anew by a "national revolution." The men of the extreme Right around the Marshal—Baudoin, Bouthillier, Jacques Chevalier, Alibert (without mentioning the presence of Maurras behind the scenes)—attributed the decline of nationalist sentiment to "red elementary school teachers." The exodus and the military retreat furnished episodes which are hardly edifying, and a whole literature has grown up around the need for a renewal of morale. *La Moisson de quarante* of Benoist-Méchin demonstrates this, as does the third volume of J.-P. Sartre's *Chemins de la Liberté*. This "national revolution" is like the "moral order" of 1871; its advocates said we were defeated because we had sinned; France must be forcibly led to virtue. All the same France had not faltered in the general mobilization, and during the retreat there were millions of acts of heroism. Therefore many Frenchmen came to believe that the reproach in respect to morale was a tactic designed to conceal the desires of the extreme Right, avid to take over power at last.

Treason? This is the regular explanation of a section of the Left. "Lucky defeat," Maurras was supposed to have said. From this to the assumption that he and his friends, in collusion with Marshal Pétain, had wanted it and prepared it, is a short step, easily taken.

A brochure of Albert Bayet sums up this impassioned thesis.[25] In fact, very few Frenchmen have accepted it. There were some typical traitors, some quasi-traitors who identified the success of their careers—which the defeat made possible—with the future of France. There were some advocates of a Fascist France, of the type of Darnand, Déat, or Doriot. But to attribute to the victor of Verdun—despite his faults and mistakes—a deliberate desire for defeat in order to further his own ambitions, remains inconceivable. Besides, the explanation of historical events by plot is appealing to the public but is generally not very satisfactory to historians.

There remains the explanation of the defeat by faulty strategy. French strategy had been based on the experience of 1918; Marshal Pétain and General Weygand were largely responsible for it. A lot of hindsight has gone into discussions of "the spirit of the Maginot Line." France had developed a purely defensive army but at the same time had formed alliances in Eastern Europe which implied offensive action. This paradox became dramatically clear on May 10, 1940. There was not a moment's hesitation in France's decision to go to the aid of Belgium and Holland instead of staying in prepared, established positions. But it is important that no official new strategy of autonomous armored divisions had been developed as Guderian had done in Germany—and de Gaulle in France. The 3,500 French tanks were stretched out the length of the frontier, while Hitler had concentrated at least 2,500 in the Ardennes region alone.

If this explanation is the most valid, as I think, I repeat in relation to the defeat what I have said of the war: that the Third Republic, which had not been able to develop a policy capable of maintaining peace, had not been any more capable of developing a strategy which would ensure its own defense. This is not a matter of squabbles among specialists, but a profound reality. Once again the French, who had vaguely sensed the problem, realized that they had not known how to adapt themselves to the modern world and that their government had not helped them. "The disaster of 1940 seemed to many the failure—in every domain—of the system and of the ruling circles."[26]

The defeat should not be analyzed only in terms of its causes, however. It raised, by its very existence, the problem of national humiliation. In a people torn by political quarrels it brought to life again certain values which had been denied or suppressed, especially the existence of a national community. The militant union member of 1936, when he thought of the boss, of the "200 families," did not include them in a "we" above the quarrels which divided them. The militant Communist said openly that he would prefer civil war of the Spanish type to a foreign war. Now suddenly, because of the defeat, it was seen that this "we" existed. The women who unceasingly distributed food and drink to unknown prisoners the whole length of the convoys, defying the German sentries, showed that they were very conscious that these were "their men." Many sincere pacifists understood at that moment what patriotic indignation was. The immense rallying of support for Marshal Pétain in 1940, like the immense rallying of support for General de Gaulle in 1944, was the visible transference to the political sphere of this unusual collective burst of sentiment.

3. *The occupation* presents striking differences from the defeat in that it did not produce such bursts of energy but gradual developments. Without doubt the presence of booted and helmeted strangers who sang as they marched, the lines of German cannon in the streets of Paris before November 1940, the tall blond SS troops in their black uniforms with the death's head, were a constant reminder that there was a French national community and that it had been mastered, humiliated, enslaved, bullied by a foreign power. Even so, it was not the sense of community which was especially fostered by the occupation, in contrast to the defeat. The occupation's great contribution to collective awareness was to make Frenchmen understand that independence and liberty are not natural gifts but the fruit of effort—hard-won acquisitions.

The occupation favored national cohesion only to a limited extent. It divided Frenchmen, initially by the demarcation line between the occupied and the unoccupied zones, until the line ceased to exist on November 11, 1942. It divided them above all in regard to their attitude toward the occupying power. The little constellation of traitors used by the Gestapo, volunteers of the

Anti-Bolshevik Legion who denounced their fellow-Frenchmen, were despised by almost everyone. But the very existence of the Vichy regime created a cleavage between those who saw in it a guarantee ("I give my person to France to mitigate her suffering," Pétain had said on June 17, 1940) and those who saw it as a shameful compromise. The history of this period shows a rapid decline of the first category and a constant rise of the second, beginning with the interview between Pétain and Hitler at Montoire on October 24, 1940, with a brief let-up at the time of the dismissal of Pierre Laval on December 13. The absurd war in Syria in June 1941, Laval's return to power in April 1942, and finally the Allied landings in North Africa reduced the *Pétainistes* to a small minority. There were nevertheless many nuances between the "collaborators," who sincerely wanted German victory because of anti-Bolshevik sentiments, the "opportunists," who worked with the Germans, the sincere enemies of Germany who continued to see in Pétain a Machiavellian destroyer of German power,[27] the "wait and see" trimmers like Admiral Darlan, whose entire concern was to determine which side would triumph and then rush to it. There were many fine differences also among the opponents of Vichy. There were those who were "waiting to see," who did not wish to compromise themselves and who whispered patriotic sentiments behind closed doors; there were the active resisters who continually risked their lives; finally, there was the mass of half-hearted resisters —Gaullists, or partisans of a "third man"—ready to resist in small ways, who for various reasons could not throw themselves wholeheartedly into the fight. No, the occupation was not a unifying force.

For the masses the essential fact was the loss of liberty—which had become immediately apparent. The French had suddenly understood the significance of the strange unanimity of the newspapers in praising the Germans, and they had learned that it was painful not to be able to say what one thought. They had grasped the importance of freedom of movement when they found themselves hampered everywhere by lines of demarcation. Finally, they had become aware of the price of individual liberty in learning that they were vulnerable to repeated arbitrary arrest and that arrest could well mean death. Certain groups of Frenchmen had known about the price of liberty in the past hundred years, but not the country as a whole. The idea that liberty was well worth fighting for—dear to the revolutionaries of 1789—had faded when liberty had become a habit. It was suddenly discovered that it is *not* a habit, but is an essential value.

The taste for liberty showed itself in all sorts of ways: listening to the BBC, for example, and violations of the demarcation line by means which gave full rein to the spirit of ingenuity. Later it showed itself in escapes over the Spanish frontier by young men who wished to get to North Africa. The taste for liberty assumed also the more dubious form of the black market. The morally acceptable idea that any food or product bought or sold outside of regular channels would escape the Germans opened the door to many compromises in which pure and simple honesty suffered.

Objectively, the occupation meant ruin. The systematic siphoning off of vital substance worked in two ways: first, by the payment of the occupation indemnity of 400 million (later 500 million) francs a day, which made it possible for Germany to buy a large part of French production; and second, by the drafting of French workers in France and then, more and more, in Germany. It is established that France paid 35 billion marks (700 billion francs) in occupation costs. Large sums were also levied by the unpaid excess of French exports to Germany over French imports from Germany in debts and clearing charges.[28]

It would obviously be unjust to compare the sufferings of the French under the occupation with that of other countries, notably Poland, which lost 6 million lives including 3 million Jews massacred in the ghettos or exterminated in the gas chambers. Famine in France was never as great as in Greece, for example. But in spite of differences in scale, France knew deportations, and executions of hostages. Of 620,000 victims of World War II, more than half were victims of the occupation or of the Allied bombings which were a direct result of the occupation.

When one continues to fight, suffering can be just as great and the ruin as complete. What distinguishes the sufferings of the occupation from those of the war is the passive quality of the former

—the sufferings are imposed by those whom defeat has made masters of the country and they are thus even more intolerable. These sufferings inevitably provoke reactions.

4. *The slight share in the common victory.* The reactions to suffering bring us to study the fourth element of the catastrophe. We must begin with the Armistice, which broke France's word to England (by the agreement of March 28, 1940) not to make a separate armistice or peace. The breaking of this promise has made France feel guilty ever since. Of course rationalizations were not lacking, and Churchill himself has recognized the most important of them: Britain's inadequate share in the Battle of France. Nevertheless the Armistice seemed to be relatively too comfortable a solution when the Allies were continuing to fight. And it had the further defect in French eyes of having rendered useless what still remained—the fleet, which was to perish stupidly by being scuttled, and the colonial empire, which might have provided territory, resources, and men to continue the war.

Furthermore, General de Gaulle's rejection of the Armistice, June 18, 1940—entirely illegal in terms of classical policy—quickly became the symbol of continuing the fight. "The flame of French resistance must not go out and will not go out." But one must realize that in June 1940 only an infinitesimal minority of the French people understood or even heard this appeal. It was a time when, in the general chaos, Frenchmen were rallying to Marshal Pétain on a large scale and the Marshal had declared categorically that de Gaulle was a traitor and the Vichy courts had sentenced him to death *in absentia*. Besides, the British attacked the French fleet at Mers el Kebir on July 3 to keep it from falling into the hands of the Nazis, which was not the way allies should act, in French opinion. Then, in September, General de Gaulle failed to take Dakar.

Nobody in France knew de Gaulle. He had written some books and articles, but thousands of Frenchmen do likewise. He had been an Undersecretary of State for a few days, but who knows the names of ministers in an unstable regime? General de Gaulle had not been able to rally a single one of the major political personalities, whatever sympathy Herriot, Blum, or Mandel might feel for him. Vichy propaganda could give free rein to the notion that he was a "mercenary" in the service of England. To anyone writing in 1962 and considering his stubbornness, this is an absurd hypothesis, but in 1940 it seemed plausible to many. Equally absurd was the opinion Roosevelt and Cordell Hull had of de Gaulle—they saw in him an incipient dictator and a sorcerer's apprentice. This mistake was also excusable, at least until the spring of 1943. After that date Roosevelt's obstinacy took on a much meaner aspect and approached personal emotional animosity. Nevertheless the feeble part played by France in the common victory, with all its psychological consequences, is to be explained in terms of these absurdities.

The notion of de Gaulle as a "mercenary" explains the slight appeal of Free France to the French in England in the summer of 1940. In November 1942 their numbers reached 70,000, according to de Gaulle.[29] The Free French Navy consisted only of small units from France and a few which had been allowed to join him from the ships seized by the British in English ports. There were not enough volunteers to man the seized ships. In addition, most of the units of the active army, headed by General Weygand, had a very unfavorable attitude toward de Gaulle and the British, whom they felt to be his masters. Most of the army remained loyal to Pétain because he had proved himself, and the army was not willing to rally to de Gaulle. When de Gaulle became one of the two chiefs of the French Committee of Liberation and subsequently eliminated Giraud, the army inevitably followed him—though reservations persisted.

American hesitation to arm the French derived largely from the idea of de Gaulle as a dictator. The general repeatedly complained that after the liberation of France, during the eight months the war had still to go, America distributed its aid in little drops. "In giving to General de Gaulle's government enough aid to equip eight or ten new divisions it would have to be expected that by the end of the winter the French army would be doubled, that it would play an enhanced role in the battle—maybe even a decisive role—and that [the Allies] would have to allow French participation in the Armistice arrangements, which Roosevelt wanted to avoid."[30] But it is possible to conclude that in seeing black designs on Roosevelt's part de Gaulle was overlooking a simple reality. Although on the one hand the occupation and its consequent ruin made France completely dependent on the Allies for arms, on the other hand the defeat had created great distrust of France. Since France had collapsed, did she deserve to have much credit extended to her? This was in fact what Hopkins said to de Gaulle: "The reason [for American policy] is above all the stupefying disappointment which France inflicted upon us in 1940 when we saw her collapse in disaster and then in capitulation. The idea we had always had of her value and her energy was overturned in an instant . . . Judging that France was no longer what she had been we could not trust her to play a great part. But we recognize what you have accomplished and we are happy to see France reappear. But how can we forget what in fact we have experienced? . . . Are we not justified in using caution in what we expect of her in bearing with us the weight of tomorrow's peace?" [31]

This is not the place to make a critical study of the American position, nor of that of Stalin at Yalta—much harsher toward France and scornful of the mere nine divisions at her disposal in 1945. The psychological element, on the other hand, deserves more of our attention.

The psychological element is closely tied to the idea of the Resistance. If de Gaulle complained of American hesitation and suspicion, it was because he felt that he drew his strength from the French insurrection against the Germans. He saw in it—without doubt correctly—an element of moral force which gave France *rights*. He felt himself supported by the Resistance and in his memoirs he has quoted the telegrams that he received—especially in the spring of 1943—showing that France was with him, at least her purest, bravest, and most patriotic elements.[32]

From this viewpoint the problem of France's slight part in the victory can be seen in a new light. *Objectively*, yes, the part was a modest one and all Frenchmen have recognized it; but *subjectively*, the Frenchmen of the Resistance, especially in France itself, fighting in the underground, hunted in the *maquis*, or furnishing information to the Allies, had the impression that they had earned more than this modest part. The geography of France and the number of German forces stationed in France because of the strategic position of the country, did not permit the type of guerrilla fighting possible in the mountains of Yugoslavia or in the forests of Russia. In providing information and in liaison, prodigious feats were accomplished, and the *Résistants* thought these should have earned them great consideration instead of distrust on the part of the Allies. The American suspicion derived not only from the fact that a good proportion of the Resistance was made up of Communists —after all in Yugoslavia the West ended by supporting Tito—but also from the nature of the Resistance itself, which stood for subversive government and elements of disorder in the eyes of countries waging a classic war.

The French therefore weighed the victory with the feeling that on the one hand they were not chiefly responsible, but on the other that their role had been systematically minimized. The celebrations of the Allies' triumph on May 8, 1945, did not have the same air of enthusiasm as those of November 11, 1918. The French celebrated the German capitulation on this beautiful May day in a cheerless atmosphere.

So the catastrophe as a whole had caused the crumbling of much of the tradition—of confidence in diplomacy and in the army, of the mistaken belief that liberty could be taken for granted, even of the idea that France was a great nation of the first rank. The French came out of the trial very bitter, also exhausted, ruined, weakened. But the catastrophe had not only this negative side; it revived a feeling which some condemned and others reduced to an instrument of domestic politics—patriotism. The word *Patrie*, banished by a section of the Left before 1939, and used by Pétain in his motto *Travail, Famille, Patrie*, had resumed its former value against the Germans and Vichy. The Communists, who in 1936 spoke only in terms of "Bread, Peace, and Liberty," now regularly used *Patrie* in their slogans. National cohesion was revived only by further spurts, but it had been proven that such spurts were possible, whereas before 1939 one might doubt it. In fact such spurts recurred periodically—in August 1944, and on the occasions of Dien Bien Phu in 1954, the referendum of September 1958, and the Algerian insurrections of January 1960 and April 1961. Finally, a very strong desire to escape further humiliation had been born. In short, the catastrophe revived the myth of the *nation* in France. It remains for us to investigate the acts of adaptation attempted, and to discuss the processes and vicissitudes with which they were accomplished.

III

THE ADAPTATION

In my discussion of the catastrophe I have emphasized certain immediate impressions of Frenchmen, but have not referred at all to their plans for the future. There are two reasons for this. The first is that if there were in fact plans, they were those of small groups, especially in the Resistance. The majority of Frenchmen, overwhelmed by the difficulties of the moment, had quite other concerns than thinking about the future. The second, even more important, is that the true and lasting consequences of the catastrophe had not yet appeared in 1945. In this connection it is enough to remind ourselves of the total ignorance at the time in France and elsewhere of the two worldwide problems that seem in the early 1960's the principal characteristics of our age—one being the bipolarization of power in the cold war and the other being decolonization.

THE NORMAL AND THE NEW

By the very facts of the Liberation and the Allied victory, the French got out of a deep chasm. From the bottom of the pit they had felt that "something must be done," but what? Indeed after any great cataclysm a nation hesitates between two directions: a a return to normalcy, or profound change. The elections of 1920 in the United States, for instance, posed this problem. Harding, champion of "back to normalcy," was elected against Cox, representing Wilsonian internationalism and the "new diplomacy"; but the blows France suffered between 1939 and 1945 were so much greater than the dislocation of the United States between 1917 and 1919 that the two situations are not comparable. Let us analyze in the French context the two notions of "back to normalcy" and "profound change."

The normal itself was pictured in the first part of this study: territorial satisfaction in Europe, attachment to the colonial empire, a will to peace to avoid bloodshed, decline of the idea of glory, and finally, as far as the governments were concerned, supremacy of political over commercial factors. All of this was in a framework of France as a great power capable of assuring her own security by herself. Faced with public opinion resolutely introversive, the governments hesitated between introversion and a moderate extroversion.

In 1945, the revival of each of the former goals appeared to be realizable.

Alsace and Lorraine, which had been annexed by Hitler, in fact were recovered; French troops entered Strasbourg on November 23, 1944. The resulting enthusiasm was no doubt a bit less than in 1918. During the war there had been many Alsatian refugees in the Massif Central and there had been some tension between the Alsatians and the somewhat backward people of the region. Very unjustly, certain "French of the interior" had accused the Alsatians of accommodating themselves easily to German annexation. But, for the country as a whole, the recovery of Alsace and Lorraine was sufficient in itself. The idea of going beyond these frontiers occurred to few people except General de Gaulle and certain members of the government.

As for the colonial empire, with the exception of the Communists and a few intellectuals, everyone thought France was lucky to have it because it had played an appreciable role in the war—as a refuge and as a source of men. It had saved France. Its soldiers —Europeans, Senegalese, Algerians, Tunisians, Moroccans—had fought with a heroism which proved that they were at the time attached to the notion of the "mother country." As a reward, reforms would be made, but reforms which would not affect the essential point: French authority. This was the theme of the Brazzaville conference of 1944. There were, of course, some difficulties in Indochina, but this was the fault of the Japanese and—everyone began to insinuate this—of American officers from China who were encouraging Ho Chi Minh to remain independent. There were some troubles in the Near East, but they were the fault of the British, who wished to eliminate France in her weakened state. Some people would speak—quoting Elliott Roosevelt—of the encouragement his father had given the Sultan of Morocco in 1943. But as a whole the empire had stood. This, moreover, had been the war aim of all French factions. De Gaulle won from Churchill on June 25, 1940, a declaration according to which "the aim of Great Britain is the complete restoration of French territory, colonial and metropolitan." [33] Giraud obtained the same promise from the United States, by the Murphy-Giraud agreements of 1943. Robert D. Murphy had written earlier to General Giraud that "the restoration of France, in all her independence, in all her grandeur and in all the area which she possessed before the war, in Europe as well as overseas, is one of the war aims of the United Nations." [34] Even the Vichy government had been concerned with the empire, in its dealings with Germany. When Darlan and Hitler met at Berchtesgaden on May 11 and 12, 1941, they mutually promised to maintain the colonial empire, except for Morocco and Tunisia, whose loss would be compensated at England's expense. The National Council of the Resistance did not hesitate over the French claim to the empire when it included in its program "the extension of political, social, and economic rights to native and colonial populations." De Gaulle proclaimed on September 12, 1944: "A hundred million loyal men live under our flag in the four corners of the world." [35]

The "back to normalcy" movement of the middle 1940's was above all the return to the introversive attitude. Public opinion was more preoccupied than ever with the problems of life at the moment when industry was producing only 25 percent of the already mediocre figure of 1939. The aspirations to return to normal were such that the government responded with demagogic measures. Bread rationing was eliminated in November 1944 (and had to be resumed in a much more severe form three months later). The government granted a rise in wages of more than 30 percent which naturally caused an uncontrolled inflation.

In October 1946 the French set up a constitution strikingly similar to that of the Third Republic, and the "return to normal" manifested itself in a return to party strife, to the detriment of all the hopes of unity, agreement, and cohesion to which the Resistance had given birth.

On the government's part there was also a return to normalcy —namely the aspiration to revive France's past greatness. The program of the National Council of the Resistance alluded to the necessity to "defend the political and economic independence of the nation, to re-establish France in its power, in its greatness, and in its universal mission." [36] But it was above all General de Gaulle who came out for this policy. On September 12, 1944, he expressed the hope "that this sort of official exile of France, from which all those who speak and act in her name have suffered, will give place to the same sort of relation which for several centuries we have had the honor and the habit of having with other great nations." He also said that "all great human constructions would be arbitrary and fragile without the seal of France." [37] The need was to "resume a place in the first rank" and "to maintain it." One of the chapters of the third volume of de Gaulle's memoirs is entitled precisely "Rank."

Now de Gaulle's policy of *grandeur* in the first phase is a remarkable copy—slightly changed—of French policy in the great epochs before 1914 and in 1919: "no more centralized Germany!"; permanent occupation of the Rhineland, which would be politically detached from Germany; the Saar, "keeping its German character," to be a separate state affiliated with France in the economic sphere. This was Foch's plan, taken up by Clemenceau in 1919, with improvements, such as the internationalization of the Ruhr. Like his predecessors, de Gaulle held that to assure re-establishment of France, Germany must lose her capacity for aggression. A return to greatness by traditional alliances was also included in his program. "There is needed a renewal in some form of that Franco-Russian solidarity which, though often unrecognized and abused,

remains nonetheless in agreement with the natural order of things."
It was also necessary to return to the Anglo-French Entente Cordiale against Germany—when differences between France and England had been resolved. "If only France and England would agree to act together in the future settlements they would have enough power so that nothing could be done which they had not themselves accepted or decided." [38] Thus it is the situation of 1914 that de Gaulle wished to recreate, with the French claims of 1919 added. Demands for slight modifications of the frontier with Italy, and the temporary designs on the Aosta valley, do not offset a striking likeness to the pattern of the past.

Opposed to the concept of the return to normalcy we find that of profound change. De Gaulle could not visualize change except in relation to the values of *grandeur* and patriotism and rebirth of national cohesion—"the winds of change are buffeting liberated France." [39] But there were other individuals and groups who wanted change, foresaw it, and prepared the way for it. In intellectual circles in the 1930's there had been an active but incoherent will to change. This "common refusal to accept the established order," this wish to put an end to decadence, had run into the obstacles of the war and the defeat; but the "revolutionary will" which it involved had spread in two seemingly opposite directions—on the one hand among the technocrats of Vichy, on the other among the intellectuals of the Resistance. [40] The catastrophe had only accelerated this process.

From both the Resistance and Vichy it was not new programs which emerged but a new state of mind. The return to normal was not possible. Boldness was called for. If boldness on the domestic front led to certain major nationalization measures, such measures figured at the beginning of the Fourth Republic only in the attitude of the Communists, who were powerful at the time. This is not the place to describe their system. The Communists in France were not innovators in comparison to the great Soviet party; their aim was the conquest of power and they tried to achieve it first by the infiltration of Resistance organizations (between August and October 1944), and then by legal means, through acquisition of one-third of the ministerial offices, combined with a powerful effort in elections. Finally after the break-up of Tri-partism in May 1947, they tried to achieve it by the great subversive strikes of 1947 and 1948, but they failed.[41] The result was that the impulses toward profound change might have been reduced to certain inconsequential words and articles if France had not had to face harsh reality and if on the other hand a new state of mind had not been created.

The truth is that among the upper classes in France a new generation had appeared, to whom the catastrophe—what General de Gaulle called *la faillite*—had given a large dose of concrete realism. The new state of mind was a *mystique* of realism. In this *mystique* the concepts of rank, glory, and traditional power were considered secondary by a large section of the elite. For these people the national goals—once security was attained—were economic expansion and European integration. Later the Common Market would represent a synthesis between the "Europeans" and those who favored economic expansion.

We must, then, examine the French "Neo-Realism" and "European spirit" and compare them to the "policy of *grandeur*, second phase" of General de Gaulle, who returned to power in 1958. But first we must survey what can be called the "harsh lesson of facts."

THE HARSH LESSON OF FACTS

The facts quickly showed that a return to normal was impossible. A few examples will suffice to make this convincing. First, the entire Gaullist policy of 1944–1946 failed; the objectives of the occupation of the Rhineland and the dismemberment of Germany simply crashed with the refusal of the powerful Allies to accept them. The French could see clearly that what was permitted to a great power—the USSR's dismemberment of Germany—was not permitted to a small power, France. The Russians could dismember East Germany because they had 150 divisions; France could not dismember West Germany—she had only 9 divisions. It was not possible to obtain such concessions merely through the good will of Allies who had their own ideas and could not be persuaded to change. The objective of detaching the Saar from Germany and attaching it economically to France seemed likely to be attained as a sort of consolation, and the Anglo-Americans accepted the idea. But it finally failed because the local population, feeling themselves to be German and knowing that they had the support of the government and the people of the new Germany, declared themselves in favor of rejoining the motherland.

The same was true of the Gaullist policy of alliances. The Franco-Soviet alliance, far from assuring France of the support of a powerful partner in her diplomatic dealings, in no way prevented the USSR from following a consistently hostile policy, beginning with Stalin's opposition at Yalta to granting an occupation zone to France. To understand this it is enough to read the memoirs of General Catroux, French ambassador in Moscow, published in 1952 and entitled *J'ai vu tomber le rideau de fer*. As for the British alliance, it was officially achieved by Léon Blum at the beginning of 1947, but one could soon see that it was only a platonic and sentimental gesture—Britain's real policy was to place Anglo-American cooperation above everything else. France could not help feeling that she was not a great power at a time when the USSR and the USA were developing atomic weapons and when on the level of conventional arms the French could barely muster a few divisions, and those thanks to United States military aid.

Even more, it was becoming clear to all but the Communists and a very small group of neutralist intellectuals that the danger no longer came from Germany, as in "normal times," but from the USSR. This "agonizing reappraisal" was brought about in 1947–1948. For the majority, the problem was to prevent the Communists from seizing power in France, and to prevent the Red Army from getting any nearer to French territory. To do this France would have to assure herself support of the only really great Western power, the United States. Now the conditions of American protection were, first, the unification of West Germany —France gave in on this point by the London Agreement of June 2, 1948—and then the rearmament of West Germany. The French resisted this inch by inch from 1950 to 1955 and then gave in. The Atlantic Pact and the nuclear shield of the United States could well be thought of as a bitter necessity and could give rise to a certain sourness toward the protector, but it *was* a necessity. To

338

have need of economic aid, of protection, and of military aid, merely in order to survive and not even to resume one's "rank," was humiliating at a time when France was aspiring to the greatness of the past, but it was indeed the harsh lesson of facts.

The level on which this lesson was hardest to learn, the most painful for France, was certainly that of decolonization. The loss of Syria and Lebanon could still be attributed to the underhanded action of the British—eternal rivals and enemies of France in the Near East. This is another instance of explanation by plot. At the beginning of the conflict in Indochina one could still believe that the trouble was caused by American advice, or Soviet advice. But the Indochina war was to last from December 1946 to July 1954 and events showed more and more that Indochina could not be reconquered. It became evident that Vietnam was profoundly stirred by basic forces and that decolonization was not a plot but a basic phenomenon of our times. Of course, not all Frenchmen understood this; even today certain groups want to hang on to what remains and they find a supporting argument in the changes in the American attitude toward Indochina. In the eyes of Americans the situation in Indochina changed from a colonial war, which they disapproved of, to an anti-Communist war. So why could not the war in Algeria, for example, be presented to the Americans as another anti-Communist war? Since the Americans did not see it this way, could not one say again, it is a plot to make us lose our last important possession? A plot of the American oil companies desirous of taking our place in the exploitation of the oil of the Sahara?

This reasoning shows that the devout partisans of the return to normal are the same people who explain decolonization by reference to plots, whereas those who submit to the lesson of facts see in decolonization the manifestation of an irresistible historical movement. Naturally, the majority of Frenchmen have come around to this last thesis, but one must clearly understand that this has been strange and disconcerting. For generations young Frenchmen have been taught that French power was relative to the size of the colonial empire, that the French were better colonizers than others, that the Blacks and the Arabs liked and welcomed them. If this were not so, how could one explain the heroism of the colonial troops in the Italian campaign, for instance? How is one to understand the rate at which everything collapsed—and why Morocco, Tunisia, Guinea, then Black Africa and Madagascar, finally Algeria, chose to separate from France and often showed themselves willing to fight for their independence? It is probable that in a few decades all this will seem like a brief episode, but, for the French, these years have seemed a rude and painful initiation to new realities.

Finally, France discovered that there are only two great powers and that she is not one of them, that decolonization is an irresistible movement which she vainly tried to stop.

The Algerian War seems at first sight to contradict this acceptance of decolonization, as well as my assertion that French public opinion is generally introversive. It is important to note that what has made decolonization in Algeria so violent and so painful was not the fact of French possession of Algerian territory but the existence of a European population which has no other home. The *colons*, although many of them are not of French origin, have been French *citizens* for generations. As a result, many Frenchmen of the *metropole* reasoned thus: we had a right to abandon Indochina, the Near East, and Black Africa but we have no right to abandon a million Frenchmen who happen to live in Algeria. It follows that some other solution, different from mere decolonization, must be found for Algeria. This reasoning explains the rise of *Algérie Française*, the 1959 proposal to "integrate" Algeria with France and also the plan to partition Algeria in the manner of Palestine. Though decolonization in general seems to have been purely a matter of foreign policy, the Algerian problem, to many, was literally a domestic problem.

The Suez affair of 1956 is a striking demonstration of the connection between the discovery of France's real weakness and the new awareness of the inevitability of decolonization. Two nations which could legitimately consider themselves as the third and fourth powers in the world (omitting China) tried to force a very weak nation, formerly a protectorate, to take back a decision it had taken, the nationalization of the Suez Canal. The operation got underway but it was harshly stopped by a vague threat from the USSR and violent moral pressure exerted by the United States, by the newly independent nations, by most of the noncolonial powers, and by a substantial proportion of British and French public opinion. Putting an end to what has been called the "gunboat policy," the Suez affair was the final revelation of the *impossibility of the return to normal.*

One cannot compare the attitude of the French to that of the Germans or the Italians, who had been stripped of their colonies as a result of defeat and of the decision of foreign powers, but one can compare it to that of the British. In comparing the attitudes of England and France in this respect we find more differences in degree than differences in substance. The British, no doubt more realistic, had understood that independence must be granted to India, too large a piece of empire to be kept by an exhausted nation. They sought to maintain ties through the Commonwealth system, but these ties imposed adjustments in British foreign policy in many cases, so as to avoid positions too different from India's. More and more, colonial emancipation has become the British method. One wonders if in countries with a large European population like Rhodesia, the British will not develop reactions similar to those of the French in Algeria. One wonders also if the Commonwealth ties will not become intermittent. The great difference between the two nations stems precisely from the fact that the British had not experienced catastrophe. The catastrophe had led France to try to "keep what she had," while the British, continuing their accustomed ways, have simply continued to follow a process (of decolonization) already begun. The British, conditioned to decolonization ever since 1783 by the establishment of the dominions, by the promise of independence to Egypt in 1922, by the granting of independence to Iraq in 1930, by the reforms of 1919 and 1935 in India, were not shattered by the acceleration of the movement. For the French, what created special difficulty was that after the national catastrophe of 1939–1944, decolonization appeared to be another national catastrophe. Though in the 1960's almost all Frenchmen have learned the "harsh lesson of facts," it is not surprising to see many officers like Marshal Juin, politicians of the Right like Jacques Soustelle and of the Center and Left like Georges Bidault and Robert Lacoste, refusing to recognize the lesson and accusing the chief of the government (de Gaulle) of treason because he was the first leader to learn this lesson thoroughly.

THE FRENCH NEO-REALISTS

With a few rare exceptions, successive French governments between de Gaulle's departure from power in January 1946 and his return in June 1958 followed a tortuous and hesitant policy toward all these problems. Their actions can be described as a compromise between the return to normal and adaptation to new conditions. The big positive decisions were all taken by governments which were extraordinary—that is, different from the average. It was the unified socialist government of Léon Blum that took the decision to wage war in Indochina in December 1946, and it was the government of Mendès-France that decided to put an end to this war in July 1954 and to repress the insurrection of the Algerian nationalists on November 1 of that same year. As a general rule, the policy of the Fourth Republic consisted in carrying on what already existed. Governmental instability, also as a general rule, had two results. First, any change of policy risked a break-up of the fragile coalition on which the government rested and was therefore to be avoided if the government wanted to remain in power. Second, the weakness caused by instability gave the high-ranking civil servants, especially in distant posts, greater freedom and authority to act. Thus, French policy in the Saar was directed by a "proconsul," Colonel (later Ambassador) Gilbert Grandval, who in effect imposed his own solutions on successive cabinets. Thus also, the removal of the Sultan of Morocco in August 1953, a very serious matter, was decided not by the very weak government of Laniel and Bidault but by local administrators. The same was true of the arrest of the Algerian national leader Ben Bella and his companions.

It is not in the actions of the cabinets of the Fourth Republic, then, that the main efforts at adaptation are to be sought. A reading of the *déclarations d'investiture* in which the French premiers set forth their programs—with the exception of those of Mendès-France to which we shall return—is very disappointing. One finds a clinging to the *status quo*, to the Atlantic Alliance or the war of

Indochina for instance. The leaders did not try anything new. At the time of the fight over the European Defense Community, the policy was even more unclear. The government declared itself in favor of the EDC, but because sending the treaty to the Assembly for ratification would have been a serious risk, means were invented to avoid this harsh necessity. The means, found by an able and subtle man, René Mayer, in January 1953, consisted in the announcement that the plan would be submitted for ratification only after certain preconditions had been met. These preconditions all involved difficult negotiations: to find a European "statute" (legal standing) for the Saar, which displeased Germany, and to obtain supplementary guarantees that British and American troops would remain in Europe, which irritated the Anglo-Saxons.

It was thus not within the cabinets—with the one exception mentioned—that the effort at adaptation was found up to 1958, but in the interesting and significant *milieux* of the high-ranking civil servants, the engineers and businessmen, the journalistic and academic circles—in short in a kind of typical French intelligentsia. It is an intelligentsia of action, not like the intelligentsia of the snobs and dilettantes of the salons in England, described by Aldous Huxley in *Those Barren Leaves*. The members of this group were not exactly technocrats; but rather those who drew from the catastrophe the conclusion that France must be a responsible nation and who tried to act, each in his own sphere, toward that end. Let us call them the French Neo-Realists.

Louis Armand, when he was Président-Directeur-Général of the Société Nationale des Chemins de Fer Française, undertook to make the French railroad system, which had been completely ruined by the war, the most efficient in the world. François Bloch-Lainé, Directeur Général de la Caisse des Dépots et Consignations, contributed largely to the launching of new housing construction in France. Jean Monnet, the instigator of so many revolutionary ideas, belongs in this category by definition. In the nationalized industries, the managers worked for and achieved successes: the best per capita production in Europe in the coal mines, great hydroelectric and thermoelectric projects thanks to Electricité de France, the export of Dauphines thanks to the monopoly of Renault, the construction of the Caravelle by Sud-aviation. One could add many other examples.

I grant that it is a bit arbitrary to lump together these "producers" and the civil servants who helped them. I grant that there were rivalries between them, that there was far from total coordination between the Planning Commission and the Committee for Atomic Energy on the government level, or, on the level of private enterprise, between organizations as different as the Chambre Syndicale de la Sidérurgie Française and the Centre des Jeunes Patrons. Nevertheless I wish to show that in their actions there are striking analogies which are much more significant than their differences.

The French Neo-Realists had as their first aim success in their own line, without worrying too much about political quarrels and the mediocre quality of politicians. It is not at all certain that they were committed to the "national interest" and the *"grandeur* of the nation," but this possibility is not to be excluded either. The important fact is that personal feeling, as far as action was concerned, took a subordinate place; concrete success was the important thing.

As a result, in contrast to the traditionalists, the Neo-Realists placed economic matters above political matters. The priority given by them to such values as expansion, productivity, and the quality of goods and services is characteristic. This is literally the *"cultiver votre jardin"* of *Candide,* interpreted in its true sense, that is, not only "let us mind our own business and not bother with the outside" but "let us apply ourselves actively and intelligently." "Let us find in action the cure for all our ills, our divisions, our quarrels." Besides, as Alfred Grosser has said, "Economic modernization had burst the traditional modes of thought and action. This modernization is at the same time the cause and the effect of the eruption in France of a technical civilization, which made itself felt as early as the last years of the Fourth Republic. Political thought is entirely transformed by it—instead of being inspired by tradition it must take into account the constant transformation of the world in general and of France in particular." [42] As W. W. Rostow would say, France had reached the level of "high mass consumption."

With priority given to economic factors, "extroversion" recovers its rights in two ways. On the one hand, there is the conviction that economic expansion is the best means to assure independence. On the other hand, expansion necessitates a shifting of attention to foreign commerce. Foreign policy, therefore, should aim more at seeking concrete methods to improve foreign commerce than at seeking prestige.

If this new hierarchy of priorities is accepted, traditions give way to considerations of economic returns. Decolonization, for instance, becomes necessary in every case where the maintenance of ties is no longer possible. Again, relations with Germany must be good, because trade between the two nations is an economic necessity. The systematic anti-Communism of American policy must be tempered by the necessity of trade with countries to the east. Costly colonial wars, the luxury of a "striking force," and in a general way, all imperial policy, the policy of power for its own sake, is disapproved of by the Neo-Realists. Since security implies American protection, they believe it is better to assure it by concessions than to put up a vain and futile resistance to the opinions of France's allies, which would risk a break in relations, with a consequent loss of the security France must have in order to continue her expansion.

Mendès-France expressed this Neo-Realism, at least symbolically. He envisaged what he called "the policy of choice" in relation to French foreign policy. This was the first truly realistic expression of the need for adaptation. In a speech at the time of his first unsuccessful bid for power in June 1953 he said, "I have already said that the fundamental cause of the ills which engulf the country is the multiplicity of tasks it is trying to undertake at once: reconstruction, modernization, equipment and development of overseas nations, raising of the standard of living, social reform, exports, the war in Indochina, the maintenance of a large and powerful army in Europe, etc. Now events have confirmed what reflection permitted to be foreseen. To govern is to choose, however difficult the choices may be." He was not absolutely hostile to the tradition because in the same speech he spoke of three men as his models: Poincaré, Blum, and General de Gaulle, three men who "have left an indelible mark on my thinking." But the past is not a panacea. "No nation, however glorious its history, can base its authority on the respect inspired by its past. The sacrifices made and the battles won long ago are an example to us but cannot be the currency of our diplomacy." [43]

A year later, June 17, 1954, Mendès-France took office. He showed more clearly this time the hierarchy of his choices: bring to an end the war in Indochina and the quarrel over the EDC, in order to liquidate the past. Then, "a coherent program of recovery and of expansion destined to ensure the gradual improvement of conditions and the economic expansion of the nation." [44] No doubt he did not have time to carry out this plan, but he nevertheless showed that, like the Neo-Realists, it was in these measures that he saw France's great opportunities.

Neo-Realism has sometimes taken the form of *cartierisme* (from the name of Raymond Cartier, publisher of *Paris-Match*). This consists in the wish to hasten decolonization. "To do the opposite of what former prudence counseled, to accelerate instead of putting on the brakes. To transfer the greatest possible amount of responsibility to the Africans as fast as possible—at their own risk." [45] In other words, all suggestion of France's civilizing mission has disappeared. Colonization is seen only in terms of economic viability. Since it is no longer viable, the empire should be abandoned in favor of withdrawing into the "national hexagon." [46]

THE EUROPEANS

Parallel to the priority of economic considerations among the tendencies discernible in France since 1945 is the spirit of European integration. It would not be correct to say that all Neo-Realists are essentially "European." The Chambre Syndicale de la Sidérurgie Française opposed the Schuman plan; the EDC divided the French along different lines from those of traditionalists versus Neo-Realists. On the other hand, the Common Market has produced a synthesis between the two groups. Louis Armand and Jean Monnet are convinced "Europeans," and are among those responsible for the drive which has been made toward European integration.

But the category of Europeans is larger. It includes also the idealists, the partisans of a *mystique* of Europe who want to create a larger nation. It includes those who, avid to rediscover a certain greatness and convinced that France cannot any longer achieve it by herself, want to transpose the traditional greatness to the level of Europe. It includes neutralists and semineutralists who are bothered by the idea of domination by the United States and who see in the creation of a strong Europe the only means to emancipate themselves. One finds "Europeans" from Paul Reynaud and Antoine Pinay on the Right all the way to Maurice Faure (Radical) and Guy Mollet (Socialist) on the Left—taking in the whole of the Mouvement Républicain Populaire on the way. Robert Schuman, one of the pioneers of the movement, belongs to the MRP.

The European idea is unquestionably gaining ground in the ruling circles in France. It prevailed with the majority of deputies of the Fourth Republic, if one excludes the Communists and Gaullists. France took the lead in most of its ventures: the Council of Europe in 1948 and 1949; the Schuman plan for the Coal and Steel Community in May 1950; the Pleven plan for the European Army in October 1950; and the revival of the European idea after the failure of EDC in 1956, a revival which finally led to the achievement of the Common Market and Euratom.

The study of these developments will not be undertaken here, but a few general remarks are necessary. Two obstacles which still hindered the movement of European integration in the middle 1950's have disappeared: French suspicions of Germany and the "economic inferiority complex" which was related to the notion of Germany's inescapable superiority. The solution to the problem of the Saar in 1955–56 brought the discovery that there was no longer *one single* territorial quarrel between France and Germany. The old tradition of the "hereditary enemy" collapsed with a suddenness which astonished the French themselves.

It may seem difficult to explain Franco-German *rapprochement*, and some have seen in it nothing more than the deep personal sympathy and mutual admiration which de Gaulle and Adenauer have shown for each other since their first meeting. This is not a sufficient explanation, for there is also a real *rapprochement* at the popular level. France and Germany certainly do not feel affection for each other, but I believe that there exists a profound awareness of mutual advantage in close collaboration. To create this awareness, certain negative myths had to be eliminated. On the French side, as late as 1953 and 1954 during the EDC debates, the fear of the German will to dominate and the fear of being submerged by Germany's superior economic power were still very much alive. On the German side there was a myth that the French were not responsible partners, which is documented by well-meaning but dangerous books like Frederick Sieburg's *Dieu est-il français?* and Herbert Luethy's *France against Herself.* In short, this is the attitude the Germans call *"Franzosische Schlamperei."*

The enormous economic expansion of France since 1953 has greatly weakened the myths of both sides. The French have discovered with surprise that they can compete in many industrial sectors; this knowledge enables them to discard their economic fears. The Germans have discovered that the French are serious competitors and therefore much more "responsible" than they had thought. It could be said that the change took place when the price of French steel fell below the price of German steel.

The disappearance of these negative reactions—the French inferiority complex and the German superiority complex—coincided with more positive factors, such as the settlement of the Saar question and the discovery, especially since 1958, that they can support each other effectively in foreign policy. The solidarity of Adenauer and de Gaulle against Macmillan on the Berlin question is an example. The most spectacular result of this mutual support has been the progress of the Common Market at the expense of the free-trade zone advocated by the British. Franco-German solidarity allows a point of view opposed to Britain's to prevail on the European level. On the world level, within the Western Alliance, it enables Europe to exert much greater influence on American policy. One can therefore say that France and Germany are joined in a marriage of convenience which has turned out to be happy, in spite of the fact that it is not a marriage based on romantic love. Franco-German reconciliation progresses despite the tragic memories of the occupation, much less because of solidarity in regard to the USSR than because the two partners have discovered that they are fundamentally equal and necessary to each other.

The acceleration of decolonization since 1954 has been another favorable factor. Formerly there seemed to be a sort of choice between the reinforcement of ties with the French Union and the reinforcement of ties with European neighbors. These two groupings seemed to be mutually exclusive. There was indeed a proposed synthesis, "Eurafrica," but this did not attract France's European partners. The ups and downs of the French Union and then of the *Communauté* dissipated many doubts and swung the balance in favor of the European community.

There remains a series of profound differences among France's "Europeans." Some are for "policy first," in the traditional manner. Their aim is to arrive at political integration which assumes the creation of a supranational authority. For them economic integration is only a *means* to the end of a United States of Europe in one form or another as the Prussian *Zollverein* favored German unity based on Prussia. Others care little for the objective of this formula which they think unrealistic and distant. For them economic integration is an *end in itself* and will develop what is essential—that is, national prosperity. Curiously, this is General de Gaulle's attitude. He is an adherent of "politics first," but on the level of France. His larger solution is a "Europe of nations" and if he proposes the creation of a "confederation" it is with the retention of sovereignty by the member states. Maybe he only conceives this political confederation as a means by which France, supported by partners which she would represent in the concert of powers, could again attain the "first rank." It is evident, however, that this solution would not be easily accepted by the other partners. Meanwhile General de Gaulle, contrary to all predictions, actively favors the development of the Common Market, whose economic advantages to France are obvious.

The inclusion of Great Britain in the Common Market has been both feared and desired, depending on whether one belonged to the "politics first" group or to the "economics first" group. Those emphasizing "politics" have feared that British membership would retard for a long time the progress toward political integration of Europe. Those emphasizing "economics," who are quite indifferent to such a goal, have seen in British adherence a proof of the value of the Common Market and in any case a diplomatic victory for France.

In all, and in spite of many variations, it can be said that the group of "Europeans" is larger than that of the Neo-Realists, which it overlaps considerably. Significantly, all the influential French newspapers and weekly magazines of large circulation are fundamentally "European": *France-Soir, Paris-Match, Le Figaro,* even *Le Monde.* This is probably the greatest proof that after the catastrophe and after the failure of the return to normalcy the principal effort at adaptation by the French is the discovery of a new goal—for some a new ideal—namely, the creation of a unified Western Europe.

POLICY OF GRANDEUR, RECENT PHASE

It seems that General de Gaulle, although moved by a totally different conception of the national interest, and although advocating a Europe of nations rather than the integrated Europe of the "Europeans," has recently come to share a number of views with them. His clear firm position has always been that the greatness of France is the supreme goal to be sought. "The positive side of my mind convinces me that France is not really herself except in the front ranks, that only vast undertakings are capable of offsetting the disintegrating elements of her people. In short, France cannot be France without greatness." [47]

Such a goal may seem very different from that of the Neo-Realists. The General is typically a man of extroversion, for whom foreign policy has first priority, whereas Neo-Realism is introversive by definition and gives priority to profits and the raising of the standard of living, and not to the "dream of domination." [48] But, as Stanley Hoffmann has so well said, "Some criticisms of 'grandeur' are based on a misunderstanding of the General. His *mystique* is not a quest for anachronism, a vain nostalgia for past greatness, a fruitful drive for restoration . . . When he talks to the French about their greatness, then and now, it is in order to get them to adapt to, and to act in, the world as it is, not in order to keep them in a museum of past glories. It is flattery for reform." [49]

The best proof that this interpretation is right is the General's evolution in regard to these "vast undertakings" by which the country will achieve greatness. In 1940 the undertaking was to keep the flame of resistance burning, that France *as France* should continue to fight: "What is the use of providing the auxiliary forces for another power? No! For the effort to be worthwhile not only Frenchmen but France must carry on the war." [50] In 1946 the undertaking was to resume "rank," to keep the empire in a revised form, to destroy the threat of Germany by dismembering her. What are the "vast undertakings" which General de Gaulle now offers to the French, still in the name of greatness? There are fundamentally two.

The first is economic expansion. "The condition which will determine the entire future of France is for her children to unite in a great national task . . . What task? the development of France! This is the immense opportunity that offers us power, harmony, greatness . . . This huge renewal must be the business and the prime ambition of France" (May 8, 1961). "We French must rise to the rank of a great industrial power or resign ourselves to decline" (June 18, 1960). "We will pursue a vast development—scientific, technological, academic, economic . . . which leads to prosperity, influence and power" (December 31, 1960). "Once again, we are a nation in the midst of revolution, which knows that its own development is the source of prosperity and power" (press conference, September 5, 1961).[51]

The second great undertaking is decolonization. "It seems to me contrary to the present interest and new ambition of France to remain bound by obligations and burdens which no longer fit her power and influence . . . It is a fact . . . [that] decolonization is our interest and is therefore our policy" (press conference, April 11, 1961). "As a world power, we must complete this enterprise of decolonization which we have already pursued so far" (Mont de Marsan, April 12, 1961). "For many reasons our national interest is to disentangle ourselves from futile costly burdens and to let our former subjects work out their own destiny. All the better if new relations of friendship and cooperation are established, as is the case with twelve states in Black Africa and with the Republic of Madagascar! But in any case, good sense, our aim, our success, can be called decolonization" (July 12, 1961).

On these two points of economic development and decolonization, General de Gaulle, with a different ultimate goal, *grandeur*, reaches the same conclusion as the Neo-Realists, who care little for *grandeur*, or at least consider it out of date. Raymond Aron wrote in 1959, thinking that it was criticism of the General, "the greatness of France will not be measured either in the number of square kilometers over which the *tricolore* flies . . . or by the rate of economic growth, or by the height of our skyscrapers. It will be the by-product of a double success—economic modernization and continuity of culture." [52]

General de Gaulle calls this continuity of culture the "*mission humaine*" of France. "We have always had a humane mission and we have it still; policy must adapt itself to our genius" (press conference, November 10, 1959). Aron writes, "France will be great in the eyes of the world in the exact measure that she fulfills herself." De Gaulle obviously goes further: "France must fulfill her mission as a world power. We are everywhere in the world. There is no corner of the earth, where, at a given time, men do not look to us and ask what France says. It is a great responsibility to be France, the humanizing power *par excellence*" (Bordeaux, April 15, 1961).

As for the "Europeans," they cannot avoid realizing that the Common Market was saved in 1958 from the British plan for a free-trade zone—which would have deprived it of its positive aspects—exclusively by the tenacity of the two leading statesmen of Europe, de Gaulle and Adenauer, who were also the builders of a solid and lasting Franco-German reconciliation.

In these circumstances of so many overlapping aims, what are the essential criticisms of General de Gaulle on the level of foreign policy? One can discern three types of criticism by the Neo-Realists:

1. The General absolutely insists on creating—from motives of a futile *grandeur*—a French atomic striking force, which is very expensive. The majority of foreign and French experts are extremely skeptical of the possibility of France's creating a "useful force"; in fact, General Gallois alone dissents. Under these conditions, why not stick to the conventional arms which the NATO partners want to see France develop? But the General relates this

matter to *grandeur*. "It is both the right and the duty of the continental European powers to have their own national defense. It is intolerable for a great state to have its destiny subject to decisions and acts of another state, no matter how friendly it may be" (April 11, 1961). The only argument one can advance in favor of the Gaullist policy is hypothetical and based on the possibility that it might prepare the way for the establishment of a European deterrent. As Aron says, "If [France] continues to dream of domination without possessing the means, she might as well resign herself to becoming absorbed in European unity. A united Western Europe would have the resources necessary for a 'grand policy.' She could send rockets to the moon and accumulate a thermonuclear stockpile." I need not add that Aron and many other writers are skeptical of this possibility.

2. General de Gaulle tends to relate greatness to isolation. His temperament fosters this, to be sure. "It is by acting as the inflexible champion of the nation and of the state that it will be possible for me to gain followers and even enthusiasts among the French, and to gain from foreigners respect and consideration . . . In short, handicapped and alone as I was, and precisely because I was, I had to reach the top and never come down." [53] In the 1960's this isolation consists in not deferring easily to the opinion of the Allies; in refusing to integrate French forces in NATO; in not taking advantage of the opportunity for maneuver in the United Nations—"*le machin*"—afforded by twelve newly created states whose language is French; and in remaining inflexible and intransigent. The critics may well denounce in this attitude the danger of losing France's partners. At a time when the nation's ultimate protection comes from the American deterrent, wouldn't it be better to strengthen the ties with the United States and increase her interest in defending Europe—as England and Germany do? Even if the General is right, it is a mistake (as André Fontaine says often in *Le Monde*) for France not to adjust herself in a spirit of compromise to certain views held by her allies.

3. Above all, the Neo-Realists see in the idea of *grandeur*, in "national ambition," in the emphasis on foreign policy, a dangerous illusion. The appeal for great enterprises made in September 1961

was answered by a wave of strikes in the nationalized industries—electricity, gas, railroads—not to mention agitation by the peasants and the butchers. To the idea of *grandeur*, realism at once opposes tangibles: a greater share in the profits of expansion for the working class; strong measures in underdeveloped rural areas in many French provinces; and, most worthy task of all, the safeguarding of democracy threatened by extremists. These are the objectives of those who have their feet on the ground, so to speak, compared to him who towers above the clouds. If it is objected that these charges are often brought by shortsighted people against men of vision, the reply might be that while seeing far, one must not neglect concrete reality. Woodrow Wilson was a victim of such a dichotomy between the future and goals which are temporary but dear to the hearts of men. In seeing in his opponents only *"la hargne, la rogne, la grogne,"* and in disregarding the possible support of organized groups such as parties and unions, does not General de Gaulle risk the total loss of his ideal of national ambition in the long run—as he did in 1946?

The Europeans, for their part, direct their criticisms at de Gaulle's rejection of a supranational authority, of real political integration.

For him integration means the absorption of France into a new entity and he considers that such absorption would in fact bring about obliteration and disappearance of France's supreme value. General de Gaulle is in favor of the Common Market, but no one is under any illusion that he has much use for Euratom and the Coal and Steel Community. No doubt he advocates a plan of "vast confederation" for Europe, but it is a confederation of independent states. There is a suspicion among France's allies that such a confederation is, in the General's mind, only a way of getting the support of other European states for French goals. In brief, the French "Europeans" reason that at the very moment that the concept and emotional myth evoked by the idea of the nation need revision, General de Gaulle rushes to the defense of a form of nationalism they think outmoded. This nationalism, the supreme goal for newly created nations, should no longer be the supreme goal in Europe. In their eyes, it is a fearful anachronism.

IV

CONCLUSION

◇◇◇

In comparison to the *tradition*, and following the *catastrophe*, the picture of the present ideal values held by the French is quite confused. The Algerian War, which, in contrast to decolonization, has jeopardized the interests of one million French Europeans and a substantial minority of Moslems who wish to remain French, has increased the confusion to an extraordinary degree. Among those who totally disapprove of the Secret Army extremists there is a group of sincere and honest Frenchmen who consider Algeria French and who hold that a nation has no right to eject some of her children from her body; they suffer bitterly from everything they consider a retreat. But this is a very small group in metropolitan France. The referendum of January 1961 resulted in a 75 percent majority "yes" answer and only 24 percent "no." "Yes" meant acceptance of the extension of decolonization to Algeria. On this point the Neo-Realists as well as de Gaulle knew they had a substantial majority. Of the 24 percent "no" it seems reasonable to consider that 20 percent were Communists who favor rapid decolonization but are basically hostile to the Fifth Republic. There remains about 4 percent partisans of *"Algérie Française,"* a sort of residue of the tradition of colonial expansion, not a large movement. The referendum of April 8, 1962, with 90.8 percent "yes" and 9.4 percent "no" confirms this. Among those who voted "no" there are certainly many anti-Gaullists of the Left, who favor the independence of Algeria although they oppose de Gaulle. Besides, only a minority of the supporters of *Algérie Française* approve the terrorist methods of the Secret Army. There are very few Fascists in France.

So we arrive at the crucial question: when General de Gaulle is no longer in power, which of these changes taking place in French foreign policy will last? After the "normal" of pre-1939 and the futile attempt to "return to normal" of 1945, will a new "normalcy" be achieved?

Only the study of basic French opinion will yield a few plausible answers. It goes without saying that the attitude of France—barring world disaster—remains and will remain basically introversive. Let us cite an essential commentary of the Institute of French Public Opinion (based on Gallup polls) concerning this attitude: "Asked about urgent problems about the government's first task, the public first mentions domestic issues and among them those which deal with material existence: wages, prices, standard of living, housing, or employment. Only events in which individuals are to some extent directly involved and whose repercussions in national life are obvious and perceptible at the individual level . . . can make this concern with everyday matters . . . take a subordinate place. The affairs of Indochina, and then of North Africa in general, and finally of Algeria . . . are examples of such movements . . . Concern for peace, general anxiety about the balance of power, international politics, systems of alliance in which France is involved, never appear until later and then only at the back of the average mind. They do not constitute for the public the prime object of French policy." [54]

This assumption explains another characteristic of the "normal." As in the past, but now even more so, France is satisfied with her territorial limits in Europe. This is the spirit of the hexagon. In all political groups from the narrowest *cartierisme* to the most ambitious *gaullisme*, the present territorial limits of France are absolutely not in question.

On the contrary, whereas we have seen that the policy of colonialism was formerly generally approved by the masses—despite their indifference—now the great majority of Frenchmen accept decolonization. One might even say that General de Gaulle has been successful in showing the French that decolonization is an imperative necessity of our time, that it is a fertile source of friendship among peoples—in short, that it is a "vast undertaking."

At the point where it becomes necessary to analyze specific ways of protecting the security of the hexagon, one can no longer find such substantial majorities. France has chosen the Western camp and this is little discussed. To conclude from this that the French are convinced adherents of the Atlantic Pact would not be accurate, however. The wish to escape a possible war between

East and West means that there is in fact a substantial portion of neutralists. A poll of December 1957 indicated that in case of a war between East and West, 21 percent of the French wish to be in the Western camp, 3 percent in the Eastern camp, 51 percent in neither camp. (Curiously, in the same poll the percentage of Communist voters was 8 percent for the West, 29 percent for the East, and 49 percent for neither camp.) [55]

Similarly, in regard to European union there is a substantial majority of partisans and few convinced opponents (55 percent to 9 percent in December 1957).[56] But ideas concerning the nature of this union were pretty hazy. Thus the increasingly enthusiastic acceptance of the Common Market by the French, especially by industrial firms and many professionals, and the inclusion of agricultural affairs in the Common Market in January 1962 despite the reluctance of France's partners, do not necessarily imply a vigorous movement favoring the *political* integration of Europe. The Common Market has proved that it stimulates economic expansion. In this sense it is approved. France is largely abandoning her restrictionist Malthusian attitude and there now exists a *mystique* of expansion. On this point where de Gaulle and the Neo-Realists meet, a new tradition is being created. But, since de Gaulle does not join the "Europeans" on the political plane, there is as yet in France only the beginning of a possible tradition of political unification of Europe.

On the notion of a "French mission" in the world, it is probable that there is a rather wide agreement among Frenchmen. The French, at least the educated elite, are very proud of their culture. They like knowing that it plays a role in the world. The appearance on the international scene of twelve new states which consider French their national language and two others (Mauritania and Madagascar) which consider it one of two national languages, and four more (Cambodia, Laos, Morocco, and Tunisia) which consider it the principal language of international negotiations, shows that the French language maintains a solid position. The French rejoice in this. The budget for "cultural relations" is never attacked. The adding of technical cooperation to cultural cooperation, as reflected in the 1958 "Plan of Expansion and Reconversion," shows that the French keep the idea of a mission. But a cultural nationalism, a "scarcely disguised French-centeredness" continues. Alfred Grosser has ably shown the development from "pointless socializing" to a much broader and more serious participation in cultural exchange.[57]

Let us note the conclusion of a high-ranking civil servant, Stephane Hessel, in a still unpublished report on the role France can play in the world: "More than any other nation France should be able to replace her military power, even her economic leadership, both outdated, by cultural leadership of the nations which she has led to political maturity." From these efforts and attempts to adapt to a new "normal," we must remember this: it is not certain that the policy of *grandeur* will survive de Gaulle, for realism is constantly gaining. But it would be a mistake to believe that such a concept—*grandeur*—is totally opposed to French aspirations. The catastrophe, because it brought many ideas into question, humiliated the country, upset the balance of power, and helped to give the French a new emotional patriotism. This is no longer jingoistic. People do not burst into tears at the sight of the flag, but they will not accept further humiliation, either. The art of General de Gaulle has been to wipe out humiliation several times in his life. This has appeal for the people and he has felt it. Speaking of his 1946 departure from public life he wrote, "Nevertheless, while the personnel of the regime gave in to the euphoria of resuming old habits, the mass of the people, on the contrary, withdrew into sadness. With de Gaulle's departure there departed also a breath from the summit, a hope of success, the ambition of France which bore up the national soul." [58]

The Fourth Republic died partly because it was limited to the attitude of introversion. It would be well for the General's successors not to lose sight of the fact that a nation needs a certain pride, however realist she may be. In this sense there continues to be a French nationalism. Except for groups which dream of the past, however, it is no longer a nationalism of expansion and domination, but merely a desire to have a proper place in the world. The French adapt themselves out of realism but they do not admit that this adaptation means the loss of their independence and their originality.

SIX AUTHORS IN SEARCH
OF A NATIONAL CHARACTER

François Goguel

For a Frenchman to express at the same time what he thinks of the foregoing studies and his own opinion of the problems they deal with is a fascinating and difficult task. The basic questions are: What changes have taken place in France in the last thirty years? What are their causes, immediate and underlying? Do these changes represent a passing phase in the history of French society or should one expect to see them proceed at an accelerated rate? In the latter case, they would mark a fundamental development in French history.

The task is fascinating because in certain respects no one can ever have sufficient perspective on matters he is involved in or evaluate the real significance of gradual changes in his own environment. It is very instructive for a person to learn how others see him, how they interpret the development of his career or personality. It is no less instructive for a person taking part in the daily life of a nation and in certain of its subcommunities to learn from foreign observers who are well qualified, objective, and well disposed how they view the evolution of his society and the role of its component parts.

The task is difficult, however, because it implies that he can resist two contradictory temptations. There is the temptation of being so carried away by the point of view of the foreign observers, and so convinced that they see more clearly than one could oneself, that one concludes they are always right. Another temptation is to protest against unwonted judgment, against evaluation which seems to derive from a surface view or a certain lack of proportion; to feel some annoyance at oversimplified or over-harsh judgments; and, finally, to reject without scrutiny the validity even of the attempt to elucidate from the outside problems in which one feels too intimately involved to accept the possibility that others might offer a solution.

Of these two temptations, the first is the one I had to struggle against most often in reading the chapters of Stanley Hoffmann, Charles Kindleberger, Laurence Wylie, and Jesse Pitts. (I do not mention Jean-Baptiste Duroselle, as he is a fellow Frenchman.) All of them know my country so well and know how to express their feelings about it with such delicacy that I think it would be impossible for the most sensitive French nationalist, after reading their chapters, to feel the kind of xenophobic reaction aroused by other studies of France which lack intimate knowledge of French realities and the indispensable minimum of real sympathy for France, even though they are written with clear-cut concern for scientific objectivity. The reader should, therefore, not expect me to deny consistently the value and scope of the observations of my American friends in this book. The reservations or criticisms I shall express of some of their ideas have more often arisen from a second reading than from my initial reaction.

The task is also difficult for another, more personal, reason. I am not involved in these studies merely as a Frenchman. Between 1933 and 1939, during the great depression, I shared in the activities of two of the groups, subsequently publications—*Esprit* and *Nouveaux Cahiers*—which, before the Second World War, contributed to the re-evaluation of values and social structures which French society had inherited from the past. Stanley Hoffmann, in particular, attaches great importance to these groups. Five years as a prisoner in Germany prevented me from joining the men from these groups who took part either in the Vichy government or in the Resistance, but in 1945 I resumed participation in *Esprit*, whose criticism of the "established disorder" continued to follow the line created by Emmanuel Mounier in 1932. Even though, in the last ten years, my activity has been increasingly oriented toward analysis based on political science—assuming that it is a science—rather than toward the "revolutionary" trend of *Esprit*, the partial coincidence of my studies with those of the other authors of this book still poses a problem: Do I not run the danger of disagreeing with certain of the observations merely because they do not coincide with my own former conclusions? Can I remove myself sufficiently from what I have thought and written since 1945 to recognize that I have made more than one mistake and that I therefore should not be too dogmatic in my present opinions? The reader may be able to answer these questions. At least he should know that I am conscious of the particular difficulty of my task. The honor of writing this concluding chapter makes me very much aware of the obligation to be as honest and objective as possible.

How can I attempt to sum up the significance of the foregoing chapters?

France has experienced since 1945 a basic economic transformation. Continual and extraordinary technical progress in industry and commerce, an increase in production, and the development of foreign trade have brought about a striking contrast between the postwar period and the interwar period. From an economy whose stability often seemed inherently connected with immobility, France has moved to an economy marked by a regular and prolonged expansion whose rate of growth compares favorably with that of other Western European nations. From an economy geared essentially to the domestic market, which she tried to keep to herself by protectionism, France has moved to an economy which no longer fears competition and even seeks it, because she feels confident of being able to compete with her neighbors, especially Great Britain and Germany. The inferiority complex which French industrialists formerly had in relation to German and British industry has almost entirely disappeared.

Corresponding to this economic renewal, there have been changes in the structure and values of society which are less complete but incontestable. Social, professional, and regional differences in France today are less hard and fast and less conspicuous than formerly. The tendency toward greater uniformity is seen in the material aspects of life, transformed by modern equipment, and also in mental and psychological attitudes, determined by news media ever more direct and uniform.

Nevertheless, especially in the realm of values, directly connected with the system of formal education, a certain number of factors operate to check and delay social change, which has not yet followed economic change to its logical conclusion. The lag in social change can place certain obstacles in the way of extending to all regions and sectors of the economy the modernization of production and distribution.

Despite the lag, however, one cannot deny that changes in values and in social structure have developed in the last fifteen years in a sufficiently clear way and on a broad enough scale for them to be considered irreversible.

The same is not true in the political sphere; the adaptation of France to the world of the second half of the twentieth century, so largely accomplished in economic affairs and already well advanced in the social order, remains almost wholly to be worked out and implemented in political terms. In foreign policy France today seems, in many respects, to have begun to adapt herself, although not without painful shocks. I refer to decolonization and to the fact that despite sudden reversals (the rejection of the European Defense Community is the best example), France has, on the whole, understood and accepted the fundamental necessity of the economic unification of Europe, which in turn inevitably implies a corresponding political unification in one form or another.

Within the nation, however, neither the political forces (in the organization of the parties, their programs, ideologies, and methods), nor institutions (in structure, balance, and in the relations between different elements of public power) have changed in such a way as to enable the state to function satisfactorily. This explains the contrast, so striking under the Fourth Republic, between the rejuvenation of the country and the embarrassment and instability of the political leaders, who could not formulate and carry out a coherent program. In one sense General de Gaulle's rise to power and the overwhelming confidence which the country has manifested in him in the referenda of September 1958, January 1961, and April 1962—submerging its usual partisan divisions—

are results of the incapacity of the traditional parliamentary state to face up to its responsibilities in the preceding period. The problem of the adaptation of the French system to the contemporary world is not thereby solved, however; it is simply postponed. In a sense, the solution may have been made still more difficult because of certain aspects of the government France has had since 1958.

Profound transformation in the economic sphere, changes in the organization and values of society (albeit less rapid and less complete), immobility and nonadaptation in the strictly political sphere: such is the conclusion of the several studies in this book. With this general conclusion I cannot but agree. In the following pages I shall risk trying to qualify the other essays and to analyze in detail the reasons for the postwar changes—economic, social, and political—and their significance.

In the identification of the factors responsible for change, certain fundamental themes unify the various chapters of this book. In some cases the underlying unity is more obvious than in others. The factors responsible for change discerned by the authors are in many cases the same, whatever the particular field under discussion. The obstacles to change also operate simultaneously—though not always to the same extent—in economic affairs, in society, and in the political sphere.

The major factors responsible for change in France since the end of World War II were not produced internally. It was not by a spontaneous movement that the French economy and society have evolved with such speed that they present today a situation that in many respects differs in *kind* rather than merely in *degree*. Externally-induced traumas stimulated these changes.

The first of the shocks was caused by the great depression of the 1930's. France reacted all the more awkwardly to this event because she was affected later than other nations by repercussions from the fall in world prices, from the slowdown of business in the United States, Germany, and Great Britain, and from the disorganization of currencies—developments which were at once the consequence of and the empirical remedy for the world crisis.

Then came the outbreak of war, which constituted a double

setback for French foreign policy since 1919. French policy had had two aspects; the "security" of the nation had been sought both by the classic method (alliances and armaments) and by the newer method of collective security through law, embodied in the League of Nations. Up to about 1934–35, the parties of the Right preferred to support the classic method while those of the Left preferred collective security. The foreign policy of Briand, between 1925 and 1932, tried to reconcile them. From 1935 on, that is, after the signing of the Franco-Soviet Pact, both the Right and Left were divided between those who advocated resistance to totalitarian policies and those who favored regular "appeasement" at the price of concessions to "revisionist" claims. The fluctuation of France's diplomatic action before 1939 and her tendency to line up with the British are no doubt to be explained in great part by these divisions and by the place domestic policy increasingly took in determining the attitude of politicians and public opinion toward foreign policy. What is certain is that the very fact of the outbreak of war in September 1939 completed and made clear the defeat of both tendencies in French diplomacy—resistance and appeasement—because the advocates of both wanted above all to avoid war.

The defeat of 1940, brought about in six weeks, constituted another trauma, a very violent one, whose complex results were made worse in the following years, first by the occupation and then by the Resistance. It is true that the defeat healed certain basic divisions which had traditionally divided French society. The shock, caused from outside, certainly was a source of a process of unification. At the same time, however, the different attitudes toward "collaboration" and toward the policy of "wait and see," the controversy over support of General Giraud and General de Gaulle brought about new divisions in the national community.

Finally, beginning in 1944, the ambiguity of France's international position is important. She was in the camp of the victors but not as a full partner. Difficult relations with her allies, French need for American aid to reconstitute the economy, the problems posed by the worldwide phenomenon of decolonization in Indochina, Morocco, and Tunisia at first, then in Algeria, and finally—in a less dramatic way—in Black Africa, have continued, in varying degree, to affect France as shocks of external origin, with results that were complex and sometimes contradictory.

On the whole, there is no doubt that the authors of the foregoing chapters are right when they say that these phenomena from outside the French hexagon—from Black Friday on Wall Street in 1929 to the Algerian rebellion of 1954 and the Evian agreement of 1962—were the fundamental causes of changes in French economy and society in the last thirty years.

It may be that the foreign origin of these changes explains why the *political* adaptation of France to the new kind of world has been the most difficult kind of adaptation. The fact that France has had to undergo some changes by necessity rather than by choice may explain why a not inconsiderable segment of public opinion can still today incline to the view that the era of changes, whose causes appear to be external, is merely a temporary phase, bound to end soon, after which the situation will return to "normal," that is, to the *status quo ante*.

Another factor of change, particularly emphasized by Laurence Wylie but alluded to by the other authors, is that economic and social changes have, in a way, been self-perpetuating, to the extent that their intensity has persuaded individuals and families that the pathetic effort after 1919 to reconstruct French habits and the traditional (pre-1914) style of life was futile and bound to fail. This is a psychological factor which I consider to be basic. Instead of persisting in the effort to hold themselves back (especially demographically, but in other ways also), an effort which led no-where, Frenchmen began, in a kind of despair, to live from day to day. An unforeseen hope was born from this despair, when people perceived that this more empirical attitude, more open to change, far from leading to catastrophe, opened up new perspectives for individuals and families. The new perspective may be disconcerting from the point of view of tradition, but it also has many advantages.

Doubtless it has led to numerous social changes, for example the increasing replacement of the "extended" family by the "nuclear" family as the basic unit of society (including the liberation of the younger generations from the domination of parents and grandparents); the decline in the importance of inheritance in middle-class milieux; and, in the upper classes, new attitudes toward work. Frenchmen have given up trying to revive the past.

The spectacular extension of technical progress in all spheres of private life as well as in the economy, the new role of intermediate groups and associations between the individual and the state, especially in economic affairs, the acceptance of economic planning and of state intervention in production and distribution as a natural thing—these other essential factors of change in France in the last fifteen years are probably derivative. They were made possible, and sometimes were even initiated, either by the external shocks to French society and economy or by the fundamental psychological change resulting from the shocks, which manifested itself in a renunciation of the futile effort to restore the past.

The factors leading to change have not been able to make their full effect felt because there are others which continue to hold in check the changes in present-day France. Most of these stem from the traditional values of French culture. I believe myself to belong to the category of Frenchmen conscious of the impossibility for France in 1939—and probably as early as 1919—to reconstruct the social structure, economic organization, and style of life of her people as they had been before the World Wars. Yet I must admit my resistance to the penetration of certain modern techniques into my private life, although I am well aware that they are powerful forces for change in society. I refuse to own a television set, I prefer the printed word to the radio as a source of news, and I do not go to the movies as often as three times a year. This attitude certainly derives from a desire to preserve a personal style of life inherited from the past, considered more civilized and more human than one which would result from yielding to all the facilities of modern technology. This small example shows how fidelity to a certain conception of culture can be a hindrance, or at least a check, to the transformation of society—if it is indeed true that the development of the mass media is an essential factor in that transformation.

The prime reason that certain traditional values of French culture can slow or block changes in society, however, stems from the educational system. In many respects, to be sure, French educational tradition favors the present changes. The Cartesian spirit, the emphasis on mathematics, the general rational approach based on science certainly favor economic planning and technical progress, but this is not true of a certain traditional conception of humanism, based on the superiority of what is old, whether in the theatre, in painting, in architecture, or in literature. The public interest provoked by polemics in the press about changes in the old sections of French cities, the "sacrilege" of constructing modern apartment houses beside monuments of the past, and the public concern to defend the rural landscape against the invasion of factories and urban centers are revealing in this respect.

A plan to build housing for fifteen thousand persons on the outskirts of Paris was resisted by certain administrators because it would spoil the landscape painted half a century ago by Claude Monet. In general, French public opinion seems to me unresponsive to the argument of modern architects when they ask the right to substitute their works for those of their predecessors and justify themselves by pointing to the Romanesque churches which gave way to Gothic cathedrals or to seventeenth-century buildings which could not have been built except by the destruction of medieval buildings. André Siegfried, during the last years of his life, wrote many articles opposing changes in the Jardin des Tuileries whose purpose was to facilitate traffic in Paris; public opinion supported him. This respect for the past and suspicion of contemporary works, or at least the desire to keep them on the outskirts of cities where they cannot present such a striking contrast to the works of the past, are very indicative of an attitude which prevails in the circles which set the tone of French public opinion. These mental attitudes cannot help delaying and holding in check changes in society even as material changes actually take place in French life.

Laurence Wylie is decidedly right in saying that the place given to history and geography in the school curriculum, which gives children the impression that their lives will be largely determined by the past and by the geographical setting, does not predispose them to accept or to initiate rapid and complete social change.

The organization of education constitutes, without a doubt, a factor of social immobility even more important than the content of instruction. The entrenched divisions between the lower degrees and the highest, between general instruction and technical instruction, between the several faculties on the one hand and the whole university establishment and the *grandes écoles* outside the university on the other, are hard to overcome. There is a kind of academic corporatism in France, which values all the levels of instruction with their elected bodies, composed of teachers of various types, who, even if in theory they are only advisory, possess administrative power which is often decisive. The advantage of this organization is to guarantee academic freedom vis-à-vis the state. Its disadvantage is to hinder reform, especially in the relatively numerous cases where it is an unwritten law that these bodies make no decision except unanimously.

The material difficulties in French education in the last fifteen years are perhaps due less to insufficient state financial support (which is greater than is sometimes realized) than to a series of interlocking problems. The structure and established hierarchy of academic organization has been jealously defended at a time when the number of students has risen sharply. At the same time the training of new teachers by traditional methods, culminating in difficult examinations, is hampered by the low birth rate in the group born before 1940, from which new teachers must be recruited. Moreover, economic expansion has attracted into other fields young men who might otherwise have gone into teaching.

It was physically impossible to provide secondary instruction exactly like the traditional instruction in the *lycée* when the number of students quadrupled while that of new teachers remained the same. This was nevertheless what was attempted, and it is hardly surprising that the attempt failed.

Reforms in the educational structure are nevertheless taking place. An effort is being made to overcome the rigid divisions, to allow or facilitate passage from one academic category to another, to modify curricula and methods. Academic inertia makes the actual implementation of these changes slow, and I do not doubt that this is one of the basic causes of the lag in social change.

Family attitudes are also involved. If the number of students at the highest level who come from peasant or working-class background is still too low, it is partly because parents of gifted children in these social groups often fear that if they urge their children to undertake advanced study they will lose contact with them, whereas they hope that children oriented toward technical instruction will still speak the same language. This attitude is an important cause of the widespread tendency in France for a family's progress from class to class to take place in two steps instead of one. The son of a farmer will become an elementary teacher or a minor official; the grandson may become a member of a university faculty or *Inspecteur des Finances*. It is easy to understand and, up to a point, to sympathize with the human and family reasons which explain the preference for such gradual rise in social status rather than a more rapid rise, but it cannot be disputed that there are disadvantages in this check on social mobility.

The attitude and the traditional reflexes of French citizens toward the state probably constitute still another basic factor of resistance to change. For a long time the majority of Frenchmen considered the state much less as a body dependent on them, for whose proper functioning they had a responsibility, than as a sort of foreign body, a necessary evil perhaps, against which the wise course was to take many precautions to prevent state action from weighing too heavily on individuals and on families. This explains the long-continued refusal to recognize the right of the state to intervene in economic affairs, except to protect vested rights (*situations acquises*) threatened in the natural course of events. It also explains the tendency to consider that the wise citizen should use his vote not to give the government power but to keep it weak, by setting up the legislature as an opposition capable of defeating the natural tendency of public authority to push its power too far. "Resistance to power is more important than reforming action," wrote the Radical philosopher Alain forty years ago. Many French voters—often even among those who support the Communists—act as if this were in fact the guiding principle of their vote. It is hardly necessary to explain why such an attitude provides a very effective counterweight to the changes, economic, social, and political, which come about either from various pressures on France from the outside world or from causes of change lying hidden in French society.

In all, despite these powerful negative forces, there have been considerable changes in French society in the last fifteen years, as the reader will have realized in reading the foregoing chapters. In each field (even the political, despite the lag) there are particular causes of change in addition to the general causes operating in all fields. The particular factors help to overcome the forces of resistance. I shall now try to analyze these particular causes of change in the economy, in society, and finally in political life.

What seems most striking in Charles Kindleberger's excellent analysis of the causes of recent expansion in the French economy is that in many respects he attributes economic growth more to psychological or socio-psychological factors than to strictly economic ones. He concludes that it is a state of mind which has changed, largely under the influence of the external shocks France endured between 1930 and 1950. The changed psychological outlook was all that was needed for pre-existing factors of expansion—held in check until recently by the immobility of French society—to be, so to speak, liberated and allowed free play to achieve their full effect. The high technical quality of French methods of production does not seem to me an entirely new fact—far from it. What is new is that business management has allowed technological progress freedom to develop and has even favored it by making the required investments.

There are, nevertheless, facts which do not bear on psychology and which it is useful to recall in order to grasp thoroughly all the aspects of the contrast between the interwar French economy and the French economy since the Second World War. France's losses between 1914 and 1918, which reached the enormous figure of 1,400,000 men, certainly contributed in great part to the perpetuation of a static rather than a dynamic state of mind in France in the 1920's and 1930's. (One notable result of these losses was the abnormal prolongation of leadership for the older generation.) This static mental state could not help being reinforced by the stagnation of the French population. Since the population did not increase between 1919 and 1939, it was possible for the concept of a totally stable society not to seem absurd.

During the Second World War, on the contrary, France did not suffer a human blood-letting comparable to that of 1914–1918; and after 1945 a moderate but lasting rise in the birth rate brought about a regular and uninterrupted increase in the population of about 300,000 a year. In these conditions, the whole ideal of stability lost its foundation. Growth in the economy seemed to be a necessary consequence of the increase in the number of Frenchmen.

What accounts for the reversal of the demographic pattern? Why should a people whose birth rate fell constantly for eighty years suddenly experience a steady rise in the birth rate? It is all the harder to answer these questions because the population growth is not confined to France. In the last fifteen years an identical demographic change has taken place in other Western societies.

In the case of France, it is certain that measures to raise the living standard of families with children, taken under the *Code de la Famille* in 1939 and increased after the Liberation, have contributed to the rise of the birth rate. These measures are not enough in themselves to explain it, however. Personally, I think Laurence Wylie is entirely right in considering that the disappearance or lessening of demographic restriction stems to a great extent from the fact that many groups which between the two World Wars had not renounced the effort to restore the traditional, pre-1914 style of life, and who saw in small families a means to this end, have finally understood the impossibility of going back. As soon as they were resigned to living in the present they abandoned family restriction, since its purpose had disappeared. By doing so, they brought into existence a new kind of future, based on economic growth rather than on stability, on work rather than on savings.

For population growth to affect the economy, it was also necessary for people to recognize the essential connections between them. In this respect, probably the rejuvenation of business leadership, started during the war and occupation and accelerated since, played an important part. Stanley Hoffmann underlines the fact that through both the Vichy government and the Resistance the years 1940–1945 offered opportunities of leadership to men influenced by the thinking of the 1930's. This meant that their action would be consistently oriented toward reexamination of the traditional structures and values of French society. Mr. Hoffmann's observation is certainly correct.

Nevertheless, I wonder if the fundamental cause of the shift in the French economy from stability to expansion does not lie in the very situation of the economy immediately after World War II, a situation whose conditions implied in themselves the necessity of growth.

On the one hand, it is a fact that the material needs of the French people, after five years of penury, inevitably created a powerful demand for goods. On the other hand and above all, the former equilibrium of the balance of payments, based on investments outside France, could not be reestablished because these investments had been liquidated. It was therefore necessary that the reconstruction of France's economy after the war include a transformation of its structure. The new equilibrium could not be conceived without a growth in exports, implying an increase in production, reduction of production costs, and the abandonment of protectionism through tariffs. In short, the given elements of the French economic situation after the war demanded a profound transformation. It seems reasonable to assume that this fact not only contributed largely to the modification of the general state of mind—by replacing the former desire for stability with a desire to expand—but also helped the new leaders to whose role Stanley Hoffmann attaches such importance, in carrying out their policy.

It should be underlined, however, that even if, in an over-all study of changes in France, the substitution of a growing economy for a stagnant economy and the decline of a Malthusian attitude become indisputable facts, there are still marked geographical differences which affect these changes. The increase in population really affects only one third of the country, principally because of the internal migration which draws labor to the industrial regions. One would certainly be mistaken to conclude from this that economic modernization is not manifest throughout France, but it does not take the same form everywhere. In many rural regions it takes the form of a reduction in the number of jobs at the same time that agricultural production has increased—compared to the pre-war period—through mechanization. Even in regions where the population is declining, modernization is physically in evidence, not only because of farm machinery but also in the farmers' houses and in their style of life, thanks to household appliances. There remains in these regions, nevertheless, a population deficit which prevents them from participating fully in the general transformation of French society, from the psychological point of view. In some places migration is the cause; in regions where the average age is abnormally old there is a low birth rate, and the result is the same. This is an essential element in the policy of regional development, whose purpose is to assure a balanced economy in all regions by creating alongside agriculture an industrial sector extensive enough to maintain demographic equilibrium. This policy, although successfully launched, is far from achieving its goal. So long as it is not completely implemented, we cannot consider the continuation of over-all economic growth as wholly certain. Without a lessening of geographic disparity the less-favored regions, although they are making progress in absolute terms, will consider themselves at a disadvantage in comparison to regions with expanding industries. The social and political consequences of economic growth thus risk being delayed in some parts of the country by regional inequalities whose disappearance was the precise object of the policy of regional development.

These observations do not constitute objections to Charles Kindleberger's conclusions; they tend merely to qualify and supplement them. Just because the recent modernization and growth of the French economy stem essentially from psychological factors, resentment arising from geographical inequality in modernization and growth is very important. Such resentment threatens the cohesion of the national community. This is ironic in that national cohesion seems, in many respects, to be among the most important consequences of the disappearance of the Malthusian attitude and the over-all economic growth which goes with it.

Laurence Wylie and Jesse Pitts, in their studies of changes in France since the Second World War, have considered not only the structure of society but also its system of values. These two types of phenomena, structure and values, are certainly connected, but the nature of the connection is not always easy to discern. To what extent do values affect structure? Conversely, how much does change in structure involve changes in values, sooner or later? In any case it is clear that study of structure and its changes lends itself more easily to objective observation than analysis of values and their changes. The former are evident, almost visibly, in group and individual life and they are often embodied in legally defined institutions which can gradually adapt their organization and rules to fit changing reality. It is conceivable, for example, that a study of the family might be based primarily on a full analysis of marriage contracts. If the various types were precisely analyzed in terms of space and time, they would provide an objective basis for over-all interpretation of change in family structure, and it may be that analysis based on this kind of evidence would produce the most useful study of changes in the substance and role of family values.

Mr. Pitts presents a model of the French value-system and so does Mr. Wylie. I do not mean to deny the worth or interest of their attempts in noting that the two models have nothing in common. The Pitts model features the ideas of aristocracy, prowess, and peer groups, whereas that of Wylie emphasizes certain conceptions of reality, time, and the nature of man. Both seem to me partially true—thus also partially untrue, or at least, incomplete. They are useful to the extent that they permit an observer to bring to light phenomena which might otherwise be overlooked, but I feel that it is dangerous to place too much reliance on these constructions, however ingenious they may be. To my mind, they are working hypotheses, that is, tools of research, rather than verified and certain conclusions.

Possibly my reservations stem from a personal weakness: I lack inclination as well as aptitude for handling abstractions and I have a built-in suspicion of the over-systematized. I must admit that the first part of Pitts' chapter and the last part of Wylie's—each devoted to French values—are the parts of their analyses I find hardest to accept.

This hesitation does not mean that I think either Pitts' interpretation, based on the aristocratic ethos or the idea of prowess, or Wylie's interpretation, based on French attitudes toward reality, man, and time, is without foundation. I willingly concede that certain aspects of French society are explained by their theories, but I think that other aspects are left out and that these models, used exclusively, risk distorting the observer's sense of proportion. For example, there is no doubt that French civilization has been deeply affected by Catholicism, as Pitts says, and, more exactly, by the unique form Catholicism has taken in France. But whether the distinction between the "doctrinaire-hierarchical" and the "aesthetic-individualistic" aspects of the influence of Catholicism fully corresponds to reality seems to me doubtful.

I shall avoid proposing a third model for French values, but in order to make clear my attitude toward the two models presented in this book, I must note what seem to me some important omissions in *both* of them. I feel that any model of French values is essentially incomplete if it does not include the influence of Voltairianism, so widespread in the middle class in the nineteenth century, and of that scientific rationalism whose domination only began to diminish just before the First World War. It seems to me that many French political and social reflexes of the mid-twentieth century show the undoubted influence of these two forces. The school controversy, in particular, cannot be explained otherwise.

Curiously, Marxism does not seem to have had the same influence. Its effects have been felt only in the narrow circles of the intelligentsia. The working-class philosophy (*ouvrièriste*) of the mid-nineteenth century and the anarcho-syndicalist thought of the early twentieth century seem, on the contrary, to play an appreciable part in the constellation of values of certain elements in French society today.

The omission of these elements no doubt explains my reluctance to accept either the Pitts or Wylie formulation of a synthesis of French values. I think that such formulations are doomed to fail, at least partially, because French society, over the generations, has had not *one* but *several* systems of values. Their respective importance varies from time to time; for example it is probable that the system influenced by Catholicism is becoming more and more important and it is possible that Marxist values are also developing. Pluralism remains the rule, however, and it is no doubt one of the fundamental obstacles to the unification of French society into a real community. Even when social structure becomes more unified, there is more than one interpretation of this evolution because the original systems of values are distinct and each of them tends to develop only in such ways as will preserve the essential characteristics that distinguish it from the others.

Pitts and Wylie, so different in their formulations of values, show marked agreement in their comments on structure, though they are considering very different levels of French society.

Pitts begins by describing the traditional situation and then reviews both the factors of change in recent years and the changes themselves. He is considering society as a whole, but I do not think I am mistaken in concluding that his analysis is essentially Parisian. Given the role of Paris in France and the fact that there are few problems which at some point do not manifest themselves in the capital, the Parisian character of his interpretation does not at all mean that he neglects or ignores the real situation in the provinces.

Wylie's point of departure is different: he looks at society from the viewpoint of the two rural communities whose life he has shared and whose structures and problems he has explained so well. The first part of his essay takes up recent transformations in France, specifically the aspects of psychology, technology, demography, education, the trends toward democratization and state intervention, and the effects of these various factors on social integration. His concrete local observations (so instructive even for—perhaps primarily for—a Frenchman) are documented by precise references to the way in which the factors analyzed develop on the national scale, but such generalizations serve only to give a framework for the particular phenomena in Roussillon and Chanzeaux. Thus it is only after carefully reviewing certain realities that he analyzes the factors of resistance to change in France which stem from education, social organization, the symbols of French society and its system of values.

It is noteworthy that the analyses of Wylie and Pitts, though worked out in such different ways, one, so to speak, at the grass-roots level of French villages and the other from the point of view of French society as seen from Paris, arrive at conclusions which are to a great extent the same. Pitts' reference to the transformation of associations—no longer bands of comrades but representatives taking an active administrative part in the framework of a real common interest—fits exactly the democratic administrative groups Wylie describes as developing in Chanzeaux under the influence of the Catholic Church, such as an employment agency and an organization to participate in a system of school buses. With allowances for certain transpositions, one may say that their conclusions on change seem identical whether it is a question of technological change, changes in family structure, acceptance of the state as more than the guarantor of *situations acquises*, the influence of movements inspired by Catholicism like Centre des Jeunes Patrons or the Jeunesse Agricole Catholique, the enlargement of local communities to include new activities with which the individual is concerned, or the trend toward a more uniform style of life and point of view. I shall not dispute Wylie and Pitts on these matters because I personally think they are right, with certain minor qualifications.

I would like, nevertheless, to take up from another point of view the problems discussed so successfully by these two writers. I shall summarize briefly what seem to me the essential changes in French society in the last thirty or forty years, so as to bring out some of the aspects which their chapters do not emphasize as much as I would have done.

First, there is a visible phenomenon, which must strike anyone who visits France after an interval of several years: the growth of the Paris region. Its population has doubled since the early twentieth century while that of France as a whole has increased only 15 percent. Sixty years ago one Frenchman in eleven lived within the neighborhood of the capital; today one in six lives there. Despite measures taken to decentralize this in some respects monstrous growth, it would be unrealistic to expect to stabilize the ratio short of one in five.

Furthermore, metropolitan concentration is not confined to the Paris region, although the population statistics do not always make this clear because the administrative units of towns are far from coinciding with the agglomerations of population. To a lesser degree, concentration exists in the neighborhoods of most of the big cities and many of the middle-sized cities. Suburbs tend more and more to merge with the urban center itself. The result is that more than one Frenchman in four today lives in a metropolitan area of more than 100,000 inhabitants.

People often tend to picture France as a land of moderation (*mesure*) as is seen in the famous hexagon, about whose symbolic meaning Laurence Wylie has made such perceptive comments. France is visualized as the chosen center of a civilization which combines harmony with diversity thanks to the equilibrium maintained between the several provincial cultures.

In many respects this is no longer true. On the contrary, there is growing tension between static regions—whose relative importance is diminishing or which are gradually losing population—and dynamic regions where population and wealth are concentrated. The static regions believe themselves to be unjustly condemned to perish and they demand that the state make a special effort to revive them by modernizing their economy. In the dynamic regions, despite their progress, technical development is nevertheless still a need if the individuals and families living in them are to be assured the kind of material existence which fits the exigencies of our time.

There is thus a competition between the needs or claims of the two kinds of regions and this competition inevitably gives rise to some tensions. The contrast between France northeast of a line from Le Havre to Grenoble, where industry and population are concentrated, and the part southwest of the line, which feels that it is being sacrificed because it is losing population and because with some local exceptions the new industrial decentralization does not extend to them, threatens to become a major problem in future years if some way of lessening it cannot be found. The troubles arising over the use of the natural gas of Lacq, in the Basses-Pyrénées, illustrates the problem. The southwest region would have liked priority in the use of this new source of energy, or at least a preferential price, but the industry of the region is not sufficiently developed to make use of it all. The gas of Lacq is therefore sent by feeders to the industrial regions in the north of France and the resulting industrial development seems likely to accentuate present regional differences rather than to diminish them.

Other structural problems arise from the continuation, in the middle of the twentieth century, of administrative units established at the end of the eighteenth. Laurence Wylie refers to the obsolete character of the *départements*. One might qualify what he says by pointing out that a century and a half of common experience has created deeper ties among the inhabitants or natives of a *département* than might be thought at first sight. The fact that groups of provincials living in Paris almost all reconstitute, spontaneously, the departmental framework is very revealing. It should be added that as the administrative tasks of the communes grow more burdensome, the difficulties arising from the fact that an increasing number of the old units are insufficiently populated to support public services essential for contemporary living, become more and more complicated. The creation of new rural districts with a minimum population of several thousand persons would be the only way to overcome these difficulties, but local patriotism in the present communes opposes such reform, and Michel Debré's efforts (between 1959 and 1962) to promote it have up to now been ineffective. Such a reform means a regrouping of small communities, which do not relish the idea.

Where an agglomeration of population which crosses the lines of several communes creates administrative difficulties, the problem is not the same, because it has been possible to create urban districts. A special district has been imposed by law on the departments and communes of the Paris region. Here also local patriotism and departmental, even municipal, particularism stubbornly continue to oppose necessary reform. The best proof lies in the fact that in the Parisian region the reforms have had to be imposed by law because the administrative units concerned could not agree.

379

In short, there is a contrast between rapid change in the real structures in which people actually live and immobility in the legal structures by which people are supposed to be governed. The realities change but the changes are not reflected in institutions because of people's ignorance of the reforms that change implies and because of the ingrained tendency to defend vested positions.

The occupational structure of France has undergone well-known quantitative changes. Between 1906 and 1954 the proportion of persons in the active population employed in agriculture fell from 43.2 percent to 27.4 percent, the proportion employed in industry and transportation rose from 32.6 to 41.2 and the proportion in the tertiary sector—commerce, services, and administration both private and public—rose from 24.2 to 31.4. Within the tertiary sector the number of persons in government jobs has doubled. French society, like other Western societies, although later than some, is changing in the direction of rapid decline in the agricultural sector, considerable growth in the industrial sector, and rapid expansion in the tertiary sector. This is a sign of growing complexity in the organization of society.

Even more important than this quantitative change are the qualitative changes within these categories. What I have to say on this point will do no more than confirm, from a different point of view, many observations of Laurence Wylie and Jesse Pitts; it will supplement their comments on certain subjects.

Changes in the agricultural sphere are perhaps the most important, but any résumé of the subject risks distorting the reality, which varies according to regions. The diminishing number of farmers has coincided with an increase in production, thanks to the technological revolution. This means that the output of each farmer is considerably greater, but the share of agriculture in the national income is nonetheless diminished, partly because the rise of output in industry is still greater and partly because the price of agricultural products could not be maintained at a profitable level for all the producers. One reason for the great unevenness of profits is the lack of a sure foreign market, a situation which the Common Market may be called upon to remedy in the coming years. But the main cause is to be found in the same discrepancies of French life discussed before: regional differences.

A minority of specialized farmers, concentrated in certain regions, possess substantial capital resources and they exploit their land at a high technical level. They are set apart from the majority of farmers who grow a variety of crops and who lack resources and sometimes the technical know-how that would permit them to modernize their methods by specializing. The specialists tend to use the situation of the general farmers to ask for a rise in prices, although such a rise would do nothing but increase their own profits without solving the problems of the traditional farms of mixed crops, whose yield is not great enough for a rise in prices to provide sufficient capital for modernization. What mixed agriculture really needs is credit for investments; technical training; and, finally, greater flexibility in the traditional legal system governing rural land ownership to create larger production units and allow recourse to cooperative methods.

For a long time, the organizations representing agricultural interests have been divided by their political allegiances. Some (in the Rue d'Athènes and Rue Scribe) were dominated by the representatives of the landed aristocracy. Others (in the Boulevard St. Germain) were dominated by middle-class representatives who belonged to the Radical Party. The traditional leaders of agriculture —whether Right or Left—came mostly from the rich regions of specialized agriculture. Most of them, noble or middle class, did not really belong to the peasant group.

This social framework is in the process of breaking up. The key fact is that in recent years the ideological and partisan divisions have tended to give way to a cleavage based upon regional differences and on differences between generations. The cooperative movement and the unions, especially the Jeunesse Agricole Catholique, have had a profound effect in rural circles and have produced among the peasants militant, capable individuals anxious to take the lead in the organizations representing agriculture. This is not a mere matter of changing faces; it means that in agriculture's claims on the government, reforms of structure to meet the needs of peasant mixed agriculture will take precedence over traditional pressures for a rise in prices. Such a change in the leadership of agriculture has already begun: today a member of the Centre des Jeunes Agriculteurs, a native of Aveyron, is Secretary-General of the Fédération Nationale des Syndicats Exploitants Agricole which, as recently as three years ago, was still the spokesman of large-scale specialized agriculture. The very existence of this offensive by the younger generation, usually representing poor regions of mixed agriculture, means that the old political divisions between organizations of Right and Left are losing much of their importance. Regional solidarity and that of age-groups makes the leaders of the older organizations form a common front against the new "Young Turks" who have breached their former monopoly.

This change in leadership brings up another problem. Because they are so conscious of the peasants' situation, the Jeunes Agriculteurs leaders sometimes give the impression of deliberately confining themselves to very narrow considerations, occupational, cooperative, and local. Perhaps this tendency is related to the role played in their education by the Jeunesse Agricole Catholique. Certain Catholic circles are inclined to emphasize professional and local communities too much. I am tempted to say to "sanctify" them. This propensity involves a concomitant incapacity to place the problems of a particular social milieu in the perspective of the more general economic and political factors in the nation as a whole. Such shortsightedness runs the risk of nullifying efforts which are, in themselves, very worthwhile. A refusal to visualize the political problems of the nation to which the peasant belongs can prevent many of the benefits to be expected from the new kind of agricultural leadership from being realized.

These dangers can be avoided, however. The main point is that agriculture at the very time its relative position in French society is declining (and largely because of this decline) seems to be undergoing important internal changes. It is to be hoped that these internal changes will help French agriculture to deal with the problems created by the technological revolution (which has already occurred) in such a way as to really contribute to their solution by the state.

The working class, too, has experienced important internal changes since the early twentieth century. Fifty years ago, the working class was still not far removed from the artisan class; twenty-five years ago it seemed to be evolving into an undifferentiated mass of interchangeable workers who often moved from one industry and even from one "specialty" to another. Politically, the working class before 1914 was deeply influenced by the somewhat utopian hopes of French nineteenth-century Socialism. Between the two World Wars an increasing proportion of industrial workers, seeking compensation for the painful aspects of their lives, found it in the myth of the Soviet Revolution. Finally, since 1945, profound changes have been taking place.

These postwar changes result partly from economic expansion, from the consequent rise in the standard of living, and from improved social legislation; but they result much more from the great progress in French industrial techniques. Indeed, technical progress has transformed the physical conditions of manual labor in many branches of industry. The new techniques, whether or not they extend to the point called automation, seem to be giving rise to a new type of working class, whose members, instead of performing undifferentiated tasks which make them interchangeable, are becoming more and more specialized professionals. This recalls the old artisan class, but the framework is totally unlike that of the small workshops of the nineteenth century. Where this change is most complete—that is, in wholly automated factories—it is said that the worker's job of tending the machines is similar to the job of supervising complex experiments in scientific laboratories. The workers, far from being interchangeable, are attached to the business by the technical training it has given them, which is not always applicable elsewhere. The managers of the business, for their part, are interested in keeping the workers because their technical training constituted a major expense. These factors result in a common desire for stability on the part of the wage-earner and the employer, a new and very important fact. To hold their workers in a situation characterized by economic growth, the management is willing to make collective agreements like the "Renault contract," guaranteeing a regular increase in wages, security of employment, and a substantial improvement over the retirement allowances provided by the general system of social security. The traditional relations between management and labor are completely transformed by these new working conditions.

The psychological reaction of the workers to this situation is not a docile and satisfied attitude. Workers in the new industries, because of the way their remuneration is related to output and because of their concern for real stability of employment, are louder than workers in less advanced industries in demanding the right to be informed about the economic, technical, and commercial administration of the industry, and even the right to share in this administration. From this point to the claim that their unions have a right to be heard when national economic policy is formulated is only a step. The workers sense the importance of national economic policy for the business which employs them and therefore its importance for them. Without doubt this explains why the proportion of union members is much higher in automated industries (like oil refineries) than in other industries. The new kind of unionism is less political and more realistic than before 1939, even when the unions remain faithful to the Confédération Générale du Travail.

The "new working class" in the new industries, or in industries which have had a technical revolution, is certainly still a minority, but it plays a pilot role and workers in other industries seem to follow its lead and adopt its attitudes. The workers in the shipyards of St. Nazaire recently asked for contracts guaranteeing job security, which formerly would have been inconceivable in a branch of production which has been always very sensitive to economic fluctuations. This is undoubtedly an example of contagion from the new industries. These workers asked, "why should our comrades who build automobiles be more protected than we are against periodic unemployment? It is up to management and to those who formulate national economic policy to provide reliable markets for industry, which will ensure employment to the workers." The continuation of economic growth for more than ten years has fostered the conviction that the government now possesses means to prevent a depression like that of the 1930's.

Prosperity has modified the attitudes of both management and workers. It has led management away from Malthusianism. Among the workers it has diminished the importance of compensatory myths—such as the realization of a Socialist society by imitating the USSR—and it focuses the workers' concern on more realistic considerations such as the control of economic policy by representatives of labor and the continual improvement of the position of workers. This, of course, does not mean that the working class has become conservative.

All of these are only trends, more or less clearly manifested in various regions and industries. But there seems to be no doubt that a very important change in the working class is well launched.

As for the middle class, the qualitative changes are more difficult to sum up. Another result of the improvement (and therefore the growing complexity) of industrial, commercial, and administrative techniques is that there is today a sub-group in the middle class which is experiencing an expansion similar to that of the most favored element in the working class, but still distinct from it. This group includes technicians trained in vocational schools, designers, engineers with average education—a whole category of men whose general education is different from that of engineers trained in the *grandes écoles* and who often approach social and political problems with an attitude conditioned by their training and their occupation. Their frame of mind is characterized by an interest in concrete matters, concern for output, emphasis on efficiency, and suspicion of abstractions. Opposition to parliamentary government seems to be involved also; in fact they do not think in classic "political" terms at all. It appears that voters from this group were largely responsible for the unstable character of French elections after 1945 as compared to elections before 1939. This group supported the Mouvement Républicain Populaire in 1945 and 1946; the Rassemblement du Peuple Français in 1951; Mendès-France in 1956; and the Union pour la Nouvelle République (de Gaulle) in 1958. This political behavior, combined with a desire for efficiency, surely contributed to a situation in which the French type of parliamentary government could not succeed because it could not function properly without a stable balance of power between the various groups in the National Assembly.

To summarize briefly the changes in the middle class, I think emphasis should be placed on the type of education its members receive. Formerly their education was primarily legal or literary; today it is scientific and technical.

It should be added—although Laurence Wylie has made the essential point—that some middle-class groups, such as small shop-keepers and artisans, now feel their existence threatened by the recent economic changes and the resulting trend to concentration in all spheres. This is true not only in Chanzeaux and Roussillon but also in the cities. Politically, this feeling has been another cause of instability, as the temporary success of Poujadism in 1956 shows. Despite the decline of that form of protest, the problem which caused it remains, and there is a danger that in coming years it will be further complicated by the addition of Europeans repatriated from Algeria to the section of the middle class threatened by economic, social, and political changes which are in the process of transforming France.

This leads us to the third aspect of changes in France treated in this book, an examination of the difficulties the French political system has had in adapting to the new economic and social realities.

At the beginning of this essay, in summarizing what seemed to me the over-all conclusions which could be drawn from the studies in this book, I said that France's political adaptation to the world of the second half of the twentieth century was clearly lagging behind the changes in the economic sphere and in social structure. This is, indeed, the lesson to be learned not only from Stanley Hoffmann's chapter, where the problem is the subject of profound study, but also from the allusions to the life and functioning of institutions in the chapters of Charles Kindleberger, Laurence Wylie, and Jesse Pitts. I subscribe fully to this conclusion.

It would be possible, nevertheless, to maintain the contrary. Since the middle of 1958, in fact, the political institutions of France have undergone a deep transformation which has had repercussions not only in a relative sense, but upon the very nature of the forces which influence political institutions. The differences between the Fifth Republic and the Third and Fourth Republics are clear and substantial. Is this not proof that political adaptation—necessitated both by internal changes in French society and changes in France's relations with the outside world—has really taken place or is in the process of taking place?

This raises a question which I think useful to consider before going any further: why cannot the striking political change in France since 1958 be considered to be on the same level of significance as the economic and social changes discussed above?

It is undeniably true that, since June 1, 1958, political power has been exercised by General de Gaulle, first as Premier and since January 1959 as President of the Republic, for a length of time, to an extent, and with an authority which present a total contrast to the power of his predecessors in the Third and Fourth Republics, whether as chiefs of state or as Premiers.

The political overturn of 1958 arose, on the one hand, from a particularly difficult problem, decolonization in Algeria, where about a million Europeans lived among nine million Moslems, and, on the other, from the presence of a man outside all the usual categories, General de Gaulle. The role played by de Gaulle from 1940 to 1945 and his wholly exceptional personality give him a prestige and leeway for action which cannot be measured in the same terms as those for other political leaders. Only very indirectly can this political upheaval be attributed to the previous regimes' inability to adapt to new economic and social circumstances. Rather, the fact that these changes began to make themselves felt under the Fourth Republic allowed its leaders to take credit for them and thus to maintain, even to believe sincerely, that their political system really met France's needs. They were able to believe that a most unusual situation and a conspiracy had been required to overthrow their system.

The acceptance of the 1958 overturn of political institutions by the men of the traditional political class in France has, therefore, been merely apparent or partial. By "political class" I mean *parlementaires*, actual and potential; leaders of national and local political organizations; newspapermen; and officials of local government. Their support of General de Gaulle in June 1958 is to be explained primarily by the fact that the assumption of power of the former leader of Free France seemed at the time the only alternative to civil war and the only way to preserve fundamental civil liberties against a Fascist-type threat. The acceptance by the political class of the constitution submitted to the citizens in September 1958 was partly due to its parliamentary aspects—in line with traditions the political class was accustomed to—and partly because the confidence of the people in General de Gaulle was so obvious that it would have been awkward for the political class to set itself in opposition. The way in which they accepted the constitution's *implementation*, which considerably infringed upon parliamentary tradition—that is, by protesting without ever really opposing it—can only be explained by the fact that the Algerian problem quickly convinced them that General de Gaulle alone was in a position to offer a solution acceptable to opinion in France.

This acceptance was a matter of circumstances rather than of principles. In fact the political class, the men who for decades had been the only intermediaries between the people and political power and the only group to exercise such power, thought almost from the beginning that General de Gaulle's regime was merely a transitory interval, made necessary and even useful by the circumstances, which it would be both easy and desirable to terminate when the circumstances changed.

In these circumstances, one of the basic tasks of the new regime was to entrench itself. To do so, it would have been necessary, first, to create and develop political forces devoted to the new Republic and capable of gradually replacing the old forces when they did not choose to adapt themselves to the new structure. It would have been necessary, second, to apply the rules of the new constitution in such a way as to make them increasingly acceptable to the representatives of the traditional political organizations. One could easily foresee that although the political class could not oppose the new regime in 1958, it would quickly develop a good many reservations about it. In brief, the task of entrenchment called for renewing and enlarging the political class and at the same time obtaining its support.

Neither the circumstances nor the character of the men involved lent themselves to such a program. Furthermore, the attitude of the traditional political class toward power and toward the man who visibly embodied it, President de Gaulle, was soon so distrustful, not to say hostile (except in relation to his Algerian policy), that the General accentuated his tendency to appeal to public opinion for support, "above all intermediaries," as he was to put it himself in a television speech during the campaign preceding the referendum of January 8, 1961. Disregarding the parties and their leaders, considering them to be merely secondary elements of political life, expecting of the Assemblies set up by the constitution of 1958 only a mechanical enactment and support of his own political initiatives, excluding all protests or any active participation in formulation of national policy in its important aspects, de Gaulle acted more and more clearly as if French political life had only two poles: the President of the Republic and the French people. By his trips around the country, by his speeches, by using the technique of the referendum, he has constantly tried to create and maintain a direct bond of confidence between the people and himself.

This analysis is not made in a spirit of criticism or attack. Its object is merely to describe what has occurred as objectively and as exactly as possible, not to determine whether it might have possibly been avoided. Besides, I believe that the responsibility is divided between the traditional political class and the leaders of the new regime. The representatives of the traditional political class, shocked by the abrupt break with former habits and by the way in which the new constitution was put into effect, did not make the effort to adapt which would have allowed them to play a role, diminished perhaps, but effective, in the determination of national policy and in the operation of political institutions. As early as the first months of 1959 they were not making this effort. It may be that they yielded (more or less consciously) to the desire *not* to resume responsibility for the functioning of a regime which their reflexes—formed by the Fourth Republic—made them consider both abnormal and transitory. For their part, General de Gaulle and his first minister, Michel Debré, did not attach enough importance to the psychological aspect of their relations with Parliament and the party leaders to be able to heal the growing break between themselves and those traditional forces. This was because they were almost wholly absorbed in other concerns, de Gaulle in the big problems of Algeria, foreign policy, and defense, and Debré in the implementation of a large-scale policy of administrative and social reform and in the consolidation of national recovery in the financial, monetary, and economic spheres.

However this may be, the results of this state of affairs seem to me indisputable. In the summer of 1962, four years after de Gaulle's return to power and over three and a half years after the constitutional referendum of September 28, 1958, the institutions of the Fifth Republic, operating in a spirit which uses the parliamentary elements of the constitution less and less, are not rooted in the country. The political class tolerates the institutions with growing impatience and usually invokes the theory behind the institutions only in order to criticize its implementation. Public opinion in general, whatever its continuing attachment to General de Gaulle and the authority it acknowledges in him, shows no confidence in the regime aside from the person of its leader.

This is why one cannot consider that the changes in French political life and institutions in the last four years are of the same nature as the economic and social changes. There is nothing to assure their continuation because they are too exclusively tied to General de Gaulle. His disappearance from the scene, or the rise of circumstances which would adversely affect his prestige and popularity in the country, might suddenly create a political void in France. In such case, many forces would try to fill the void, but it is impossible to predict how and by whom it would be accomplished.

Thus is justified the "suspended judgment" by which Stanley Hoffmann ends his excellent analysis at the beginning of this book. Thus is justified also the conclusion that recent political change in France does not correspond to recent economic and social change.

In order to discern the reasons for this lag and to evaluate its scope, one must look far back in the past, as Stanley Hoffmann has done. France's policy cannot be understood without taking into account her history, as well as her sociology and psychology. French habits and reflexes in public life are really still largely determined by the past. This is true of the political class and of the average citizen; it is without doubt the fundamental reason they find it so difficult to adapt to changes required by the contemporary world.

I personally consider Hoffmann's picture of what he calls the "republican synthesis" of the Third Republic remarkably accurate. After more than eighty years of instability and of alternations between authoritarian regimes and popular regimes, the Third Republic was able to establish itself solidly and to endure, despite the ideological and political divisions in public opinion, because it had limited goals. The role of the state, according to the men who ruled France from 1875 to 1914, should be to stabilize society, not to transform it. The preservation of *situations acquises* was the fundamental and ruling precept of the regime, which channeled the forces of change into symbolic areas rather than concrete ones (examples are found in the problems of relations between Church and State and of the relationship of the Church to education and society). Between 1875 and 1914, the state intervened in the economic sphere only to a limited extent; it fostered the development of means of transport, and, especially, it enacted protectionist policies whose purpose was to crystallize the existing economic structure and, notably, to conserve the dominant agricultural sector, although this sector was falling ever more behind in comparison with the agriculture of other countries. Whatever the scope and significance of the economic changes of this period, they were certainly not brought about by systematic state action. Charles Kindleberger has shown that historians of the French economy do not agree in their interpretation of these changes. Furthermore, the state sought to slow down change by its fiscal measures, favoring small individual enterprise as much as possible and overtaxing the more modern, centralized industries.

In social matters too, the state under the Third Republic did not seek to play an initiating role; it sought to preserve the *status quo*. In so doing, moreover, it was faithfully carrying out the will of the majority, which wanted no striking changes but desired, on the contrary, simply the maintenance of the traditional values and style of life.

There was, nevertheless, a paradox imbedded in the system. Both Right and Left opposed and defended the regime. In political and religious matters the regime, being republican and characterized by clear hostility to Catholicism, had to deal with opposition from the Right, whose traditions and sympathies had been primarily monarchist at first and then more exclusively clerical as the course of events made the restoration of monarchy less likely. The parliamentary Republic, as a political regime, had practically no opposition from the Left, despite the growth of revolutionary unionism and the slow but steadily increasing assimilation of Marxist ideas by the Socialist parties. In matters of social policy, on the other hand, the situation was reversed. The Rightist opposition associated itself with the Republicans of the Center and Left-Center to ensure the conservation of the traditional social structure, a goal they had in common with the conservative leaders of the Third Republic, while the Socialist parties refused to share in this consensus. The Socialists opposed their evolutionary—or even, at least in theory, revolutionary—ideas to the opinion of the majority.

In short, there was a split in party alignment according to the type of problem under consideration. The Republicans of the Center and Left-Center, secularist but socially conservative, drew on the support of the Extreme Left to defend the Republic and combat the influence of the Church but drew on the support of the Right to resist change in the social structure and slow down economic changes which would have accelerated social changes.

Potentially, therefore, a considerable danger of dislocation was built into the "republican synthesis." The growth of the Socialist Party before 1914 made it possible to foresee that the time would come when the Center would have to choose between acceptance of social change and continuing collaboration with the Right. The renunciation of systematic anti-clericalism might become indispensable if the Center was to continue to cooperate with the Right in a successful defense of the established order.

The moment of choice had not yet arrived, however, when the First World War unleashed a general process of change, economic, social, and political. The Third Republic did not survive this general trend for many more decades because it had not produced a system of parties and institutions which would enable the state to meet the problems it would face in the future.

Because of the very limitations on state action which made the Republican synthesis possible, and, because of the continual see-saw of shifting majorities in connection with political and social problems, the Third Republic was a series of feeble and unstable governments. These governments were characterized by a practically sovereign Parliament and by parties with very few adherents outside the narrow limits of the political class. The parties were therefore unable to impose the least discipline on elected representatives who belonged to these parties.

Political life thus assumed the aspect of a senseless "game," played for the fun of it according to its own rules, without any real relationship with the necessity to establish an effective state, capable of resolving problems which demanded some continuity of vision and action. Political life did not connect sufficiently with reality in the economic or social spheres, or even in foreign policy. With the exception of a few specialists, Parliament paid little attention to such problems before 1914. The result was that the degree of awareness of the technical conditions underlying these problems was not sufficient to correct the deficiencies of the "rules of the game" when public life had to face something other than ideological questions or to take real decisions rather than merely symbolic ones.

The weight of pre-1914 tradition prevented the French political system between the two World Wars from reforming itself so as to be able to handle the wholly new problems France had to face after 1919. The party system remained feeble and incoherent, at least in the Center. The Socialist Party and later the Communist Party had an organization and a discipline lacking in the Center and Right. Parliamentary majorities remained fragile coalitions, liable to be completely overturned without recourse to the body of voters, as can be seen in 1926, 1934, and 1938. In each of these three years, after Left majorities had been chosen by the voters, they gave way to majorities composed of a minority which had been in opposition at the start and the most conservative elements of the former (elected) majority. The governments were even more unstable than before 1914 and their relationship to the sovereign Parliament was characterized by regular alternation between delegations of legislative power to the government and ministerial crises of increasing frequency.

At no time between the wars was it seriously planned to reform the system so as to make it capable of acting efficiently and on a long-term basis, despite evidence that the pre-1914 system had not adapted to the tasks born of World War I. The weight of habit in the political class and among the voters prevented the Socialist Party, in particular, from understanding that the economic reforms it proposed would only be made possible by a new relationship between the government and the Parliament, which would permit a real executive power to be established. The Left knew that its parliamentary majorities were essentially fragile, and the Right, by raising a hue and cry for various more or less precise programs of constitutional reform, aroused the suspicion of its opponents in so doing. Moreover the Socialists came to power too late and for too short a time to experience directly the drawbacks of the system, and the Communists, who did not want any reform government capable of efficient action, tried continually—by outbidding the democratic parties—to maintain and to re-animate the traditional "republican" opposition to any system which would give the government the possibility of leading the parliamentary majority instead of being led by it.

The weight of the past played a key role in this situation. If it was impossible to establish an effective power to dissolve Parliament—the only way to put the government in a position of power against parliamentary offensives and to guarantee that future reversals of majorities would be submitted to popular vote—it was because the dissolution of 1877 was an abortive attempt by a reactionary President of the Republic to stop the progress of the Left. If no plan to reform the political system, neither that of Millerand in 1923 nor that of Doumergue in 1934, could be discussed, it was because a sort of taboo forbade the political class to recognize that a system entirely animated and dominated by itself could need any changes. Political immobility, at least on the level of institutions and their functioning, thus became a republican dogma, more and more fiercely defended as the regime's inability to adapt became more striking.

Does not the fear that political reform would be the prelude to social change largely explain this situation? The paradox here is that the parties loudest in demanding social changes were precisely

394

the parties most clearly opposed to the political reforms without which social change could not take place. This attitude is understandable in the Communists, who could hope that the revolution would be facilitated by the impotence of the state. The attitude of the other Leftist parties can only be explained by the weight of long-established habits of thought and by an innate incapacity to recognize the changes brought about by World War I and the depression of the 1930's in the role of the state. In the last analysis, the refusal to reform the political system doubtless reflected the fact that the political class, because it was small and narrow and did not renew itself sufficiently, persisted in believing it possible and in thinking it desirable to return gradually to all the pre-1914 structures and modes of life, economic and social as well as political and ideological.

Stanley Hoffmann has shown correctly and very precisely that, from the 1930's on, this immobility stimulated various political and intellectual movements whose object was reform, economic, social and political. I should like to underline strongly that although these movements were eventually able to exercise a certain influence in the economic and social spheres through Vichy and the Resistance, it has not been the same in the political sphere. This raises the question "why?"—a puzzle which merits special consideration.

Before taking up this problem, however, it is well to draw up a balance sheet of the French political system as it was at the end of the Third Republic, that is, on the eve of the Second World War. The most striking characteristic seems to me the virtual monopoly of power by what I have called the political class, whose basic nucleus was members of Parliament but which included also future members, local party leaders, a high proportion of departmental officials, and a small number of municipal officials and newspapermen who dealt primarily with domestic policy.

This narrow group—not more than fifteen or twenty thousand persons at most—had succeeded in really confiscating the theoretical sovereignty of the people as expressed in universal suffrage. Elections, indeed, were necessarily conducted by and controlled by the political class, which was opposed to any new manner of posing the problems. Parliamentary sovereignty, the result of a distortion of the representative principle, was naturally the most striking aspect of this confiscation, even though the influence of the rest of the political class on members of the *Chambre* and *Senat* had the effect of slightly increasing the number of beneficiaries of this transfer of power. The most visible result was that the voters were never directly consulted. They were not consulted on concrete problems, as might have been the case if elections had been able to establish a clear sanction for durable and coherent government administration and a choice between specific programs. They were not even consulted on the way the parliamentary "game" was played between elections. Neither the episodic fluctuations in the composition of governments and parliamentary coalitions, nor the complete overturn of majorities as in 1926, 1934, and 1938, could really be submitted to the approval of the voters. The weakness of the political parties and their narrow oligarchical internal organization was such that it was impossible to assume that they represented the opinion of most Frenchmen.

The instability and weakness of government personnel had not presented a major hazard before 1914, because the system had been developed deliberately to limit state action to the preservation of *situations acquises*, at least in domestic problems—to which the interest of the political class was almost exclusively confined. Between the two wars, however, the state was faced with an entirely new type of problem, which could only be solved by continued and coherent action directed at renovating economic mechanisms inherited from the nineteenth century and the traditional structure of society. Probably because its leaders were haunted by the desire to return to what had seemed normal before 1914, the regime was incapable of any adaptation stronger than recourse to legislation by decree, whose intrinsic ambiguity was compounded by fundamental errors of judgment in economic matters on the part of those who were responsible for such legislation.

The system still held on the surface, but only thanks to the force of habit of the voters and of the political class. Neither seemed, on the whole, to have been influenced by those who, after 1930, had denounced the drawbacks at the same time they pointed out the necessity for profound economic and social change. Their warnings could also appear to be at least partially invalidated by the way in which French society and the political system had succeeded in absorbing the shock of the depression and of the social movements of 1936–1937. But the series of shocks from outside France—the war, the defeat of 1940, and the German occupation —could not but ruin the system.

What seems inexplicable is that France at the end of the Second World War could not learn the lesson of this collapse, and that she restored within a few years practically the identical system whose defects had manifested themselves so clearly. Despite certain modifications on the surface, the regime of the Fourth Republic, when stabilized after 1947, reproduced very exactly the fundamental traits of the Third Republic.

Why has the reforming zeal which arose from the intellectual movement of the 1930's not produced, up to now, any serious results of a political nature?

As far as the men who were influenced by this movement and later took part in the Vichy government are concerned, it is not surprising. As Stanley Hoffmann has shown, the business staff and, in a lesser way, the administrative staff of the Vichy government were able to exert influence in the economic sphere after 1945. This was facilitated by the fact that they shared a number of important views with their companions of the 1930's who had chosen the Resistance between 1940 and 1944. In the political sphere itself, however, everything which had derived from Vichy or had figured in the Vichy system was totally discredited in 1944–1945. The few correct ideas that had been able to penetrate the hodge-podge of ultranationalist (*maurrassienne*) or Fascist ideology—which took the place of theory for the leaders of the "National Revolution"— were thus underestimated after the Liberation.

But the Resistance, too, had dreamed of a political renewal. Its leaders had condemned the system of the Third Republic almost as severely as had the Vichy leaders, although they expressed it in different terms and for different reasons. How can one account for the fact that they ended up by restoring it?

A complete analysis of the problem would greatly exceed the limits of this essay, but it is necessary to indicate the main lines along which an answer might be found.

The first blow against the transformation of the French political system was struck when General de Gaulle, for reasons both domestic and international, had to allow room for representatives of the old parties in the National Council of the Resistance. This move was in opposition to the desires of his most clear-headed political assistant, Pierre Brossolette. The decision itself was probably inevitable and, in the short-run at least, justifiable. As soon as the decision was made, however, it was certain that efforts after the Liberation to establish a political regime really different from that of the weak Third Republic of the interwar period would meet opposition from within the Resistance itself. When the provisional government of General de Gaulle was established in Paris the consequences of his decision began to be apparent, especially in the debates of the Consultative Assembly and in the activity of the parties.

The tendency to restore the past system was powerfully aided at the time by the Communist Party, which clearly understood that its chances of coming to power would be increased by the existence of an intrinsically weak political regime. This explains the Communist campaign against "personal power" and its alliance with the Radicals and some of the moderates in the Consultative Assembly against the provisional government and the constitutional solutions it proposed.

There were three forces which could have and should have opposed this tendency to reconstitute the old system. First, there was the Socialist Party, some of whose leaders during the war and occupation had expressed ideas favoring the establishment of a political regime in liberated France which would give the executive—eventually in presidential form—a much bigger role than under the Third Republic. Next, there was the Mouvement Républicain Populaire (MRP), which, as a party without deep links to the past, could have approached the problem of a future political system for France without the handicap of past habits that weighed on the old parties. Finally, there were the political leaders of the

Resistance, that is, those who, having refused to line up with the old groups, were to set up a small group known as the Union Démocratique et Socialiste de la Résistance (UDSR).

The Socialists, however, having rebuilt their party, with its federations, its local units, and its prewar militants, rediscovered their old political conceptions all the more quickly as the attractions of Communism for some of their members soon made them hypersensitive to competitive bidding on the extreme Left.

The MRP, in its approach to the problem of institutions, was armed with a veritable arsenal of false ideas about democracy "organized" by contracts between powerful parties. Doubtless, also, the fear that French Catholics always have of being classified as Rightists contributed to the orientation of the MRP toward traditional Leftist attitudes and thus made the new party favorable to parliamentary sovereignty.

As for the UDSR, too weak to endure without allies, it went from a coalition with the Socialists, in 1945, to an understanding with the Radicals (in the Rassemblement des Gauches Républicaines) in 1946. The contagion of Third Republic habits spread to the UDSR very quickly because its parliamentary representatives adapted themselves fast and well to the traditional rules of the French parliamentary "game."

To tell the truth, the restoration of the old political system in France must be attributed as much to the attitude of General de Gaulle himself as to the failure of the political organizations confronted with the problem of reconstituting France's political regime. For several months, the President of the Provisional Government, absorbed in France's international problems, had to neglect domestic questions. At no time did he envisage the only solution which would have allowed his conception of the state to prevail, that is, to make himself the head of a new party and to use his prestige to organize it solidly in the country, making it the intermediary between himself and the people. He always refused to compromise what he stood for by aligning himself with any party —even a new party—and by that very fact, without realizing it, he left the field open for the manipulators of the former political class, minus those who had compromised themselves too much with

Vichy and plus a certain number from the Resistance. Despite these slight changes in composition, the political class had not changed basically either its nature or its prewar attitudes.

This is the explanation, it seems to me, of the fact that the drastic changes resulting from the war and the great need of a complete transformation in the state's sphere of action did not prevent the restoration in 1946 of a political regime which reproduced the defects of the old system. It even aggravated those defects, as a consequence of the electoral system of proportional representation.

The reasons that the Fifth Republic cannot be considered as the start of an irreversible change in the structure and conduct of French political life, outlined earlier in this essay, show that the problem left unresolved in 1945 still remains to be solved in 1962. General de Gaulle's return to power and the authority which popular confidence, usually expressed in nonparliamentary ways, has allowed him to exercise since 1958 do not in themselves constitute a solution. Indeed, the basic attitude of the political class toward the present regime—reserve, nonparticipation, even hostility—does not rule out the possibility of a new revival of parliamentarism in the French style, that is, of a system which inherently threatens the authority of the executive because government is dependent on Parliament and because the election of Parliament by universal suffrage is much more a periodic confiscation than a consecration of popular sovereignty.

Although such a restoration is conceivable, the restored system probably could not be stable, given the problems the state must deal with in coming years. One cannot help fearing that the foreseeable future of the new parliamentary "game" would give rise to an undemocratic, totalitarian regime, whether of the extreme Right or of the extreme Left. How could this risk be avoided?

A statesman of the Fourth Republic, M. Edgar Faure, said recently that the parties could not interest public opinion until they proposed something interesting. On the level of political forces, the present situation of France is characterized by a striking dualism. On the one hand, political parties continue to exist, with personnel and organizations feebler than ever, and because there is no "new blood" among their leaders and active members they go constantly around in circles, repeating the same criticisms of the regime. Although they all *say* that they do not want the reestablishment of a system like that of the Fourth Republic, they seem incapable of conceiving any other. Perhaps it is partly to mask this impotence that they resort to a kind of flight to the future—or shot in the dark —in their competitive zeal for immediate creation of a politically integrated Europe. On the other hand, outside the parties a certain number of nonpolitical groups testify by their activities to the fact that there exist, in all regions and classes of France, citizens who are not indifferent to the problems facing the state, who try to put them in concrete terms, and who want to promote the efficient solutions. Among these groups are labor union study groups, regional committees for economic expansion, student groups, and associations of young farmers—to name only a few. Each in its own sphere, different as they are from one another, these groups present an approach which contrasts with that of the established political class.

Meanwhile, the President of the Republic persists in avoiding any commitment to a group—of whatever type—and in trying (successfully up to the summer of 1962) to establish a bond of confidence between himself and the people. The indisputable reality of this bond does not mean, however, that if the voters were to elect a new National Assembly a majority might not vote for the representatives of the old parties and thus put back into the saddle the political class which has been out of power for four years.

I personally think that the chances of establishing in France an efficient democratic regime, excluding the defects of parliamentary sovereignty as seen in the Third and Fourth Republics but excluding also risks inevitable in the absence of intermediary organizations between the government and the citizens, are ultimately tied up with a renovation of the political parties. It might result from a transformation of the existing parties, through the entry of and participation by men moved by the spirit shown in the nonpolitical organizations mentioned above, but it may be that the sclerosis of the old parties is so great that it is not possible to revive them from within. One is tempted to think so from the failure of

Mendès-France's attempt (a clumsy one, to be sure) to transform the Radical-Socialist Party a few years ago.

If this solution fails, and since it is written that one cannot put new wine into old bottles, should not the groups so actively concerned with solving a number of problems under the jurisdiction of the state make strenuous efforts (although at present they are nonpolitical) to set up intermediary organizations between the people and the state, in one form or another? Without some such intermediaries there can, in the long run, be no democracy. The obstacle to this solution is the profound discredit into which the very idea of political parties has fallen in present-day France. But this lack of confidence, understandable toward parties which are incapable of dealing with the real problems of the state and excessively preoccupied with the political "game," should not extend to real parties, formed to educate the people and to express their own opinions.

It is obviously necessary that these groups which might become either real parties or their equivalent be capable and desirous of tackling not only local and professional problems but also the overall problems which France faces today because of her internal changes and her situation in the world. Perhaps therefore a sort of federation of different kinds of organizations should be established?

Whatever may develop in this respect, the reconstitution of real political forces, capable of holding their own against the representatives of the traditional political class and of embodying popular sovereignty with a minimum of distortion, seems to me more important than constitutional reform.

When General de Gaulle invited the French people to decide on October 28, 1962, that the President of the Republic would be elected in the future by direct universal suffrage instead of by the small electoral college established in 1958—a college in which representatives of less than 40 percent of the population had the majority—he denied that he was preparing a switch to a presidential system. However, his initiative has once more raised the French political problem in institutional terms.

This reform is intended to consolidate the practices which

have shaped the actual role of the presidency during the last four years. If it does, one may ask whether it will not lead, in the future, to the abolition of the Premier's responsibilities before the Assembly, perhaps even to the elimination of a premiership distinct from the presidency and to a further reorganization of the rights which the executive enjoys vis-à-vis Parliament.

However, one can imagine that political circumstances after de Gaulle could bring forward a President, elected by a small majority, and a Premier, chosen by such a President, both of whom would give up the use of the procedures and powers that the constitution of 1958 puts at their disposal to strengthen their authority vis-à-vis Parliament. Thus, without any further constitutional amendment, a mere change in the practices could lead to something like a restoration of the Fourth Republic.

Consequently, everything leads one to believe that the basic problem is that of the renovation of political parties. It is difficult to assess whether this renovation will have been speeded up or delayed by the conflict which the referendum of October 28, 1962, provoked between General de Gaulle and the traditional political forces.

The "suspended judgment" by which Stanley Hoffmann concludes his analysis of the political situation in France, whose economy has been transformed and whose social structures are in the process of renewal, seems to me fully justified. I think the future will depend essentially on what happens to the political forces of this society in the next few years.

It does not seem necessary to add any special comment on Jean-Baptiste Duroselle's chapter concerning changes in France's relation to the rest of the world since 1945. His absolutely pertinent remarks, because they are written by a Frenchman, perhaps could be better commented upon by an American. I would like to underline, however, how correct I think is his point that foreign policy is far from taking first place in French public opinion. In this respect there is a considerable difference between General de Gaulle and the average Frenchman. The opposition parties seem to want to use the theme of an integrated Europe—almost the only thing on which Independents, Demo-Christians, Radicals, and Socialists can agree—as a weapon to combat a regime which considers it preferable not to act hastily, not to establish a politically unified Europe too soon. Any peoples who found the decisions of such a supranational Europe to be against their interests would certainly rebel against them. An attempt by the French "Europeans" to establish a supranational organization would entail sure disappointment for them as well as for foreigners who see in it a convenient way to "get France under control" by fostering the fall of a regime and a man whose *raison d'être* they think will disappear now that Algeria is independent. The French will not commit themselves emotionally either to or against an integrated Europe, or a Europe of states, and if the question were put to them in this form, their answers would very likely be given in terms of purely domestic considerations.

In concluding this essay, it is impossible not to pay homage to the quality of the studies in this book. The five authors give a picture of France's present situation and of the problems it raises which I think is profoundly accurate, on the whole. They recognize what has been done these past ten years, while concealing nothing of what remains to be done and the present difficulties. Concerning the factors in recent economic change, they have been able to disentangle those which France has in common with all Western Europe from those which are specifically French. They analyze the causes of change but also the elements which block change. Above all, they have brought out the crucial importance of the political problem, which must be solved or else everything gained in the economic and social spheres will be jeopardized.

Despite the uncertainty of the future, it seems to me that the over-all effect of these chapters is an encouraging impression, that of a rejuvenated people who have succeeded—infinitely better than could have been foreseen at the time of their Liberation—in rebuilding the structure of their economy, in initiating transformations in society, and in adapting themselves to the world in which France plays a role—diminished but still important in many respects.

After the victory of 1918, France had a period of decadence

because that victory, gained with the aid of allies, had cost France too much and had placed her in a position that exceeded her means. Since the defeat of 1940, France, liberated by allies rather than by her own efforts (however real, costly, and effective these were), has had an extraordinary revival—this book proves it. The revival, which is still incomplete, took place partly because France in 1944 was at the bottom and could not fail to rise, but also because France has found in herself the will and outside herself the aid—in the Marshall Plan—without which her adaptation to an entirely new world would not have been possible.

THE AUTHORS

(All the contributors have published books and articles about France. Only their most recent major writings are named here.)

Stanley Hoffmann, Associate Professor of Government, Harvard University. *Le Mouvement Poujade* (1956); *Contemporary Theory in International Relations* (1960).

Charles P. Kindleberger, Professor of Economics, Massachusetts Institute of Technology. *Economic Development* (1958).

Laurence Wylie, C. Douglas Dillon Professor of the Civilization of France, Harvard University. *Village in the Vaucluse* (1957).

Jesse R. Pitts, Associate Professor of Sociology, Wayne State University, Detroit. *The Family and Peer Groups* (1960).

Jean-Baptiste Duroselle, Professor at the Fondation Nationale des Sciences Politiques, Paris, and Director of the Centre d'Etudes Internationales. *Histoire diplomatique de 1919 à nos jours* (1953); *De Wilson à Roosevelt* (1960).

François Goguel, political scientist, Secretary-General of the French Senate. *La Politique des partis sous la Troisième République* (1946); *France under the Fourth Republic* (1952).

NOTES

Stanley Hoffmann, Paradoxes of the French Political Community

1. J. H. Clapham, *The Economic Development of France and Germany 1815–1914* (Cambridge, Eng., 1923), p. 53; Edmond Goblot, *La Barrière et le niveau* (Paris, 1925), p. 6.
2. Flaubert's Bouvard and Pécuchet represent those two lines pretty well.
3. Cf. Jean-Paul Sartre's definition of the bourgeois: "le moyen terme élevé à la toute-puissance," in *Situations II* (Paris, 1948), p. 157.
4. See David S. Landes' and John E. Sawyer's essays in *Modern France*, ed. E. M. Earle (Princeton, 1951) and Jesse R. Pitts, *The Bourgeois Family and French Economic Retardation*, unpublished thesis, Harvard University, 1957.
5. See Michel Crozier's articles in *Esprit:* "La France, terre de commandement" (December 1957, pp. 779–798), and "Le Citoyen" (February 1961, pp. 193–211); also Laurence Wylie, *Village in the Vaucluse* (Cambridge, Mass., 1957).
6. I have relied here on François Bourricaud, *Esquisse d'une théorie de l'autorité* (Paris, 1961), a theoretical essay partly based on experiments by U.S. sociologists Ralph K. White and Ronald Lippitt. Bourricaud does not specifically apply his findings to the French case.
7. See Jean Lhomme, *La Grande Bourgeoisie au pouvoir, 1830–1880* (Paris, 1960), although the author often falls into the Marxist or pseudo-Marxist fallacy I have mentioned.
8. Note the belated and grudging recognition of "groups" (rather than parties) in the rules of Parliament under the Third Republic; cf. Jean Waline, "Les Groupes parlementaires en France," *Revue du droit public et de la science politique*, November–December 1961.
9. Harry Eckstein, *A Theory of Stable Democracy*, Princeton Center of International Studies, Research Monograph no. 10 (1961).
10. This is the theme of Nicholas Wahl's study in *Patterns of Government*, ed. S. Beer and A. Ulam (New York, 1958).
11. See Eugen Weber, *The Nationalist Revival in France* (Berkeley, Calif., 1959).
12. It is worth noting that ever since the 1890's the agrarian program of French Socialists had become a mere defense and illustration of small property—thus clearly sacrificing the "productive" thrust of original Marxism to a concern for justice-in-distribution characteristic of the stalemate society; also, the economic policies of the Blum cabinet in 1936–37 were as protectionist as those of his predecessors.

13. See, for further elaboration, my article "Aspects du Régime de Vichy," *Revue française de science politique*, January–March 1956, pp. 44–69.

14. See Charles Micaud, *The French Right and Nazi Germany* (Durham, N.C., 1943).

15. E.g., the *X-Crise* movement founded by students of the Ecole Polytechnique during the depression.

16. E.g., the labor newspaper *Syndicats*, the periodical *Les Nouveaux Cahiers*, and the business organization Comité de Prévoyance.

17. For a similar study, see Jean Touchard, "L'Esprit des années 30," in *Tendances politiques de la vie française depuis 1789* (Paris, 1960).

18. See Jacques Bardoux' book, *L'Ordre nouveau face au communisme et au racisme* (Paris, 1939).

19. The *plan du 9 juillet* (1934) shows in its text and in its list of signatories a fine case of generalized but nevertheless significant confusion.

20. On two movements in which *planistes* were particularly prominent—Libération-Sud and the Organisation Civile et Militaire, see Arthur Calmette, *L'OCM* (Paris, 1961), and Christian Pineau, *La Simple Verité* (Paris, 1960).

21. See the study of the school by Janine Bourdin, in the *Revue française de science politique*, September–December 1959, pp. 1029–1045.

22. Remember Aragon's wartime poems ("mon parti m'a rendu les couleurs de la France . . .").

23. The most edifying story is that of the movement of Les Compagnons de France; see issue no. 27 (1943) of *Métier de chef*, which tells most of it.

24. See *Positions d'ACJF, 7 ans d'histoire au service de la jeunesse de France* (Paris, 1946).

25. The artistic association Jeune France, sponsored by Vichy, became a breeding ground for numerous talents that were to become famous in postwar France.

26. See on this point *La Vie de la France sous l'Occupation*, vol. I (Paris, 1957), the statement by René Belin, p. 145.

27. See Henry W. Ehrmann, *Organized Business in France* (Princeton, 1957), chaps. II–III.

28. See Adolphe Pointier's embattled testimony in *La Vie de la France sous l'Occupation*, vol. I, pp. 275 ff.; also *Les Paysans et la politique*, ed. H. Mendras and J. Fauvet (Paris, 1958), *passim*.

29. See for instance the famous program of the Conseil National de la Résistance in *Les Idées politiques et sociales de la Résistance*, ed. B. Mirkine-Guetzévitch and H. Michel (Paris, 1954), pp. 215 ff. See also Marie Granet, *Défense de la France* (Paris, 1960), pp. 280 ff.; also Calmette (note 20 above), pp. 44 ff.

30. Continuity is well demonstrated by the case of Aimé Lepercq, who was the head of one of Vichy's main business committees (coal mines) and later a member of the OCM and de Gaulle's Finance Minister.

31. See for instance Belin's reference to a letter of de Peyerimhoff, the head of the Comité des Houillères (*La Vie de la France sous l'Occupation*, vol. I, p. 150). Pierre Nicolle's book, *Cinquante Mois d'armistice* (Paris,

1947), is a perfect record of all the campaigns waged by small business against Vichy's Business Committees.

32. See *La Vie de la France sous l'Occupation*, vol. I, pp. 14 ff.

33. See *Syndicats paysans* during 1940–1942 (the newspaper of Jacques Leroy-Ladurie and Louis Salleron).

34. See for instance the story of such measures in postwar France in Warren C. Baum's rather one-sided book, *The French Economy and the State* (Princeton, 1958).

35. Val R. Lorwin, *The French Labor Movement* (Cambridge, Mass., 1954), pp. 78–79.

36. See M. de Calan's testimony in *La Vie de la France sous l'Occupation*, vol. I, pp. 31 ff.

37. See for instance the article by Father Renaud in *La Revue des deux mondes* of June 1, 1939.

38. See Ministère de l'Education Nationale: Commission Chargée de l'Etude des Rapports entre l'Etat et l'Enseignement Privé, June 25–Oct. 29, 1959, *Rapport général* (Paris, n.d.), pp. 14–29.

39. On Pierre Laroque's role in August 1940, see Belin in *La Vie de la France sous l'Occupation*, vol. I, p. 146. P. Laroque's role in Vichy, however, was both technical and extremely brief; he symbolizes in many ways the *"haut fonctionnaire"* at his best—professional conscience, drive, a deep concern for the public interest, efficiency, and liberalism.

40. This can be shown in the case of the poujadists and the Union pour la Nouvelle République. See the author's *Le Mouvement Poujade* (Paris, 1956) and René Rémond, "Le Nouveau Régime et les forces politiques," in *Revue française de science politique*, March 1959, pp. 167 ff.

41. The very swift evolution of *Esprit* in the latter half of 1940 is particularly interesting; so is that of the Uriage school, whose last class joined the Maquis.

42. This was the thesis of François Goguel; see his "La Politique dans la société française," in *Aspects de la société française* (Paris, 1954).

43. See for instance Marie Granet and Henri Michel, *Combat* (Paris, 1957), pp. 94 ff.

44. See René Hostache, *Le Conseil National de la Résistance* (Paris, 1957), esp. chap. II; and Colonel Passy, *Souvenirs*, vol. III (Paris, 1951).

45. *L'Oeuvre de Léon Blum: la prison, le procès, la déportation* (Paris, 1955), pp. 364, 375, 381, 388, 392, 398.

46. See Mirkine-Guetzévitch and Michel (note 29 above), pp. 287 ff.

47. See de Gaulle's *Memoirs*, vol. II, *Unity* (New York, 1959).

48. See Maurice Duverger, *Demain la République* (Paris, 1958).

49. On these points, there are many interesting remarks in de Gaulle's *Memoirs*, vol. III, *Salvation* (New York, 1960). On the role and fate of Vichy's army, see Jacques Weygand's novel *Le Serment* (Paris, 1960) and a forthcoming Harvard Ph.D. dissertation by Robert O. Paxton. On the tensions in the new army, see George Kelly, "The French Army Reenters Politics," *Political Science Quarterly*, September 1961, pp. 367–392.

50. The testimonies in *La Vie de la France sous l'Occupation*, vol. I, show how extensive had been the contacts between French civil servants

in charge of the economy and their German civilian or military counterparts.

51. See Granet and Michel (note 43 above) and Calmette (note 20 above).

52. See de Gaulle's *Salvation*, pp. 216 ff., and Alfred Grosser, *La Quatrième République et sa politique extérieure* (Paris, 1961), pp. 20 ff.

53. See for instance Thierry-Maulnier, *La France, la guerre et la paix* (Paris, 1942).

54. Grosser, pp. 33–35.

55. See *Etudes et conjoncture*, May and August 1961.

56. Pierre Massé, "French Economic Planning," *French Affairs*, no. 127, issued by French Embassy in the U.S., December 1961, p. 16.

57. See Club Jean Moulin, *L'Etat et le citoyen* (Paris, 1961), pp. 267 ff.

58. *Le Monde*, Jan. 4 and 5, 1961.

59. See Serge Moscovici, *Reconversion industrielle et changements sociaux* (Paris, 1961), chap. XII.

60. In his Sorbonne lectures on *Le Développement de la société industrielle et la stratification sociale* (Paris, 1957, mimeo.).

61. See the coming study of *Taxation in France*, Harvard Law School (courtesy of Martin Norr).

62. The Rueff-Armand report of 1960.

63. Club Jean Moulin, *op. cit.*, pp. 51 ff.

64. P. Laroque, *Succès et faiblesses de l'effort social français* (Paris, 1961), chaps. 6 and 10, esp. pp. 290–291.

65. The Christian labor confederation (CFTC) has increased its strength at the Communist CGT's expense, but only since its own left-wing *tendance* got control of it. Is it illegitimate to see in this broader workers' support for the CFTC an example of *both* greater willingness to envisage occasional cooperation with bosses and officials, since the CFTC avoids the CGT's attitude of rigid opposition, *and* continued favor for a radical form of syndicalism, since the CFTC has been almost consistently tougher than the non-Communist Force Ouvrière (CGT-FO), sometimes even than the CGT?

66. See Andrée Andrieux and Jean Lignon, *L'Ouvrier d'aujourd'hui* (Paris, 1961).

67. André Philip, *Pour un socialisme humaniste* (Paris, 1960).

68. A brief but perceptive discussion of some of France's higher education problems is J. G. Weightman's "The Sorbonne," in *Encounter*, June 1961, pp. 28–42.

69. See *Le Monde*, Nov. 29, 1961, and Michel Drancourt, *Bilan économique de la Cinquième République* (Paris, 1961), pp. 90 ff.

70. See Club Jean Moulin, *op. cit.*, pp. 187 ff.

71. See Charles Morazé, *The French and the Republic*, trans. J. J. Demorest (Ithaca, 1958).

72. See for instance two books by François Fontaine, *La Nation frein* (Paris, 1957) and *La Démocratie en vacances* (Paris, 1959).

73. See Claude Nicolet, *Mendès-France ou le métier de Cassandre* (Paris, 1960).

74. Whether a French atomic striking force could ever become a useful deterrent is a question on which there are sharp disagreements between

French and American officials, and also among the French. Two points must however be noted. (1) Those Frenchmen who doubt France's capacity to build an independent deterrent usually do not question France's atomic program. They advocate either that France's force be merely an additional contribution to the Atlantic deterrent, as is the British striking force, or that France's efforts aim at the creation of a European deterrent. (2) The more the U.S. insists not only on the dangers of nuclear diffusion but also on the need for NATO to switch from a policy of *deterring* Soviet attacks in Europe through a first-strike threat to a policy of *defending* Europe by conventional forces (and, if necessary, tactical nuclear weapons), the more the Europeans will be tempted to build their own deterrent. For to the Europeans the difference between deterrence and defense is a difference between life and death. Whereas the U.S. begins to doubt the credibility of its own deterrent for the protection of Europe, the Europeans, instead of questioning the credibility of *any* nuclear deterrence in the age of nuclear plenty, tend rather to interpret America's shift as making a European deterrent imperative.

75. It is significant that General Challe, who led the rebellion in Algiers in April 1961, and had been the military organizer of the Suez expedition, was on the other hand a convinced partisan of European and Atlantic integration.

76. Grosser (note 52 above), p. 386.

77. See the issue of *La Nef* (July–September 1961) on the French army.

78. Grosser, p. 369.

79. See for instance Maurice Duverger's books, *De la Dictature* and *La Sixième République et le régime présidentiel* (both published Paris, 1961); or Roger Priouret, "Les Institutions politiques de la France en 1971" in SEDEIS' *Futurible* no. 786, May 1, 1961.

80. See Paul Mus, *Le Destin de l'union française* (Paris, 1954). The one political impulse was the *loi-cadre* on Black Africa pushed by Gaston Defferre—but this exception did not come until 1956.

81. See Raoul Girardet's analysis in: R. Girardet, R. Rémond, J. Touchard, *Le Mouvement des idées politiques dans la France contemporaine* (Cours de l'Institut d'Etudes Politiques, Paris, 1958–59, mimeo.).

82. See my remarks in "The French Constitution of 1958—the Final Text and Its Prospects," *American Political Science Review*, June 1959, pp. 332–357.

83. This point is well made by François Goguel in the conclusion of his course, *Les Institutions politiques de la France*, III (Cours de l'Institut d'Etudes Politiques, Paris, 1960, mimeo.).

84. See Léo Hamon and Claude Emeri, "Vie et droit parlementaires," *Revue du droit public et de la science politique*, November–December 1961, pp. 1238–1248.

85. See for instance Pierre Fougeyrollas and Albin Chalandon in *La Nef*, April–June 1961, and Bertrand de Jouvenel, "Sur l'évolution des formes de gouvernement," in SEDEIS' *Futurible* no. 785, April 20, 1961.

86. George Kelly, from the epilogue of a draft manuscript on the French army, Center for International Affairs, Harvard University.

87. Wylie, *Village in the Vaucluse* (Cambridge, Mass., 1957).

88. See Gilbert Declercq in *La Nef*, April–June 1961, and Moscovici (note 59 above), p. 312.

89. For instance, the one useful technique for increasing popular participation and achieving a consensus of the electorate, the referendum, has been compromised, not so much by its plebiscitarian aspect (for when the executive asks the people for an answer this aspect is quite unavoidable) as by the extreme ambiguity of the questions and the replies. As a result, parliamentarians are once again warning against the perils of "direct democracy," and forgetting the disastrous effects of past games played in the isolation room of the House without Windows.

90. It is important to notice that what happened in the Third Republic, Vichy, and the Resistance is happening again; Michel Debré, an apostle of decentralization immediately after the war, was far less concerned with it after he became premier.

91. See Georges Vedel in *La Nef*, April–June 1961. For a more elaborate discussion of this and other points touched upon here, see the author's "Observations sur la crise politique française," *Archives Européennes de sociologie*, vol. I, no. 2 (1960), pp. 303–320.

92. See Pierre Fougeyrollas in *Preuves*, February 1962.

93. The Club Jean Moulin study on "Planification démocratique," *Les Cahiers de la République*, December 1961, p. 31.

94. See Bourricaud (note 6 above), esp. parts II and III.

95. *Ibid.*, p. 311.

96. Club Jean Moulin, *L'Etat et le citoyen* (Paris, 1961), pp. 181 ff.

97. *Ibid.*, pp. 223 ff.

Charles P. Kindleberger, *The Postwar Resurgence of the French Economy*

1. See Harry D. White, *The French International Accounts, 1881–1913* (Cambridge, Mass.: Harvard University Press, 1933); and Rondo E. Cameron, *France and the Economic Development of Europe, 1800–1914* (Princeton: Princeton University Press, 1961).

2. David S. Landes, "French Entrepreneurship and Industrial Growth in the XIXth Century," *Journal of Economic History*, May 1949, pp. 49–61; Landes, "French Business and the Business Man: A Social and Cultural Analysis," in *Modern France*, ed. E. M. Earle (Princeton: Princeton University Press, 1951), pp. 334–353; and Landes, "Observation on France: Economy, Society and Polity," *World Politics*, April 1957, pp. 329–350.

3. Jesse R. Pitts, *The Bourgeois Family and French Economic Retardation*, unpublished thesis, Harvard University, 1957.

4. John Sheahan, "Government Competition and the Performance of the French Automobile Industry," *Journal of Industrial Economics*, July 1960, pp. 197–215.

5. See, for example, the discussion by M. L. Henry in Colloques Internationaux du Centre National de la Recherche Scientifique, *Sociologie com-*

parée de la famille contemporaine (Paris: Editions du Centre National de la Recherche Scientifique, 1955), p. 67. He asserted that a brusque change in fecundity was manifest in couples married in 1943, and perhaps in those married in 1941 and 1942.

6. Pierre Clément and Nelly Xydias, *Vienne sur le Rhône* (Paris: Colin, 1955), p. 28.

7. For what they are worth as an indication of the fertility characteristics of various occupational groups, however, I offer the following 1946 census data as given in Alain Girard's paper in *Sociologie comparée de la famille contemporaine* (cited in note 5), p. 56. These are the numbers of children surviving per 100 married men aged 45–54.

Miners and terracers	272
Farmers	253
Common labor, workers, foremen	189
Shopkeepers, artisans	181
Salaried staff, liberal professions, and employers of more than five persons	170
Storeowners, employers	165
Office workers	162
Sales clerks	139

8. For their limited value, the data are suggested by listing below the departments with the highest rates of excesses of births over deaths (ten or above), and the lowest (two or below) in 1954. The national average was 6.8. It will be noted that the highest birth rates were in departments of high (and rising) income as well as high immigration, and the low birth rates were in the poor agricultural regions of the Southwest. The data are from *Annuaire Statistique de la France, 1956*, pp. 17, 18:

Ten or above		Two or below	
Moselle	13.6	Lozère	2.0
Orne	12.9	Allier	1.8
Calvados	12.3	Basses Alpes	1.5
Meurthe-et-Moselle	11.9	Corrèze	1.5
Seine-Maritime	11.5	Nièvre	1.4
Doubs	11.1	Pyrénées-Orientales	1.4
Ardennes	11.0	Haute-Vienne	1.2
Manche	10.7	Haute-Loire	1.1
Meuse	10.4	Lot	0.7
Aisne	10.2	Alpes-Maritimes	—0.9
Haute-Marne	10.2	Creuse	—3.0
Sarthe	10.0		

9. Clément and Xydias, p. 27. A more detailed table on total size of household is presented on their p. 25, but is impaired by the fact that the bourgeois and farmers maintain the "extended family" rather more than workers, employees, and small employers (36 percent and 40 percent as

against 12, 16, and 20 percent respectively). Both tables presumably relate to 1950. From the table on their p. 25 come the following data on the average number of persons per household in Vienne by occupational groups:

Higher technical staff	3.90
Liberal professions and large-scale employers	3.77
Foremen	3.27
Small traders	3.11
Artisans	2.97
Workers	2.95
Employees	2.87
Retired	1.75
Farmers (only 3 percent of total sample)	3.85
Others	2.25
Average	2.80

10. Pitts (cited in note 3 above), p. 260.

11. Robert Mendras, *Etudes de sociologie rurale, Novis et Virgin,* Cahiers de la Fondation Nationale des Sciences Politiques, #40 (Paris: Colin, 1953), p. 69.

12. G. LeFèvre, *Politique intérieure du Second Empire* (Paris: Centre de Documentation Universitaire, n.d., ca. 1953), p. 56.

13. François Perroux, "Prise de vues sur la croissances de l'économie française, 1780–1950," in International Association for Research in Income and Wealth, *Income and Wealth,* series V (London: Bowes & Bowes, 1955), pp. 59 ff.

14. Jean Lhomme, *La Grande Bourgeoisie au pouvoir, 1830–1880* (Paris: Presses Universitaires de France, 1960), *passim.*

15. John E. Sawyer, "Strains in the Social Structure of Modern France," in *Modern France,* ed. E. M. Earle (Princeton: Princeton University Press, 1951), pp. 301–305. See also, in the same volume, John Christopher, "The Dessication of the Bourgeois Spirit," pp. 55 ff.; and Jacques Fauvet, *La France déchirée* (Paris: Arthème Fayard, 1957), esp. pp. 90 ff.

16. See Henry W. Ehrmann, *Organized Business in France* (Princeton: Princeton University Press, 1957), pp. 104, 107.

17. L. A. Vincent in *Etudes et conjoncture,* February 1959, pp. 143–150.

18. See Institut National de Statistiques et Etudes Economiques (INSEE), *Mouvements économiques en France de 1944 à 1957* (Paris, 1957), p. 42, where it is noted that output grew much faster in the industries with large-scale units. With 1938 as 100, petroleum products in 1957 had an index of 199, mechanical and electrical industries 168 each, chemicals and rubber 149, metals 141, and glass, tiles, and building materials 141, compared with 101 for textiles and 104 for leather.

19. Pierre Lalumière, *L'Inspection des finances* (Paris: Presses Universitaires de France, 1959), p. 194 (translation mine). This is set out as the analysis made by the Inspection.

20. W. C. Baum, *The French Economy and the State* (Princeton: Princeton University Press, 1958), *passim*.

21. For a discussion of the changes in depreciation rules governing corporate income taxes, see Martin Norr, "Depreciation Reform in France," *The Tax Magazine*, May 1961, pp. 391–401. These changes started out as a series of *ad hoc* measures but were generalized in the 1959 tax reform.

22. See *Rapports et travaux sur la décongestion des centres industriels* (Paris: Ministère de l'Economie Nationale, 1945), vols. I–VI.

23. Michel Augé-Laribé, *La Politique agricole de la France de 1880 à 1940* (Paris: Presses Universitaires de France, 1950), p. 80.

24. See William N. Parker, "Comment" on C. P. Kindleberger, "International Trade and Investment and Resource Use in Economic Growth," in *Natural Resources and Economic Growth*, ed. J. J. Spengler (Washington, D.C.: Resources for the Future, Inc., 1961), pp. 187–190.

25. C. F. Carter and B. R. Williams, *Industry and Technical Progress* (London: Oxford University Press, 1957), pp. 179 ff.

26. Pitts (note 3 above), p. 353.

27. Cameron (note 1 above), *passim*.

28. René Sédillot notes in *Peugeot* (Paris: Plon, 1960), p. 53, that the Franche-Comté was economically stimulated after 1871 by refugees from Alsace.

29. For a discussion of how destruction can help, as opposed to the economic argument which holds that any asset which survives the war can be abandoned if it is not useful, see my "Obsolesence and Technical Change," Oxford Institute of Statistics *Bulletin*, August 1961.

30. Lalumière (note 19 above), p. 179.

31. *Ibid.*, p. 85.

32. *Ibid.*, p. 126.

33. François Jacquin, *Les Cadres de l'industrie et du commerce en France* (Paris: Colin, 1955), p. 19.

34. Bernard Vernier-Palliez, "La Régie Nationale des Usines Renault devant la concurrance," in Travaux du 3ᵉ Colloque des Facultés de Droit, *Le Fonctionnement des entreprises nationalisées en France* (Paris: Dalloz, 1956), p. 95.

35. P. E. P., "Economic Planning in France," *Planning*, Aug. 14, 1961.

36. For a full-length description of the French government's controls and their effectiveness in promoting recovery, see John Sheahan, *Promotion and Control of Industry in Postwar France*, forthcoming from Harvard University Press.

37. See Jean Meynaud, "Qu'est-ce que la technocratie?" *Revue économique*, July 1960, p. 520. See also Meynaud's book, *Technocratie et politique* (Lausanne, 1960), for references to the current French discussion of efficiency as an end in itself.

Laurence Wylie, Social Change at the Grass Roots
(Fictitious names have been assigned to the villagers in this essay.)

1. The following data on numbers of tractors on the farms of France are from INSEE, *Annuaire Statistique de la France: Retrospectif* (Paris, 1961), vol. 66, n.s. 8, p. 99:

1929......... 25,600	1950.........136,400	1955.........305,400
1946......... 56,500	1951.........151,000	1956.........396,000
1947......... 74,200	1952.........177,200	1957.........477,500
1948.........106,900	1953.........211,300	1958.........588,600
1949.........121,500	1954.........249,600	1959.........628,300

2. For the statistics on this phenomenon see M. Febvay, "La Population agricole française: structure actuelle et évolution," *Etudes et conjoncture*, August 1956, pp. 731–737.

3. The following table is left in French because of the impossibility of finding exact English equivalents for the professional categories:

Origine sociale des étudiants des universités françaises

Profession des parents	Répartition de 1000 étudiants suivant la profession des parents			
	1939	*1945*	*1951*	*1959*
Professions libérales	188	180	165	128
Chefs d'entreprise	160	165	124	63
Fonctionnaires	257	250	296	283
Employés	126	131	133	174
Artisans et petits commerçants	38	47	87	125
Propriétaires agricoles	40	37	53	49
Ouvriers d'industrie	16	15	23	30
Ouvriers d'agriculture	9	7	6	8
Propriétaires—rentiers—sans profession	98	78	47	45
Professions indéterminées	68	90	66	95
Totaux	1000	1000	1000	1000

Source: *Informations statistiques, Supplément au Bulletin Officiel de l'Education Nationale*, no. 22, June–July 1960, p. 300.

4. *Encyclopédie pratique de l'éducation en France* (Paris: Ministère de l'Education Nationale, 1960), pp. 51–52, and *Informations statistiques du Ministère de l'Education nationale*, no. 28, April 1961, pp. 101 and 121.

5. *Encyclopédie pratique*, p. 162.

6. See two articles on this subject, both with the same title, "L'Origine sociale des élèves de 6e," one by Marcelle Bidault, the other by Marcel Boret, in *L'Education nationale*, Dec. 17, 1959, pp. 10–12, and Feb. 11, 1960, pp. 4–6. See also Odette Brunschwig, "Influence des facteurs sociaux," *L'Education nationale*, June 15, 1961, pp. 4–5. This number of the periodical is devoted entirely to articles on *le cycle d'observation*.

7. Jacques Hochard writes as follows in "Les Finalités primaires et secondaires des prestations familiales," *Droit social*, May 1957, p. 309: "L'objet essentiel des allocations familiales est de permettre 'la constitution ou le développement normal des familles par l'apport d'une contribution régulière et permanente à l'entretien des personnes dont le chef de famille assume la charge.' Mais on se rend compte que d'autres buts sont poursuivis pour l'ensemble des prestations familiales en général:

    1. une politique démographique et nataliste;
    2. un encouragement au travail;
    3. une politique d'expansion nationale;
    4. l'instruction des enfants;
    5. l'encouragement de l'apprentissage;
    6. un frein à la hausse des salaires.

Ainsi les prestations familiales deviennent une récompense aux naissances multiples sous réserve que l'attributaire ne veuille pas, sans effort, tirer profit de la société et que les enfants bénéficiaires non seulement soient à charge, mais respectent certaines obligations."

8. See the discussion in Lucien Bernot, *Nouville, un village français* (Paris: Institut d'Ethnologie, 1953). Thus, on p. 206: "La père, c'est surtout celui qui rapporte la paye; c'est peut-être le seul aspect précis de sa fonction: rapporter un salaire. Mais qu'est-ce que ce salaire en comparaison de ce qu'apportent à la famille les Allocations Familiales? parfois le tiers seulement. Ce qui contribue encore à minimiser le rôle du père. La famille nombreuse a une ressource certaine, sur laquelle elle compte essentiellement: les prestations familiales: c'est là un revenu sûr, ce qui compte c'est ce que l'on touche *par* les enfants, *pour* les enfants et l'on entendra dire par quelques femmes: 's'il n'y avait que la paye du mari!' " Bernot goes on to show how the woman, unable to make ends meet, criticizes the husband because he does not earn enough and throws up to him the fact that she brings more to the family than he does. Hence frequent conflict between father and mother.

9. See P. Durand, "Les Equivoques de la redistribution du revenu national par la Sécurité Sociale," *Droit social*, May 1953, pp. 292–293.

10. Cf. Jacques Lecaillon, "Sécurité sociale et répartition du revenu national," *Droit social*, September–October 1961, pp. 490–497. He speaks of *"l'effet stabilisateur exercé par les prestations sociales;* les prestations augmentent moins vite que les ressources des catégories en perte de vitesse; elles s'opposent donc, dans une certaine mesure, à la redistribution des revenus résultant de la croissance économique" (p. 496). The italics are Lecaillon's.

11. J. Milhau, "Les Caractères généraux des revenus agricoles," *Droit social*, January 1961, pp. 11–19, esp. p. 13. See also Lecaillon, p. 493; and L. Estrangin, "La Population agricole française de 1838 à 1958," *Economie rurale*, special issue dated January–June 1959, p. 19.

12. Paul Delouvrier, *Politique économique de la France* (Paris: Les Cours de Droit, 1958), p. 16 and *passim*.

13. Pierre Breton, "Le Financement de l'agriculture," *Economie rurale*, special issue dated January–June 1959, p. 175.

14. *Le Monde,* July 15, 1961, p. 12. Translation of encyclical is in *New York Times* of the same date.

15. See for example Jean Chombart de Lauwe, "La Fin des paysans?" *Esprit,* September 1961, pp. 237–254.

16. This is strikingly illustrated by an item in the Angers newspaper *Le Courrier de l'Ouest,* Nov. 8, 1961, announcing a series of meetings at which young farmers could discuss the possibilities of cooperative agriculture:

"Le milieu agricole évolue à une cadence accélérée. Sans cesse, il faut repenser l'organisation des exploitations en fonction de l'équipement, de la main-d'oeuvre, des débouchés, du morcellement.

"L'agriculteur pourra-t-il par lui-même faire face à toutes les transformations qui s'imposent? Seul, pourra-t-il assumer toutes les fonctions de l'entreprise? Au contraire, n'allons-nous pas inévitablement vers une action de groupe, à la fois entre voisins, avec les spécialistes, et au sein des organismes professionnels.

"Consciente de ces problèmes et soucieuse de préparer les jeunes à leur avenir d'exploitants engagés dans le milieu, la JAC organise du 15 au 19 novembre, à Redon (I.-et-V.), Maison de la Retraite, un stage économique ayant pour thème: 'Vers une agriculture de groupe.'

"Ce stage s'adresse aux responsables JAC et JACF des sept départements de l'Ouest.

"Il comportera:

"—une recherche des problèmes posés, et des moyens susceptibles de les résoudre.

"—une prise de conscience des possibilités, des valeurs et des limites de différentes formes de groupement.

"—la présentation des témoignages sur des réalisations concrètes.

"A travers tout cela, la JAC et la JACF peuvent permettre aux jeunes de s'épanouir davantage, à travers leur profession et aider le milieu agricole à prendre en main, de plus en plus sa propre destinée."

17. See Andrée Michel, *Famille, Industrialisation, Logement* (Paris: Centre National de la Recherche Scientifique, 1959), pp. 260 ff.

18. Paul Valéry, *Oeuvres,* vol. I (Paris: Gallimard, 1957), p. 1025.

19. Pierre Massé, "Prévision et prospective," *Prospective,* November 1959, p. 107.

20. The basic individualism of the French, symbolically expressed in the culture from Montaigne to *Le Ballon rouge,* is not a myth. Dr. Stanley Milgram, testing students in France and Norway, found that the French students had significantly greater ability to withstand group pressure verbally expressed. *Scientific American,* December 1961.

21. "Enfin l'histoire nous montre que, soit en bien, soit en mal, il existe un lien entre les hommes des époques successives. C'est par l'effort de ceux qui nous ont précédés que s'est formée la civilisation dont nous jouissons aujourd'hui dans notre pays. Nous prenons conscience de nos responsabilités envers ceux qui nous suivront: l'histoire nous donne une leçon de *solidarité.*" G. Dez and A. Weiler, *Orient et Grèce, Classe de Sixième* (Paris: Hachette,

1957), p. 2. This book is in the widely used series, "Cours d'Histoire Jules Isaac."

22. "Le souffle général, sacré, de '89, passe sur la nation qui se retrouve et qui se dresse." *L'Union*, July 1954, as quoted by Stanley Hoffmann, *Le Mouvement Poujade* (Paris: Colin, 1956), p. 229.

23. Television address of Feb. 5, 1962, as quoted in *New York Times*, Feb. 6.

24. A rather free translation: "If the public criticizes me, I don't give a good damn. That only proves how good my division and my methods are. The more furious the public is, the better job I'm doing for the State."

25. These examples are taken from the appendix of Jean Meynaud, *Groupes de pression en France* (Paris: Colin, 1958), p. 359 ff.

26. "Le pouvoir est mal armé pour résister éfficacement à ces pressions [of pressure groups], en raison de la structure de notre administration. En effet, dans l'organisation actuelle, caracterisée par un découpage de l'administration en compartiments verticaux et cloisonnés, un grand nombre de fonctionnaires, en dépit de leur intelligence, de leur conscience et de leur dévouement, se sont habitués, en toute bonne foi, à voir dans la défense des intérêts qu'ils ont mission de contrôler, un aspect naturel et essentiel de leur fonction, aspect qui tend à éclipser ou à fausser pour eux la vision de l'intérêt général." *Rapport sur les obstacles à l'expansion économique présenté par le comité institué par le décret No. 59-1284 du 13 novembre 1959* (Paris: Imprimerie Nationale, 1960), p. 25.

27. Jacques Le Bailly said in an article during the strike: "De travée en travée, d'écurie en écurie puisqu'ils couchent presque tous là où l'on mettait les chevaux, les propos sont les mêmes et l'amertume sourd de partout comme l'eau jaunâtre qui ruisselle tout au long des parois. Les uns disent: 'On n'est pas des Américains qui déménagent tous les trois ans,' les autres rétorquent: 'On n'est pas des Russes qui, du jour au lendemain, peuvent être envoyés au fin fond de la Sibérie.'" The article was in *Match*, Jan. 13, 1962, pp. 25–29.

28. Gilbert Mathieu wrote in *Le Monde*, Dec. 30, 1962 (p. 1): "Pas plus que les Bretons ou les paysans, les mineurs aveyronnais n'acceptent d'être traités en parents pauvres dans la nation, défavorisés par rapport à d'autres régions ou à d'autres professions . . . Les Aveyronnais expriment le plus bruyamment possible leurs doléances pour amener les pouvoirs publics à intensifier l'effort (investissements d'infrastructure, subventions d'équipement, implantations d'entreprise . . .) consenti en faveur de leur région."

29. *Le Monde*, Jan. 23, 1962, p. 14.

30. As early as Jan. 3, 1962, when the strike was about two weeks old, Pierre Drouin had written in *Le Monde*: "Les avantages accordés au mineur sont attachés à son métier parce qu'il est particulièrement pénible. Pourquoi les emporterait-il avec lui s'il le quitte sans dommage physique? En vertu de quelle loi, même 'non écrite,' garantir à un jeune de Decazeville reclassé dans une usine mécanique ou chimique le statut du mineur jusqu'à la fin de ses jours? Quelle serait la réaction de ses nouveaux compagnons de travail face à ce 'privilège' gardé par l'un d'eux?"

31. *L'Express,* Jan. 14, 1960, p. 21 (underlining mine).

32. Information concerning taxation is derived from Martin Norr, *Taxation in France* (manuscript of a study made for the Harvard Law School International Program in Taxation), *passim,* and from conversations with that author. The subject is new to me and merits more extensive development than given in this text.

33. "On distinguerait dans la carte générale actuelle des idées politiques françaises six familles d'esprits, que j'appellerais la famille traditionnaliste, la famille libérale, la famille industrialiste, la famille chrétienne sociale, la famille jacobine, la famille socialiste. En d'autres termes, on discernerait six idéologies politiques françaises, lesquelles s'arrangent tant bien que mal, souvent plus mal que bien, avec des systèmes d'intérêts, et ne coïncident parfois que d'assez loin avec des groupes parlementaires, avec une représentation politique . . .

"Ces dix idées politiques sont complémentaires. Elles constituent une république platonicienne d'Idées non d'idées immobiles, mais d'idées qui marchent, et qui croisent ou diminuent, et qui par ces mouvements contribuent à la vie d'un tout: idée de la liaison du présent avec le passé; idée de la production par tout le travail actuel et acquis, de la planète à transformer par l'industrie et l'invention; idée d'un mouvement social présent accordé aux disponibilités de l'héritage chrétien; idée de la Révolution Française dans son principe et son mouvement; idée de l'avenir social dans sa capacité illimitée de transformation et dans son maximum de différence avec le passé." Albert Thibaudet, *Les Idées politiques de la France* (Paris: Stock, 1932), pp. 11, 263–264.

34. Address by General de Gaulle over French radio and television, May 8, 1961, as printed in *French Affairs,* no. 114, issued by the French Embassy in Washington, p. 3.

Jesse R. Pitts, Continuity and Change in Bourgeois France

1. E. R. Curtius, *The Civilization of France* (New York: Macmillan, 1932); Friedrich Sieburg, *Gott in Frankreich?* (Frankfurt: Societats-Verlag, 1930); Hermann Keyserling, *Europe* (New York: Harcourt, Brace & Co., 1928).

2. David S. Landes, "French Business and the Business Man: A Social and Cultural Analysis," in *Modern France,* ed. E. M. Earle (Princeton: Princeton University Press, 1951).

3. Beau de Loménie, *Les Responsabilités des dynasties bourgeoises,* vol. II (Paris: Denoel, 1947).

4. Charles de Gaulle, *Mémoires de guerre,* vol. I, *L'Appel* (Paris: Plon, 1954), p. 1.

5. A wonderful example of the delinquent community is to be found in Jules Romains, *Les Copains* (Paris: Gallimard, 1932).

6. Michel Crozier (for instance in "La France, terre de commandement," in *Esprit,* December 1957, pp. 779–797) has described, on the basis

of what he calls a "horror of face-to-face" authority relations, a pattern of French organization which fits well into our model based upon the juxtaposition of doctrinaire authority to the "delinquent community." The French worship the *idea* of authority and yet cannot endure its incarnation. Even though Crozier ignores the importance of "seductive authority" in French structures, he has pointed out the difficulty the French experience in accepting face-to-face subordination on a purely functional basis. The escape from this situation is found in the recourse to a higher authority (non–face-to-face) as umpire, in letting the situation evolve until *la force des choses* commands a solution, and more commonly by a coagulation of the bureaucratic organization into impermeable castes with little communication between each other. Here the bureaucratic procedures become rituals of membership and semifeudal rights. What was supposed to insure predictability and subordination becomes the guarantee of "in-group" autonomy. In the extreme forms we have the bureaucratic fossils described by Courteline.

7. William Kornhauser, *The Politics of Mass Society* (Glencoe: The Free Press, 1959), chap. 3.

8. The *Synarchie* was a group composed of prominent business managers who were supposed to be plotting a Europe-wide technocratic and authoritarian state centered around France. It may have existed as a set of ideas shared by a typical "delinquent community," but is most unlikely to have ever plotted constructively any more than any other delinquent community. On the other hand as a set of ideas it is alive today.

9. Henri de Bourzanel was a captain of Spahis, famous for the flowing red coat which he wore during cavalry charges against the rebellious tribes of Morocco. He was killed in 1935 the first time he charged without his coat, which he had abandoned on orders of his superior officer.

10. Leclerc de Hautecloque is the full name of Marshal Leclerc, hero of the Free French forces. Lionel de Marmier and Schloessing were Free French pilots; Rémy was the head of an underground group; Corniglion-Molinier is a pilot famous for his daring and his grandiose practical jokes (he once disguised himself as the Sultan of Morocco and was given a red-carpet welcome by a garrison); La Porte des Vaux is a navy officer famous during the war for his dash and his gay, mischievous originality; Monclar, a hero of the Free French forces, commanded the French battalion in Korea; Gilles was a great general of paratroopers; Lalande commanded the Isabelle position at Dien Bien Phu; Bigeard, a former bank clerk, became a very successful colonel of paratroopers in Algeria.

11. Michel Lagache, *Les Investissements privés et le concours financier de l'Etat* (Paris: Berger-Levrault, 1959), pp. 32–33. Cf. Jan Marczewski, "Some Aspects of the Economic Growth of France: 1660–1958," *Economic Development and Cultural Change*, April 1961. On page 372 Marczewski states that the central government expenditures for the years 1955–1958 averaged 47 percent of the *gross physical product*.

12. For the history and conceptions behind the building of this dam, see *Donzère-Mondragon*, special issue of *La Houille blanche*, Grenoble, 1955.

13. See the evaluation of the nationalized Renault firm by John Sheahan in "Government Competition and the Performance of the French Automobile Industry," *Journal of Industrial Economics*, June 1960, pp. 197–215.

14. Information on Planning Commission obtained in interviews and from a summary of the Plan's administrative structure by Pierre Massé, "French Economic Planning," an address given in England at a symposium organized by the National Institute of Economic and Social Research, and reprinted in *French Affairs*, no. 127, issued by French Embassy in the U.S., December 1961.

15. *Le Monde*, Jan. 17, 1962.

16. I. Mathelier, "Bilan de la déconcentration industrielle," *Economie et humanisme*, July–August 1962, pp. 53–65.

17. Henry W. Ehrmann, *Organized Business in France* (Princeton: Princeton University Press, 1957).

18. A good example of action which associates the trade unions, the employers, and the state has been the Association Nationale Interprofessionelle pour la Formation Rationelle de la Main-d'Oeuvre (ANIFRMO), which controls the Centre de Formation Professionelle des Adultes (FPA). One hundred five centers, specializing in job upgrading, have turned out since their inception in 1949 more than 200,000 skilled workers.

19. The Ecole Nationale d'Administration, which has functioned since 1946, and which produces most of the high civil service, has revitalized the training of its students with much greater emphasis upon economics and practical experience; for instance, students serve internships in business firms and government offices.

20. Jean Meynaud and Alain Lancelot, "Groupes de pression et politique du logement," *Revue française de science politique*, December 1958, pp. 821–860.

21. *Baroud d'honneur*, an expression which has entered the French language from the colonial wars in North Africa, describes a battle which is not meant to be deadly but rather to express the feelings of one or both parties, and which legitimizes the failure to win completely one's demands, while maintaining the legitimacy of these demands.

22. Information from Professor Georges Lavau, July 1961.

23. Adrien Dansette, *Destin du Catholicisme Français, 1926–1956* (Paris: Flammarion, 1957).

24. For descriptions of the new Catholic attitudes see Béatrix Beck, *Léon Morin, Prêtre* (Paris: Gallimard, 1952); Emile Pin, S.J., *Pratique religieuse et classes sociales dans une paroisse urbaine* (Paris: Spes, 1956).

25. Some figures mentioned by Dansette are as follows: At Vienne (1950) those who regularly go to Mass make up about 20 percent of the parish. The percentages of practicing Catholics among the population aged 14 and above are 36 percent in Tourcoing (Nord) and 12 percent in Toulouse. At St. Etienne 5 percent of the factory workers go regularly to Mass as against 60 percent of the engineers and 40 percent of the males of the "liberal professions." Jacques Maitre in his article "Les Sondages sur les attitudes religieuses des français," *Revue française de sociologie*, vol. II (1961), pp. 14–29, discusses the complexity of the problem of measuring religious attitudes.

26. René Rémond, "Droite et Gauche dans le Catholicisme Français," *Revue française de science politique*, vol. VIII (1958), nos. 3 and 4.

27. François Bourricaud, "Malaise patronal," *Sociologie du travail*, July–September 1961, and his "Contribution à la sociologie du chef-d'entreprise: 'Le Jeune Patron' tel qu'il se voit et tel qu'il voudrait être," *Revue économique*, December 1958.

28. This is an estimate derived from a sample of questionnaires which I collected in 1952–1954 giving the size of firms represented by individual members, and from Pierre-Bernard Cousté in *Jeune Patron*, May 1959, p. 101, giving the size of the membership as 3,000. Cousté claims that 12,000 employers have been members of the CJP since its inception. Ehrmann (note 17 above) is more skeptical than I am about the impact of the movement.

29. Pierre Clément and Nelly Xydias, *Vienne sur le Rhône* (Paris: Colin, 1955), chap. VI.

30. *Cahiers pédagogiques*, Feb. 15, 1959, pp. 38–45. See also issue of Jan. 15, 1960.

31. Information from Professor Arnold Kaufman of the Institut Polytechnique de Grenoble.

32. The figures on the remaining years of fathers are rough estimates based on an increase of about five years in total life expectancy and an assumption that bourgeois fathers, on the average, now are likely to be in their middle or late forties when their daughters marry, as compared with their middle fifties earlier.

33. Serge Moscovici in *Reconversion industrielle et changements sociaux* (Paris: Colin, 1961), pp. 285–288, gives data that tend to support the statement that there is more equalitarianism and certainly more common decision-making than before among the young better-paid workers, and especially those who work in the modern, dynamic factory.

34. These *"amies"* must be differentiated from *"petites amies"* (mistresses).

35. The insurance company La Paix provided me with figures (Sept. 13, 1960) which showed an increase in the number of cars and trucks in circulation of 84 percent between 1953 and 1958 while the number of body injuries in the same period increased only 13.4 percent.

36. Henry W. Ehrmann in his article "French Bureaucracy and Organized Interests," *Administrative Science Quarterly*, March 1961, pp. 534–555, sees a symbiosis between the administration and the trade associations —the latter the tail wagging the dog—which would require a strong executive as a countervailing power, still to be created, if the national interest is not to be forgotten.

Jean-Baptiste Duroselle, Changes in French Foreign Policy since 1945

1. *Lettres de M. Guizot à sa famille et à ses amis*, ed. Mme. de Witt, née Guizot (Paris, 1884), pp. 270–271.

2. Alfred Grosser, *La IVième République et sa politique extérieure* (Paris, 1961), pp. 34–35.

3. F. P. G. Guizot, *L'Histoire de France depuis 1789 jusqu'en 1848* (Paris, 1879), VII, 700, 703.

4. Maurice Reclus, *La Grandeur de la Troisième République de Gambetta à Poincaré* (Paris, 1948), p. 199.

5. *Journal Officiel: Débats parlementaires, Chambre des Députés*, March 1, 1926, vol. II, 1926, p. 1092, and Sept. 25, 1919.

6. Jules Ferry, unsigned preface to Alfred Rambaud, *Les Affaires de Tunisie* (Paris, 1882).

7. Paul Leroy-Beaulieu, *De la Colonisation chez les peuples modernes* (Paris, 1874), p. 501.

8. Cited by Henri Brunschwig, *Mythes et réalités de l'Impérialisme colonial français, 1871–1914* (Paris, 1960), p. 55.

9. *Journal Officiel: Débats parlementaires, Chambre des Députés*, July 28, 1885.

10. *Ibid.*, p. 1668; see also *Débats*, March 27, 1884, p. 935.

11. *Esprit des lois*, book XX, chap. VII.

12. *Le Figaro*, Nov. 24, 1961.

13. Anonymous, *L'Abominable Vénalité de la presse* (Paris, 1931).

14. Quoted in Georges Suarez, *Briand* (Paris, 1941), vol. V, p. 235.

15. *Lettres Persanes*, no. 91.

16. Quoted in Louis Bodin and Jean Touchard, *Front Populaire, 1936* (Paris, 1961), p. 206.

17. *Ibid.*, p. 76.

18. *Ibid.*, pp. 25–26.

19. See John B. Wolf, "'The *Elan Vital* of France': a Problem in Historical Perspective," in *Modern France*, ed. E. M. Earle (Princeton, 1951), pp. 19–31. This author seems to me to alter historical reality in claiming that the decline began in 1789.

20. Charles de Gaulle, *Mémoires de guerre*, vol. I, *L'Appel* (Paris, 1954), p. 267.

21. Alfred Grosser, *La Démocratie de Bonn* (Paris, 1958), p. 14.

22. Compare the defense of the treaty in Etienne Mantoux, *La Paix calomniée, ou les conséquences économiques de M. Keynes* (Paris, 1946).

23. Jean Martel, *Les Silences de M. Clemenceau* (Paris, 1919), pp. 262–263.

24. Alfred Sauvy in *L'Express*, April 20, 1960, cited in Bodin and Touchard (note 16, above), p. 8.

25. Albert Bayet, *Pétain et la Cinquième Colonne* (Paris, 1944). See also the much more subtle work of Marc Bloch, the distinguished historian who was shot by the Germans in 1944, *L'Etrange Défaite, témoignage écrit en 1940* (Paris, 1946).

26. De Gaulle, *Mémoires de guerre*, vol. III, *Le Salut* (Paris, 1959), p. 94.

27. See the curious book of Louis-Dominique Girard, *Montoire, victoire diplomatique, le secret du Maréchal* (Paris, 1948).

28. Frederic Jenny, "Economie et finances de guerre," in *Le Deuxième Conflit Mondial* (Paris, 1947), vol. II, pp. 520–521.

29. Marcel Vigneras, in *Rearming the French* (Washington, 1957), p. 9, estimates the number to have been only 35,000.

30. De Gaulle, vol. III, p. 32.

31. *Ibid.*, pp. 81–82. Robert Sherwood, in *Roosevelt and Hopkins*, gives only a brief account of this interview, which took place January 27, 1945.

32. See especially de Gaulle, *Mémoires de guerre*, vol. II, *L'Unité* (Paris, 1956), quoting messages from Edouard Herriot, p. 473, and from Jean Moulin, president of the National Council of the Resistance, p. 475, which show the attitude of leading Frenchmen toward France's share in the victory.

33. De Gaulle, vol. I, p. 273.

34. Murphy's letter of Nov. 2, 1942, quoted in William L. Langer, *Our Vichy Gamble* (New York, 1947), p. 333.

35. For National Council program see *Année politique, 1944-45*, p. 431. For de Gaulle speech see his vol. III, p. 306.

36. *Année politique, 1944-45*, p. 429.

37. De Gaulle, vol. III, pp. 305, 306.

38. *Ibid.*, pp. 46–47, 52, 54.

39. *Ibid.*, p. 91.

40. See Jean Touchard, "L'Esprit des années 30: une tentative de renouvelment de la pensée politique française" in *Colloques, tendances politiques* (Paris, 1960), pp. 88–120.

41. See J.-B. Duroselle, "The Turning-Point of French Politics: 1947," in *Review of Politics*, July 1951, pp. 302–328. *Tripartisme* was an attempt at coalition government, with the Communists participating.

42. Grosser, *La IVième République*, p. 405.

43. Mendès-France quotations from *Année politique, 1953*, pp. 490–491, 495, 498.

44. *Année politique, 1954*, p. 522.

45. *Paris-Match*, Sept. 1, 1956. See the comment of Alfred Grosser, *La IVième République*, p. 352.

46. France has roughly the shape of a hexagon, with three maritime sides (Channel, Atlantic, Mediterranean) and three continental sides (Pyrenees, Alps, Rhineland). French textbooks of geography and history start by stressing this symmetry, which is therefore a familiar point of reference for Frenchmen. The harmony, balance, and geometrical perfection are carried over into the concept of France as a logically balanced whole.

47. De Gaulle, vol. I, p. 1.

48. Raymond Aron criticizes this dream in his "De la Politique de Grandeur," *Preuves*, November 1959, pp. 3–12.

49. Stanley Hoffmann, "De Gaulle's Memoirs: the Hero of History," *World Politics*, October 1960, pp. 150–151.

50. De Gaulle, vol. I, p. 69.

51. All references to de Gaulle's speeches come from *Année politique*. Where no city is cited, the speech or press conference took place in Paris.

52. This and the two following Aron quotations are from his *Preuves* article of November 1959, p. 12.

53. De Gaulle, vol. I, p. 70.

54. "La Politique étrangère de la France et l'opinion publique, 1954–1955," in a special issue of *Sondages*, 1958, nos. 1 and 2, p. 10.

55. *Ibid.*, p. 130. A substantial number of abstainers in these polls is to be explained by opposition to de Gaulle's domestic policy.
56. *Ibid.*, p. 160.
57. Grosser, *La IVième République*, p. 78.
58. De Gaulle, vol. III, p. 287.

INDEX

437

438

D04708